Geography, Religio the Eastern Medite

Geography, Religion, Gods, and Saints in the Eastern Mediterranean explores the influence of geography on religion and highlights a largely unknown story of religious history in the Eastern Mediterranean.

In the Levant, agricultural communities of Jews, Christians, and Muslims jointly venerated and largely shared three important saints or holy figures: Jewish Elijah, Christian St. George, and Muslim al-Khiḍr. These figures share 'peculiar' characteristics, such as associations with rain, greenness, fertility, and storms. Only in the Eastern Mediterranean are Elijah, St. George, and al-Khiḍr shared between religious communities, or characterized by these same agricultural attributes – attributes that also were shared by regional religious figures from earlier time periods, such as the ancient Near Eastern Storm-god Baal-Hadad, and Levantine Zeus. This book tells the story of how that came to be, and suggests that the figures share specific characteristics, over a very long period of time, because these motifs were shaped by the geography of the region. Ultimately, this book suggests that regional geography has influenced regional religion; that Judaism, Christianity, and Islam are not, historically or textually speaking, separate religious traditions (even if Jews, Christians, and Muslims are members of distinct religious communities); and that shared religious practices between members of these and other local religious communities are not unusual. Instead, shared practices arose out of a common geographical environment and an interconnected religious heritage, and are a natural historical feature of religion in the Eastern Mediterranean.

This volume will be of interest to students of ancient Near Eastern religions, Judaism, Christianity, Islam, sainthood, agricultural communities in the ancient Near East, Middle Eastern religious and cultural history, and the relationships between geography and religion.

Erica Ferg is an assistant professor in the Liberal Arts department at Regis University in Denver, Colorado, where she teaches courses on Islam, Christianity, Judaism, world religions, and religious studies theories and methods. Her doctorate is in the Study of Religion, and her area of specialization is Eastern Mediterranean comparative religious history. Her research focuses on Mediterranean comparative religion, comparative linguistics, and archaeology. Prior to academia, Erica was a Persian linguist in the United States Air Force. Erica is at work on her second book, entitled *Starry Nights: A Celestial History of Religion in the Mediterranean.*

Studies in the History of the Ancient Near East
Series editor: Greg Fisher, University of California Santa Barbara, USA
Advisory Board of Associate Editors

Studies in the History of the Ancient Near East provides a global forum for works addressing the history and culture of the Ancient Near East, spanning a broad period from the foundation of civilization in the region until the end of the Abbasid period. The series includes research monographs, edited works, collections developed from conferences and workshops, and volumes suitable for the university classroom.

On the Edge of Empires
North Mesopotamia During the Roman Period (2nd–4th c. CE)
Rocco Palermo

Children in the Bible and the Ancient World
Comparative and Historical Methods in Reading Ancient Children
Edited by Shawn W. Flynn

Near Eastern Cities from Alexander to the Successors of Muhammad
Walter D. Ward

A Story of YHWH
Cultural Translation and Subversive Reception in Israelite History
Shawn W. Flynn

Migration and Colonialism in Late Second Millennium BCE Levant and Its Environs
The Making of a New World
Pekka Pitkänen

Geography, Religion, Gods, and Saints in the Eastern Mediterranean
Erica Ferg

https://www.routledge.com/classicalstudies/series/HISTANE

Geography, Religion, Gods, and Saints in the Eastern Mediterranean

Erica Ferg

Routledge
Taylor & Francis Group
LONDON AND NEW YORK

First published 2020
by Routledge
2 Park Square, Milton Park, Abingdon, Oxon OX14 4RN

and by Routledge
605 Third Avenue, New York, NY 10017

First issued in paperback 2021

Routledge is an imprint of the Taylor & Francis Group, an informa business

British Library Cataloguing-in-Publication Data
A catalogue record for this book is available from the British Library

Library of Congress Cataloging-in-Publication Data
Names: Ferg, Erica, author.
Title: Geography, religion, and sainthood in Eastern Mediterranean / Erica Ferg.
Identifiers: LCCN 2019034540 (print) | LCCN 2019034541 (ebook) | ISBN 9780367182175 (hardback) | ISBN 9780429060151 (ebook)
Subjects: LCSH: Religion and geography. | Middle East–Religion.
Classification: LCC BL65.G4 F47 2019 (print) | LCC BL65.G4 (ebook) | DDC 202/.13–dc23
LC record available at https://lccn.loc.gov/2019034540
LC ebook record available at https://lccn.loc.gov/2019034541

ISBN 13: 978-1-03-223888-3 (pbk)
ISBN 13: 978-0-367-18217-5 (hbk)

DOI: 10.4324/9780429060151

Typeset in Times New Roman
by Deanta Global Publishing Services, Chennai, India

For my Grandfather, John Ferg (1928–2014), and my Grandmother, Gurli Ferg (1929–2007).

Contents

Figures

Acknowledgments

It is a pleasure to thank the people who have helped to create this book. First, I would like to thank Dr. Andrea Stanton, Dr. Nader Hashemi, Dr. Scott Montgomery, and Dr. Albert Hernandez for their invaluable intellectual contributions and kind mentoring during my doctoral work at the University Denver and Iliff School of Theology. Dr. Greg Robbins and Dr. Mark George as well were generous in their own mentoring, and erudite in their assistance with specific chapters. I would like also to thank Dr. Amy Balogh, for whose insightful comments and camaraderie I am grateful, as well as Dr. Eric C. Smith, Dr. Catherine Orsborn, and Dr. Micah Saxton for their many and varied contributions to all stages of this project.

At Regis University, I would like to thank my wonderful colleagues for their kind and consistent support throughout the final writing phases of this book. Dr. Bryan Hall, Dr. Janet Rumfelt, Dr. April Samaras, Dr. Anna Floyd, Denise Walton, Emma Thompson, and Mary Jo Coe were extraordinarily helpful. I sincerely appreciate the support I received in this project from all of my colleagues in the College, as well as from the wider University.

Dr. Beverly Chico, Marilyn Kopelman, and Dr. Lori Willard read and commented upon an entire draft of this book, and on short notice, for which I am grateful. I would like as well to thank all anonymous readers at Routledge and at Brill who read and commented on this project. Your comments and criticisms made this a better project – thank you.

I would like to thank the many people in Colorado, Lebanon, Israel, Palestine, and Syria who assisted me in 2004 and in 2013 during fieldwork relating to this book. Your generous help made all the difference for my research. Several individuals at the Greek Orthodox Metropolis of Denver, at Saint Elias Antiochian Orthodox Church, and at Balamand University in Lebanon were invaluable in assisting me with field research. Thank you as well to the Institute for American Universities and to the IAU College of the Mediterranean for graciously hosting me as a resident fellow during summer, 2018, and for generously sharing IAU library reserves during my research and writing.

Dr. Greg Fisher, Elizabeth Risch, Ella Halstead, Lisa Sharp, and Lisa Keating, as well as all of the copy editors associated with Taylor & Francis, were extremely professional and courteous. I could not have asked for better people with whom to work.

Thank you to Dr. Kara Taczak, who was an unflagging marvel of editing assistance and positivity.

To the scores of people who are not mentioned here by name, but who helped with all stages of this book, in ways large and small, you know who you are. Thank you.

Most of all, I would like sincerely to thank my family and friends – most especially, my Mom and my Dad – for their loving support and encouragement. Thank you in particular to Wadi Muhaisen, who supported this book from beginning to end. I hope you will be happy with the roles you have played in the creation of this book – it would not have been the same without you.

Finally, I dedicate this book to my grandfather, John Ferg, and to my grandmother, Gurli Ferg. Thank you for being my greatest supporters, and my closest confidants. Your support of my academic work, your encouragement of my ideas, and your belief in me as a person have shaped who I have become. I am so grateful to have had you as my grandparents. I hope that a part of you also will live on through this book.

1 Geography and religion in the Eastern Mediterranean

This book recounts a largely unknown story of religious history in the Eastern Mediterranean.[1] Not only is the story itself little known and often misunderstood, but retelling it also offers us an unexpected glimpse into the obscured view of the religious histories of Jews, Christians, and Muslims in the Eastern Mediterranean, as well as of the agrarian bent of pre-modern religion. *Geography, Religion, Gods, and Saints in the Eastern Mediterranean* examines the influence of geography upon the development of religious ideas and motifs in the Eastern Mediterranean – motifs that remained popular in the region for millennia.

By examining these motifs, this book also opens a window onto the emergence and gradual development of regional religious communities in the Levant – in particular, the religious traditions of Judaism, Christianity, and Islam, and of their relationships to one another. Ultimately, this book suggests that although Jews, Christians, and Muslims in the Eastern Mediterranean are members of distinct religious communities, the religious traditions of Judaism, Christianity, and Islam are not, historically or textually speaking, separate. Thus, this study argues for an understanding of Jews, Christians, Muslims, and other regional religious groups as distinct but not separate in their local Eastern Mediterranean context. Shared religious practices between members of these faiths – a hallmark of the historical and textual continuities between these communities – today can be viewed as aberrant, problematic, or even religiously inauthentic. Instead, shared religious practices are a natural feature of this geographical region and of the close development therein of its religious communities. As strange as these shared practices first may appear to outside observers, this book demonstrates that shared religious practices are entirely in keeping with the authentic religious history and geographical environment of the Eastern Mediterranean.

Part One: St. George and al-Khiḍr among Christians and Muslims in the Levant

In a quiet church in Palestine dedicated to Saint George,[2] candles flicker as a small party of vow-fulfilling Muslims passes through the vestibule and makes its way down the central aisle of the church. The members of this party have come to see an icon, and to say prayers of thanks to God. They have come to the church to venerate and to fulfill their vows to a specific figure: St. George, to whom Muslims refer as al-Khiḍr, (Ar. 'the Green [One]').[3] At a monastery in Ras el-Metn, on Mount Lebanon, Muslims and Druze from the surrounding area come to see the renowned 14th-century icon of St. George/al-Khiḍr, and to make supplications and give thanks to this powerful figure. Elsewhere, Christians visiting St. George at shrines dotted throughout the Levantine mountains refer to him as al-Khiḍr – a title that most people agree refers as well to the Muslim figure.

In the Eastern Mediterranean, the Muslim figure of al-Khiḍr is in many ways identical to the Christian saint, George. Many believe that St. George and al-Khiḍr come to the aid of anyone who calls upon their assistance, and people often claim to see or to interact with these figures in dreams and in waking life. St. George and al-Khiḍr popularly are considered among the most powerful and important religious figures for Christians and Muslims in the region. In terms of popularity, they are perhaps second only to the regionally beloved figure of Mary.[4]

Over the course of the past 1,400 years, the largest religious communities in the region have been Muslim, Christian, Jewish, Alawite, and Druze.[5] All told, within the region of the Eastern Mediterranean, there are today around 190 million Muslims, 15 million Christians, and 6.5 million Jews.[6] Within just the Levantine coastal countries of Syria, Lebanon, Israel, and Palestine (and including Cyprus and portions of southern and southwestern Turkey and of Egypt's Sinai Peninsula), there are around 22 million Muslims, 6 million Jews, 5.7 million Christians, 2.5 million Alawites, and 1.5 million Druze.[7]

Back inside the church in Palestine, the Muslims who venerate or engage in veneration practices around al-Khiḍr and St. George do not consider their behavior abnormal or contradictory to their identity as Muslims. Nor is that the judgment about these Muslims by Christians who might simultaneously engage in similar veneration practices (although the parish priest might complain that more Muslims than Christians seem to come).[8] Indeed, St. George and al-Khiḍr – or, St. George-al-Khiḍr/al-Khiḍr-St. George – is understood much more as a *regional* figure of power and assistance, accessible to and respected by all, rather than as a figure belonging to any specific religious tradition.[9]

This Muslim and Christian veneration of St. George and al-Khiḍr is not new; since at least 1200 CE, St. George and al-Khiḍr have shared similar iconography and, oftentimes, they are conflated in popular imagination.[10] Furthermore, St. George and al-Khiḍr also have a regional Jewish counterpart, in the figure of Elijah.[11] Until the mid-20th century CE, Eastern Mediterranean communities of Arabic-speaking Jews and Muslims jointly venerated Elijah (Ar., الياس '*Ilyās*', '*Ilyā*', or '*Elias*') and al-Khiḍr, often at common sites.[12]

Al-Khiḍr is therefore popularly identified in the Eastern Mediterranean with both St. George and with Elijah. Because Elijah and St. George both are widely known for their actions in defense of 'true' faith,[13] linkage also is popularly imputed between St. George and Elijah. However, linkages between St. George and Elijah lie in the realm of similarity rather than that of convergence, as has been the case between al-Khiḍr-St. George and al-Khiḍr-Elijah. As a result of these conjunctions, up through the 20th century CE, joint regional communities of Jews, Christians, Muslims, Alawites, and Druze came to venerate Elijah, St. George, and al-Khiḍr at 'common sites' throughout the region.[14] Among regional religious communities, these figures popularly are considered to be something akin to a shared regional inheritance.[15]

It is this shared, regional phenomenon that underlies the impetus for this book. In 2010, as I encountered this scenario, I was immediately struck by the apparent strangeness of it. How is it, I wondered, that Muslims could come to visit a *Christian* saint? How could Christians in the region refer to their saint, St. George, as '*al-Khiḍr*', whom most people agreed was a *Muslim* figure? How could Elijah and al-Khiḍr be shared as the *same* figure between communities of Jews and Muslims? How had it come to be that, for at least the past 800 years, communities of Jews, Christians, and Muslims in the Levant – both peasant agricultural *fallāḥīn* communities, and 'city' people from the larger towns – largely had shared and jointly venerated the figures of Elijah, St. George, and al-Khiḍr – together?

This phenomenon surprised me, because it contradicted what I thought I knew about religion and religious communities in the region.[16] After all, both 'common wisdom' and my own religious studies training suggested that Muslims, Christians, and Jews were very different and quite separate, particularly in the politically and religiously contentious Levant. And that was a perspective perhaps to be expected. Most religious history texts – indeed, most textual histories of the Eastern Mediterranean region in general – are broken into discrete periods and subjects, investigating religions in an artificially sterile manner, as though they were not intimately connected to multiple strands of both past and contemporaneous influences.

In contrast, this book investigates those influences and associations in order to illuminate a single thread of interconnection in Eastern Mediterranean religious history. *Geography, Religion, Gods, and Saints in the Eastern Mediterranean* tells the story of how it is that Elijah, St. George, and al-Khiḍr came to be related in religious texts, iconography, and practices in the region. In so doing, it sheds light on a largely unacknowledged aspect of religious history in the Eastern Mediterranean: interconnection.

Textual narratives and traditional stories of these figures

Outside of the Levant, Elijah, St. George, and al-Khiḍr each are very important within their textual and lived traditions as Jewish, Christian, and Muslim figures, respectively. Outside of the Levant, however, Elijah, St. George, and al-Khiḍr are not shared in exactly the same way between communities of Jews, Christians, and Muslims, nor do these figures regularly demonstrate the peculiar characteristics mentioned below. Outside of the Levant, and thus shorn of its geographical, historical, and religious influences, these figures generally are known only by the content of their textual narratives.

The biblical Prophet Elijah is a powerful figure in the Hebrew Bible (1 Kings 17–19, 21, and 2 Kings 1–2) whose prophetic role was to ensure correct community worship of the god YHWH, or Yahweh. By virtue of his traditional inclusion at important Jewish rituals, such as circumcision ceremonies and the Passover

Seder, Elijah continues to fulfill this role. Because of his colorful narratives in the Hebrew Bible, Elijah became for millennia an enormously popular figure among multiple religious communities in the Eastern Mediterranean.

St. George is believed by many Christian communities to have been an influential, early-fourth-century CE Christian martyr. Communities within and beyond the Mediterranean revere St. George as a helper to those in need, and, by virtue of his legendary battle with a dragon, as a martial saint. He eventually was named the patron saint of more than 30 cities and countries throughout the Christian-majority world, from England to Moscow. The earliest textual narrative of St. George, and that from which all other narratives of St. George's life were drawn, is the *Acts of St. George*, an originally fifth-century CE Greek text whose most complete form is found in a Syriac-language version from ca. 600 CE.

Al-Khiḍr is a highly popular Muslim religious figure believed to have been an Islamic saint (or '*walī*'), prophet, or holy person. Al-Khiḍr is referenced in *tafsīr*/commentary to the Qur'ān as a teacher of Moses (18:60–82), is believed to come to the aid of those in need, and is revered by Muslim communities throughout the Muslim-majority world, particularly from Eastern Europe to Southeast Asia.

However, in the Levant – and only in the Levant – where these figures originated,[17] they are not only shared and sometimes conflated, they also exhibit 'peculiar' additional traits. These figures long have been associated with rain, storms, thunder, lightning, greenness, fertility, and fecundity; with the ability to appear and disappear; with mountains and high places; with local feast or celebration days of April 23;[18] and with a particular pictorial presentation: mounted upon a white horse (or standing on foot), arm raised and brandishing a weapon, poised to slay a dragon through the mouth, or to strike the death-blow upon a human foe underfoot.

In keeping with the 'peculiar' characteristics listed above, Elijah, St. George, and al-Khiḍr in the modern period each have been well studied and analyzed within their respective religious traditions. Interpreters often are uncomfortable about the figures' peculiar characteristics, which for centuries have remained the subjects of internal discussion and debate regarding the figures' religious statuses and significances.[19] The fact that the figures share these unique characteristics and convergences *only* in the Levant, where the texts and legends about Elijah, St. George, and al-Khiḍr originated, calls for the study of these figures within their original context.

A traditional religious studies perspective

From a traditional religious studies standpoint – often known as a 'World Religions' perspective – this phenomenon represents at least two paradoxes. First, there is the paradox of the figures' peculiar and shared aspects in the region of the Eastern Mediterranean: why do the figures display those peculiar aspects only there, and why are those aspects sometimes *shared* between the figures? Second, there is the paradox of communities of Jews, Christians, and Muslims in the region, for at least the past 800 years, jointly venerating these figures. Traditional religious studies discourse suggests that Judaism, Christianity, and Islam are distinct and separate religious traditions, and particularly in the Eastern Mediterranean. How is it then that these figures could be venerated in common by communities of Jews, Christians, and Muslims, and especially over such a long period of time?

The traditional World Religions perspective remains prevalent within Religious Studies textbooks and theoretical approaches.[20] This manner of organization and study focuses on discrete, comprehensive traditions, and normative beliefs and practices.[21] This is also the theoretical framework from within which most of the investigations involving Elijah, St. George, and al-Khiḍr have been undertaken. Because of that, these figures usually have been studied from *within* their individual religious traditions. Such an approach has tended to miss the figures' associations with one another, and it also has tended to misunderstand as accretive and/or anomalous the figures' 'peculiar' aspects.[22]

Most of all, what this traditional World Religions approach lacks is an awareness of the ways in which locality informs religion. That is, it does not account for the intersections of time and place that always are evident in the manifestation of a specific religious tradition. Take, for example, the religious tradition of Christianity. The texts, doctrines, theologies, and lived customs that constituted Christianity in third-century Syria are very different from those that constituted Christianity in the 20th-century American South. A traditional theory of World Religions cannot easily account for this complexity, because that particular theoretical perspective tends to view the elements that constitute a religion as part of a comprehensive, unchanging whole.

A Geography of Religion Perspective

Theories associated with the field of Geography of Religion represent a more promising approach – one which considers the ways in which locality informs religion. The field of Geography of Religion has evolved since the 1960s in various ways, but one of its more important contributions is the "contextualization of religion" that is evident in local, geographically oriented studies of religion.[23] These local studies of religion account for the intersections of time and place in analyses of specific religious traditions. That is, according to a Geography of Religion theoretical perspective, religions are inherently geographically contextualized: prevailing political, social, religious, and physical-geographical conditions evident within a particular locality are understood to influence the development and manifestation of that locality's religious traditions at any given point in time.

Returning to the case of third-century Syria, a World Religions approach might suggest that we understand the manifestation of Christianity as reflected in period-specific thinkers and texts. Within this approach, thinkers and texts often are contextualized, but those texts and thinkers tend also to be viewed tautologically, as signposts along the road of a comprehensive tradition whose final outcome already is known. Furthermore, analysis of a religious tradition within the World Religions theoretical framework, especially of that tradition in earlier time periods, has tended to be restricted to the analysis of foundational religious texts. The larger logical problem with the World Religions emphasis on texts is that often it is unjustifiably reasoned that if one understands the foundational texts of a tradition, one can thus claim to understand the tradition as a whole in all times and places, which simply is not the case.

A Geography of Religion approach, on the other hand, suggests that in examining Christianity in third-century Syria, one should consider the prevailing third-century political, social, religious, and physical-geographical conditions which combined to influence the tradition. That is, in which ways did those influences combine to affect that manifestation of Christianity in that time and place? In which ways were this tradition's customs, doctrines, and practices *lived out* in ways that were informed by the geographical locality of third-century Syria? Moreover, how were this tradition's texts, narratives, symbols, and figures influenced by those of neighboring religious and cultural forces?

Using a geographical lens

When we view Elijah, St. George, and al-Khiḍr through the lens of geography – a lens that is not restricted to inquiry from within a single religious tradition – several advantages emerge. First, use of a geographical lens allows us to view the figures in comparative perspective, both with respect to one another, and with respect to the individual figures themselves, over time. Second, using the lens of geography allows us to investigate the figures' regional influences, be they political, social, religious, or geographical. Third, a geographical investigation is not limited to a single time period. In different eras, the influences upon these figures have changed, as have the figures, themselves. Limiting this project by geography rather than by time allows us to see the fluidity of the influences at work behind the figures, as well as behind the figures' contextual alignments to one another. Finally, the use of a geographical lens helps to resolve the apparent paradoxes regarding the figures' regional 'peculiarities', as well as those involving joint Jewish-Christian-Muslim veneration of the figures. Ultimately, a geographical view of this phenomenon helps to illuminate why, outside of this region and shorn of its influences, these figures are not conflated, nor are they shared in the same way between communities of Jews, Christians, and Muslims.

Past studies

Past studies of these figures, on the whole, generally have been performed by religiously committed insiders, whose work has tended to reinforce doctrinal tenets, and to downplay, dismiss, or ignore the figures' shared aspects and origins. Secular scholarship on these figures, individually and collectively, began in the late 19th century, largely in the vein of a World Religions theoretical framework. Notable academic studies of the specific figure of Elijah are generally broken into categories: biblical, Talmudic, and folkloric; there are individual studies of St. George and of al-Khiḍr, studies of two or more of the figures in comparison, and, in a few instances, studies of all three figures.[24]

In 1969, Hassan S. Haddad argued that the similarities and linkages between Elijah, St. George, and al-Khiḍr deserved to be considered on a wider scale.[25] Haddad wrote a brief article entitled "'Georgic' Cults and Saints of the Levant," wherein he noted the similarities of Elijah, St. George, and al-Khiḍr among agricultural communities of Jews, Christians, and Muslims in the Levant. Haddad was the first to make the provocative but unsubstantiated claim that "the cults of these 'georgic' saints is a continuation, with variations, of the cults of the Baals of ancient Syria,"[26] referring to the millennia-long regionally dominant figure of the Syro-Canaanite storm-god, Baal-Hadad, as well as to Baal's regional syncretic manifestations.[27]

Haddad made this claim on several grounds: not only do Elijah, St. George, and al-Khiḍr often share elements of iconographical representation with the storm-god Baal-Hadad – 'vanquishing' posture, for instance – they also popularly are associated with the qualities for which Baal-Hadad long had been known: rain, greenness, fertility, fecundity, storms, lightning, thunder, as well as the ability to appear and disappear, and a commemoration day of April 23. Furthermore, as a native of the Levant, Haddad was uniquely positioned to have been aware, as well, of the common practices surrounding these figures between local communities of Muslims, Christians, Jews, and others.

Geography, religion, Gods, and Saints in the Eastern Mediterranean

Geographical setting of the region

As we begin this investigation, a few definitions and clarifications are in order. Although the Levant is a part of the agricultural zone known as the Fertile Crescent, throughout large sections, it is both arid and rocky. These climatic conditions are a result of the region's unique geography and geology. As we will see in Chapter Two, the Mediterranean Basin is comprised in the main of a bedrock of limestone. This type of bedrock produces in thin, rocky soils that weather quickly to form exposed rocks and caves. Furthermore, owing to the geographical position of the Levant at the meeting point of three continental plates – the African, Arabian, and Eurasian – large sections of the Levant are mountainous where the plates collide, and gradually descend to the east to form a rocky plain. This geographical diversity largely has shaped the region: historically, the multiformity of geographical conditions impeded political consolidation between regions, affected the course and character of local rivers, and helped to create a zone of fertile land for rain-fed farming on the lee sides of the mountains, with steeply declining amounts of moisture in the desert lands to the east. Levantine geography, as this book demonstrates, has profoundly shaped the religious notions of the people who have lived there.

How we usually think of religious history in the Levant

Scholars and laypersons in religious studies often think anachronistically of religious history in the Levant, and in the wider Eastern Mediterranean, as a region peopled with individuals who share our modern notions of religious identities. They often envision discrete, theologically mature communities. Such a view reflects a modern religious perspective that is both historically inaccurate, and was, until relatively recently, impossible to create.

Discrete, theologically oriented religious communities largely are a product of modern, literate cultures. Only modern, literate cultures are associated with the religious and political infrastructure necessary to produce mass literacy, to create and maintain numerous buildings for worship, and to produce, equip, and support trained religious personnel who could mold and police religious identities. Before the 20th century in the region, such conditions were impossible to meet.[28]

Text-based religious perspectives, which are characterized by a focus on the text and especially on the exclusivity of theological messages, require mass literacy. Pre-modern cultures lacked the capacity for mass literacy, and in the absence of such text-based religious perspectives, people neither wanted nor needed to conceive of their religious identities as theologically 'pure', and distinct from others' religious identities.[29] Indeed, in the ancient world, and even up through the early modern periods in history, people conceived of their religious identities less in terms of 'religions' or 'beliefs', and more in terms of which gods they followed, and which rituals they practiced.[30] Furthermore, allegiances to gods largely were not exclusive.

Despite the admonitions of canonical texts and the decrees of religious councils, which we will encounter in this book, most people in the region, throughout most of history, were religiously opportunistic and pluralist: one could and did follow those gods who were powerful, and one could and did engage in those 'magical', sacrificial, and amulet-driven practices and other rituals that were considered *effective* – irrespective of, in lieu of, and-or in concert with – a 'primary' religious orientation.[31]

Furthermore, most cultures of the Near East were both interconnected and mutually dependent. These "cultures interacted with each other and were interrelated. This means that acculturation not only took place between 'Greek', 'Roman', and multiple 'Near Eastern' cultures, but also *within* Near Eastern cultures and religions."[32] To be sure, religious identities were "dynamic," "multifaceted," and "continuously developing," and "there is never one 'religious identity' that is transmitted across periods."[33] But the degree of interaction, overlap, and interrelation between religious cultures of the Near East was far greater than is often presented in most religious history texts about the Eastern Mediterranean. Discrete, insular, theologically exclusive religious communities in the Eastern Mediterranean largely are a product of modern political and religious influences, in that they are based upon literate communities and involve the consequent ascendency of textual religion. Such are modern religious perspectives, however, and should not anachronistically be projected upon earlier time periods.

Popular religion

Our modern perspectives about religious identities – in particular, the predominance of *textual* religion – occlude an accurate understanding of religious history in the Eastern Mediterranean. In a modern sense of the definition, we tend to think of 'popular' or 'folk' religion as those religious practices and notions that diverge from the core theological teachings of a religious tradition. Furthermore, we tend to think of the core teachings of a religious tradition as synonymous with textual, canonical religion. Oftentimes, these categories are termed 'high' and 'low' religion, with high religion equating to textual, orthodox religion, and low religion referring to all other or 'folk' religious practices and notions that deviate from the textual perspective.

The problem with this notion of popular religion is two-fold: first, it is inaccurate, as it is only makes sense from a modern perspective. That is, when we try to apply this framework to historical analyses, it collapses. The notion of 'popular religion' commits the error of imputing the extensive, inherited corpora of developed theologies back upon earlier times. Indeed, when we set out to examine the ways in which 'popular', non-canonical, and non-orthodox practices and notions deviate from canonical texts, we forget that, in earlier times, these orthodoxies and canonical texts were *in the process of being created* alongside – and out of – the popular religious cultures of the day. This error relates to a second flaw regarding the conceptual category of 'popular religion': it presumes that the development of canonical, orthodox religion was the earlier, original act.

Canons and orthodoxies develop out of the popular religious cultures of their day – irrespective of which religious tradition or culture is being examined. Popular or 'low' religious practices and notions do not diverge or devolve from 'high' canonical religion at some point in history. Indeed, it is the other way around. That which comes to be deemed by its community as 'canonical' or 'orthodox' originally developed out of contemporaneous, as-yet non-canonical religious practices and notions.

'Popular' or non-canonical, contemporaneous religion always exists alongside and in simultaneity with the development of 'canonical', orthodox religion. Both phenomena, naturally, continue to develop independently of one another. Insofar as canonical religion becomes associated with political power, as we shall see below, canonical religion has tended to have a greater influence upon most of the population.

Agrarian religion

Notions of popular religion are flawed because of the conceptual limitations of language, and because of the errors in reasoning often committed around those notions. Instead, a far more effective way to conceive of what is meant by the term 'popular religious practice', particularly in the Levant, is through the category of 'agrarian religion'. As James Grehan points out in *Twilight of the Saints: Everyday Religion in Ottoman Syria and Palestine*, agrarian religion is a notion which cuts across the limitations of categories such as popular, high/low, and urban/rural to highlight a "fine attunement to the essentially agrarian conditions of everyday existence."[34] "As much urban as it was rural, it was the expression of an entire social and economic order whose rhythms were tied to the slow turnings of the seasons, and finely attuned to the vagaries of earth, sky, and environment."[35] This was an experience actually shared by all, regardless of distinctions in social class, location, age, and gender.

Agrarian religion in the Levant, in Grehan's formulation, is driven by geographical influences, and is characterized by sacred sites, essential agricultural needs, shared religious culture, and saints and holy figures. Sacred sites are intimately related to geography, and are often hulled from the rocky landscape or simply created around natural wonders. In the Levant, sacred sites consist of holy mountains, noteworthy rock formations, and caves – especially caves with access to subterranean water.

Agricultural concerns, foremost among them water, droughts, and crop yields, shape the contours of agrarian religion. Another hallmark of agrarian religion is diminished sectarianism. Lacking the mass literacy and religious infrastructure necessary for rigid or distinct religious identities, people in the agrarian, premodern religious culture of the Levant shared linguistic and cultural traditions, as well as the same agrarian needs for survival. Furthermore, people shared not only the same spaces, but the same religious history. This is particularly noteworthy among Levantine communities of Jews, Christians, and Muslims of the past two millennia, whose shared religious history involved common biblical religious figures, narratives, and texts.

Among the more prominent features of agrarian religion in the Levant is a prevalence of saints and holy figures. The saint is the most identifiable figure in agrarian culture.[36] This phenomenon is related both to the agrarian needs of everyday existence, which the saint or holy figure helps to meet, and to the prevalence of a common pool of legendary and heroic figures in the Near East. The relatively small size of the Levant, as well as the development therein of related religious communities, contributed to the existence of a common pool of legendary and heroic figures, popular narratives, and powerful motifs in the region.

In addition, the saint or holy figure helped to provide for medical needs in agrarian cultures that lacked basic health care and medical knowledge. People long believed that demons caused illness, physical deformity, and especially the psychological and mental problems they deemed 'madness'. Accordingly, saints, who had the power to expel demons, were considered a ready source of miraculous medical cures.

Saints in agrarian religion were associated with tombs, pilgrimages, and vows for favor and fame in exchange for supplications met. Related to the cult of saints were efficacious remedies, cures, and protections that could be found in powerful images, icons, magic, amulets – pictorial and written – as well as in the act of the blood sacrifice, a ritual long practiced throughout the Near East.

Agrarian religion, in attending to the harsh conditions of life, and in being shaped by the geographical environment, dominated pre-modern, pre-literate religion in the region. Scholars of religious studies tend to think of historical religious peoples in the region as being theologically distinct from one another. However, before the ascendency of mass literacy, textual religion, and a concomitant rise in exclusive sectarian religious identities, religious communities in the Levant were marked more sharply by a shared agrarian religious culture than they were differentiated by distinct doctrinal characteristics.[37] Geographical and geological conditions, which change very slowly, underlie agrarian religion in the Levant. Agrarian religious culture is therefore naturally slow to change,[38] and associated with a *longue-durée* perspective. These phenomena and characteristics associated with agrarian religion endured in the region for a very long time, and only began to be eclipsed during the course of the twentieth century, CE.[39]

Canonical religion

'Canonical religion' or 'institutional religion' as used in the book are terms closely associated with two concepts: a canon of authoritative religious texts,[40] and notions of religious orthodoxy. Both concepts, canonicity and orthodoxy, usually require sufficient political power to enforce particular doctrines, promote specific texts, and establish categories of orthodoxy and heresy.[41] Canonical religion, as mentioned above, takes several centuries to develop. It is also not uniform, as competing communities within a given religious tradition differ with respect to authoritative texts and theological notions.

A major difference between canonical religion and agrarian religion is the reliance of the former on written texts.[42] What we think of today as a 'canonical' text often began as an oral story or series of oral traditions, and was at various points in time written down and circulated among specific communities, in different textual renditions. As the political or internal power of a religious tradition reached sufficient implementation levels, one or more of those textual renditions was selected by religious officials for inclusion in a 'canon' of authoritative, 'authentic' texts. When selected texts take on the revered and often divine statuses associated with canonicity, they tend to change very slowly over time.[43] In that way, written texts tend to anchor, stabilize and shape the contours of orthodoxies.[44]

Moreover, early religious texts often represent polemical arguments about how things ought to be – that is, early or foundational religious texts are texts largely in evidence of a contemporaneous religious culture (or of the 'previous' religious culture, from a later temporal perspective) – rather than reflecting the precepts of their own majority-religious environment. For that reason, in this project, we will examine the Baal Cycle as a document in evidence of ancient Near Eastern religious groups; the Hebrew Bible as a document in evidence of Canaanite, Egyptian, and other ancient Near Eastern religious groups; the New Testament as a document in evidence of Second-Temple Jewish groups, among others, of the first century, CE; the Acts of St. George as a document in evidence of fifth-century CE Roman, Hellenistic, Christian, and Jewish religious groups; and the Qur'ān as a document in evidence of the late antique religious world, and in particular of the various Christian, Jewish, and Arabian polytheistic groups of the day.

Historiographical method

With regard to historiographic method, this book will take as its guide the *longue-durée* geographical model of historical time mentioned above and proposed by Fernand Braudel in 1949.[45] In examining this historical phenomenon within the Eastern Mediterranean, this book will suggest that geological time and linguistic time are two of the deepest and slowest-changing elements of time affecting human history in the Eastern Mediterranean.

At the lowest level, geography and geology affect the climatological realities of life and agricultural production in the region. Although climate in the Eastern Mediterranean occasionally has changed since 7000 or 6000 BCE, in this book, climate in the region will be considered *generally* characterizable by three dry years out of every ten.[46] Furthermore, the stable general pattern of climate will be described herein as a significant and determinative element of influence upon the region, as well as of its long-lived geographical motifs.[47]

I suggest linguistic history as a slightly faster-moving layer of time in this model. Historically, the Levant has been a region dominated by the Eastern, Central and Northwest branches of the Semitic language family, save for the late-fourth-century BCE introduction of Greek, and the introduction of Latin in the early centuries of the Common Era.[48] Finally, I suggest religious history as a faster-changing level of history in this regional model, and political history as the fastest-changing level of history in the Eastern Mediterranean.

What this book examines and why

Texts, images, and sites function like artifacts that can tell us a great deal about the societies in which they were produced. They represent moments-in-time; each text, image, or site functions like a small window into history. In order to geographically contextualize each of the figures under examination, so that we may understand them each as a product of time and place, this book investigates the figures' important texts, images, and sites.

Each text, image, or site is examined for evidence of contemporaneous religious, political, and geographical influences. In so doing, we see in each text, image, or site, wider evidence of time and place, as well as reflections of specific religious traditions. We also see in each text, image, or site evidence of agrarian religion and of the influence of geography in phenomena such as sacred mountains, rocks, and caves; in agricultural concerns, involving crops, water, drought, and harvests; in shared religious cultures, where sectarian identity is diminished; and in the prevalence of saints and holy figures, tombs, demons, images, icons, magic, and sacrifice. We see as well in each text, image, and site evidence of developing orthodoxies in religion. Through a common pool of compelling Near Eastern figures, narratives, and motifs, we see evidence of the ways in which older ancient Near Eastern religious traditions in the Levant are related to Judaism, Christianity, and Islam. Finally, we see as well in this examination a view into the interconnected histories of Judaism, Christianity, and Islam in the Levant, and into their particular conceptions of monotheism.

It should also be noted that despite the equal focus in this project on the figures of Baal-Hadad, Elijah, St. George, and al-Khiḍr, in practice today, the most commonly venerated of these figures are St. George and al-Khiḍr, among limited communities of Muslims and Christians in the Levant. This reflects regional demographics over the past 800 years, and, in particular, turbulent 20th-century political history.[49] Most notably, these effects include the institution of political borders between countries created after World War I, as well as the establishment of the state of Israel. Both of these political events had the effect of creating exclusive access for specific persons to formerly open-access sites. Despite the fact that shared regional practices involving Jewish communities and the figure of Elijah are no longer as prevalent as they once were, both the figure of Elijah and the popular practices of Jewish communities are crucial for an accurate understanding of this historical phenomenon.

A third 20th-century political event that has diminished these practices, as well as the size of the modern Muslim and Christian communities who engage in them, is a rise in exclusivist theological interpretations. These exclusivist theological orientations largely can be correlated to the ascendency of textual religion, with the growth of political Islamist movements, and with an increase in general sectarianism as a consequence of 20th- and 21st-century political events.[50] From a perspective of exclusivist theology, shared religious practices often are condemned as 'folk, 'inauthentic', 'confused', or 'improper'.

Why does this matter?

Influence of geography on religion

Religious beliefs, ideas, symbols, and practices naturally are informed by the social and geographical conditions in which their theologies are elaborated.[51] Geography does not drive religious belief, but it has a distinct shaping influence. This influence exists in a religious culture for as long as geography can be said to be the most influential factor on human life. In the case of the need for rainfall for survival in the arid Levant, geographical motifs associated early on with the figure of the storm-god remained powerful and efficacious in Levantine culture and gradually became associated with related and successive figures from among regional religious traditions.

Continuity of motif

This book suggests that the figures' 'peculiarities' – relating to rain, storms, thunder, lightning, greenness, fertility, and fecundity, as well as the ability to appear and disappear and associations with mountains and high places, local feast or celebration days of April 23, and the vanquishing of a serpent or dragon – are in fact simply a continuation of powerful and efficacious motifs related to regional geographical needs. Hasan Haddad first suggested that the figures Elijah, St. George, and al-Khiḍr were each "a continuation of the cult of the Baals of Syria."[52] This book suggests, in conclusion, that although the figures chronologically are related in various ways to one another, each of the figures – including that of the storm-god – became associated with powerful and efficacious geographical motifs in Levantine and wider Near Eastern culture. These motifs originated in geographical needs that emerged in simultaneity with – and in some cases predated – the figure of the storm-god Baal-Hadad.

There is a notion in the field of archaeology that is known as 'continuity of cult'. From this perspective, archaeologists note that oftentimes the same sacred site (if not the same outright structure, or portions of the same structure located at that site) can be reused *as* a sacred site by successive dominant groups. That is, as archaeologists dig, they notice that underneath important religious structures or cult sites, there often lie even earlier important religious structures or cult sites, and so on. The meaning, significance, rituals, and belief structure associated with the site changes under successive groups, but the site itself retains a kind of sacred power and continuity as a 'cult' location.[53]

This notion of 'continuity of cult' is a helpful analogy for understanding the continuity of important regional geographical motifs that this book highlights. In this sense, the phenomenon takes place in a religious rather than in an archaeological sense. The motifs themselves remain powerful and efficacious in agrarian religious culture, first, because people living in successive generations continue to feel the same acute need for rain and crop growth. Second, because these motifs are cultural phenomena, the motifs themselves pre-exist successive generations, who are taught to recognize the motifs as efficacious and powerful.[54]

In a manner very similar to the functioning of 'continuity of cult', in 'continuity of motif', the motifs come to be associated with related and successive important regional religious figures. Thus, powerful, efficacious, geographically influenced motifs that we could identify as having appeared in very early eras continue to be employed over long periods of time, but become associated with religious figures whose religious significances vary, even though the figures themselves inseparably are related to one another. This book documents how this process takes place for each of the figures under examination, and in so doing also helps us to see the relationships between the figures, as well as the relationships between their respective religious traditions. Ultimately, *Geography, Religion, Gods, and Saints in the Eastern Mediterranean* suggests that these geographical motifs are shared by these figures, over a very long period of time in the region, *because they share the region.*

The gradual emergence of Judaism, Christianity, and Islam

Despite commonly held beliefs, religions are not born fully formed, nor do they begin wholesale with founding figures. Religions arise out of their own contemporaneous religious, political, and geographical environments – often as a reaction to another contemporaneous religious tradition – with the emergence of a small early community. Eventually, this community begins to record essential ideas in texts, often to employ images, and to frequent sites (and sometimes to re-employ already-extant images and sites, as in the 'continuity of motif' notion highlighted in this project). Naturally, these are not linear processes, but can take place simultaneously. Gradually, larger religious communities grow out of these early groups, and religious 'traditions' – with their attendant theologies, rituals, practices, and beliefs – form and develop over the course of centuries.[55]

Likewise, this book demonstrates that religious traditions in the Levant emerged in a gradual process of formation and contradistinction from one another. Because of that, Judaism, Christianity, and Islam can be said to be distinct religious traditions, but not religious traditions that historically are separate.

Significance and implications

In challenging a traditional narrative of separation between these religious traditions, in challenging an understanding of premodern, preliterate, agrarian religion in the region as primarily theologically oriented, and in highlighting the shared religious practices of the region, this book offers an innovative departure from the traditional literature on regional religious history. It has implications for the study of religion in the Eastern Mediterranean, and it asks us to rethink our general perceptions of Judaism, Christianity, and Islam, as well as human history in the region.

This book also illuminates a common pool of legendary and heroic figures, popular narratives, and powerful geographical motifs specific to the Near East. It argues as well for monotheism as a specific strand of religious thought that characterized Jews, Christians, and Muslims in contradistinction to one another, and in contradistinction to a Near Eastern religious environment that was dominated by polytheistic religious traditions.

The relationships and continuities between Baal-Hadad (and, subsequently, as we will see, Levantine Zeus and Jupiter), Elijah, St. George, and al-Khiḍr in the Levant that are uncovered by this book provide a critical case study for helping us to understand a broader phenomenon involving geography and religion. In the field of religious studies, this phenomenon, and the arguments derived thereby, still are largely unspoken: the need to recognize regional specificity even for global religions, and the need to recognize regionally specific relationships between religious traditions.

In a modern sense, this book also has contemporary political implications. It helps us to remember that there are elements of cultural commonality that long have connected people in the Levant to one another, to the land, and even across time. Furthermore, there are elements of cultural commonality, such as can be seen in the modern associations between St. George and al-Khiḍr among communities of Christians, Muslims, Alawites, Druze, and other local religious communities, which also *bind* religious groups in the Middle East.

Finally, in demonstrating that the religious traditions of Judaism, Christianity, and Islam are not – historically or textually speaking – separate, this book contradicts the claims of modern austere and exclusivist religious groups who accentuate difference and divergence between these religious traditions and their local communities. *Geography, Religion, Gods, and Saints in the Eastern Mediterranean* reveals the shared phenomenon involving St. George, al-Khiḍr, and Elijah as authentic both to the historical heritage of the Eastern Mediterranean, and to the region's shared religious practices. In so doing, it recovers an interconnected religious history of the Eastern Mediterranean that today remains largely unknown.

Summary

Chapter Two of this book, "Levantine geography, history, and agrarian religion" surveys the region of the Eastern Mediterranean as a whole: geography, climate, and weather. This chapter gives an impression of the region sans modern political borders and discrete historical periodization, and surveys regional geography, geology, and climate. Part Two of this chapter provides summaries of political, religious, and linguistic history in the region, beginning in the Bronze Age. Part Three of this chapter contrasts the vicissitudes of changing political history with long-lived elements of agrarian religious culture, giving an impression of the Levantine agrarian religious experience as a whole, and over time.

Chapter Three, "Canaanite religion and the storm-god Baal-Hadad," focuses on the figure of the storm-god Baal-Hadad, situating the analysis by discussing the ancient Near Eastern storm-gods among whom Baal-Hadad emerged, and then focusing on Baal-Hadad, the Western Syrian and Coastal Canaanite storm-god. This chapter examines Baal-Hadad's most important text, the Baal Cycle; his iconographical representation, the Baal Stele; and two sites associated with Baal-Hadad – Baalbek and Mt. Sapan. It suggests that the influential motif of the storm-god defeating a serpent or dragon may originate in meteorological phenomena, and examines, as well, the ways in which the figure Baal-Hadad influenced the Greek-Levantine cults of Zeus (e.g., Zeus-Baal) and the Roman-Levantine cults of Jupiter (e.g., Jupiter Dolichenus), in the Levant. Over the course of about 1,000 years, cults dedicated to Zeus (and then to Jupiter) gradually came to supplant Baal worship in the region. This chapter highlights those narratives and motifs associated with Baal-Hadad that resonated in the subsequent figures of Elijah, St. George, and al-Khiḍr: associations with the defeat of a serpent or snake – a narrative shown to have a long life, indeed, throughout the region – stormy theophanic imagery, such as rain and storms and lightning; associations with Mt. Sapan and other high places; associations with fertility and fecundity and the seasonal cycle; and recurrent disappearance and return.

Chapter Four, "The Hebrew Bible and Elijah," focuses on the figure of Elijah, situating the ancient Israelites and the biblical tradition as it emerged in the ancient Near East. In particular, special attention is paid to the ways in which the biblical tradition emerged from within an ancient Near Eastern and 'Canaanite' religious environment that was dominated by Baal (Baal-Hadad) worship. This chapter focuses on the biblical narrative of the prophet Elijah, whose narratives in 1 and 2 Kings involve the eradication of Baal worship in defense of the true god, Yahweh. This chapter then examines the ways in which Elijah remained an enormously popular and influential figure throughout the wider Near East, from the second half of the first millennium BCE, and well into the first and second millennia CE, known for his defense of the 'true' god. Late-antique-period Elijah is of particular importance for this study, both in terms of his biblical-narrative relationship to the figure of St. George, and in terms of popular late antique stories that involve Elijah and Moses, and which connect Elijah to the figure of al-Khiḍr, as well.

Chapter Five, "Early Christianity and St. George," focuses on the figure of St. George by contextualizing the first-century CE emergence of Christianity from among communities of Jews and against the backdrop of Roman state polytheism and the mixed religious milieu of the first centuries of the Common Era. This chapter examines the etymological origins of the name 'George', and suggests that etymology might link the early Christian cult of 'saint' George to contemporaneous local cults to Zeus-Georgos. This chapter also analyzes the earliest hagiography of St. George, the Syriac-language *Acts of St. George*, demonstrating the contemporaneous religious and political forces of influence in the text; among them, the narratives and motifs of Elijah, wherein St. George was presented as a defender of the *true* god, in the exact manner as Elijah's narrative in 1 and 2 Kings. The chapter also examines material evidence for the cult of St. George in the Eastern Mediterranean, focusing on the changing iconography of St. George. Particular attention is paid to the ways in which the changing iconography of St. George is related to contemporaneous Roman polytheism, developing Christianity, to the figure of the storm-god, and to Levantine agrarian religious influences.

Chapter Six, "The emergence of Islam and al-Khiḍr," situates the emergence of the Qur'ān (and later Islam) within its late antique political and religious contexts, dominated by the contemporary Melkite, Jacobite, and Nestorian sects of Christianity, by rabbinic Jewish traditions and the Talmudic texts produced in the academies at Babylonia, and by Arabian polytheistic traditions. This chapter then contextualizes the al-Khiḍr narrative (Q. 18:60–82), a pericope known as 'Moses and the Servant', which is a wisdom literature story about the nature of God's mysterious justice. It investigates as well the earliest exegetical (*tafsīr*) identification/naming of the 'servant' in the narrative as 'al-Khiḍr', and suggests that the *tafsīr* reference to 'al-Khiḍr' likely was an epithet for the figure of late antique Elijah. This chapter examines the figure of al-Khiḍr in the Eastern Mediterranean, through al-Khiḍr's linkages in text and in popular belief with the figure of Elijah, as well as through his characteristics of greenness and fertility, which were similar in the region to those of Elijah, and, in the wider Levant, to those of St. George. Finally, this chapter begins to characterize shared practices around these figures in the Eastern Mediterranean, as communities of Christians, Jews, and Muslims there grew and evolved together from the eighth-ninth century CE onward.

Chapter Seven, "Eastern Mediterranean Shared Religious History," refocuses the discussion on the shared practices between communities of Muslims, Christians, and Jews in the modern Eastern Mediterranean. It suggests implications about the relationships between these figures as revealed by this study, and surveys conclusions about the gradual emergence and development of Canaanite religion, Judaism, Christianity, and Islam; about the pervasiveness and durability of agrarian religion; about gradualism and continuity in regional religious history in general; and in particular about the theological distinctiveness of Judaism, Christianity, and Islam. Chapter Seven concludes with thoughts on the influence of geography upon the development of geographical motifs – such as that of the vanquishing of a serpent or snake – that remained popular in the region for millennia, on the shared religious culture of the Eastern Mediterranean, and on the historical and religious authenticity of regional shared religious practices.

Notes

1 I consider the Eastern Mediterranean to be those countries that line the Eastern border of the Mediterranean Sea from Southern Anatolia to Egypt. The terms 'Eastern Mediterranean' and 'Levant' will be used interchangeably in this book. While the term 'Eastern Mediterranean' can sometimes include Greece or even Italy and Libya, it will not here. Instead, 'Eastern Mediterranean' will be used interchangeably with 'Levant', but both terms will be limited to the region of the Levant: those modern countries which comprise or are near the Eastern border of the Mediterranean Sea basin: Southern and Southwestern Turkey, Syria, Cyprus, Lebanon, Israel, Palestine, and Egypt (especially the Sinai Peninsula). 'Levant' can also include the modern country of Jordan, and it does so here. 'Levant' is etymologically French (derived from Middle French and ultimately from the Latin term '*Levāre*', meaning 'to raise'), but it generally corresponds with the term (and with the countries referenced in) المشرق '*al-mashriq*'. In Arabic, as in French and Latin, '*al-mashriq*' – similar to '*Levāre*' – refers to 'the place of (sun)rise', or 'the 'East'.

2 St. George is believed to have been martyred in c. 303 CE, and is commonly depicted atop a white horse, poised to vanquish a dragon or serpent. See Chapter Five.

3 الخضر '*al-khiḍr*' (alt. '*al-khaḍir*', i.a.) is referenced in *tafsīr*/commentary to Q. 18:60–82. See Chapter Six.

4 This statistic is drawn by the author, and is based upon the total number of regional Christian churches, as recorded by the ARPOA project at the University of Balamand, which are dedicated to the figure of Mary, and which outnumber regional Christian churches dedicated to any other figure or saint. The second-most-common church designation is to St. George. http://home.balamand.edu.lb/ARPOA.asp?id=12737. See also Victor Sauma, *Sur Les Pas des Saints au Liban,* 2 vols. (Beirut: FMA, 1994), appendices, for statistics on the marked prevalence of St. George churches in Lebanon. This statistic is further informally drawn from ethnographic research in the region, and also is based upon the prevalence of Mary icons, pictures, and souvenirs, which also outnumber those available for any other regional figure or saint. Icons, pictures, and souvenirs of St. George also are highly common. Because this data is drawn from informal observation, it is difficult to be precise about the relative prevalence between regional figures and saints of icons, pictures, and souvenirs for sale, although St. George images and souvenirs abound.

5 It should be noted that many Alawite and Druze communities consider themselves a part of the Muslim tradition – of the *Ithnā 'Asherī* ('Twelver') and *Ismā'īlī* ('Sevener') Shi'i branches, respectively. However, most larger Sunni and Twelver-Shi'i communities dispute Alawite and Druze wholesale inclusion into mainstream Islam. Furthermore, Alawites and Druze arguably are distinct religious traditions, with their own places of worship (sometimes), communities, and histories. Therefore, the Alawite and Druze communities are addressed in this project individually. Druze prefer to call themselves '*Ahl al-Tawḥīd*', 'The People of Unity'. 'Druze' will be used in this project because of the prevalence of this name in Western scholarship. Alawites are believed to have been founded as a sect during the ninth century CE by Ibn Nuṣayr, and are sometimes known as *al-Nuṣayrīyyah.* Although 'Alawite' (Arabic) and related 'Alevi' (Turkish) communities share a linguistic root in and reverence for the Muslim figure of 'Ali, as well as associations with the Twelver-Shi'i branches of Islam, these communities have significant

religious, historical, linguistic, and political differences between them. Thus, Turkish-speaking Alevis and Arabic-speaking Alawites, while in some ways religiously similar and jointly considered in this project, are, in reality, distinct communities.

6 Counting communities in Turkey, Syria, Cyprus, Lebanon, Israel, Palestine, Jordan, and Egypt. Unless otherwise noted, population statistics herein (general and religious) are drawn from the Pew Research Religion and Public Life Project: http://www.pewforum.org/2012/12/18/global-religious-landscape-exec/ and from the CIA World Factbook: https://www.cia.gov/library/publications/the-world-factbook/. These sources are imperfect, but are used here because they contain recent and continually updated demographic data. Islam is the largest religious tradition in Eastern Mediterranean countries. Muslims make up around 54% of the population in Lebanon, 87% in Syria, and 97.8%, in Turkey. Within Muslim-majority populations, Sunni Islam predominates, although, in Lebanon, 27% of the population is Shi‘i, 15–30% of the population in Turkey is Alevi, and, in Syria, around 12% of the population is Alawite. Christians make up 2% or fewer of the population in Turkey; to 2–3%, in Israel and in Palestine; 3%, in Jordan; 10%, in Syria; 10%, in Egypt; 40.5%, in Lebanon; and 78%, in Cyprus. According to Laura Robson, "Recent Perspectives on Christianity in the Modern Arab World," the "major Christian branches in the Middle East are the Eastern Orthodox churches, which are especially prominent in Syria, Lebanon, Israel, Palestine, and Jordan; the Maronite church, located primarily in Lebanon; and the Coptic Church, in Egypt. Smaller Catholic, Assyrian and Protestant communities are scattered throughout the Levant, Iraq, and North Africa." Laura Robson, *History Compass*, vol. 9 (April 2011): p. 313. Judaism can be found in small communities (less than 1% of the population) in Turkey, Syria, Lebanon, and Egypt; at around 14%, in Palestine, and at 75% of the population in Israel. After Islam, Christianity, and Judaism, the most sizeable religious communities in the region are the Alawites and the Druze. In Palestine, the Druze constitute less than 1% of the population; in Israel, they make up about 1.6% of the population. In Syria, Druze amount to about 3% of the population, and Lebanon, where their community is largest, the Druze community comprises about 5.6% of the total population.

7 All figures for Syria are ca. 2014 CE, and do not account for the population-disruption effects of the Syrian war.

8 William Dalrymple, *From the Holy Mountain: A Journey among the Christians of the Middle East* (New York: Henry Holt and Company, 1997). On the subject of modern Christian-Muslim veneration of al-Khiḍr and St. George, see also Chapter Seven.

9 The designation 'all' is specific to the particular demographic makeup of the space under examination. In general, veneration of al-Khiḍr among the Alawites and the Druze is just as prevalent as it is among mainstream Muslim communities (although sometimes al-Khiḍr is understood in slightly different ways or associated with different figures among Alawite and Druze communities than he is among mainstream Muslim communities).

10 See Suad Slim; Al-Khiḍr being referred to as '*Abu Ḥarba*', the 'father of war/"the lance"', Hassan S. Haddad, "'Georgic' Cults and Saints of the Levant." *Numen* 16, no. 1 (1969): 21–39. See also Josef Meri, *The Cult of Saints Among Muslims and Jews in Medieval Syria* (Oxford: Oxford University Press, 2002), 4.

11 Elijah is referenced in the Hebrew Bible at 1 Kings 17–19, 21, and 2 Kings 1–2.

12 See Josef Meri, *The Cult of Saints among Muslims and Jews in Medieval Syria* (Oxford: University Press, 2002). See also Josef Meri, "Re-Appropriating Sacred Space: Medieval Jews and Muslims Seeking Elijah and al-Khadir." *Medieval Encounters*, 5, 3 (1999): 237–264.

13 Many ethnographic interviews, including with a Greek Orthodox church official in Balamand, Lebanon relayed that people who live in the region view St. George and Elijah both as victorious defenders of 'true' faith. Also, iconography in churches dedicated to St. George and to Elijah reinforces that narrative, as well as other narratives from

the *Acts of St. George*, and from the Hebrew Bible passages related to Elijah (1 Kings 17–19, 21, and 2 Kings 1–2). The Hebrew Bible narrative of Elijah depicts Elijah as the defender of the 'true' God, YHWH, in the face of predominant Baal worship; see Chapter Four. In the *Acts of St. George*, St. George intentionally was depicted employing similar motifs to that of Elijah in the Hebrew Bible account; most prominently, St. George was depicted as a defender of the 'true' God, Jesus Christ; see Chapter Five, 163–167.

14 'Common sites' can refer to sites that are or were jointly visited by multiple religious communities, and/or to sites specific to one of the religious figures that previously had been dedicated to another of the figures. Political influences during the 20th century have affected the joint veneration of these figures, especially the figure Elijah.

15 This was an overwhelmingly common response to my field research questions about joint or shared practices around these figures.

16 Meredith McGuire describes this experience as researchers encountering "assumptions, embedded in their field's basic definitions," that "get in the way of understanding the phenomenon they are observing. The realization comes as a jolt, because it means that the way we have learned to think about a phenomenon is now hindering our ability to understand what we are observing." Meredith B. McGuire, *Lived Religion: Faith and Practice in Everyday Life* (New York: Oxford University Press, 2008), 19.

17 By 'originated', I mean where they first appeared in written texts and in lived religious traditions. Also, these figures have been known by the characteristics and shared in the manner described herein in the region of the Levant (see the definitions of 'Levant', and of 'Eastern Mediterranean', above). Such can also be the case in surrounding regions, for instance, into Southeastern Europe and Central and Southeastern Asia. However, in some surrounding areas, the figures' characteristics and relationships differ, and are specific to their own geographical and cultural environments.

18 Only in Turkey is this the feast date for the figure Elijah, where he is known as a conflation of both Khiḍr and Elijah in the name *Khizrilyas* (also spelled 'Chidrelles' in the 17th-century travel account of Antoine de Busque). Oya Pancaroglu, "The Itinerant Dragon-Slayer: Forging Paths of Image and Identity in Medieval Anatolia." *Gesta*, 43, 2 (2004): 151–164. Most Christian calendars designate Elijah's feast day as July 20. The general feast or celebration day for both St. George and al-Khiḍr in the Eastern Mediterranean is April 23, except in the Orthodox churches, where the feast day of St. George is moved to May 6 if the calendar date of Easter falls on or after April 23.

19 For instance, in the case of al-Khiḍr, there has been significant internal debate over his spectacular disappearance and peculiar status as an immortal, and in the case of St. George, there has been significant internal debate over the historicity of St. George, to the extent that, in 1969, Pope Paul VI demoted the official feast day of St. George (already of waning official status) to an optional memorial.

20 This perspective has been challenged, but remains the predominant approach. See for instance Tomoko Masuzawa, *The Invention of World Religions* (Chicago: University of Chicago Press, 2005). See also Talal Asad, "The Construction of Religion as an Anthropological Category," in *Genealogies of Religion: Discipline and Reasons of Power in Christianity and Islam* (Baltimore, MD: Johns Hopkins University Press, 1993), 27–54.

21 Kim Knott, "Geography of Religion," in *The Routledge Companion to the Study of Religion*, 2nd ed. (New York: Routledge, 2010): 478. This perspective refers to 'separate silos' of religions.

22 See, for instance, Samantha Riches, *St. George: Hero, Martyr and Myth* (Gloucestershire, UK: Sutton Publishing, 2000). Riches claims that St. George's association with the dragon is a 'late-medieval accretion' to his narrative, rather than associating it with a prevalent motif in the Eastern Mediterranean. Riches' perspective reflects a majority of opinion among modern St. George scholars, which I challenge as a major premise of this book. See in particular Chapter Two, 65–70; Chapter Three, 161 and 178; and Chapter Seven, 245–248.

23 Richard W. Stump, *The Geography of Religion: Faith, Place and Space* (Lanham, MD: Rowman and Littlefield, 2008): 177. See also Knott, 476–491.

24 Biblical: Cogan 1964, Bronner 1968; Talmudic: Lindbeck 2010; and folkloric: Segal 1935, Schram 1997. Notable academic studies of St. George include Budge 1930, Riches 2000, and Goode 2009. Academic studies of al-Khiḍr include Ocak 1985, Franke 2000, Ghanami 2000, and Halman 2013. Academic studies of two or more of the figures have generally focused on two of the figures in comparison, such as St. George and Khiḍr in Hasluck 1929; Laird 1998, 2011; Dalrymple 1997; Bowman 2007; Wolper 2003, 2011; Elijah and al-Khiḍr in Augustinovic 1972; Meri 1999, 2002, or, in two instances, all three figures, in Canaan 1927; Ḥaddad 1969). In 1927, Taufik Canaan's study, *Mohammedan Saints and Sanctuaries in Palestine*, recorded and described the shrines that existed at that time in Palestine, and noted that, in many instances, shrines to Elijah, St. George, or Khiḍr were frequented by Jewish, Christian, and Muslim visitors at each, and that the names used for the 'saints' by visitors at each site were relatively interchangeable, i.e., Elijah/'*Ilyās*'/'*Ilyā*' and St. George being also called Khiḍr, and vice-versa.

25 Haddad, H.S. "'Georgic' Cults and Saints of the Levant," *Numen*, 16, Fasc. 1 (April 1969), 21–39.

26 Haddad, 22.

27 Also note that there is an inconvenient overlapping of names at work here. Hassan Haddad (spelled in Arabic with an aspirated Ḥ and two Ds) is the author of a work concerning the Syro-Canaanite storm-god, Baal-Hadad (spelled with a non-aspirated H and a single D). Haddad, from the *ḥdd* root, in Arabic, means to sharpen/delimit/demarcate, and *ḥadad* means 'blacksmith' (i.e., one who sharpens; see Hans Wehr, 187–188), and is today a common surname among Christians in Syria, Lebanon, and Palestine. Etymologically, as we will see, the earliest meaning of Hadad (*hdd* root) was onomatopoeically related to thunder (see Chapter Three). While potential aural relations between *ḥdd* and *hdd*, as well as the cultural trails suggested by this etymology, are interesting, the name similarity here is simply a coincidence. For more on the dragon-slaying myth with which the storm-god Baal-Hadad is associated, see Robert D. Miller II, *The Dragon, the Mountain, and the Nations: An Old Testament Myth, Its Origins, and Its Afterlives* (Explorations in ANE Civilizations 6. Eisenbrauns 2018).

28 James Grehan, *Twilight of the Saints: Everyday Religion in Ottoman Syria and Palestine* (Oxford: Oxford University Press, 2014). This perspective is adopted, as well, in this book.

29 Grehan, 190–192.

30 Shaye J.D. Cohen, *From the Maccabees to the Mishnah*, 2nd ed. Library of Early Christianity Series (Louisville, KY: Westminster John Knox Press, 2006), 50–52.

31 Evidence of porous, pluralist, and opportunist religious practices abounds, in religious texts and in other historical writings, in the examples found in this project, and in several recent works on the subject. Among them, see Michael Blömer, Achim Lichtenberger, and Rubina Raja, eds. *Religious Identities in the Levant from Alexander to Muhammad: Continuity and Change*. Contextualizing the Sacred 4 (Turnhout, Belgium: Brepols Publishers, 2015). See also Grehan, 150–156. See also Chapter Two, 37–50.

32 Blömer, introduction to *Religious Identities in the Levant from Alexander to Muhammad*, ed. by Blömer, Lichtenberger, and Raja, 3–4, emphasis added.

33 Blömer, 3–4.

34 Grehan, 140. See also Virginia Burrus and Rebecca Lyman, who argue that the notion of a realm of 'popular' religion, that is distinct from or even opposed to the religion of the elite, is untenable. Virginia Burrus and Rebecca Lyman, "Shifting the Focus of Christianity," in *A People's History of Christianity*, vol. 2, *Late Ancient Christianity*, ed. Virginia Burrus (Minneapolis, MN: Fortress Press, 2005), 14.

35 Grehan, 16.

36 Grehan, 62–70.

37 Sectarian differentiation in agrarian religious settings seemed to have been most pronounced in the realms of birth, marriage, death, and burial. See Chapter Two.

38 See Grehan, 16. "To reconstruct these patterns fully would require research encompassing many long centuries. The history of the long term – the only proper yardstick for agrarian religion – is beyond the scope of the present study."

39 See Chapter Two. See also the work of Fernand Baudel, who argues that the deepest levels of historical influence, such as geological, tend to be the slowest-changing. *The Mediterranean: And the Mediterranean World in the Age of Philip II.* 2 vols. Translated by Siân Reynolds. (Berkeley, CA: University of California Press, 1995), original 1949. See also Grehan, *Twilight of the Saints*.

40 'Canon' in this project will refer to a set of texts that have met a standard established by a community that sets them apart from other texts. Canon is conceptual – it exists in the mind of a person or group making a judgment about whether a text meets a certain standard. Communities also often imply by the term canon a 'whole,' or 'closed' set of texts, although the canon is only 'whole' or 'closed' from the specific perspective of that community. 'Scripture' as will be used herein: scripture *functions* in certain ways or *does* certain things or is *used by* a community in certain ways. As Wilfred Cantwell Smith argues, "people make a text into scripture, or keep it scripture: by treating it in a certain way." Smith, Wilfred C. *What is Scripture? A Comparative Approach* (Minneapolis, MN: Augsburg Books, 2000), 18. The concept of 'scripture' in Judaism, Christianity, and Islam is a highly debated topic. What constitutes scripture is as varied as the communities making the judgment. For the purposes of this study, I will classify scriptures loosely, so as to be inclusive of many variations while still treating this subject (not indefensibly) in the aggregate: those texts which constitute for their community a 'divine' message, as well as (often) lower-status texts which are related (commentary, exegesis) to the higher-status divine-message texts. 'Canons' in Judaism, Christianity, and Islam, as will be used herein: a compendium (which of course varies by sect) of religious texts (often scriptural in nature) that have met a standard established by the community that sets them apart from other texts. For the purposes of this project: in the case of Judaism: the canon of the Hebrew Bible as commonly attested by the mid-second century CE, as well as Rabbinic and Talmudic writings associated with the Oral Torah. In the case of Christianity: the canon of the New Testament and the Old Testament as of Bishop Athanasius' 367 CE Easter Festal Letter, as well as hagiographical accounts of saints' lives. In the case of Islam: the canon of the Qur'ān as of the 650 CE "Uthmanic Codex," as well as the major collections of Sunni and Shi'i *tafsīr* and *ḥadīth*.

41 Part of the development of canonical religion takes place through the work of tradition-specific commentators and exegetes, who "participated in each religion's development of its own distinctiveness in belief, worship, and thought, and, at the same time, contributed strongly to the differentiation and distance between the three faith communities [of the religious traditions of Judaism, Christianity, and Islam]." See Robert C. Gregg, *Shared Stories, Rival Tellings: Early Encounters of Jews, Christians, and Muslims* (Oxford, UK: Oxford University Press, 2015), xiv. Additionally, Gregg argues that exegetically 'competitive' scripture interpretation, of shared narratives, between religious commentators, functioned as a "singularly powerful force in the early divergence between Christians, Jews, and Muslims, and in their separation into discrete, independent religious cultures," Gregg, 598.

42 People in agrarian religious cultures, of course, did revere the written word – in particular, that of scriptural texts – as itself divine and imbued with supernatural power. See Grehan, *Twilight of the Saints*, 153.

43 All texts change over time, as a result of human scribal, redactive, or translational error or intention. 'Canonical' texts, however, tend to change more slowly because of the prohibitions and divine status often implied in being deemed 'scripture' and 'canon'.

44 Of course, through the continual work of commentators and exegetes, orthodoxies are not unchanging. "Scriptures and their meanings were not fixed or static, but always unfolding – vital and current precisely because they were creatively renewed and refreshed." Gregg, *Shared Stories, Rival Tellings*, 598.

45 Braudel, *The Mediterranean: And the Mediterranean World in the Age of Philip II* (Paris: Colin, 1949).

46 Frick, Frank S. "Palestine, Climate of" in *The Anchor Bible Dictionary*, Vol. 5 (New York: Doubleday, 1992), 126. See also Eric Cline, *1177 BC: The Year Civilization Collapsed* (Princeton, New Jersey: Princeton University Press, 2014), 123 and 126. See also Chapter Two, 24–35.

47 Frick, 126, quoting Amiran, D.H.K. "Land Use in Israel," in *Land Use in Semi-Arid Mediterranean Climates*. UNESCO International Geographic Union. Paris, 1964.

48 Although the Romans politically dominated the Levant beginning in the mid-first-century BCE, and the Latin language came gradually into some use thereafter, it is not possible to give a simple date for the introduction of Latin in the region. Additionally, a majority of people continued to speak Greek and Aramaic even when Latin was in administrative use.

49 See Chapter Seven, 256–258.

50 See also Chapter Two, 48–50.

51 John Hinnels, ed. *Routledge Companion to the Study of Religion*, 2nd ed. (New York: Routledge, 2010), 13.

52 Haddad, 22.

53 An interesting recent example of 'continuity of cult' exists in the northern Iraqi city of Mosul, at the 'Nabi Yunus' Islamic shrine and mosque there dedicated to the 'Prophet Jonah'. The Nabi Yunus shrine in Mosul is located on the edge of what was the historical city of Nineveh, capital of the Neo-Assyrian Empire from 911 to 609 BCE (see also Chapter Two, Part Two: Summary: Levantine political history). According to narratives from both the Qur'ān and the Hebrew Bible, Yunus/Jonah reportedly traveled to Nineveh to warn its citizens that they would be destroyed unless they repented their sins (Jonah 1:1–4:11; Q. 37:139–148). Many Muslims believe that the Prophet Yunus' bones were buried at the site, and that the remains at the site also included a tooth from the whale in whose belly for three days Jonah had swam when first he had attempted to avoid his commission from God to Nineveh. Prior to the site becoming an Islamic shrine and mosque, the site itself had earlier been the location of a monastery, during the Christian period. Most likely, the bones that were located at the Nabi Yunus shrine were interred there in 701 CE, upon the death of Christian patriarch Henanisho I, of the denomination that is today known as the Church of the East. These Christian origins of the site were reportedly what spurred members of the Islamic State to declare that, according to their narrow interpretation of the Qur'ān and of legitimate Islamic practice, the site itself was idolatrous rather than holy, and should be destroyed. On July 24, 2014, militants placed explosives on the inner and outer walls of the mosque and destroyed it. This was an enormous cultural loss, but it did serve the inadvertent purpose of having revealed underneath a 3,000-year-old Assyrian palace, complete with limestone slabs that bore the names of neo-Assyrian kings, rock reliefs of hitherto-unknown depictions of neo-Assyrian women, and a rock engraving of a Lamassu, mythical stone creatures who guarded the entrances of Assyrian palaces. See Khoshnaw, Namak, Adeane, Ant, and El Gibaly, Lara. "Explore the IS Tunnels: How the Islamic State Group Destroyed a Mosque but Revealed a 3,000-Year-Old Palace." BBC News: Nov. 22, 2018. Retrieved from https://www.bbc.co.uk/news/resources/idt-sh/isis_tunnels

54 For more on this process, see also Pierre Bourdieu, *The Logic of Practice*, trans. Richard Nice (Redwood, CA: Stanford University Press, 1990).

55 This development process continues for as long as the religious tradition exists.

2 Levantine geography, history, and agrarian religion

Part One: Levantine geography

The collision of the African, Arabian, and Eurasian continental plates millions of years ago formed the area for the Mediterranean, and in the process forced upward the complex of mountain ranges that line it. Gradually, the eastern and western ends of the Mediterranean joined, trapping the prehistoric Tethys Ocean for eons until it eventually evaporated, leaving behind a basin of limestone bedrock. Then suddenly, at some point nearly five million years ago, the Atlantic Ocean crashed through the Strait of Gibraltar in a spectacular waterfall that lasted 100 years, creating the modern Mediterranean Sea.[1]

Unique as a geographical region in being defined by a sea rather than by a continent, the only connections of the Mediterranean to the larger oceans of the world are through the Strait of Gibraltar, which separates Africa and Europe by just nine miles at its narrowest point, and through the Suez Canal, a manmade waterway that since 1869 CE has linked the Mediterranean with the Red Sea. The Mediterranean Sea and the mountainous continents that rise around it thus form a self-focused unit, which share not only weather patterns and climatic zones, but also a common geological and human history.

That shared history is the focus of this chapter, which examines the geological, climatological, and agricultural history of the Levant (Figure 2.1). It provides an overview of the political, religious, and linguistic history of the region, as well as detailing the long-term phenomenon known as 'agrarian religion', which is itself largely related to and shaped by the region's geography. The historical backgrounds presented in this chapter undergird the remainder of the book, and highlight, as well, the elements of continuity in history, culture, and lived experience that have been shared by peoples in the region over the past several thousand years.

Indeed, a fundamental argument of this book is that there have been far fewer breaks than commonly believed between compelling religious concepts among changing communities living in the Levant over time.[2] To that end, this book is conceived of as a counterpoint to the notion that the Eastern Mediterranean region in which this phenomenon plays out, and its history and religious traditions, can be divided into discrete units, with distinct borders. Such borders in cognition – political, temporal, and religious – have limited a thorough understanding of the region, and its longer-term continuities.

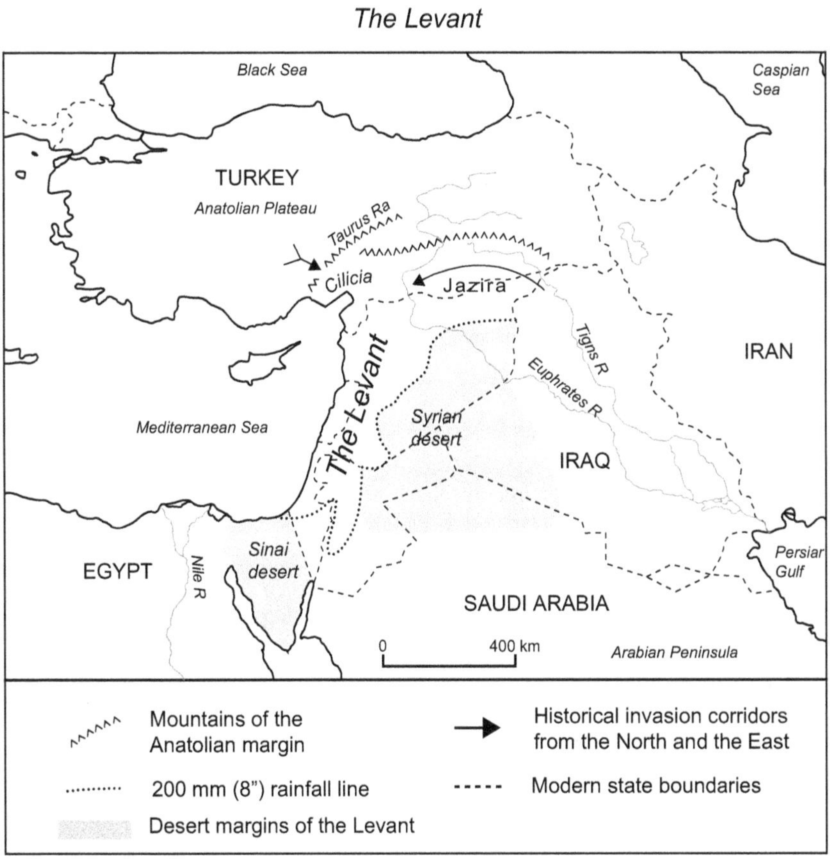

Figure 2.1 Map of the Levant

Geology

From its widest stretch, spanning from Gibraltar to Lebanon, the Mediterranean Sea extends 2,300 miles. Its north-south dimensions vary greatly, although a maximum length of 680 miles stretches between modern-day Venice and the north African country of Libya. The landlocked nature of the Mediterranean Sea effectively isolates it from the tides of the great oceans of the world, so that its own tides are primarily the result of the effects of the moon and the sun on the sea itself.

Because of the narrow entry and exit points through the Strait of Gibraltar of incoming Atlantic Ocean water and outgoing Mediterranean Sea water, the water temperature in the Mediterranean is warmer than in most seas. The Mediterranean also is saltier than most seas, and thus it can support fewer species of marine life than can the larger oceans. The generally warm and arid climate of the

Mediterranean, along with the effects of regularly unimpeded sunshine, combine to evaporate the sea at a rate of about 57 inches annually. This process further salinizes the Mediterranean, although annual rainfall, watershed from the Black Sea and the Nile River, and incoming colder water from the Atlantic Ocean generally replenish the lost water. Regional climate and agriculture are affected by the Mediterranean Sea, and so the fortunes of those who live around it are intertwined with the fortunes of the sea itself.

Climate

About 12,000 years ago, the climate of the Mediterranean approached its current conditions.[3] The Mediterranean is temperate and tropical, with two seasons: cool and wet in the winter from October to April, and hot and dry in the summer, from May to September. During all seasons, temperatures are moderated by proximity to the sea. The pattern of winds fluctuates from season to season and within different parts of the Mediterranean. During the winter, the jet stream, which guides areas of low pressure, shifts into the Mediterranean. A series of low-pressure centers form over the relatively warm Mediterranean Sea and move eastward; depressions also can move in from the Atlantic and become strengthened over the warmer Mediterranean Sea. As these air masses absorb the moisture of the sea, they pour rain onto the sea and nearby continents, and thus the preponderance of rainfall comes to the Mediterranean during the winter season. Winter, in fact, can be very stormy, dangerously raising the sea levels and threatening trade and transport.

Summer around the Mediterranean is hot and dry, and because most of the rain falls during the winter, during the summer season, streams can be intermittent. Areas near the sea can be humid and very hot, although the coastal mountains are often much cooler. Waterspouts, intense rotating columns of water and spray that are formed by a whirlwind occurring over the sea – essentially, tornadoes that appear to rise out of the sea – are a climatological feature of the Mediterranean Sea region. That is the case as well in the Eastern Mediterranean, about which we will see in Chapter Three.[4]

The rainy season begins again in the Eastern Mediterranean in October or November, in the form of heavy thunderstorms. Winter storms move eastward across the Mediterranean Sea, reach the landmass at the northern part of the Eastern littoral (southern Anatolia around Antioch, near modern-day Antayka, Turkey), and turn and move in a southeasterly direction across the inland areas.[5] Moisture-laden winds move up the coastal mountains of the Levant, where they condense and precipitate before crossing, leaving a dry area on the lee side of the mountains. Thus, the western coastal mountains of the Levant attract most of the regional rainfall, creating an area of rain-shadow to the east. As in all areas of the Mediterranean, variation in precipitation from year to year in the Eastern Mediterranean can be great. One year may bring twice the yearly average; the next year, only half, and variation in precipitation between zones of the Mediterranean is often substantial.[6]

About 70 percent of the average rain in the Levant falls between November and March. Influenced by altitude, latitude, and proximity to the Mediterranean, rainfall is unevenly distributed, decreasing sharply to the south and to the east. In the extreme south, average yearly rainfall is less than 100 mm (4 inches); in the extreme north, it can be as much as 1100 mm (43 inches).[7] Rainfall varies from season to season and year to year, and precipitation often is concentrated in destructive storms. In the Near East, a rainfall line (isohyet, on maps of the region) of at least 200 mm (8 inches) per year demarcates areas of arable land. Areas certain to be cultivable must fall within the 400 mm (12 inches) isohyet (see Figure 2.1). In the southern Levantine area of modern-day Israel and Palestine, for instance, only about one third is cultivable.[8] Droughts are frequent in the Levant, and in general, its climate can be characterized by three dry years out of every ten.[9] The combined realities of aridity and frequent drought have had an enormous influence on the kinds of religious motifs that developed in the Eastern Mediterranean.

Geography of the Levant: Regions, mountain ranges, rivers and water sources, and flora

The Levant is demarcated by several geological barrier zones. To the north are the Taurus Mountain ranges, which transition to the different climatic and cultural zone of the Anatolian plateau. To the northeast, the Levant descends into the steppe grasslands of the area between the Euphrates and Tigris rivers, known historically as Mesopotamia. To the east and to the south are the Syrian and Arabian deserts, distinguishing the Levant from the lower Tigris-Euphrates river system, as well as from the vast arid expanses of the Arabian Peninsula. To the southwest, the largely empty Sinai Peninsula separates the Levant from Egypt and the lower Nile. To the west is the Mediterranean Sea. These limits enclose an area about the size of Italy, which today is roughly coincident with the modern states of Syria, Lebanon, Israel, Palestine, and Jordan.[10] The entire region extends some 400 miles from north to south, and between 70 to 100 miles from west to east.

The Levant itself consists of three distinct geographical zones that run parallel from north to south. In the far west is a narrow strip of land known as the coastal Levant, with many seaports and agricultural areas. The center of the Levant consists of a zone of coastal mountain ranges, and in the east, descending eastward toward the Syrian and Arabian deserts, is an interior zone of plateaus and plains. One of the reasons why the Levant never coalesced into a single political unit is because of the geographical compartmentalization between these zones: coastlands, mountains, and interior plains, all of which have no natural center. Travel between or across the zones, and even within them, always has been difficult. The coast, in the west, and the interior plains, in the east, are open both from the north and from the south, which made these areas regular invasion points from Anatolia and northern Mesopotamia, as well as from Egypt and from outsiders to the west. Moreover, the mountains, as a barrier to travel, hinder communication between the coast and the interior plains, and thus exacerbate cultural differentiation between the Mediterranean ports and the inland cities.[11]

The mountains separating the coast from the interior are the principal physical feature of the Levant, comprising a north-south line of hills and mountains parallel to and immediately inland from the Mediterranean shoreline. These mountain ranges begin with the high Amanus Range (Nur Dağlari) of Cilicia, in the north, followed by the al-Nuṣayrīyyah Mountains that line the Syrian coastline. One mountain in particular from the Nur Dağlari range, located just north of the modern Syrian city of Latakia, is very important to this book: known to modern-day inhabitants as *Kılıç Dağı* in Turkish, and as جبل الأقرع *jebl al-āqra'* in Arabic, it has been known as Mount Hazzi to the ancient Near Eastern Hurrians and Hittites, as Mount Saphon/Sapan to ancient Canaanite inhabitants, as Mount Zaphon in the Hebrew Bible, as Mount Kasios, in Greek, and as Mount Casius in Latin. In this book, most frequently it will be referenced as Mount Sapan, as Mount Kasios, or as *jebl al-āqra'*. The location of this mountain is coincident with the land mass of the northernmost part of the Eastern Littoral of the Mediterranean basin; as such, it is exactly the area where winter storms from the Mediterranean turn and move overland to the south and the west.[12] As a geographical feature long related to climatic patterns, to navigational practices, and especially to regional religious history, this mountain figures prominently throughout the book.

South of the Nur Dağlari range, the extensive Mount Lebanon range parallels the Lebanese coastline. A southern area of the Mount Lebanon range juts to the northeast to form the Anti-Lebanon mountains, creating between them what is known as the Beka'a valley and the agricultural zone. Farther south is the Carmel Mountain range, dotting the Israeli coastline south of the city of Haifa. Southeast of the Carmel Mountains lies the Palestinian or Judean highlands or "hill country," which extend southerly and grade slowly into the Negev Desert. To the east, and parallel to the Palestinian highlands, lie the Transjordan Hills, which extend all the way south to the Gulf of Aqaba, in the Red Sea. Between the Palestinian Highlands and the Transjordan Hills lies the Jordan Rift Valley. Forced below sea level by the collision of the African and the Arabian continental plates, the Jordan Valley and the Dead Sea created there by runoff constitutes the lowest physical place on the earth, at about 1,300 feet below sea level.

Mount Lebanon is located at the geographical center of the Mediterranean mountain ranges, and only two gaps punctuate these ranges of coastal mountains. The northernmost gap is named the Homs Gap, located at the political border between modern-day Lebanon and Syria along the Mediterranean coast, and extending eastward to the Syrian city of Homs. The southernmost gap is called the Galilee Gap, and it extends from the Mediterranean Sea just north of the city of Haifa eastward to Lake Tiberius (the Sea of Galilee). These gaps in the central mountain ranges that line the Levant are significant not only as geographical features, but also because they function as the Levant's only zones of west-east access between the Mediterranean Sea and the interior plains.

Being located exactly at the convergence of three continental plates – the African, Arabian, and Eurasian – thus has formed the topography of the Levant, creating its three topographical zones: coastal plains in the west, a central band of mountain ranges, and plains and plateaus in the east. This continental-plate convergence also accounts for another very important geographical feature of the Levant: frequent earthquakes.[13]

Rivers and water sources

There are three primary rivers in the Levant. The Orontes River, in the north, originates near Baalbek in the Beka'a Valley, and flows for 355 miles northeast through Lebanon and Syria, then west and southwest into Turkey, exiting into the Mediterranean near Antakya (ancient Antioch). The Orontes River also is called locally in Turkish and in Arabic the '*Asi*, 'Rebel' River, because, unlike any other regional river, it flows to the north rather than to the south. The Litani River also originates near Baalbek and flows 87 miles southwest through the Beka'a valley, turning due west and flowing sharply out of the Lebanese Mountains into the coastal plains and Mediterranean Sea at a location north of the city of Tyre.

Historically, the Orontes River also has been known as Τυφῶν 'Typhon', by the Greeks, etymologically related to the Greek word for 'smoke', or 'storm', and named after the fearsome, serpent-headed storm monster defeated by Zeus.[14] In Latin, and likely in earlier local languages, the Orontes River was known as the Draco, or the 'dragon' river.[15] The name of the Litani River is derived etymologically from the Semitic root *ltn*, corresponding, according to many sources, to the mythical sea creature Lotan ('Leviathan'), in the Hebrew Bible, whom Yahweh defeated. Historically, the Greek demon Typhon also was associated with the Hebrew Bible figure of Lotan. These associations highlight the interconnected nature of regional myths and point out historical linkages between these specific myths and regional rivers, which will be discussed in coming chapters; especially in Chapter Three. Most importantly for this study, the Orontes (Typhon/Draco, 'dragon') river long has been associated, because of proximity, with Mount Sapan/Mount Kasios/ *jebl al-āqra'*, the prominent mountain located just north of the modern coastal Syrian city of Latakia on the Mediterranean, which long was considered the home of Baal-Hadad, the Storm-God.[16]

The Jordan River originates in tributaries in the Lebanon and Anti-Lebanon mountain ranges and also in tributaries from the Golan of Syria and Israel. These tributaries join in the Huma Valley, forming both the Jordan River and filling the Sea of Galilee. The Jordan River flows 156 miles south from the Sea of Galilee through the Jordan valley and along the Jordan rift, descending finally into the Dead Sea. Hundreds of smaller – and often seasonal – rivers and tributaries flow westward from the coastal mountain ranges along the folds of the coastal mountains.

People living in the more-arid interior plains are watered by a few surface lakes, as well as smaller rivers such as the 43-mile-long Yarmouk, an eastward-flowing tributary of the Jordan River that comprises part of the modern border between Israel, Jordan, and Syria, and drains into the Hauran Plateau in northern Jordan. In addition to direct rainfall, peoples in the Levant are watered by underground aquifers. Aquifer fields in the Levant, used for drinking water and for agriculture, primarily are shallow – close to the surface of the land – and are recharged by area streams, rivers, and lakes, which are, themselves, naturally affected by rainfall levels.[17]

In the Levant, Syria's main water sources are the Euphrates and the Orontes Rivers; Jordan depends upon the Yarmouk and Jordan Rivers; Iraq depends upon the Euphrates and Tigris Rivers; Lebanon's sources are the Litani and Orontes Rivers, as well as several smaller rivers which flow westward from the coastal mountains; Israel depends upon water from the Sea of Galilee and the Coastal and Mountain Aquifers; Palestine depends on the Mountain Aquifer, which mainly is located underneath the West Bank, and Gaza depends upon the Coastal Aquifer. In the West Bank and Gaza, access to water is limited by the Israeli government, which motivates many people to sink unofficial wells into local aquifers and further destabilizes the continued viability of these resources.

Historical water preservation and transportation methods: Cisterns and qanats

In the arid climate of the Levant, where precipitation is concentrated during the winter months from November to March, and the summers are hot and dry, it has been essential to capture the winter rainfall for use later during the year. The historical use of cisterns throughout many parts of the Levant and the wider Middle East has served as a ready water source during the summer, as well as a crop-yield-extender in areas where rain-fed farming is employed. Deep, plaster-lined cisterns cut into the limestone bedrock at a depth of 5 to 25 meters and positioned to capture a maximum quantity of winter rain can store water for as long as two or three years.[18]

Because of the uneven distribution of land that falls within the rain-fed farming zone, historically throughout the Levant and the wider Middle East it also has been important to employ creative water transportation methods. This could be achieved by two types of hydraulic systems: open canals, or underground channels, known as *qanats*. Open canals were suitable where it was possible directly to tap into the waters of a river, but *qanats*, of Iranian origin, consisted of an underground channel dug along a precise shallow gradient and connected to the surface by a series of vertical shafts. The underground tunnels collected their water as it drained through the soil – usually commencing at the base of a mountain or alongside a river – and ran gradually downhill at 50–60 km toward its destination. *Qanats* often collected water in large cisterns from which the water could be transferred to nearby fields via open channels, and, properly constructed, could have an operational life of a century or more.[19]

Flora

The flora of the Mediterranean is remarkably similar around the east and west of the sea, as it was in most of North Africa, as well, before processes of desertification crept up to the sea.[20] Most plant life around the Mediterranean coastal and mountain areas is comprised of *maquis*, a dense scrub vegetation that is hardy and drought-resistant. Maquis is made up of evergreen shrubs and trees, such as oak, pine, olive, and laurel, as well as *garigue*, a low, soft-leaved cover of bushes, bunchgrasses, and aromatic herbs like juniper, lavender, and sage, all of which grow well in the dry soil of the Mediterranean, and which produce the region's characteristic scent.

Agriculture

The history of agriculture is inextricably related to the history of soil. An ideal type of agricultural soil, called loam, is made up of a mixture of clay, silt, and sand, and allows for free air circulation, good drainage, and easy access to plant nutrients, such as nitrogen, potassium, and phosphorus.[21] The character of a soil reflects topography, climate, and biology, as well as the local geology underneath the soil, which provides the raw materials from which soil is derived. The geology of a region controls the kind of soil produced, because as rocks break down, they crumble into particular types of soils. Granite disintegrates into rocky soils, whereas basalt produces clay-rich soils. Limestone, the bedrock of most of the Mediterranean basin, mainly dissolves away, leaving behind rocky landscapes with thin soils and caves.[22]

The history of agriculture also is inextricably related to humans. Communities of humans spread out from East Africa to Western Asia, reaching the Levant around 100,000 years ago, and arriving at the Western end of the Mediterranean in Spain approximately 40,000 years ago. Paleolithic humans in the then-abundant ecosystems gathered plants, caught fish and crustaceans, and hunted mammals.

As humans adapted to the natural environment, the technology they created to do so became more complex and powerful through time. After the most recent Ice Age and during a time of warming climate, broadly speaking, from about 12,000 to 10,000 years ago, communities of humans in the Mediterranean basin began to adopt new methods of living within the natural environment. These methods involved the seasonal cultivation of food plants, like grain-bearing grasses, as well as bringing herd animals and their migrations under human direction. Groups of people in fertile areas along the Syrian hills and near the annually flooded lakes in the Nile Valley began to harvest wild grains between 14,500 and 13,000 years ago, and eventually to save and plant seeds from one season to the next.[23]

Once it was taken, that step of saving and planting seeds enabled the feeding of more people in the community, as well as the survival of larger, more sedentary populations in limited areas. Domestication of plants improved the dependability of the food supply and enabled larger populations, but it also required a settled community to care for crops. Along with agriculture came weaving, pottery making, and the fashioning of lighter, more sophisticated stone tools and weapons, a well-attested characteristic of the Neolithic period. The major early crops in the region were barley, wheat, oats, rye, legumes, and flax. Farmers selected seeds from the best plants after the harvest for planting in the following year, enabling the growth of new varieties of crops.[24]

As important as was the domestication of plants to Neolithic people was the domestication of animals. Sedentary farmers also began to keep tamed species, but the early work of domestication was undertaken by migrant peoples who, rather than following herds of grazing animals in order to hunt them, began gradually to protect herds from predators and to control their annual movements. Most herders were not nomadic wanderers, but practiced transhumance, the movement of herds to higher mountains in summer, and lower areas in winter. Pastoralism developed first in the Near East with goats and sheep, and later with cattle, pigs, and donkeys, because these animals were adapted to land where grassland, brush, and forest interpenetrate.[25]

The Levantine regional population began to grow rapidly as the domestication of wheat and legumes increased food production. By about 7,000 BCE small farming villages were scattered throughout the Levant. The first farmers relied on rainfall to water their crops. They were so successful that, by about 5,000 BCE, the human population occupied virtually the entire area of the Middle East suitable for dryland farming. This, in turn, increased pressure to extract more food from the land, and led to a major revolution in agricultural methods: irrigation.[26]

Irrigation

The early, river-based irrigation civilizations, such as those in Mesopotamia and Egypt, became history's first great empires. Water was vitally important and life-giving: during those periods in history when the water flow was interrupted, either naturally or through human causes, crop production fell, surpluses dissipated, dynasties toppled, and starvation and anarchy threatened the entire social system.[27]

In fact, the way water resources presented themselves seems to have exerted a strong influence on the nature of a society's political system. Historically, irrigation cultures have been accompanied by centralized states with large bureaucracies. However, rain-fed farming could not produce the food surpluses, population densities, and grand civilizations that were enabled by irrigation.[28] It seems, therefore, that physical geography has impacted the Eastern Mediterranean region in yet another way: the Levant's lack of large, annually flooding rivers that could be harnessed for irrigation – and its extreme reliance on rainfall for agricultural needs – may also have impeded the political consolidation of the region.[29]

Changes over time to land and agricultural practice

Changes in climate often resulted in changes to agriculture, but sometimes changes in agricultural practices also changed the natural environment. Erosion, a natural process essential to soil formation, also can be sped up dangerously – and sometimes swept away altogether – by human practices such as deforestation, irrigation, and plowing.[30]

From antiquity, through the Middle Ages, and into the modern periods, agriculture was the basic economic activity of the Levant. In antiquity and the Middle

Ages, agricultural production was dominated by the Mediterranean staple crops of grains, olives, and grapevines.[31] During the Middle Ages, over nine-tenths of all peoples in the Mediterranean lived on the land in an agricultural, rural setting, and new crops such as sugar cane, citrus fruits, melons, and strawberries were introduced.[32] Grazing animals – cattle, sheep, goats, and pigs – were important as food and clothing sources, and horses, mules, and donkeys were used for transportation and drafting. These animals grazed on fallow fields and enriched them with manure.

The most important raw material for the textile industry in the pre-modern era was wool, and sheep were among the greatest number of grazing animals. Demands for wool increased the sizes of flocks, increasing their impacts on forests and grasslands and contributing to soil depletion and erosion, because sheep are notoriously destructive of vegetative cover.[33] Timber always was in great demand for shipbuilding and other construction, heating, metallurgy, ceramic manufacture, and sugar refining. Because the shores and hills of the eastern Mediterranean largely had been exhausted of their timber resources by the older civilizations of Syria, Mesopotamia, and Egypt, until the modern era wood had to be sought from northern areas of costal Anatolia.[34] Indeed, a landscape barren of trees is a characteristic of the modern Eastern Mediterranean. For instance, *jebel al-āqra'*, the Arabic name for Mt. Kasios/Mt. Sapan, the consequential mountain along the northern Levantine coast, mentioned above and located at the border between modern-day Turkey and Syria, means in Arabic the "'bald' or 'stark' mountain," and refers to the deforested state of the mountain.[35]

In the Early Modern Period, beginning in the 17th century CE, agriculture continued to consist of the Mediterranean staples, but it also was supplemented by green vegetables, and root crops. New plants from the Americas also appeared, including maize, potatoes, and tomatoes, and crops from the east, including rice and cotton, began to be raised in the Ottoman Empire (1453–1923 CE) and in Egypt. In the Ottoman Empire, agricultural production beyond the level of subsistence was taxed by the state to finance military and bureaucratic endeavors, and wood, as a source of fuel for warmth, cooking, and smelting, remained the dominant source of energy.[36]

During the Modern Period, beginning in the 19th century CE, changes to materials and processes spurred by the industrial revolution resulted in unprecedented impacts upon the natural environment. Mechanization – the use of metal machines driven by power generated from a heat source – of both trains and agricultural practices was a challenge throughout the Mediterranean, because of its soils and diverse topography. However, changes to long-distance travel and trade brought by the steam engine began rapidly to transform Eastern Mediterranean trade and travel during the late 19th and early 20th centuries.[37] Agricultural mechanization in the eastern Mediterranean made only minor inroads until the mid-20th century, until which time at least 80 percent of the population had remained agrarian, producing crops such as grains, tobacco, rice, cotton, grapes, cereals, olive oil, sugar, oranges, and dates.[38] Today, less than 10 percent of the population, on average, in the Eastern Mediterranean is engaged in agricultural work.[39]

Over the course of the 20th century CE, changes to production methods and tools were extensive, and the effects of those changes upon local populations and civic infrastructure were tremendous. In 1800 CE, the population of Istanbul, the Levant's most populous city, was approximately 750,000, and had grown to 1.4 million by 1924 CE. In Beirut, the population in 1860 CE was 10,000, and by 1914 CE it ballooned to 150,000. Between 1917 and 1937 CE, Cairo grew from 800,000 to 1.3 million. Infrastructural resources also grew during the 20th century, but improvements often kept poor pace with population growth. Water and sewage systems, gas, electricity and telephone services, buses, tramways, and motor traffic increased in the Eastern Mediterranean during the 1920s and 1930s CE.[40]

Large-scale mass production of agriculture began in the eastern Mediterranean after World War II, further speeding population growth, and raising the levels of animal waste and pesticides in regional rivers and seas. Enormous human-driven changes to the land of the Levant during the 20th century CE have caused the emergence of several environmental problems, particularly during the past 50 years. Among those environmental problems are water pollution and low reserve, air pollution, detrimental mass agricultural practices, desertification of arable land, loss of biodiversity among plant and animal species, as well as potential food shortages.[41] Human-driven damage to natural systems during the relatively brief Modern Period thus has been greater than that of all previous times combined.[42]

Conclusion

Geological history in the Eastern Mediterranean is one of change: changes to land and to climate that have been the results both of natural and human processes. However, until very recently – the mid-20th century CE – among the most stable and continuous human economic and sustenance activities in this region has been agriculture and farming. One of the more fundamental changes to patterns of lived human experience, therefore, to have taken place in the Levant during the past few thousand years was that of 20th-century CE mechanization and mass agriculture, which have enabled most inhabitants no longer primarily to be engaged in agricultural work. This diminution in the prevalence of agricultural work seems to have gone hand-in-hand with other modernizing changes – such as the advent of mass literacy – that have affected regional religious practices (even if those changes seem to have had somewhat less effect on long-lived regional geographical motifs).

Another continuity evident in this analysis is that of the long-term regional dependence upon rainfall for agricultural needs. Because the Levant is arid and lacks the kind of major irrigational rivers that predictably flood and deposit soil-enriching silt, agricultural peoples in this region for most of its inhabited history primarily have relied upon rainfall, which also feeds rivers, aquifers, and water storage and preservation technologies, for their farming needs. Still today, agricultural use accounts for some 70% of regional water usage.[43] Of course, all early human agricultural communities needed rain and water to survive, but in the arid environment of the Levant – a region frequently in drought – the essential need for rain long has been acute. The pervasiveness of this regional need for rain has affected groups of humans living in the Levant throughout history, regardless, of course, of political, religious, or linguistic affiliations, and has contributed immensely to the development of regional motifs involving rain, storms, and agricultural needs – particularly those we examine in this book.[44]

Part Two: Levantine political, religious, and linguistic history

As the only land bridge between the continents of Europe, Asia, and Africa, the Levant has been well traveled by peoples and empires throughout history. Primarily due to an interrupted geography that impeded political consolidation, but also because the Levant lacked great rivers for irrigation and trade (and thus administration), the Levant never coalesced as a single political unit. On occasion, it was ruled from within by an internal ruler or dynasty, but for most of its history, the region of the Levant has been subsumed by larger powers.

By and large, the centralized, irrigated empires – and their historical successors – to the north, east, and southwest of the Levant have at various times exchanged control of all or parts of the Levant. Historically speaking, even when areas of the Levant were not under the direct control of surrounding superpowers, those areas tended nonetheless to be politically and culturally influenced by nearby neighbors: Anatolia and northern Mesopotamia influenced the north; Mesopotamia and Persia influenced the eastern interior plains; outsiders from the west influenced the coastal areas; and Egypt influenced the southern lowland areas.

Part Two of this chapter is designed to provide an overview of the ways in which human history in the Levant has overlain regional geography. This section will outline the political, religious, and linguistic backdrop of the human stage upon which the major story in this book unfolds. In so doing, this section serves also to highlight linguistic and religious linkages between and among changing political eras.

The political history section of this chapter is divided into time periods, so as to give an historical impression of the region as a whole, and over time. I am mindful, of course, that each of these periods and designations is or could be the subject of significant and important debate as to when and how and even whether it is constituted. Also, the Levant regularly was subject to combined, contested, and region-specific rule, and the region is of course not a monolith. Conscious of these important caveats and debates, I offer the following overviews as background information, and as support for my argument that Levantine history, like Levantine religion, properly is appreciated when viewed in the aggregate. Summaries of religious history (traditionally understood), and linguistic history follow at the end of this section.

Summary: Levantine political history

ca. 6000 BCE Regional settlements
ca. 3000 Coastal cities
ca. 2334–2250 Akkadians (Sargon I – rule extends to the Syrian coast)

ca. 2000 Amorites / Canaanites / Syro-Palestinian city-states (Aleppo, Byblos, Damascus, Jerusalem, Ugarit., i.a.)
ca. 1550–1350 Egypt controls northern and southern Levant
ca. 1350–1200 Hittites control the northern Levant; border with Egypt at town of Qadesh
ca. 1100 Arameans in the interior; Philistines in the southern coast; Phoenicians in the northern coast; Hebrews in the hill country
ca. 1000–929 Hebrew Kingdoms; thereafter Israel in north 929–722 and Judah in the south 929–586
911–609 Neo-Assyrians
609–539 Neo-Babylonians
539–332 Persians
332–323 Greeks
312–63 Seleucids
312–198 Ptolemies
140–37 Hasmoneans
63 BCE–395 CE Romans
395–610; 627–636 Byzantines
610–627 Persians
636–661 Rashidun Caliphate
661–750 Umayyads
750–978 Abbasids
860–905 Tulunids
935–969 Ikhshidids
978–1071 Fatimids
1071–1098 Seljuks
1098–1187 Frankish Crusader Kingdoms
1187–1250 Ayyubids
1250–1516 Mamluks
1516–1923 Ottomans
1920–1940s French, British Protectorates
1940s– Syria, Lebanon, Israel-Palestine, Jordan, Iraq

Summary: Traditional Levantine religious history

Religious concepts do not exist in a vacuum, gradually contacting similarly pristine religious ideas. Indeed, it is a premise of this project that religious ideas are inseparable from and connected by other regional, political, and temporal influences – including the influences of nearby religious groups. Additionally, the summary here represents a traditional understanding of regional religious history. As will be argued in Part Three, and demonstrated throughout the remainder of this book, daily religious life for most people of the region, throughout most of history, was and should be characterized far more by the agrarian concerns of everyday existence than by modern notions of institutionalized religions, with their attendant doctrinal differences and boundary concerns. Nevertheless, it is useful here to delineate with broad brushstrokes the particular periods of regional *emergence* of certain doctrinal religious complexes, in order to demonstrate a general historical and temporal pattern against which this project is set.

From approximately 2000 BCE (and before), the Levant could be characterized primarily by so-called 'Canaanite' as well as other ancient Near Eastern religious traditions. Beginning in approximately 1000 BCE Hebrew traditions began to emerge out of Canaanite and other ancient Near Eastern religions; these grew and consolidated into what we now call Judaism during the seventh and sixth centuries BCE. In the mid-sixth century BCE, under Achaemenid rule, Zoroastrian religious ideas appeared in the region, as did Greek religious concepts in the final third of the fourth century BCE, and Roman in the mid-first century BCE. Christian traditions emerged in the Levant during the mid-first century CE, as did Jewish Rabbinic traditions. Islamic religious traditions emerged in the Levant in the mid-seventh century CE; Islamic sectarian traditions such as the Druze and Alawites in the 11th century CE; western Roman Christian traditions appeared during the 11th and subsequent centuries CE, Protestantism appeared in the Levant beginning in the 19th century CE.[45]

Summary: Levantine linguistic history

Noting that this characterization is drawn broadly and that linguistic traditions also are inextricably related to politics, one observes that major regional languages of the Levant have come from the Semitic language family. Akkadian was the first administrative *lingua franca* of the Near East; Northwest Semitic languages such as Aramaic, Canaanite, Ugaritic, and Hebrew emerged and dominated in the Levant following the 13th century BCE. During the Persian Era in the sixth century BCE, Aramaic became the general regional language of administration, and this was matched by spoken varieties of Aramaic; the Syriac dialect of Aramaic emerged in the first century of the Common Era. Aramaic remained a primary spoken language of the Levant for over a thousand years, until well into the tenth century CE. From the final-third of the fourth century BCE Greek became a language of administration and was spoken in some communities (Greek remains the primary language of the Greek southern half of the island of Cyprus); in the early centuries of the Common Era, Latin became an administrative language and, in some instances, supplanted Greek, although Latin was not widely spoken. Instead, Arabic gradually displaced spoken dialects of Aramaic (and some Greek) after the seventh century CE. The major spoken language of the Levant and the wider Near East through the modern period has been Arabic (and, since the 11th century CE, Turkic languages in the north of the Levant), although modern state formations such as that of Israel in 1948 have introduced Modern Hebrew as a major regional spoken language.

Part Three: Levantine agrarian religion

Most scholarship about Levantine religious history presumes that people's religious identities and everyday practices reflected the kind of doctrine, law, and texts that anchor canonical religion, envisioning historical religious communities as mirroring those of *modern* sectarian religious identities and communities.[46] However, everyday religion in the Levant, as it actually was practiced, was shaped far more by "the essentially agrarian conditions of everyday existence"[47] than it was oriented around orthodox notions of religion. What is more, this kind of agrarian religious practice and perspective remained the dominant mode of religious expression in the Levant well into the early 20th century CE.[48] Rather than being characterized by texts, canons, and law, it is geography itself that left the most enduring stamp on Levantine premodern religion and culture.[49]

This way of thinking asks most readers to reconsider what they know about religious history.[50] Unless otherwise noted, Part Three of this chapter largely is based upon the pioneering scholarship of James Grehan on the topic of agrarian religion. Grehan's work sets a new path for a more-accurate understanding of pre-modern religious practice in the Levant, and fundamentally it resonates with the religious historical picture revealed by this book, as well. *Geography, Religion, Gods, and Saints in the Eastern Mediterranean* offers an illustration of agrarian religion in practice.

Infrastructure, religious professionals, and illiteracy

While most scholarship about Levantine historical religion presumes that religious expressions were characterized by institutional or canonical religion, in the way we think of those concepts today, infrastructural realities on the ground suggest that that could not have been the case. For one thing, the possibilities for 'canonical' religious identities entirely were predicated upon the religious infrastructure that was required to impart, enforce, and police orthodox belief and practice. Religious structures, religious experts, literacy, and the social and political apparatuses that attend these institutions, all of which are necessary for orthodoxy to prevail, always were sorely lacking in the Levant, and deeply imbalanced when they did exist.[51]

Grehan's work surveyed Ottoman Syria and Palestine between approximately 1600 and 1800 CE, and was based upon written pilgrimage accounts, as well as Ottoman administrative records dating from the *Tanzimat* (1839–1876 CE). Although Grehan's analysis was limited to the early modern period, that time period in regional religious history represents the only possible point in time – other than during the 20th century CE – during which regional religious infrastructure could have been robust enough to impart, enforce, and police orthodox belief and practice. That makes the early premodern period, from 1600 to 1800 CE, useful as a framework for understanding Levantine historical religious expressions into even earlier periods, as well.

That is, if modern religious identities are a product of the religious infrastructure necessary to impart and enforce orthodoxy, and such infrastructural requirements were only earliest realizable in the region during the 20th century CE, then all regional peoples, socially and economically marked until the 20th century CE, as we have seen in Part One, by the 'agrarian concerns of everyday existence',[52] necessarily would have shared similar notions of agrarian religious practice and identity. Furthermore, Grehan himself suggested that many aspects of the notion of agrarian religion constitute a useful framework for understanding regional religious history into time periods much earlier than those he researched, but admitted that his work simply could not encompass the necessary scope to demonstrate that end.[53] This book, on the other hand, does allow us to examine the presence, scope, and functioning of agrarian religious orientation in the Levant into much earlier time periods.

Early modern religious structures such as mosques, churches, and synagogues may have existed at a basic level in the few larger towns in the region, but religious architecture everywhere else was rudimentary.[54] Religious personnel – those trained in religious teachings and who could make careers out of imparting sanctioned religious knowledge – could be found overwhelmingly in the towns, but not in the countryside, where many people lived.[55] Furthermore, deficiencies in education, and particularly in literacy, were pervasive until the period of modern state reform. Premodern religion thus was not dominated by institutional religion, because the religious establishment simply did not have the means to enforce or "correct" religious belief across the population.[56] Furthermore, that infrastructural reality was not differentiated between townspeople and peasantry, who usually were equally illiterate and uninformed.[57] Most people in the region, throughout most of history, were religiously opportunistic and pluralist: one could and did follow those gods who were powerful, and one could and did engage in those 'magical', sacrificial, and amulet-driven practices and other rituals that were considered *effective* – irrespective of, in lieu of, and-or in concert with – a 'primary' religious orientation.[58]

Agrarian religion

Instead of being defined by orthodox thought and practice, Levantine religion in the premodern period was shaped by geographical and climatological realities, and dominated by magic men; sacred stones and caves; water cults; holy trees; haunted landscapes; spells, talismans and icons that could aid in fertility or act as magical shields that protected against demons and the misfortune and mental disturbances caused by them; by visions and dreams; blood sacrifices; prayer; and a common religious culture that paid little attention to sectarian difference.[59] The "core obsession" of agrarian religion was "managing a hostile and uncertain world."[60]

Saints and magic men

Saints or 'holy men' sat at the head of agrarian religious culture.[61] Moreover, the Levantine cult of saints transcended sectarian affiliation. People of all religious backgrounds looked first to the saints, who, in everyday worship in agrarian religion, functioned as the most important intermediaries between heaven and earth.[62] While saints sometimes were unusually holy men, they just as often were notable figures from religious history: prophets and legendary figures,[63] as in the cases of Elijah, St. George, and al-Khiḍr.

One of the most compelling powers that saints wielded, and that which people most appreciated, was the saints' mastery of the arts of healing. In a time of rudimentary medical care, which consisted mainly of natural and dietary remedies and treatments, mortality was high, and sickness was common. Saints' powers in the areas of healing and protection carried with them, as well, an implied capacity for equal harm and vengeance,[64] and thus they also were thought of as great protectors.

Tombs

Deficiencies in religious architecture, especially in the countryside, resulted in tombs – rather than mosques, synagogues, and churches – functioning as the central religious and institutional structures in the region. Worshippers, both male and female, were motivated by the terrestrial concerns of the health of their children, animals, loved ones, for increased rain, for the growth of crops, the return of missing relatives, and for fertility.[65] Worshippers came not only to pray and plead for intercession with God; they sought basic legal services and protections, and so tombs also functioned as social gathering sites. The veneration of saints and holy persons at their shrines furthermore flourished equally among all religious communities. "These customs were, in fact, neither 'Muslim', 'Christian', nor 'Jewish'. They had nothing to do with official religious doctrine."[66]

The longevity of a saint's cult reflected that saint's abilities. If sufficient numbers of people believed in that saint, their cult would endure.[67] That is particularly notable for this book, because the cults to Baal-Hadad, Elijah, St. George, and al-Khiḍr have existed for a very long time, indeed. In the case of Elijah, St. George, and al-Khiḍr, the centerpiece of a tomb or shrine dedicated to them could be either a fragment of their person – as in the case of the ubiquitous pieces of St. George located throughout the Mediterranean. More often, the hundreds of sites were created around a place associated in some measure with one of the figures: a miracle that had occurred there, a dream in which a benefactor had been told to create the shrine there, a 'high place'/on a mountain, and/or a site long associated with one or more of the figures.[68] During a fieldwork interview in August 2013 at the St. George Monastery of Ras el-Metn, on Mt. Lebanon, I was told that the monastery itself had been built, as a Christian monastery, during the 12th century CE, for the very reason that a local Druze leader had encountered al-Khiḍr in a dream, and he had been instructed by al-Khiḍr to pay for the building of a monastery to himself – that is, St. George – on that exact site.

Sacred landscapes: Stones, caves, water cults, and the powers of nature

Holy scripture – whether Muslim, Christian, or Jewish – described Syria and Palestine as the locations of divine revelations and other important occurrences,[69] and local people literally could find evidence for this everywhere.[70] But those scriptural ties to the land were related to the power of the landscape itself, which was intimately tied to the region's geography and geology. Indeed, nothing reveals the deeply intertwined relationship in the Levant between religion and geology better than the popular use of stones.[71]

The geology of the Levant is of course ultimately related to its bedrock of limestone, which, as it weathers, mainly dissolves away, leaving behind rocky landscapes with thin soils and caves.[72] Unsurprisingly, perhaps, local people used piles of stones to mark holy sites among the landscape. Among what was a mainly illiterate population, as well as for foreign travelers, piles of stones were often the only possible map to holy sites that they could use.[73]

With so many rocks dotting the landscape, it is not always easy to tell why worshippers venerated some rocks and not others. A general rule seems to suggest that people believed that rocks with unusual physical properties might have been formed by supernatural forces. One field of stones, of a markedly plump and round shape, were thought to be ancient melons that the prophet Elias (Elijah) had turned to stone in order to retaliate against a peasant who had denied him charity.[74] The most famous rock specimen in all of Palestine was of course that of the rock underneath the Dome of the Rock in Jerusalem. Muslims believed the indentation in the rock to be the footprint left by the Prophet Muhammad on his Night of Ascension, Christians believed the footprint was that of Jesus Christ, and Jews said that the footprint belonged to Abraham. The stone was of course able to bear these competing stories, which simply serves to highlight a popular reverence for the rock itself.[75]

Ancient manmade stone formations from earlier eras likewise were revered, and, although their original meaning(s) often were forgotten, these stones were incorporated into the stories of contemporaneous religious groups. South of Damascus, for instance, was an ancient stone column, commemorating the victories of Egyptian pharaoh Rameses II (r. 1279–1213 BCE), that locals in distant later centuries referred to as the "Rock of Job."[76]

Caves, another geographical feature relating to the limestone bedrock of the Mediterranean, also inspired a general reverence. Many of these caves or grottoes were not much more than shallow gashes or narrow twisting tunnels in the earth. Local peoples of all sects believed that the caves and grottoes were themselves holy places, as well as linked to one another, through a network of subterranean tunnels. Several St. George sites in the Levant are associated with caves and grottoes, such as the well-known cave of St. George, located at Jouneih Bay in Lebanon.[77]

As we saw above in Part One, no major irrigational rivers flow through the Levant, although several minor rivers arise as a result of snowmelt in the Levantine mountains. The development of a reverence for water was of course quite natural in this arid environment. Sources of water were believed to flow under the eye of watchful spirits, who needed recognition and tribute. In propitiation, villagers would not hesitate to offer sacrifices to some local saint who presided over a vital stream, spring, or well.[78] The aridity of the region, as well as the reliance therein, for agricultural purposes, on water from the sky, led as well to the development of a long-term reverence for the god long considered to be the abode of the sky and its lifegiving rains – the Storm-god Baal-Hadad.[79]

As late as 1927, Taufik Canaan, during one of his tours of the Palestinian countryside, came upon a peasant woman who was desperate for children. Watching her prepare a sheep for sacrifice, he was astonished to learn that she was offering it "to the sea":

> In this seemingly pagan gesture, which dispensed with any pretense of appealing to the prophets or at least to some local saint, a sort of submerged nature worship briefly surged to the surface. Not yet archaic, even at the beginning of the twentieth century, these reflexes continued to lurk within the folk imagination of the Middle East.[80]

We will see far older antecedents of this 1927 ritual, as well, in Chapters Five and Seven: from the Canaanite narrative of Astarte and the Sea, to the Hittite Song of Ullikumi, to the Egyptian tale of Rennenutet and Yamm; even to the Greek legend of Perseus and Andromeda, the tale of a woman attempting to appease the sea long lived in the Levant.[81]

Haunted landscapes: Spirits and demons

Wandering throughout the land were spirits and demons. Everyone, common person and religious professional alike, believed in the existence of this realm of beings. The spirit world contained a diverse population: angels, demons, and genies/(*jinn*). For the most part, the human and spirit worlds stayed apart, especially if humans wisely stayed within their own settlements. Spirits, however, could go anywhere, and were known to reside in dank and gloomy spaces. Caves were automatically presumed to be the dwelling spots of spirits, in part because of the presence of water, which likewise tempted the spirits into bathhouses, cisterns, wells, and springs.[82] Demons and malicious spirits were apt to come closer, however. They could besiege entire communities or launch assaults on individual households. One variety of evil sprites, the *'afrit*, could make their homes on housetops, and sneak into corners and hearths or behind doors and walls.[83]

One particular demon, known in Arabic as '*al-Qarīna*' (the 'female demon who haunts women/childbeds' and is still in modern Arabic the term for the deadly pregnancy-related medical condition called 'eclampsia'); in Hebrew and among Jews as 'Lilith' ('*Lîlît*', female demon, from '*Lîlîtū*', referring to a Mesopotamian female class of demons, and etymologically derived from the Semitic root *lyl*, or 'night'); in Coptic Egypt as '*Alabasandria*'; in Greek during the Byzantine period as '*Gylou/Gyllou*'; and, in the Levant during the first centuries of the Common Era as '*Abyzou*', or as '*Obyzou/Obyzouth*', was a malign female spirit who, herself infertile and maniacal with envy, preyed on newborn infants and women convalescing from childbirth.

'*Abyzou*' probably is derived from the Akkadian term '*Apsu*', a name for the primordial cosmic sea (specifically, freshwater with a kind of religious, fertilizing quality). As such, by whichever name she is known, this demon often is pictured with serpent-like attributes on amulets, or with the living-venomous-snakes-for-hair of the Greek Medusa, usually being whipped or vanquished by a more-powerful god, saint, or holy figure.[84] As we will see again in Chapter Five, this notion of a female demon who threatens pregnancies or newborns was ubiquitous throughout the Levant for millennia, and is a good example of the kind of continuities in belief and practice that are characteristic of agrarian religion.[85]

Demons and sickness

In a premodern and agrarian religious context, physical illness, in general, as well as what we might consider today 'mental illnesses' often were diagnosed as a form of possession or demonic attack. Without medical explanations for various medical conditions, such as fits, fainting spells, or uncontrollable seizures, people sought causes in the realm of the spiritual world.[86] Because mental illness was considered a form of demonic possession, agrarian religious knowledge suggested that only a saint, with their concomitant ability to vanquish demons, could contend against such an adversary.

St. George, who very famously had defeated a demon/dragon, was considered particularly adept at that specific skill. Near the Christian city of Bayt Jala, next to Bethlehem, was a monastery of St. George, where peasants from around Palestine would bring their worst cases of mental disturbance. Even as late as the early 20th century, 'mad' individuals were kept chained, day and night, to the walls of the church there. According to the monks, St. George himself revealed when the madness had ended. Appearing as an old man, he would remove their neck chains, and when the monks made the discovery the next day, they knew whom to discharge.[87]

Likewise, in his funding request from the late 19th century, "Appeal for the First Home of the Insane on Mount Lebanon," Christian missionary Theophilus Waldmeier wrote:

> In the neighbourhood of Bethlehem is a convent called El Khudr. It is dedicated to St. George the Dragon Killer, and stands under the superintendence of the Oriental Orthodox Christian Patriarch of Jerusalem. The legend tells us that St. George killed the dragon, *and that the dragon was a demon, and in consequence of this the people believe that St. George is also able to subdue and cast out demons*. Therefore, the monks of St. George's convent have a few small cells appropriated for the madjaneen [insane]. However, it appears that St. George has not succeeded in killing all the demons, as there are still, I am sorry to say, many demons who take possession of the people. In these cells the insane are half or quite naked, with heavy iron chains round their necks, running through a hole of the wall of the cells into the church of St. George, where they are fastened round a stone pillar.[88]

Moreover, we see in the regional account from an even earlier era, during the fourth century CE, the then-contemporary-as-well belief that "madness" was caused by demons. In Epiphanius' partisan account in his *Panarion* of the Jew, a certain Jewish figure named Josephus was *able to drive a demon from a madman* by sprinkling water, upon which he had first made the sign of the cross, over the madman – despite the fact that he himself had not (yet) converted to Christianity, by saying " 'In the name of Jesus of Nazareth who was crucified, *come out of him, demon*, and may he have his health'. The man let out a mighty cry and fell prone, foaming greatly at the mouth and writhing."[89]

Magical shields: Spells, talismans, icons

The perils of the spiritual world of agrarian religion required several forms of defense. One could simply say a prayer or utter the name of God, but a talisman was the strongest measure of defense. Common at all social levels and particularly among women, the use of talismans had little to do with formal religious belief and was one of the many areas of agrarian religious practice where sectarian religious boundaries were irrelevant.[90]

Although from a modern religious perspective it may seem surprising, in the agrarian religious context of the Levant, all men of religion were treated as potential experts in magic. Religious knowledge and training were not, however, required for magical skill. Mystics, sorcerers, and wise women met the demand from all social levels for talismans and charms. Both townspeople and villagers, men and women, rich and poor, hung them around necks, placed them over doors, slipped them into children's clothing, and affixed them to livestock.[91]

The most sophisticated types of talismans and amulets were those containing the written word. Since literacy was so rare, these objects were the hardest to create, and would have required the skills of a religious expert. The most powerful word was the name of God, and the most elaborate amulets contained entire verses from the Qur'ān or Bible. The exact source of such materials "did not matter as much as its status as scripture," which was the means by which it derived its power.[92] Talismans and amulets that harnessed the power of writing are another example of a long-lived agrarian religious practice. For as long as the practice of writing has existed in the Levant, amulets bearing writing have been considered among the most powerful of apotropaic objects one could possess.[93]

In an illiterate, agrarian religious context, holy texts themselves often functioned as communal talismans. During community crises such as plagues or droughts, the local ulama of the city of Homs would adorn the head of a long procession to implore God for mercy and deliverance with their prized seventh-century copy of the Qur'ān. Christians used their texts in the same manner, positioning themselves underneath a copy of the Bible, in order to ameliorate afflictions like headache and back pain. In serving these functions, the Qur'ān and Bible lost much of their textual qualities: most participants in these ceremonies did not, and could not, read them. For the vast majority of the population, they simply functioned as magical objects.[94] As we see in Chapter Five, Christian icons functioned in much the same way.

Visions and dreams

People turned to an array of magical objects to manage their interaction with the spirit world, and vigilance was especially critical at night.[95]

Nighttime also brought with it a second portent: visons and dreams. Pursuing guidance and foreknowledge, some people would spend the night at tombs and shrines, where, in sleep, they could seek otherworldly inspiration. On Mt. Carmel outside of Haifa is a cave that contains a shrine to the prophet Elijah, who also is identified there with al-Khiḍr. For a small fee, Druze, Christian, and Jewish pilgrims spend the night there, hoping to encounter Elijah/al-Khiḍr. This practice, as we will see as well in Chapters Four and Seven, was common for centuries at the cave on Mt. Carmel, and continues even up to this day.[96]

One of the most prized encounters one could have in sleep was that of al-Khiḍr. "They spoke of fleeting visits in dreams, meditative trances, or sudden flashes of illumination. Like the prophet and other religious sages, al-Khiḍr could deliver messages, possibly orders to move to another town and study under new masters, or small dollops of advice and instruction."[97]

A common language of veneration

In many gestures of prayer and devotion, religious boundaries in a Levantine agrarian religious context could not really be classified as Muslim, Christian, or Jewish. Such practices and rituals freely were available to worshippers of all backgrounds. Nowhere was this convergence of posture and motion more apparent than at shrines, where sectarian identity was diminished, anyway. Petitioners would have routinely presented themselves, for example, through the act of prostration, which did not belong to any single religious tradition.

> Though prostration is today regarded as a quintessentially Muslim gesture, many Middle Eastern Christians and Jews would have used it, in one manner or another, in their churches and synagogues. … Thus, Christians visiting the Holy Sepulcher in Jerusalem found nothing odd about practicing circumambulation at the church, no matter how obviously it might conjure up Muslim customs in Mecca. It simply was one of the rituals that worshippers might conduct anywhere throughout the region.[98]

Regular worshippers in an agrarian religious environment cared little for formal theological distinctions. They crossed boundaries and participated in rituals that, from a doctrinal or strictly sectarian standpoint, they "ought" to have shunned.

People unapologetically swore oaths to each other's saints and holy men, all of whom were respected. This willingness to invoke saints, irrespective of sectarian 'religious identity', was common throughout the agrarian population. People did not hesitate to observe each other's fasts and holidays.[99]

> Faced with some overwhelming need, Muslim villagers had no aversion to baptizing their children or having holy water sprinkled over them. To their way of thinking, the rituals had no outward sectarian significance. Baptized children did not thereby become Christian, and at most would acquire nothing more than a Christian godfather. In turning to baptism, Muslim families sought mainly to enlist magical aid against illness, possession, or misfortune. … In participating in these obviously Christian rituals, Muslims had no thought of leaving their religion. They sought only the spiritual blessings of the mass, which had its own recognized potency. All of these measures were an outgrowth of a rugged peasant pragmatism that had no use for doctrinaire hair-splitting. Muslims credited Christian prayers and benedictions, no less than those of their own religious community, as having an undisputed value and sanctity.[100]

These kinds of common rituals could make it challenging to sort between religious communities. Practitioners themselves did not care about such identifications; it only was literate authorities – and most often outsiders – who sought to identify particular practices with one sect or another.

> Did they care about their blatant trampling of Islamic doctrine? No more than Muslim villagers elsewhere in Palestine, who would routinely mark heaps of grain with the sign of the cross and they went about winnowing the harvest. The gestures had acquired all the apparent weight and naturalness of tradition, which had long since rendered them time-honored and innocuous. If asked about their origins, no one could really explain. Distant forefathers had hit upon tried and true techniques for conveying piety and calling down blessings. Nothing about these customs seemed intrinsically "Christian."[101]

Shared religious practices helped to promote toleration among groups. Despite doctrinal differences, members of every religious community were able to acknowledge that their religious traditions "had sprung from the same general source, including prophets, legends, and landmarks that appeared in all the holy books."[102] Moreover, conversion of religious architecture, as well as of the local population, had been taking place for centuries. By the late medieval period, the region slowly had accumulated a Muslim majority, and many houses of worship had changed hands. Still, often without the least harassment, local Christians could enter and to pray in mosques that previously had been churches. At another mosque, which had once been a Church of St. George, Christian worship was so routine that the Christians of Homs paid for half of all the oil burned in the lamps. Muslims demonstrated a corresponding casualness about praying at churches, coming in with the same desires they brought to shrines, in a quest for blessings that eclipsed concerns about sectarian affiliation.[103] Before leaving for battle against the militias of Nablus, in 1735 CE, Bedouin chieftain Ẓāhir al-ʻUmar stopped at the Church of the Virgin in Nazareth. He prostrated at the door, rubbed his face in the dust, and prayed to the Virgin for victory, promising to supply the church with oil for the rest of his life, which, apparently, he did.[104]

Multi-confessional presences likewise were built into the very design of many regional churches. At the Church of the Holy Nativity, in addition to the Christian altar, there also were two other prayer-niches: one pointed in the direction of Mecca, and the other faced Jerusalem. At the St. George church of Bayt Jala, the icon of St. George, whom, of course, Muslims identified with al- Khiḍr, was hung in the direction of Mecca, so that Muslims' direction of prayer was aligned with the painting.[105]

The Levantine shared religious culture eminently was visible on religious holidays as well, in which every regional religious group participated. Grouped together into the community of the quarter or the village, they shared the same social rhythms and expressed communal solidarity in these public celebrations.[106]

How religious identity mattered in Levantine agrarian religion

The existence of a common religious culture certainly did not erase sectarian consciousness. Most people would have received something like a "homespun catechism," being aware of the basics involving the holy books, fundamental prayers, and important figures from their own religious tradition.[107] Still, few people possessed more than a rudimentary knowledge of the tenets of their religion.

> When pressed for explanations, few members of any religious community could muster more than the simple propositions held universally by Muslims, Christians, and Jews alike: the existence of God, of heaven and hell, and of angels and demons. Beyond this basic knowledge, nearly everyone knew the names of the great prophets and a few saints and could distinguish between the holy books of the different religions (without, of course, having direct access to any of these texts themselves). Other details were hopelessly abstruse and lay beyond their full grasp and deliberation.[108]

Distinctive religious communities were maintained, and sectarianism enforced, however, primarily through birth, marriage, taxes, and death practices. Intermarriage (even between different denominations of the same religion) was unthinkable. The main effect of these marriage prohibitions was to prioritize one sort of social boundaries.[109] The same reasoning applied to death practices. Each religious community buried its dead together in its own cemetery, where they would lie only with members of the same community. On the other hand, funerary customs, involving wailing, relatives performing the corpse-washing, and visiting graves, were nearly identical among all the regional religious communities.[110]

In an agrarian religious context, sectarian religious identity mainly had to do with social and political status. This mostly was evident during acts of conversion, in which one 'faith' ostensibly was left behind for another. "Conversion amounted to a declaration of a new social and political status. ... Both sides recognized it as a fundamentally social transformation."[111]

The end of agrarian religion

Religious communities and identities in the Levant became more recognizably 'religious' in a modern sense – that is, "anchored in private conscience and belief" along with the advent of mass modernity, with improvements in medical techniques,[112] and with the diminishment of regional agrarian identity.[113] Additionally, during the 19th and 20th centuries, local religious communities in the Eastern Mediterranean began to be categorized and separated by European Colonial administrators, creating legalistic communal boundaries and divisions where previously they had not been present in the same manner.[114] In later, post-Ottoman spaces, ethnic and religious minorities began to be banned from national territories, just as occurred during the events of the Balkan wars in 1912 and 1913, the departure of the Muslim population from the Balkans, the Armenian massacre in Anatolia in 1915, and the enormous transfer of the Greek Orthodox population from Turkey in the era of Kemal Attaturk: "During such conflicts, entire communities were forced to abandon their homes and holy sanctuaries, to leave room as it were for the construction of homogenous national territories."[115] Along with these developments came a heightening of sectarian awareness that was accompanied by a shift to a "more strictly scriptural interpretation of religious tradition."[116]

These changes were also directly related to the development of mass literacy, which was realized in the region by the mid-20th century CE.[117] Literate religious cultures generally tend to emphasize the distinctiveness of their religious texts, and thus to be more ideological in orientation. In these religious environments, sectarianism and religious difference are accentuated. When religious adherents are able to study and learn scripture, scripture becomes the new core of their religious experience.[118] "Wherever this guiding logic [i.e. regarding the primacy of literate religion] established itself, *religion would turn into a 'set of propositions' to be held and advocated with unshakable conviction.*"[119]

This privileging of the scriptural word, for which the common believer could now produce an unmediated reading, was related as well to the 20th-century development, among the region's religious communities, of exclusivist religious identities. In this reorienting of religion around textual knowledge,

> older forms of piety were now denounced as superstition and nonsense. The landscape was emptied of its population of spirits and demons. The shrines were forsaken. Magic lost its efficacy and ceased to have the power to charm, possess, or intimidate[120]

The presence and persistence of agrarian religion in the Levant is obscured largely because of our modern literate religious outlooks. Today, and in part because most religious communities "participate in truly global modes of belief and ritual which, for the most part, would have been unimaginable to earlier generations," they "read history through imaginative gaps that distort it beyond recognition. They take perspectives that have arisen entirely out of contemporary political struggles and cultural movements and project them backwards in time."[121] Worse still, they misrepresent everyday religion, misreading religion as it was practiced before the development of mass literacy. The practices and beliefs of everyday religion in the Levant were not found in doctrine, law, and religious texts, but in the needs and patterns of the local environment.[122]

Agrarian religious culture faded gradually with the emergence of mass society, which overwhelmed and surpassed the ancient agrarian functioning of the world.[123] Marked in the main by mass urbanization and diminishing of agrarian social and economic organization, older religious patterns nonetheless were slow to be abandoned. In the countryside of Lebanon, it took until decades after World War II before communal prayers for rain ceased.[124]

Geography left the most enduring stamp on premodern religion and culture

Ultimately, Grehan's work on agrarian religion suggests that if we are really going to look for demarcations, or 'zones of cultural coherence' in religion, we would do best to think in terms of geography, "which left the most enduring stamp on premodern culture."[125] Geography was a "mighty constraint, which bound minds and ideas, no less than bodies and goods." Agrarian religion in the Levant "encompassed people of different religious backgrounds, who nonetheless held the same notions of spirituality and piety – precisely because they lived together and shared the same local culture."[126] Indeed, one need only call to mind the 19th- and 20th-century reactions of Christian and Jewish missionaries from Europe, who, upon settling in the Middle East, immediately saw that sharing a 'common religion' with groups of local peoples had failed to make those people or their customs, rituals, and beliefs seem any less foreign. The religious history of the Levant is thus not what it might at first seem. Indeed, "far greater than the religious differences between premodern Muslims, Christians, and Jews are those that separate modern religiosity from its folk antecedents."[127]

Despite the developments in the Levant of mass literacy, urbanization, modern medical treatments, and the diminishment in regional social and economic organization and identity, we still see elements, continuing even until today in the Levant, of agrarian religious culture and its long-lived shared religious practices. By examining the ancient Canaanite storm-god, Baal-Hadad, Jewish Elijah, Christian St. George, and Muslim al-Khiḍr, as well as the geographical motifs they share, *Geography, Religion, Gods, and Saints in the Eastern Mediterranean* offers a firsthand account of the ways in which agrarian religion in the Levant has linked regional figures and religious communities over time, as well as of the power, legacy, and persistence of the region's shared agrarian religious practices.

Notes

1 Unless otherwise noted, geological information in this chapter is taken from J. Donald Hughes, *The Mediterranean: An Environmental History*. Nature and Human Societies Series, Mark R. Stoll, ed. (Santa Barbara, CA: ABC-CLIO, 2005).

2 Others have recently speculated about such long-term continuities; this book highlights one. See also Michael Blömer, Achim Lichtenberger, and Rubina Raja, eds. *Religious Identities in the Levant from Alexander to Muhammad: Continuity and Change*. Contextualizing the Sacred 4 (Turnhout, Belgium: Brepols Publishers, 2015); and Grehan, *Twilight of the Saints*.

3 Hughes, 4. Many instances of changes in weather, both naturally occurring and human-caused, have taken place over the past several thousands of years. However, the larger Mediterranean climatic pattern has remained generally stable since the end of the last Ice Age in approximately 10,000 BCE.

4 See Chapter Three, 67–70.

5 Frank S. Frick, "Palestine, Climate of" in *The Anchor Bible Dictionary*. Vol. 5 (New York: Doubleday, 1992), 126. See entire article at 119–126.

6 Hughes, 6.

7 Carl Mehler, ed., *National Geographic Atlas of the Middle East* (Washington, D.C.: National Geographic Society, 2003). See also Frank S. Frick, 122.

8 http://www.weatheronline.co.uk/reports/climate/Israel-and-Palestine.htm

9 Frank S. Frick, "Palestine, Climate of" in *The Anchor Bible Dictionary* Vol. 5 (New York: Doubleday, 1992), 126. Quoting Amiran, D.H.K. "Land Use in Israel," in *Land Use in Semi-Arid Mediterranean Climates* (UNESCO International Geographic Union: Paris, 1964).

10 William Harris, *The Levant: A Fractured Mosaic* (Princeton, NJ: Marcus Wiener Publishers, 2003).

11 Harris, 15.

12 Harris, 4.

13 Most of the cities of the Levant have been shaped and partially destroyed by earthquakes. For instance, the city of Antioch suffered from devastating earthquakes in 184 BCE, 37 CE, and 115 CE, to highlight just one 300-year period of its history. Refer as well to a 19th-century CE description of Antioch: "Earthquakes and the changing floods of the stream have over-turned and covered with silt the palaces of the Greek and of the Roman city, yet as I stood at sunset on the sloping sward of the Noṣairiyyeh graveyard below Mount Silpius [a foothill of Mt. Sapan/Kasios], where my camp was pitched, and saw the red roofs under a crescent moon, I recognized that beauty is the inalienable heritage of Antioch." Gertrude Lowthian Bell, *Syria: The Desert and the Sown* (New York: Tauris Parke Paperbacks, 2016. First published London: William Heinemann, 1907), 299–300. See also Chapter Three, 67–70.

14 See the account of Greek historian Strabo (*Strábōn*), ca. 24 CE: "They say that Typhon was struck by the thunderbolts [of Zeus, the Storm-God] (he was a dragon[drakon]) and he fled in search of a way underground. He cut into the earth with his coils, making the channel for the river, and by diving into the earth be broke upon the spring. The name of the river derived from this" (Strabo C750-1), quoted in Daniel Ogden, *The Legend of Seleucus: Kingship, Narrative and Mythmaking in the Ancient World* (Cambridge, UK: Cambridge University Press, 2017), 123; bracketed information my own.

15 The sixth-century CE Antiochene bureaucrat John Malalas tells us in his account of the founding of the city of Antioch "Antigonus laid out his city of Antigonia beside the Drakon ('Dragon') river, as then did Seleucus his city of Antioch, though in the

days of these kings it [the Drakon river] had changed its name to the Orontes." Quoted in Ogden, 115.

16 Harris, 4, 7. See also Chapter Three, 67–70; 80–83.

17 For aquifer reserves, see Mehler, 72. See also Howard A. Cohen and Steven Plaut, "Quenching the Levant's Thirst," *Middle East Quarterly*, 2, no. 1 (1995): 37–44.

18 Marcus Milwright, An Introduction to Islamic Archaeology, *The New Edinburgh Islamic Surveys*, ed. by Carole Hillenbrand (Edinburgh: Edinburgh University Press Ltd, 2010), 64. Quoting James Pace, "The Cisterns of the al-Karak Plateau" *Annual of the Department of Antiquities of Jordan* 40 (1996), 369–374, and John Oleson, "Water Supply in Jordan Through the Ages" in *The Archaeology of Jordan*, MacDonald, Adams and Bienkowski, eds. (Sheffield, UK: Sheffield Academic Press, 2001), 604–608. For an interesting study of the use of crosses as apotropaic devices in fifth- and sixth- century CE Byzantine cisterns, see Stephen D. Humphreys, "Crosses as Water Purification Devices in Byzantine Palestine," in *Trends and Turning Points: Constructing the Late Antique and Byzantine World*, Matthew Kinloch and Alex MacFarlane, eds. (Leiden: Brill, in press).

19 Milwright, 65.

20 Steven Solomon, *Water: The Epic Struggle for Wealth, Power, and Civilization* (New York: Harper Perennial, 2010), 17.

21 David R. Montgomery, *Dirt: The Erosion of Civilizations* (Berkeley, CA: University of California Press, 2007), 15, 17–18.

22 Montgomery, 18.

23 Hughes, 20.

24 Hughes, 20.

25 Hughes, 21.

26 Montgomery, 36.

27 Solomon, 25.

28 Solomon, 21–22.

29 Solomon, 24–27.

30 Montgomery, 16. Erosion, which increases the amount of dirt that flows into nearby rivers, can also cause ports located near the mouths of rivers to silt over and to "move" inland, a common form of environmental change. An example of this can be seen in southern Mesopotamian cities, such as Uruk and Eridu. During the early Bronze Age, ca. 3300 BCE, these cities were located closer to the Persian Gulf, but because of the effects of silt deposition from the Euphrates and Tigris rivers caused by extensive irrigation, these former Mesopotamian cities are today located 150 miles inland from the Persian Gulf.

31 Hughes, 66.

32 Hughes, 61, 68.

33 Hughes, 70.

34 Hughes, 71.

35 See above, p. 28.

36 Hughes, 98.

37 Hughes, 125.

38 Hughes, 117.

39 Anthony O'Sullivan, Marie-Estelle Rey, and Jorge Galvez Mendez, "Opportunities and Challenges in the MENA Region," *Organization for Economic Co-operation and Development* (OECD, 2011), 21–22.

40 Hughes, 114–115.

41 Hughes 138–178.

42 Hughes, 134.

43 See Cohen and Plaut, 34.

44 Since the mid-20th century, peoples throughout the Levant have devised technological solutions to address the essential need for water from rainfall in an arid region,

through programs such as direct aquifer extraction, the creation of reservoirs and dams, and plants for seawater desalinization and reclamation of wastewater. However, due to mismanagement and overuse, all water sources are endangered, and even programs such as these do not eliminate the continuing regional need for water from rainfall and aquifers. Such programs can serve, as well, to exacerbate political tensions over scarce water resources between regional inhabitants. See Cohen and Plaut, 37–44.

45 On Protestantism in the Middle East, see Ussama Makdisi, *Artillery of Heaven: American Missionaries and the Failed Conversion of the Middle East* (Cornell, NY: University Press, 2009).

46 See also Eric C. Smith, who argues that these are "categories we impart from the present back onto the ancient world." *Jewish Glass and Christian Stone: A Materialist Mapping of the 'Parting of the Ways'*, Routledge Studies in the Early Christian World (New York: Routledge, 2017).

47 Grehan, 140.

48 Grehan, 21.

49 Grehan, 207. See also the work of Fernand Baudel, who argues that the deepest levels of historical influence, such as geological, tend also to be the slowest-changing. *The Mediterranean: And the Mediterranean World in the Age of Philip II.* 2 vols. Translated by Siân Reynolds (Berkeley, CA: University of California Press, 1995), original 1949.

50 See also Eric C. Smith, *Jewish Glass and Christian Stone*, who argues that we can only perceive and understand what our categories allow us to understand.

51 Grehan, 21.

52 See Part One; Grehan, 140.

53 "Within this persistent framework, only recently abandoned, [agrarian religious culture] could tolerate, and even encourage, many little ruptures and innovations in prayer and observance, ritual and architectural forms, and in the distribution and location of shrines (among many other possibilities). To reconstruct these patterns fully would require research encompassing many long centuries. This history of the long term – *the only proper yardstick for agrarian religion* – is beyond the scope of the present study. We will confine ourselves here with the period running from the late seventeenth to the nineteenth century, right as this older religious life was entering its historical twilight." Grehan, 16 (emphasis added). See also Fernand Baudel, who argues that the deepest levels of historical influence, such as geological, tend also to be the slowest changing. *The Mediterranean: And the Mediterranean World in the Age of Philip II.* 2 vols. Translated by Siân Reynolds. (Berkeley, CA: University of California Press, 1995), original 1949.

54 Grehan, 23–42.

55 Grehan, 43–53.

56 Grehan, 60. See also Rebillard and Rüpke, who argue that "On the contrary, in many situations religious institutions struggle to draw and enforce boundaries and to impose identities." Éric Rebillard, and Jörg Rüpke, "Introduction: Groups, Individuals, and Religious Identity," in *Group Identity and Religious Individuality in Late Antiquity*, Éric Rebillard, and Jörg Rüpke, eds. CUA Studies in Early Christianity, edited by Philip Rousseau (Washington, D.C.: The Catholic University of America Press, 2015), 11.

57 See also Virginia Burrus and Rebecca Lyman, who argue that the notion of a realm of 'popular' religion, that is distinct from or even opposed to the religion of the elite, is untenable. Burrus and Lyman, "Shifting the Focus of Christianity," 14.

58 Evidence of porous, pluralist, and opportunist religious practices abounds, in religious texts and in other historical writings, in the examples found in this project, and in several recent works on the subject. Among them, see Michael Blömer, Achim Lichtenberger, and Rubina Raja, eds. *Religious Identities in the Levant from*

Alexander to Muhammad: Continuity and Change. Contextualizing the Sacred 4 (Turnhout, Belgium: Brepols Publishers, 2015). See also Grehan, 150–156.

59 Grehan, all.

60 Grehan, 63.

61 Grehan, 62.

62 Grehan, 63.

63 Grehan, 86.

64 Grehan, 81.

65 Grehan, 103. See also Josef Meri, *The Cult of Saints Among Muslims and Jews in Medieval Syria*, Chs. 2 and 3.

66 Grehan, 88.

67 Grehan, 89.

68 Multiple fieldwork interviews.

69 For more on the 27 shared narratives between the Bible and the Qur'ān, see Gregg, *Shared Stories, Rival Tellings*, xiii.

70 Grehan, 116.

71 Grehan, 116–117.

72 See Chapter Two, 25–29; 31.

73 Grehan, 118–119.

74 Cf. Q. 18:77, 82. See also the ca. 1000 CE tale of Rabbi Joshua and Elijah, first recorded in Arabic among the Jewish community at Kairaoun, Tunisia, as a part of the work *al-faraj ba'd al-shiddah* ('relief following distress') composed by Rabbi Nissîm b. Ya'aqobh b. Shâhîn, who was best known under his Arabic title, Ibn Shāhīn. The Arabic original was published by Julian Obermann, *Studies in Islam and Judaism: The Arabic Original of Ibn Shâhîn's Book of Comfort, known as the Ḥibbûr yaphê of r. Nissîm b. Ya'aqobh* (New Haven, CT: Yale University Press, 1933). An English translation can be found in William M. Brinner, *An Elegant Composition Concerning Relief after Adversity: by Nissim ben Jacob Ibn Shāhīn*, Yale Judaica Series, Vol. XX, edited by Leon Nemoy (New Haven, CT: Yale University Press, 1977). See also Chapter Six, 210–211; 218–223.

75 All of the examples in this paragraph from Grehan, 121.

76 Grehan, 123. See also Chapter Three.

77 Grehan, 128. On the 'networks of subterranean tunnels connecting holy places', see also Chapter Six, 213–214. For more on the shrine at Jouneih Bay, see https://365daysoflebanon.com/2016/05/18/the-patron-saint-of-beirut/comment-page-1/#comment-1621.

78 Grehan, 130.

79 See above, Chapter Two, 26–27. See also Chapter Three, 65–75.

80 Canaan, *Muhammadan Saints*, 135–136.

81 Grehan, 140. See also Chapter Five, 174–175 and Chapter Seven, 250.

82 Grehan, 144.

83 Grehan, 145.

84 See Mary Margaret Fulghum, "Coins Used as Amulets in Late Antiquity," in *Between Magic and Religion: Interdisciplinary Studies in Ancient Mediterranean Religion and Society*. Greek Studies: Interdisciplinary Approaches (Lanham, MD: Rowman & Littlefield, 2001), 139–148. See also Jeffrey Spier, "Medieval Byzantine Magical Amulets and Their Tradition." *Journal of the Warburg and Courtald Institutes*, 56 (1993): 25–62. See also Chapter Five, 169–170.

85 Grehan, 146. See also Chapter Five.

86 Grehan, 148.

87 Grehan 149. See also Chapter Five, 161–162; 164 81n.

88 Theophilus Waldmeier, *Appeal for the First Home of the Insane on Mount Lebanon* (London: Headley Brothers, 1897), emphasis added.

89 MacMullen and Lane, *Paganism and Christianity, 100–425 C.E.: A Sourcebook* (Minneapolis, MN: Fortress Press, 1992), 6–7. See also the translation of Epiphanius'

account, *Panarion*, 30.4–12, in J. P. Migne, *Patrologia graeca* (Paris: Garnier, 1857–91), 41, col. 109ff.; translation by MacMullen and Lane, emphasis added. See also Chapter Five, 161–162; 164 81n.

90 Grehan, 150.
91 Grehan, 152–153.
92 Grehan, 154.
93 See also Christopher A. Faraone, *Vanishing Acts on Ancient Greek Amulets: From Oral Performance to Visual Design*, Bulletin of the Institute of Classical Studies Supplements (London: University of London Institute of Classical Studies, 2012).
94 Grehan, 154.
95 Grehan, 156.
96 See Chapter Four, 126–128. See also Chapter Seven, 240–241.
97 Grehan, 158. See also Chapter Six, 187–188; 223–229. See also Josef Meri, *The Cult of Saints Among Muslims and Jews in Medieval Syria.*
98 Grehan, 177.
99 Grehan, 178.
100 Grehan, 179.
101 Grehan, 179–180.
102 Grehan, 182. For more on the 27 shared narratives between the Bible and the Qur'ān, see Gregg, *Shared Stories, Rival Tellings*, xiii.
103 Grehan, 183.
104 Grehan, 183.
105 Grehan, 184, also quoting Canaan, *Mohammadan Saints*, 14–15.
106 Grehan, 186.
107 Grehan, 191.
108 Grehan, 58.
109 Grehan, 193.
110 Grehan, 193.
111 Grehan, 194–196.
112 Grehan, 205, quoting John Gulick, *Social Structure and Culture Change in a Lebanese Village* (New York: Wenner-Gren Foundation for Anthropological Research, 1955), 94.
113 Grehan, 194.
114 Earlier of course the Ottoman millet system functioned to "categorize" and "separate" religious communities, but this distinguished between indigenous religious communities in a less-distinct manner than that of colonial administrators.
115 Maria Couroucli, "Sharing Sacred Spaces – A Mediterranean Tradition," in *Sharing Sacred Spaces in the Mediterranean: Christians, Muslims, and Jews at Shrines and Sanctuaries*, Albera, Dionigi and Maria Couroucli, eds. *New Anthropologies of Europe*, edited by Matti Bunzl and Michael Herzfeld (Bloomington, IN: Indiana University Press, 2012), 1–2.
116 Grehan, 196.
117 Grehan, 53–56; 205–206.
118 Grehan, 196–197.
119 Grehan, 197–198 (emphasis added).
120 Grehan, 198.
121 Grehan, 206.
122 Grehan, 207.
123 Grehan, 205.
124 Grehan, 205.
125 Grehan, 207.
126 Grehan, 207.
127 Grehan, 208.

3 Ancient Near Eastern religion and the storm-god Baal-Hadad

Part One: Introduction

One morning in February of 1928, Syrian farmer Mahmoud Mella al-Zir was plowing land along the Eastern Mediterranean coast, about a kilometer inland from the bay which is today called in Arabic *Minet el-Beida* (the 'White Harbor'). As his plow cut through the soil, its steel tip ran into a heavy stone just underneath the surface. Mahmoud went over to examine the obstruction and discovered a stone slab. Removing the soil above, he slowly raised the slab to discover underneath a subterranean passageway which led downward into an ancient tomb. Inside the tomb, Mahmoud discovered several objects, which he sold to an antiquities dealer. Soon, the local authorities were notified of the find at Minet al-Beida, and shortly thereafter, a French-Protectorate archaeological team was dispatched to the site. It soon became clear that what Mahmoud Mella al-Zir had uncovered that spring day was not only a tomb, but an entrance to the necropolis of Ugarit, one of the ancient world's most important lost Mediterranean cities.[1] The textual and material discoveries that eventually were drawn out of the soil at Ugarit have come ultimately to shine a valuable light upon both the ancient world, and upon the Biblical text.[2]

The textual and material remains at Ugarit represent our most comprehensive source of Canaanite religion and culture outside of the Hebrew Bible.[3] Canaanite religion, consisting of the cultural and religious traditions of western Syria and the Levant beginning in at least the second millennium BCE, did not disappear in the late Bronze Age or even the Iron Age, contrary to both common wisdom and claims made in the Hebrew Bible.[4] Instead, as we will see in this chapter, elements of Canaanite religion lived on long into the first millennium BCE, influencing subsequent regional religious traditions well into the first centuries of the Common Era.

In the remains of the city of Ugarit, the temples of Baal and Dagān (a northwest Mesopotamian deity often called Baal's father and regularly equated with the supreme god El or '*Ilu*), dominated the city. [5] Second in size only to the great palace, the Baal and Dagān temples required a large number of priestly and support staff, and worship in these temples most likely functioned as a kind of state religion.[6] As demonstrated in Chapter Two, agricultural peoples in the Levant long have relied upon precipitation from the sky to provide sufficient water for crop growth, and accordingly "one of the central themes in native religion [at Ugarit and the greater region] was the desire for the god Baal to provide adequate rain so that the crops might flourish and the harvest be adequate."[7]

The figure of the storm-god was a vital component of ancient Near Eastern religions, and not simply at Ugarit.[8] The motif of the storm-god is well attested throughout the ancient Near East.[9] For millennia, the terror of the storm, with its howling winds, thunder, lashing rain, and bolts of lightning, constituted either a theophany itself, or the basis for a description of theophany.[10] But the storm-god was not important only because of the storm. As a divine figure, the storm-god came in many places to represent a fusion of concepts surrounding both the storm and fertility. Eventually, in the evolutionary processes of most groups, the storm-god evolved within the mythical realm to become among the most prominent gods of local panthea,[11] and, within several cultic and historical settings, to be known as a fearless warrior, as the provider of sustenance for society, and as the preserver of all life.

Among these broad-level similarities, however, the storm-god was understood within different cultural settings in different ways. Regional storm-gods, in the same manner as the figures in this study, were themselves geographically contextualized; that is, situated within a complex of various natural and historical processes. Furthermore, the actual functions of a particular storm-god cannot properly be understood unless that storm-god is examined within its specific geographical and ecological environment. Indeed, the major factors of difference in manifestation, appearance, and powers between and among storm-gods in the ancient Near East largely is attributable to the geography of the region in which that storm-god evolved.[12]

In order to understand the context in which Baal-Hadad emerged in Syria and coastal Canaan, we briefly examine first the older and contemporaneous storm-gods of major regions within the ancient Near Eastern world: southern Mesopotamia, northern Mesopotamia, Syria, Anatolia, and coastal Canaan. Then, we begin the major work of this chapter, the geographical contextualization the figure Baal-Hadad. First, we will examine the Baal Cycle text unearthed in excavations at Ugarit, which arguably is the most important and influential text related to Baal-Hadad. We examine next an important iconographical representation of Baal-Hadad, known as the Baal Stele, which also was uncovered at Ugarit. Finally, we investigate two important sites and cult locations dedicated for millennia to Baal-Hadad: Baalbek, in modern-day Lebanon, and Mt. Sapan/Hazzi/Kasios/Casius/*Jebl al-āqra*', the important mountain described above in Chapter Two that is located on the Mediterranean coast between the modern-day countries of Turkey and Syria. Baalbek and Mt. Sapan are particularly notable because Baalbek is linked, via the Orontes River (earlier known as the *drakōn* or 'dragon' river) to Mt. Sapan, long known as the mythical home of the storm-god.

Throughout this chapter, we will also note the ways in which the storm-god, and the geographically and perhaps meteorologically influenced narrative of the defeat of a serpent or dragon, remained compelling and relevant within Levantine culture throughout the first millennium BCE and into the first half of the first millennium CE – long after the destruction of Ugarit. In particular, we will observe both Greek and Roman narratives and sites relating to Zeus-Baal and to Jupiter, respectively, who functioned locally as the Greek and Roman equivalents (and continuations) of Baal-Hadad.[13] As we will see, beginning in the fourth century BCE, regional cults to Zeus and to Jupiter gradually began to supplant those to Baal-Hadad. The mythological narratives and functions of Zeus and Jupiter, and their cults, largely continued those of Baal-Hadad from much earlier eras, and flourished into the first centuries of the common era.

The storm-god in the ancient Near East

The terrible display of power and force in the storm, with its loud thunder and dark clouds stretching across the horizon, but also its life-giving capacity in relation to water, crop growth, and human survival, cannot be underestimated – this most powerful of natural phenomena was identified as the 'storm-god' and associated with a variety of names and figures in different eras.[14] According to Daniel Schwemer, the most important – and those directly deserving of the title of the ancient Near Eastern 'storm-gods' – are the Semitic "Hadda," known by various names, and linked to Syro-Palestinian Ba'lu/Ba'al, Hurrian Teššub, Urartian Teišeba, Hattian Taru, and Hittite-Luwian Tarḫun(t).[15]

Southern Mesopotamia, northern Mesopotamia, Syria, and coastal Canaan

Differences in the ecological and topographical features between hilly northern Mesopotamia and flat southern Mesopotamia are key to understanding different modes of thought concerning regional storm-gods. Peoples in the north and west, dependent on the whims of the weather, resorted to cultic rituals to obtain moisture from the skies. Peoples in the south depended primarily on the fortunes of the rivers – and their characteristic seasonal floods – to provide them with water which they diverted and controlled to irrigate fields.[16]

The Sumerian god in southern Mesopotamia responsible for storms, wind, lightning, rain, and thunder was called Iškur. His name was written with the same word-sign that also stands for the Sumerian word /im/, 'wind, storm'. The worship of Iškur extended back into the prehistoric period, but written evidence of his cult comes from the pre-Sargonic era, ca. 2400 BCE. Iškur-Adad, as Iškur came to be known during the Old Babylonian period (2000–1600 BCE),[17] generally belonged to the less important of the great gods, which likely reflects Babylonian geography and agricultural practices: "The storm-god as bringer of rain has no role in the agrarian rituals of Babylonia, where agriculture was characterized by irrigation."[18]

In northern Mesopotamia, Syria, Anatolia, and coastal Canaan – those parts of the ancient Near East characterized by rainfall agriculture and dry farming – storm-gods venerated there "occupy a more significant position among the great gods than in Babylonia."[19] Daniel Schwemer considers the natural starting point of a typological examination of the phenomenon of the ancient Near Eastern storm-god to be that of the Assyro-Babylonian storm-god Adad, but also notes that extensive contacts between the regions and cultures of the ancient Near East led to "identifications and syncretisms between typologically similar deities with different names. Conversely, local forms of the same god could be worshipped under various different names or epithets within one cultural context."[20]

Adad, originating in the earlier Semitic storm-god figure 'Hadda', was known, much like the Semitic languages, over the whole Near East. In different regions and different eras, various profiles developed of the god called 'Hadda', and its phonetic variants: Hadda/Haddu/Hadad, Adad, and Addu.[21] The first textual reference to the god Hadda comes from cuneiform texts in the north Syrian city of Ebla, during the middle of the third millennium BCE.[22] Hadda – *not* a member of the Southern Mesopotamian Sumerian pantheon – was the earliest deity identified with the devastating regional storms of northern Mesopotamia. His name, *hdd*, quite likely is derived from the Semitic root that means 'to demolish with violence, with a vehement noise', 'the sound of rain falling from the sky', and 'thunder', all of which aptly describe the function of a storm-god within a rain-agriculture setting.[23]

By the start of the middle Bronze Age (1800–1600 BCE), Adad/Hadad was identified with the Hurro-Hittite storm-god Teššub/'Teshub' in cult centers such as the city of Aleppo, in Syria. For the first time during this period, sources also start to become available for the Syro-Palestinian area generally known as 'Canaan' that shed light on the worship of Haddu (that is, 'Baal-Hadad') in the Levant. Because of the geography of coastal Canaan, and because "a connection between storm- and mountain-gods is typical for landscapes in which cloud-topped mountains can be observed," Hadad in the Levant long was associated with the towering Mt. Sapan on the Mediterranean coast, as well as with protection over sea-faring.[24] Hadad became regarded as the deity *par excellence* throughout the entire region, and his role both as a fierce warrior and a beneficent provider and protector is well attested in his cult's remarkable diffusion and popularity throughout Syria and the surrounding countries.

Hadad was designated by many names and given various titles in Western Syria and Canaan. Among them, his title or epithet as *Baal*, 'Lord', which emphasized his prime position over both men and gods, was eventually used in conjunction with Hadad or even in place of it, and in subsequent centuries Baal became this deity's proper name throughout the Levant.[25] Interestingly, in modern Arabic, *b'l* /بعل also means 'lord'; it can refer to the Western Semitic storm-god, Baal-Hadad, and it furthermore means "land or plants thriving on a natural water supply."[26]

Baal-Hadad was perceived in the arid Levant as hot-tempered, fickle, and even bellicose, galloping across the sky in his dark and ominous storm-clouds, either showering beneficence on his beloved people, or punishing them or their enemies by visiting destructive drought and famine upon them. Though general cult centers existed for Baal-Hadad throughout the Levant, he also was not confined to a particular city.[27] In the region,

> use of the original epithet Ba'lu as a personal name of the Semitic storm-god, Haddu, as primarily attested in texts from Ugarit for the late Bronze Age,

> *continued without interruption in the Iron Age cultures of Syro-Palestine and South Anatolia.* The storm-god is always called Ba‘al in Phoenician texts; the ‘Canaanite’ storm-god is also called Ba‘al in the Old Testament.[28]

Indeed, Baal-Hadad remained the storm-god par excellence throughout the Levant from the late Bronze Age and well into the first millennium BCE.[29]

Yahweh

In contrast to the other supreme gods of the ancient Near East, Yahweh originally does not seem to have been a storm-god or fertility god. Yahweh emerged in northern Arabian geological and cultural contexts as a warrior god, and his mythical and historical texts in the Hebrew Bible focus on his leading followers around the southern regions of Canaan and Transjordan and eventually settling with them on both sides of the Jordan River during the two centuries spanning the Late Bronze Age and Iron Ages.[30]

The Hebrew Bible, and the figures within it, including the god Yahweh and the Prophet Elijah (as we will see in Chapter Four), as well as the living Hebrews and followers of Yahweh, emerged within a Canaanite cultural, religious, and agricultural environment.[31] In that Canaanite environment, Baal-Hadad and his fertilizing showers were the dominant religious and economic forces. Therefore, Yahweh largely would have become a viable deity to the Canaanite-Yahwists to the degree to which he came to resemble some of the compelling aspects of Baal-Hadad, even if Yahweh should not strictly be classified as a storm-god.[32] Those most compelling aspects of Baal-Hadad included his theophoric storms, powers of fertility, and powers over the rain. Within the Canaanite agricultural environment, therefore, "Hebrew poetic, prosaic, and historical sources therefore attributed to Yahweh most of the mythical characteristics of Baal, in the process using identical mythical and cultic language attributed to the Syrian storm-god."[33]

Part Two: Storm-god Baal-Hadad Text – the Baal Cycle

The Baal Cycle, so named because it is comprised of a series of related textual narratives concerning Baal, was excavated at Ugarit (the city accidentally discovered by Mella al-Zir, modern-day Tell Ras Shamra) between 1930 and 1933 CE. Consisting of 3,000 verses written in an archaic form of Ugaritic,[34] over six tablets and traditionally divided into three sections, the Baal Cycle chronicles Baal-Hadad's rise to kingship among the pantheon of Canaanite gods.[35]

The tablets were excavated from what has been called the ‘library of the High Priest’, located between the two temples to Baal and to Dagān on the acropolis. The tablets are moderately well preserved, although the narrative is far from complete and is fragmentary or completely missing in several areas. The original length of the cycle is unknown, although the tablets remaining comprise 1,830 lines. Estimates for the original text run as high as 5,000 lines, in part because the cycle shows signs of multiple stages, which may suggest a long period for the development of the cycle.[36]

Dating of the extant Baal Cycle tablets depends upon the attribution of their scribe. Traditionally credited to the scribe Ilimilku (or Ilimalku), whose name is recorded in the colophon at the end of *CAT* 1.6 VI, the tablets generally have been dated to the middle of the 14th century BCE. Because of the clear consistency of the scribal hand throughout the tablets, it is believed that Ilimilku produced the entire series of excavated tablets.

The primary evidence for dating the tablet to the mid-14th century BCE lies in the fact that the same scribe's name – Ilimilku – appears on two Akkadian legal tablets dating from that time. However, the name 'Ilimilku' may have been common in Ugarit, and there is no solid evidence that those two scribes were the same person. Furthermore, a discovery of a new Ilimilku Ugaritic text in the early-12th-century destruction layer of the house of Urtenu (a prominent official in the court of King Niqmaddu IV, who reigned in the late 13th century BCE) seems to point to a later date for the scribe, which is an opinion shared by many connected to the archaeological Mission de Ras Shamra. Thus, the tablets date to sometime between the mid-14th and early 12th centuries BCE; approximately 1350–1190/85 BCE, during a time that included both Egyptian and Hittite direct and indirect political control of Ugarit.[37] When Ugarit was destroyed in the early 12th century BCE, it was never again inhabited, marking an end to a settlement site that had lasted some 6,000 years.[38]

The Baal Cycle can of course be investigated for contemporaneous religious, political, and geographical influences in numerous ways. Here, we will make do with but a few examples, and from which we draw important thematic categories. These examples of contemporaneous religious, political, and geographical influences upon the Baal Cycle have been selected from among many possibilities because of their importance for our study: the following thematic categories we will draw (the defeat of a sea/serpent/dragon; the stormy theophanic imagery of Baal-Hadad; protection or destruction from Baal-Hadad; his association with Mt. Sapan and other high places; Baal-Hadad's association with seasonal fertility and fecundity; and the regular disappearance and return of Baal-Hadad) comprise several important regional motifs upon which the other figures in our study also will draw, and which are intimately related to the region's geography.

The Baal Cycle is traditionally divided into three major episodes: (1) the conflict between Baal and Yamm, whose name means both 'Sea' and 'River' (*CAT* 1.1–1.3 I or II); (2) Baal's palace-quest (*CAT* 1.3 III–1.4 VII); and (3) the conflict between Baal and Mot, whose name means 'death' (*CAT* 1.4 III-1.6 VI).[39] First, we will review a summary of the narrative before examining the episodes individually for their religious, political, and geographical contexts.

Summary of the Baal Cycle

The Baal Cycle presents a vivid story of the establishment of the kingship of Baal. Baal's struggle for kingship with other powerful gods throughout each of the three episodes is set amidst a royal society of various deities and their abodes, each of which represent various aspects of the world known to cultures of the ancient Near East, and especially to the peoples of Ugarit. "Through Baal's struggles for power, the Baal Cycle interrelates humanity, nature, and divinity, and thereby yields an integrated political vision of chaos, life, and death." [40]

The opening of the first tablet is not preserved, but the remains we have begin with El/'*Ilu*, the father-god of the cosmos, in conversation about plans to attack Baal with Yamm, the god of the sea, whose name *ymm* means 'sea' and who is interchangeably called *nhr*, meaning 'river'.[41] That Yamm, the god of the sea, is also referred to as 'river' may indicate that in the ancient world there was less distinction between the concept of a 'sea' and of a 'river' than there is in contemporary notions of these terms. In ancient conceptions, and because of their twisting and writhing shape (as viewed from above, or from a distance) rivers often were associated with snakes or serpents. Attributable perhaps as well to the fact that rivers always flow into a sea or larger body of water, it may have been natural to conceptualize the terms 'sea' and 'river' in very similar ways – it all appearing to be one continuous and obviously interlinked body of water. Next, all the gods are summoned to El's feast, at which El proclaims his support for Yamm. El then gives his messengers a message to deliver to Anat, a goddess usually understood as Baal's sister, which today is lost but may describe the impending construction of a palace for Yamm and perhaps the planned destruction of Baal.

The second tablet begins with lines that have not been preserved, but the narrative continues with Kothar the craftsman's response to El's messengers, and his journey again to speak with El, whereupon Kothar prostrates himself in front of the king of deities. Kothar is told to build Yamm-Nahar an extensive palace, and the remaining lines are too broken to translate. The gods Shapshu and Athtar converse about El's favor in the remaining lines of Column I, and Column II opens with Baal's messengers delivering a message to Yamm vowing Yamm's destruction for having risen against Baal. Yamm then sends his messengers to decree to El's council that they should give up Baal, son of Dagān, that Yamm may seize Baal's gold. Yamm's messengers approach the council feast where the gods are present, including Baal and El.

When the assembled council recognizes Yamm's messengers approaching, they lower their heads in deference. Baal rebukes them by asking why they defer to Yamm's messengers and declares that he will himself answer Yamm's messengers. Yamm's messengers arrive at the feast and, as instructed by Yamm, they do not bow at the feet of El, and instead they recite their instructions to El and to the assembled gods: give up Baal, son of Dagān, that Yamm may humble Baal and possess his gold. El responds to the messengers that Baal is Yamm's slave and will bring tribute to him. Baal is angered and hits Yamm's messengers with a striker; Anat seizes Baal's right and the goddess Athtart his left, demanding to know why he struck the messengers. Baal speaks directly to the messengers and says, "I myself say to Yamm, your lord, your master, Judge River, hear the word of the Annihilator Hadad ... bow down."[42]

Only a few words of Column III are preserved, but it appears from those remaining that the column may have described a declaration of battle by either Yamm or Baal or both, sent via messengers. Column IV describes the first conflict between Yamm and Baal, whereupon the goddess Astarte proclaims Baal's demise. Kothar-wa-Hasis then speaks to Baal, encouraging him to defeat Yamm and assume his eternal kingship. In assistance, Kothar makes a weapon for Baal, calling it '*Yagarrish*', 'he may drive', which Kothar declares that Baal can use to drive Yamm from his throne. The weapon leaps from Baal's hand like a raptor, striking the torso of Prince Yamm, who does not fall. Kothar makes another weapon, which he calls '*Ayyamarri*', 'he may expel all', which he declares that Baal can use to expel Yamm-nahar from his throne and dominion. This weapon leaps from Baal's hand like a raptor and strikes Yamm between the eyes. Yamm collapses to the earth, dead, and Baal dismembers him, destroying Yamm-Nahar.

The goddess Astarte instructs Baal to "scatter, O Cloudrider" (*rkb 'rpt*, or 'Cloudrider', is a common epithet for Baal), and Baal goes out and scatters Yamm's remains. At that point other deities recount Baal's victory and proclaim Baal's kingship: "Yamm is dead!" "Baal reigns!" and the third tablet begins with what Smith and Pitard argue is the final scene of the first episode: Baal's great victory feast of sumptuous food, wine, music, singing, at which Baal's daughters, 'Pidray,' meaning 'Light,' and 'Tallay,' meaning 'Rain,' are present.

Episode two details the construction of Baal's palace – the marker of his kingship and dominion over all other gods. It begins on *CAT* 1.3 II with Anat's preparations for and undertaking of several battles: she a beautiful and scented adolescent maiden who is nonetheless a vicious and bloodthirsty warrior covered in the gore of her vanquished. After her battles, she returns to her house and washes/purifies herself, and applies cosmetics, taking out the harp and the lyre and singing songs to Baal and his daughters.

Baal then instructs his messengers to deliver a message to Anat, before whom they are to prostrate themselves:

> For a message I have, and I will tell you, a word, and I will recount to you, the word of tree and the whisper of stone, the converse of Heaven with Hell, of Deeps with Stars, I understand the lighting which the Heavens do not know, the word people do not know, and earth's masses not understand. Come and I will reveal it in the Midst of my mountain, Divine Sapan, in the holy mount of my heritage, in the beautiful hill of my might.[43]

When Baal's agriculturally named messengers Gapn ('Field') and Ugar ('Vine') arrive at Anat's abode, she mistakes their visit for a warning that an enemy has arisen against Baal; Anat shakes in fear and warns her visitors about the many enemies she has fought or destroyed, such as 'Desire, the Beloved of El'; 'Rebel, the Calf of El'; 'Fire, the Dog of El'; and 'Flame, the Daughter of El'. Included in this category of enemies, she names Yamm, whom she describes both as *tnn* 'Tunnan' or 'Tinnīn', and as *ltn* 'Twisty Serpent', the "potentate with seven heads; *tnn* and *ltn* also make an appearance as adversaries of Yahweh in the Hebrew Bible."[44]

Gapn and Ugar assure her that there is no threat to Baal, and they impart their message and invitation to come to Mt. Sapan to see Baal. Anat journeys there and Baal laments to Anat that he has no house like the other gods; that he needs a palace to complete his kingship. He expresses his wish to Anat that she asks El for permission for Baal to build a palace, and Anat assures him that she will do so, and El will heed her request, lest she beat him up.

Anat journeys to El's abode where she is not received by El, having to speak with him from an outer chamber. The lines following are too damaged to interpret, but it appears that Anat did not succeed in her quest, because in the following scene, Anat returns to Mt. Sapan and Baal proceeds with a second plan, to enlist the help of Athirat (also pronounced Asherah, a name frequently appearing in the Hebrew Bible), the mother of the gods and the wife of El, to convince El that Baal should have a palace.

Baal then sends messengers to Kothar-wa-Hasis to complain about his lack of a palace and to request that Kothar fashion gifts for Athirat. Kothar creates several elaborate household items of silver and gold, and Baal and Anat go together to Athirat to deliver the gifts. They find Athirat engaged in domestic duties along the seashore, and when she spots Baal and Anat, she immediately becomes frightened, thinking they have come to make war. Noticing the gleam of silver and gold, however, she realizes they have brought her gifts and rejoices in them. Baal and Anat plead their request to Lady Athirat of the Sea over a banquet, and although the following lines are damaged, Lady Athirat apparently agrees, as the narrative next moves to her servants preparing for travel to El.

Appearing before El Athirat entreats the father of the Gods that "Our king is mightiest Baal, our ruler, with none above him… [but] Baal has no house like the gods." El relents and grants her request; delighted, Lady Athirat then responds that El is so very wise, because "now Baal may enrich with his rain, may he enrich with rich water in a downpour. And may he give his voice [thunder] in the clouds, may he flash to the earth lightning."[45]

Anat rejoices to deliver the news to Baal, who begins preparations for the building of his palace. He gathers the finest materials of silver, gold, and ore, and sends for Kothar-wa-Hasis to quickly create for him a large and magnificent palace. Kothar suggests installing a window in the place but Baal refuses, and Kothar responds that Baal will relent on the issue of the window. Kothar creates an extravagant palace of gold fired by wood from Lebanon cedar, and Baal, referred to in this section as 'Hadd', rejoices by preparing a grandiose divine banquet for the assembly gods.

Baal then embarks on a victory tour of sorts, where he receives the obeisance of cities and towns across the wide region. At this point in the narrative, Baal is truly enthroned, among both the gods and humanity. Shortly afterward Baal reverses his decision against the window, instructing Kothar to open a window in the place. Kothar opens the window, a "break in the clouds," and Baal gives vent to his voice. He thunders far and wide, the earth shakes, and the enemies of Baal hide. Baal sees that he is the lord of east and west, and he sits enthroned in his house with a cedar spear in his right hand. Baal notes that none can challenge him, but in a move that will prove portentous, he sends a delegation far away, to the underworld of the god 'Mot', 'death'.

Although Baal declares that he alone reigns over the gods and men and "satisfies the multitudes of the Earth," instructing his messengers to inform Mot of his enthronement, Mot responds that he, Death, is hungry and has an appetite like the lion in the wild, and that he will tear Baal apart, consume him; that Baal will descend into Mot's gullet. He dares Baal to invite him, and promises that he will consume Baal, for not even the god who satisfies the multitudes of the Earth and who defeated "Litan, [*ltn*] the Fleeing Serpent, annihilated the Twisty Serpent, the Potentate with Seven Heads," can escape death.[46]

Although frightened, Baal surrenders to Mot. Baal travels to Mot's underworld, described as a 'pit', a land of filth, and a low throne upon which Mot sits. Baal declares himself Mot's servant forever, and Mot rejoices. Baal visits and feasts with the divine council one final time, and he is then commanded to descend into 'hell' (into the earth), and to "take your clouds, your winds, your bolts, your rains with you."[47] Ball acquiesces but is first allowed to make love with a heifer "in a field of Death's realm," and she conceives and bears a boy.[48]

Baal, having been found fallen dead to earth, is announced as dead and mourned and lamented by El, father of the gods, who cuts himself, covers his head in dirt, and wears sackcloth. El cries, "Baal is dead! What of the peoples? The son of Dagān! What of the multitudes?"[49] Anat also mourns greatly for Baal, and wonders what will become of the peoples now that Baal, son of Dagān, is dead.

Anat descends into the underworld and with the help of the goddess Shapash 'Divine Lamp," or 'sun', to search for Baal. Anat locates Baal and loads his body onto her back. She carries Baal to the summit of Mt. Sapan and buries him in a divine pit in the Earth. She slaughters buffalo, oxen, sheep, deer, mountain goats, and donkeys as offerings for mighty Baal, and then she, El, and Athirat discuss possible successors to Baal from among the gods. However, none of the possible successors matches up: one is too weak to run like Baal or handle the lance as he does, and another is too slight – when he sits on mighty Baal's throne, his feet do not reach the footstool, and his head does not reach the top.

Anat mourns and longs for Baal, and in her rage at Mot she grabs him by the hem of his garment and orders him to return her brother. Mot brags about devouring Baal, and in her grief Anat seizes Mot, splits him with a sword, winnows him through a sieve, burns him with a fire, grinds him in a millstone and sows him in a field.[50]

El has a glorious dream that portends Baal's return, where "if Mightiest Baal lives … Let the heavens rain oil, the wadis run with honey, then I will know that Mightiest Baal lives, the Prince, Lord of the Earth, is alive."[51] El laments to Anat that the furrows of the fields are parched, and wonders where is Mighty Baal, that he might restore the ploughed land. Anat enlists the help of the goddess Shapash, 'Divine Lamp' or 'sun', to look for Baal, at which quest she is presumably successful – it is difficult to say because of a gap in the text – because Baal is returned to the land of life, seizes and defeats all pretenders to his throne, and resumes his dominion over the Earth. The narrative next turns perhaps to a description of a seven-year period of agricultural prosperity, wherein Mot then complains to Baal that he has been filled with shame. Baal and Mot then engage in an epic battle for supremacy, and they both fall, indicating perhaps that neither ultimately triumphs, and that the cycle between "life," and "death," as represented by them, is everlasting.

Analysis of influential geographical motifs from episode one: Baal vs. Yamm

Like all literature, the Baal Cycle emerged out of human cultural experience. Influenced by the religious, political, and geographical contexts in which it was composed, this text is replete with indications of its influences.[52] As Smith and Pitard point out, in addition to political, religious, and social elements which can be read in the text, the Baal Cycle also displays direct evidence of "language relationships with royal land grants, lamentations, curses, diplomatic correspondences, hymns, magical incantations, legal terminology, numerical sayings, and certainly other genres lost to modern readers."[53] Additionally, its authors display a profound sense of reverence for the divine, which they portray as deep and unknowable. Amid such a rich contextual backdrop, we will focus here on the three major episodes of the cycle, 1 – Baal vs. Yamm, 2 – Baal Enthroned on Mt. Sapan, and 3 – Baal vs. Mot, as well as on particular themes which emerge from these episodes, such as the defeat of the sea/serpent/dragon; stormy theophanic imagery; associations with Mt. Sapan and other high places; associations with fertility, fecundity, and the seasonal cycle; and regular disappearance and return. These geographically influenced themes come to comprise the geographical motifs upon which the other figures in this book also will draw.

Motif of the defeat of a sea/serpent/dragon

The Baal Cycle depicts a royal society, involving various deities and the natural realms over which those deities held power, in a manner that reflects aspects of both the political and natural worlds known in the culture of ancient Ugarit.[54] But as we have seen above, the cycle itself – and/or elements from it – are likely far older than the 14th- to 12th-century BCE version of the myth excavated at Ugarit. Among those older elements is the narrative of Baal's defeat of Yamm, whose name means 'Sea', and who is also called '*nhr*', 'River', a narrative which is linked with both earlier and later narratives of defeat of the 'Sea', and of order overcoming chaos.

The character of Baal's enemy, Yamm, and Baal's ensuing cosmic authority after Yamm's defeat, are central elements of this compelling myth, which has many ancient Near Eastern counterparts. "The base myth is that a dragon slayer, god or man, slays a dragon that represents both chaos and water."[55] Robert Miller argues on the basis of linguistic analysis that this base mytheme originated in and is preserved in Indo-European languages, hypothesizing that the myth was known to speakers of Proto-Indo-European (PIE), whence it spread to other societies. On the bases of linguistic and archaeological evidence, he adopts the position that speakers of PIE originated in around 4000 BCE in the landmass area between the Black Sea and the Caspian Sea known as the Pontus Steppes. During the fourth millennium BCE, some of those PIE-speakers migrated to Anatolia, while others migrated in around 1800 BCE to Iran and India, explaining the common linguistic and formalistic elements of this myth among geographically disparate groups.[56] Miller further uses linguistic evidence to argue that the oldest of all the extant dragon-slaying myths is the Hittite myth,[57] that this myth directly inherits from PIE times, and that it is from the region of Anatolia, from sometime during the fourth millennium BCE.[58]

According to Daniel Schwemer, "the mythologeme of the victory of the new king of the gods over the chaotic sea probably originated in the Eastern Mediterranean, but it spread so early that the individual lines of the tradition's history can no longer be traced."[59] Robert Miller argued, as we just saw above, that the myth can, indeed, be traced through analysis of PIE language roots used in individual versions of the myth. Nevertheless, Schwemer and Miller's conclusions about the origin of the myth – for Miller, the Pontus Steppes and Anatolia, and for Schwemer, the Eastern Mediterranean – need not be mutually exclusive. The Pontus Steppes and Anatolia occupy overlapping territory, as do Anatolia and the Eastern Mediterranean. Moreover, all three areas, the Pontus Steppes, Anatolia, and the Eastern Mediterranean, are located along large bodies of water. In any event, these regions, certainly, are proximate, and help to give us a set of geographical references for the earliest versions of the base myth of a dragon-slayer vanquishing a dragon who represents both water and chaos.

Powerful and compelling over a wide area, another important Near Eastern counterpart to this narrative is the Babylonian epic *Enuma Elish*. This cosmogonic myth narrates the Mesopotamian gods Ea and Anu's defeat of Apsu, the primordial Fresh Water, as well as of the god Marduk's defeat of Tiamaat, Salt Water, and from whose slain body Marduk created the world.[60] Together, Apsu and Tiamat represent the watery forces of chaos, and Marduk is the god who defeats the sea/serpent/dragon.[61] The long-lived ancient Near Eastern mytheme of a storm-god's battle against the cosmic sea widely was known and utilized by peoples throughout the region long before the dynasties at Ugarit and Babylon recorded these myths in their extant traditions involving the gods Baal-Hadad and Marduk.[62]

Regarding the form of this myth from Ugarit in the Baal Cycle, Robert Miller argues that it is an amalgamation of several other storm-god epics, and that it combines Northwest Semitic (Amorite) elements, Hittite elements, Hurrian elements, and perhaps even Indo-Aryan elements.[63] The Baal Cycle version of this myth involves the storm-god slaying the sea, depicted as a dragon, after the other gods cower in fear. Although the Baal Cycle is not a cosmogonic myth like *Enuma Elish*, in that it does not describe the creation of the cosmos, "the mountain of Baal, Mount Zaphon, and to an extent the human king as Baal's agent, still become symbols of security against defeated chaos."[64] It is, in fact, Mount Sapan – or, Mount Hazzi, to the Hittites, Mount Kasios, to the Greeks, and Mount Casius, to the Romans – as a bulwark against the chaos of the god Yamm-'sea', also referred to as 'Ullikumi', 'snake', in the Hittite myth; as '*nhr*', 'river', '*tnn*', 'snake', '*ltn*', 'twisty serpent', in the Ugaritic myth; as 'Typhon' the serpent or as 'drakōn', 'dragon', in Greek myths; and as 'Draco', 'dragon', in Latin – that form many of the fundamental common elements of Eastern Mediterranean narratives. We will see more below about the influential role of Mount Sapan, as well as of the ties between these Hurro-Hittite, Canaanite, Greek, and Roman myths in the Eastern Mediterranean.

Meteorological and Theophanic imagery of Baal-Hadad

The ubiquitous motif of a storm-god defeating the sea may also draw upon geological and meteorological imagery, such as the natural weather conditions prevailing along the Levantine coast. In particular, these geological and weather events may include the phenomenon of the rainstorm moving eastward across the Mediterranean Sea and onto land,[65] the meteorological phenomenon known as a waterspout, the flooding of regional rivers, and the frequent occurrence of earthquakes. Such meteorological and geological imagery regularly is referenced in Mesopotamian, Biblical, and Greek literature. "From Zancle to Timnath-serah, from the Bay of Naples to Sodom, eighth-century men explained oddities they found in the landscape by inventing 'just-so' stories."[66] Ancient peoples everywhere thus created stories to explain the natural phenomena they were powerless to control, such as storms, rain, wind, lightning, natural gasses arising from the earth, earthquakes, and volcanoes.[67]

In modern Arabic traditions lasting through at least the 20th century CE, the '*tannīn*' (from the Semitic *tnn*) still is understood to be a mighty serpentine monster, and it refers as well to the meteorological phenomenon of a waterspout. This natural phenomenon appears at first like a dark snake arising from the sea and reaching to the clouds.

Meteorologically, a waterspout is a column of cloud-filled air rotating over a body of water; water inside of it is made up of condensation from the cloud. Waterspouts can occur in all sea areas, but form more frequently in areas of coastal irregularities, like bays and gulfs, than they do on the open ocean.[68] Although it appears otherwise, a waterspout does not 'spout' from the water, but instead descends from a cumulus cloud.

The first stage of waterspout formation consists of the surface of the water taking on a dark appearance where the vortex of otherwise-invisible rotating wind reaches it. Next, light and dark bands start to spiral out from that dark spot on the water, and then a swirling ring of sea spray begins to develop around the dark spot. A visible, twisting waterspout starts to form, and a mature vortex can be identified as a waterspout that reaches from the surface of the water to the clouds overhead. The average waterspout has a diameter of around 165 feet and lasts between five and ten minutes, while the largest waterspouts can have diameters of 300 or more feet and last for as long as an hour. Once the flow of warm air into the vortex weakens, which often happens if a waterspout contacts the land, a waterspout collapses.[69]

Arabic literature preserved from the tenth century CE relates a tradition, popular at that time, that '*tanānīn*' ('dragons') originate as black wind on the bottom of the sea, come to the surface, and reach the clouds in the form of cyclones (that is, waterspouts). According to this text, people believed tanānīn to be black snakes whose destructive power continued until 'cloud angels' forced them out of the sea, and placed them in the land of 'Yajuj and Majuj', where the cloud angels bombarded them with hail.[70] Hasan Haddad notes that this same story seems to be reflected in a Hittite-era bas-relief from the Gate of Lions in Malatya from the 12th or 11th century BCE, depicting the storm-god and his son attacking a coiling serpent. Most scholars agree that this image from the Gate of Lions represents the narrative of the Hittite storm-god Tarḫuna defeating the snake Illuyanka by means of the storm. The details of this image also appear to be similar to Mas'udi's legend involving tanānīn in the sea being bombarded by hail.[71]

Theophanic descriptions of the divine in many ancient Near Eastern cultures very often took the form of natural phenomena related to the storm, and thus it would be unsurprising if myths involving storm-gods were likewise based in meteorological explanations for natural phenomena.[72] Recall that the base myth of the storm-god defeating the sea/serpent/dragon likely originated in the region of the Pontus Steppes, located between the Black Sea and the Caspian Sea, in Anatolia, or in the Eastern Mediterranean.[73] Each of these areas borders large bodies of water where waterspouts occur. In July of 2018, a summer storm system in the Black Sea produced multiple waterspouts over a few days, in one case stunning vacationers with a spectacular display at the Russian resort town of Gelendzhik Bay, along the Black Sea.[74]

Waterspouts often form near coastal irregularities like bays, and owing to the geology of the Mediterranean Basin, most of the landmass that borders the sea is mountainous.[75] Where the mountains are high enough, they affect the regional air and weather patterns.[76] This is not unlike the topography found at the Bay of Antioch, where Mt. Sapan (today called in Turkish *Kiliç Daği* and in Arabic جبل الاقرع *jebl al-āqra'*) sits at the one end, in a manner very similar to the Bay of Naples, in Italy.[77] In November of 2018, a water spout in the bay neighboring Naples, at the town of Salerno, moved directly into the city, making for a dramatic international news event and damaging property, but not injuring anyone.[78]

Waterspouts are visually stunning and often frightening natural phenomena to witness, but greatly destructive waterspouts are a rarity. When they do happen, though, people long remember these events. In the Mediterranean country of Malta in 1555 CE, a catastrophic waterspout hit the Grand Harbor, sinking four of the prized galleys of the Knights of St. John, and killing more than 600 people. [79]

Likewise, the Orontes ('dragon', from *tnn*), Litani (from *ltn*), and all seasonal rivers and streams in the Eastern Mediterranean region can flood dangerously and erratically. In 300 BCE, Seleucus Nicator founded the city of Antioch, located near Mt. Kasios on the Mediterranean coast and next to the Orontes ('Dragon') River, building it on a

> complicated site between the Orontes and the slopes of Mt. Silpius [a foothill of Mt. Kasios]. From the outset, Antioch had to cope with seasonally

> torrential streams, and primarily the Parmenios, and to a lesser degree, the Firminus [these are the names of seasonal streams near Antioch]. Their seasonal runoff affected the southeastern boroughs and the whole of the Orontes' left bank. [The Emperor] Justinian's so-called Iron Gate with its successive overhauls is testimony to these environmental pressures as well as to the resilience of the Antiochenes. Planted deep in the gorge between Mt. Silpius and Mt. Staurin [another foothill of Mt. Kasios], it served both as a gate and dam, and was the city's last grand effort to curb the vexations caused by these erratic waters.[80]

Indeed, the flooding Orontes and nearby rivers have been a known danger in the region for millennia. Still to this day, the Orontes river poses a threat to the communities in the Amuq Valley. Generally during the months of August through October, the river is at low-flow. In the rest of the year, the water level in the rivers depends on precipitation, and when great storms hit, the rivers flood. In 2003, a disastrous inundation caused the banks of the Orontes to overflow, and "local *tells* looked like islands in the sea."[81]

Sixth-century CE Antiochene historian John Malalas, reprising an earlier account from Pausanias of Antioch (ca. 358 CE), preserved an even earlier Greek narrative about Perseus' battle against the dragon river:

> When there was a storm, the river adjacent to the city of the Ionitans flooded badly. At that time it was called the Drakon, but now it is called the Orontes. Perseus asked the Ionitians to pray. In the course of their prayers and with their mystic rites a ball of thunderbolt fire came down from heaven, which put a stop to the storm and checked the streams of the river.[82]

Baal's theophany in the storm was a revelation of his powers of control over the heavens and the waters of the earth, by which he rendered the earth fertile. Baal's self-disclosure was associated with rain, winds, fire, storms, lightning, clouds, and mountain tops. Baal often was described as the "Rider of the Clouds," which were the chariot by which he thundered across the sky.[83] These theophanic descriptions are important not only for the ways in which they incorporate meteorological and other natural phenomena, but also because they become important motifs upon which, in different measure, the other figures in our study, Elijah, Saint George, and al-Khiḍr, will draw.

Destructive natural phenomena like waterspouts, flooding rivers, and earthquakes are deeply impactful meteorological events to which humans are helplessly subject. These events can seem, even still today, to be the fault or the will of a god or gods. In a contemporary context, we may think of phenomena like waterspouts and flooding rivers all to be related to sky storms, just as we today think in categorically different terms about what we perceive to be the characteristics of a sea and of a river. But just as what we perceive shapes our understanding of the phenomena we encounter, so, too, for peoples in living the ancient Near East and into the common era. As Robert Miller wrote, "to the human observer, the writhing and convulsing surface of the sea appears living, a fantastic malevolent beast."[84] Stories of the sea and the river as serpents and dragons – as actors in and of themselves – were used to explain the callousness of destructive meteorological phenomena. Likewise, demons, rather than illnesses or imbalances, were used to explain maladies of all sorts. In addition to the explanations inherent in these notions, in both cases, equally powerful opposing forces, such as storm-gods and saints, could be invoked to offer some measure of control over and protections against these monsters and other caprices of nature, biology, and fortune.

Kingship: Protection or destruction

At the heart of the *Cycle* is the literary and religious narrative of Baal's kingship; his rise to power and dominion over the other gods, over the humans of the Earth, and over the forces of nature – particularly, over the waters. By this means, Baal ruled not only the gods but the earthly realm as well, and he showed his beneficence – or his wrath – upon those whom he chose.

In the *Cycle*, Baal was portrayed both as a great warrior and a representation of war and destruction, but also as a beneficent helper to those whom he favored. Contemporaneous political rulers of the time therefore attempted to place themselves in Baal's favor by means of rituals and offerings, constructing temples, invoking his name in treaties, and naming themselves and their houses after the deity.[85]

But the theme of Baal's kingship, which provided either protection or destruction, was attained in the *Baal Cycle* not simply through the actions of Baal alone; he was helped greatly by his allies, such as the craftsman of the gods, Kothar-wa-Hasis, who provided Baal's weapons, and by Anat, always ready to do battle on behalf of Baal against greater enemies. Many elements of the power dynamics in the *Baal Cycle* also may reflect the political situation of Ugarit, which was a coastal buffer state existing for centuries amidst and between the more powerful empires of the Hittites, Egyptians, and other empires.[86] Certainly, the theme in the *Baal Cycle* of the great gods communicating by means of messengers, and regularly interacting amid or with the threat of battle, seems to reflect in the narrative the political realities of the day.

Analysis of influential geographical motifs from episode two: Baal enthroned on Mt. Sapan

Baal's traditional home, the place where his palace is built, and even the meeting location of the conflicts between Baal and his major enemies, is the divine mountain known as *ṣpn*, Mt. Sapan. In Akkadian, this influential mountain is known as *ba'lişapûn.* In Hittite, the mountain is known as Mt. Hazzi, , in the Hebrew Bible as Mt. Zaphon, in Greek as Mt. Kasios, in Latin as Mt. Casius, in Arabic as الأقرع جبل *jebl al-āqra'*, and in Turkish as *Kiliç Daği*.[87] Baal battles Yamm at Mt. Sapan (*CAT* 1.1 I 4–5) and Mot there as well (*CAT* 1.6 VI 12–13), and this mountain is also the site of other divine battles involving a storm-god. The Hurrian and Hittite myth of the storm-god and Ullikumi takes place at Mt. Hazzi, and Zeus fights Typhon on Mt. Kasios, as well.[88]

Here we see evidence not only of a long-term common pool of religious material involving the motif of a storm-god's conflict at Mt. Sapan, but evidence of the influence of geography, as well. At over 6,000 feet in height, this preeminent mountain is the highest peak on the northern section of the Levantine coast. As such, it creates a meteorological zone which attracts the clouds around it and which thus receives the heaviest annual rainfall in the region – over 57 inches – making Mt. Sapan, which literally towers over all other places, a fitting home for the regional storm-god.[89]

Greek and Roman associations with the storm-god and Mt. Sapan

Several regional cultures have considered this influential mountain to be the home of a storm-god, and one who defeated a sea monster to attain kingship. Interactions between Greek-speaking peoples and the peoples and locations of the Levant have taken place for millennia, both before and after the late Bronze-Age destructions. As Greek political control of the region grew in the fourth century BCE, following the conquests of Alexander III of Macedon (the 'Great'), naturally the Greek names both for this influential mountain, and for the river which was visible winding and wending its way into the sea just to the north, became these features' prominent names, and about which regional myths already were told:

> The thunderstorms that today break over Mt. Kasios, the modern Jebel Aqra, ever did so, and the mountain had long been recognized by the native peoples as the site of a primeval battle between a thunderbolt-wielding storm-god and a dragon. Accordingly, the thunderbolt-related cults of Seleucia-in-Pieria and Antioch almost certainly continued, directly or indirectly, pre-Greek forebears. Greek tradition avidly embraced this notion of an archetypal battle between a storm-god and a dragon at Mt. Kasios: the storm-god became Zeus, and the dragon became Typhon. As the storm-god was based on the mountain-top itself, home to thunderbolts, so the dragon came to be identified with the serpentine river Orontes at the mountain's foot. It had been transformed at the place of defeat. The Greeks then elaborated this basic myth with a suite of analogue and sequel narratives.[90]

There are many dragon-slaying myths in Greek mythology. Only the dragon Typhon, however, is associated with the Near East, and Typhon is arguably the most celebrated of dragons, according to Greek texts that can be traced to at least 700 BCE.[91] Writing in 24 CE, the Greek historian Strabo preserves this account of Zeus' battle against the dragon Typhon, who both created and *became* the river Orontes:

> The river Orontes flows past the city [Antioch]. It originates in Coele-Syria, and thence is taken underground, but it returns its stream to the surface,

> and, advancing through Apamea to Antioch, flows close to the city and then debouches into the sea near Seleucia. The river was formerly called Typhon, but changed its name to that of the man who built a bridge across it, called Orontes. They tell that somewhere here occurred the events concerning Typhon's being blasted with the thunderbolt and the Arimoi ... They say that Typhon was struck by the thunderbolts (he was a dragon [*drakon*]) and he fled in search of a way underground. He cut into the earth with his coils, making the channel for the river, and by diving into the earth he broke upon the spring. The name of the river derived from this.[92]

In Hesiod's *Theogony*, Zeus was said to have flung Typhon into the ground and to have trapped him below Mt. Etna, in explanation for this thundering volcano. A similar narrative is found in Pseudo-Apollodorus, ca. 100 CE:

> When the gods had vanquished the Gigantes, Ge in anger consorted with Tartaros, and brought forth in Kilikia ['Cilicia' is a southern region of the Anatolian Peninsula located along the Eastern Mediterranean] Typhon the most monstrous of all her children. Down to the waist he was human in shape, but big enough to overtop the mountains; his head often touched the stars; his hands reached the east and the west, and from them started a hundred snaky heads. Below the waist he had serpentine coils that reared and hissed. There were wings all over his body, bristly hair on his head and cheeks, fire in his eyes. He attacked heaven with hissing and shouting, and he hurled rocks and breathed out fire. The gods on seeing him fled to Egypt, where they transformed themselves into various animals. While Typhon was afar off, Zeus flung thunderbolts at him. When Typhon drew nigh, Zeus scared him with a *harpe* of adamant [a sword-like weapon of mythical hardness and indestructibility] and pursued him to Mt. Kasion [Mt. Kasios] in Syria. Seeing that he was wounded, Zeus then came to close quarters. But Typhon, casting his coils about the god, caught him, wrested the harpe from him, and cut the sinews of his hands and feet. He lifted Zeus on his shoulders and carried him through the sea to Kilikia, where he deposited him in the Corycian Cave. The sinews he hid in the skin of a bear and stored them there with Delphyne, half-snake, half-woman, to guard them. However, Hermes and Aigipan contrived to steal the sinews, and fitted them on to Zeus again. Thus Zeus, having recovered his strength, suddenly appeared in the sky on a chariot drawn by winged horses. Brandishing his [thunder] bolts, he pursued Typhon to Mt. Nysa. Here, the monster was deceived by the Moirai; for, believing that it would increase his strength, he tasted of mortal fruit. Pursued further to Thrace, [Typhon] carried on the fight round Mt. Haimos and hurled whole mountains at Zeus. But the thunderbolt forced these mountains back upon him, till [Zeus] deluged the range with [Typhon's] blood.[93] [Typhon] essayed to escape through the Sicilian sea [the Strait of Sicily, located between Sicily and Tunisia]. But Zeus finally crushed him beneath Mt. Aitne [Mt. Etna], from which the fiery blasts of the thunderbolts that were flung can still be seen to issue.[94]

Robin Lane Fox points out that eighth-century Euboan Greeks who established a community north of Mt. Sapan in the Eastern Mediterranean region of Iskenderun/Alexandretta (modern-day Hatay, Turkey), saw their own Mt. Olympus in Mt. Sapan (which they called Mt. Kasios, after 'Mt. Hazzi', the Hurro-Hittite name for the mountain). In that way, Mt. Kasios functioned as a kind of "Olympus of the Near East."[95] Moreover, it was an informal Greek and Roman convention not to ascribe stories involving similar-seeming myths and landscapes to a "new" or "foreign" god, but to associate them with their own gods and myths.[96]

Indeed, such eighth-century Greek attribution may not have been in any way artificial. Earlier Mycenaean-era Greek contacts during the Late Bronze Age with the Hittite and Canaanite communities around Mt. Sapan would have made both Mt. Sapan and the storm-god who lived there familiar to later Greeks through the medium of myth. Fox notes also that Greek μύθοι 'muthoi', or 'tales' also rely on community notions of a distant, more splendid past, which, for eighth-century Greeks, may have been reflected in tales and stories that originated in late Bronze-Age Mycenaean culture.[97] Early Mycenaean-era Greek contact with the Hittite and Canaanite communities around Mt. Sapan

> left its mark on Greek stories about the gods which then lived on for the next three or four hundred years, passed on by word of mouth. These half-remembered tales were then greatly confirmed when [Euboan] Greeks returned and settled once again on the Levantine coast at al-Mina beside Mt. Hazzi. … We should think of an initial Bronze Age encounter, confirmed by Greeks from Euboea when they established a firm presence on the north side of Mt. Hazzi [in the 8th century BCE]. … After all, the mountain was still the same potent and dominating force in people's lives. … When tremendous thunder rolled off the mountain, the lightning flashed and the sea began to swell off al-Mina's beach, any Greek would wish to know the divinities of the place. They would ask their neighbors and … learn of the stories which the landscape and songs "of the sea" and "of kingship" on Mt. Hazzi had kept alive.[98]

Greeks at settlements in the region north of Mt. Sapan during the eighth century BCE and afterward built shrines to 'Zeus Kasios' on the mountain, as Zeus the Greek sky god shared many elements in common with the storm-god Baal-Hadad. Indeed, Greek myths involving the figure of Zeus likely were influenced during the Mycenaean-era by contacts with the Levant and with the regionally dominant figure there of the storm-god.[99] 'Zeus Kasios' became a Greek equivalent to Baal-Sapan on the mountain and was venerated at shrines there and at high places throughout the region for hundreds of years.

Fox also notes that while communities of travelling Greeks long "saw" the location of *a* battle between Zeus and Typhon at geographically appropriate sites all around the Mediterranean, including the mountain of Mt. Sapan/Kasios, Homerian *textual* references to the Zeus-Typhon battle location in the *Iliad* refer to a location other than Mt. Sapan; specifically, Fox identifies that textual location with the Bay of Naples, in Italy, with its thundering Mt. Vesuvius located next to the sea.[100]

Mt. Vesuvius is of course one of Europe's three-largest active volcanoes and is therefore geographically similar in many respects to Mt. Etna, Europe's largest active volcano, located in modern-day Sicily. In just the same way that Mt. Sapan functioned for Greek-speaking communities as a "Mt. Olympus of the Near East," Fox argues that the similar geography of Mt. Sapan and the Orontes River with that of Mt. Vesuvius and the Bay of Naples naturally invoked for Greek-speaking travelers the same Pseudo-Apollodoran myth involving the battle of Zeus and Typhon.[101] When the 19th-century archaeologist and writer Gertrude Bell visited the same Bay of Antioch, near Mt. Sapan (which, in 1907, she referred to as the "Bay of Seleucia" and "Mt. Cassius," respectively), she herself noted the exact same geographical similarities: "The Bay of Seleucia is not unlike the Bay of Naples and scarcely less beautiful … The Orontes River flows through sand and silt further to the south and the view is closed by a steep range of hills, culminating at the southern point in the lovely peak of Mount Cassius which takes the place of Vesuvius in the landscape."[102]

Lastly, Fox notes that extreme geological features like Mt. Vesuvius, Mt. Etna, and Mt. Sapan, with their frequent earthquakes, also invited other 'just so' explanations. The shaking of the earth could be referenced as the location(s) where Typhon, trapped underground – trapped, according to Hesiod's *Theogony* and echoed in Pseudo-Apollodorus, under Mt. Etna – thrashed and writhed about, especially when attacked by Zeus. Describing eighth-century BCE Greek travelers, and the ways in which similar landscapes 'naturally' explained or confirmed both geological and geographical phenomena as well as myths, Fox wrote:

> Manifestly it was Typhon's lair, and the scene of the Storm God's victory. But one question remained: where was the serpent nowadays? Some said he had been vanquished in the sea; others, that his bloodstains were visible on the nearby cliffs. But others, as Homer knew, said that Zeus, even now, was 'lashing' him from time to time while the ground above him shook. This 'lashing' cannot be by the Cilician shore. Its abysses and the Corycian cave are the results of erosion, not of earthquakes. … It belongs at the heart of our Euboeans' travels, supporting the view that it was they who first discovered Typhon in the cave on great Mount Hazzi [the Hittite name for Mt. Sapan] as they traveled to and fro between north Syrian and the Cilician shore.[103]

In 300 BCE Seleucus Nikator, a general of and successor to Alexander III of Macedon, founded the cities of Seleucia-in-Pieria, Antioch, Laodicea, and Apamea, together known as the 'Syrian Tetrapolis', along the coast and the inland plain of Seleucid territory in Syria.[104] Upon founding these cities, Seleucus sacrificed to Zeus on Mt. Kasios, and had local coins struck at Seleucia representing Zeus and his thunderbolt. First-century CE Roman historian Appian of Alexandria wrote that when Seleucus set about the build the city, "a portent of thunder preceded the foundation, for which reason he [Seleucus] consecrated thunder as a divinity of the place … the inhabitants worship thunder and sing its praises to this day."[105] Later, 6th-century CE Greek chronicler John Malalas of Antioch also recorded that before founding the city of Seleucia-in-Piera, Seleucus had made a sacrifice to Zeus on Mt. Kasios, and that he did so on April 23.[106]

During subsequent (and long-lasting) Roman rule in the region, both the name of the storm-god and the name of the sea monster were Romanized to Jupiter (the Roman equivalent of Zeus) and to Draco ('dragon' for Typhon), respectively. Among the many regional Near Eastern manifestations of Jupiter, the Roman god Jupiter Dolichenus became, by the year 200 CE, a highly popular god throughout the entirety of the Roman Empire. Originally, Jupiter Dolichenus had been the main god of Doliche [Dülük], a minor town in the north of ancient Roman Syria that is today a part of modern Turkey.[107] The similarities between Jupiter Dolichenus, depicted as a "menacing god standing on a bull and brandishing his weapons – a double-axe and a thunderbolt," with the Near Eastern storm-gods like Hadad, Teshub, and Baal were long apparent to observers.[108]

Given the length in time between the cults of the storm-gods, however, and the cult of Jupiter Dolichenus, scholars had been divided on the issue of whether Jupiter Dolichenus represented a "continuity of cult" with the earlier Iron Age, or whether the Roman worshippers of this god simply had appropriated a regional iconic image. Recent archaeological work carried out at the main sanctuary of Dülük (known today as Baba Tepesi), however, has yielded sufficient evidence to demonstrate that

> the sanctuary continuously was occupied from the early Iron Age to Late Antiquity. There is no evidence of a hiatus or a violent destruction antedating the Christian era, which clearly speaks in favor of continuity and a direct link between Jupiter Dolichenus and the Ancient Near Eastern Storm God.[109]

In the Eastern Mediterranean, religious continuities between the Bronze and Iron Age storm-gods with Zeus and Jupiter of the Greek and Roman periods was a natural feature of regional religion, given the geography they all shared. Even 'outsider' Roman emperors such as Trajan, who visited in 114–115 CE, and Julian, who visited in 363 CE, also made offerings and improved shrines to Zeus Kasios on the summit of Mt. Sapan, at sites which originally of course had been dedicated to Baal-Hadad.[110] Greek Mt. Kasios and Roman Mt. Casius functioned, indeed, as an epicenter of more than 1,000 years of Greek and Roman worship in the Levant, continuing the importance of this mountain and its myths from antiquity into the first centuries of the Common Era.[111]

Analysis of influential geographical motifs from episode three: Baal vs. Mot: Disappearance and return and the seasonal cycle

The episode of Baal's conflict with Mot has clear seasonal agricultural overtones and appears to have been employed in part to explain that the kingship of Baal was limited; i.e., limited to the seasons during which Baal seemed evident and effective – fall, winter, and spring, when the rains fell, and the lands became green.

During this episode, the dramatic attempt of Anat to rescue Baal in the underworld, and her harvest treatment of Mot, 'death', display evidence both of the common pool of compelling contemporaneous religious narratives circulating in the ancient Near East, and the influence of climate and geography. In the first instance, the passage involving Anat's search for Baal in the underworld strongly echoes the Mesopotamian saga of Tammuz and Inanna. The traditions about both Baal and Tammuz are similar in their deaths and perhaps as well in their returns to life; both Baal and Tammuz are related – in different ways – to agricultural fertility; and their divine consorts, Anat and Inanna, respectively, both mourn and search for them in the underworld.[112]

In the second instance, Anat's extreme grief-driven harvest treatment of Mot, wherein she splits him with a sword, winnows him through a sieve, burns him with a fire, grinds him in a millstone and sows him in a field, precedes Baal's return to life as evidenced in the return of agricultural life to the world of the living, and her "harvest" act, itself, originates in the realm of agriculture.[113]

Thus, another influential geographical theme about Baal that emerges from this episode of the Baal Cycle is that of Baal's regular disappearance and return. Intimately connected with the cycles of the seasons and with regular regional droughts, Baal may have seemed to disappear in the summer, when it is dry and hot and the rains do not fall (to say nothing of the regular experience of drought in the Levant, during which time Baal must have seemed painfully callous and/or powerless),[114] but people understood that he was not dead and gone forever. Baal was engaged in a cycle of regular return, during which time he would make his return known in the autumnal thunder that resounded around the peaks of Mt. Sapan, and when he would shower beneficence in the months afterward upon the world of the living.

The importance of rain in all three episodes of the Baal Cycle

The centrality of rain to the life and economy of people at Ugarit is foundational in the portrayal of Baal in the cycle. Smith and Pitard argue that each of the three primary episodes in the Baal Cycle appear to come to a climax with the appearance of Baal's rains and related theophoric powers. For instance, in the first episode, the weapons used by Baal against Yamm in *CAT* 1.2 IV represent lightning, which is often an accompaniment to rains. In the second episode, Baal's thunderous theophany from the open window in his palace concludes Baal's enthronement scene, and likely refers to the return of the rainy season in fall. Finally, in the third episode involving Baal and Mot, Baal's return to life was connected to the return of his rains after a long period of dryness (*CAT* 1.6 III 4–7), which itself was connected both with Anat's harvest activity involving Mot, and also again with the return of the rains in fall. Smith and Pitard argue that this threefold rain-imagery was deliberate and intended to reinforce the portrayal of a triumphant Baal sending his life-giving rains.[115] Such a portrayal of Baal would well suit a region where rainfall represented the primary source of water for life and agriculture.

The Baal Cycle as a source of numerous compelling Levantine religious motifs

Because the Baal Cycle – itself impacted, as we have seen, by physically and temporally nearby religious, political, and geographical influences – exemplifies major elements of religious belief among the Canaanites of the Levant, it should also be understood as expressing "the heart of West Semitic religion from which Israelite religion largely developed."[116] The original god of Israel may have been El (perhaps before this god merged among ancient Israelites with Yahweh, the god from the south), the deities Baal and Athirat/Asherah, likely among others, were worshipped and condemned in ancient Israel as recorded in the Hebrew Bible (see 1 and 2 Kings and Chapter Four, below), and the depictions of Yahweh as an enthroned king, or as a stormy god in theophanic description, resemble depictions both of El and of Baal, respectively, in the Baal Cycle.[117]

Many of the narratives and motifs of the West Semitic religious milieu that are found in the Baal Cycle passed into ancient Israelite culture as described in the Hebrew Bible. These were then passed into the New Testament and into other Jewish works of the Second Temple period. Such compelling figures, narratives, and motifs in turn survived in Christian writings and in rabbinical works of the Common Era, and even into the text of the Qur'ān and subsequent regional religious texts.[118] Many compelling motifs in the Baal Cycle – whether as a part of agrarian religious culture or which found their way into specific religious texts – enjoyed a long history well after the destruction of the city of Ugarit, and it can confidently be claimed that the early forms of many formative religious concepts in Western civilization and in the Near Eastern religious traditions of Judaism, Christianity, and Islam can be located in the Baal Cycle.[119]

Part Three: Storm-god Baal-Hadad image: The Baal Stele

The Baal Stele, also known as 'Baal of the Lightning', arguably has been among the most important items excavated at Ugarit. It was found on May 28, 1932 CE, located at a depth of .65 m (2.1 feet) underneath the surface, overturned and at an incline, among a pile of large blocks and within a sanctuary situated next to the grand temple. The stele itself was carved out of a single block of white limestone which may have been quarried near the site of Ras Shamra. The stele measures 1.42 m tall (4.8 feet [.791 inches]), .5 m (1.64 feet) wide at the base, .47 m (1.54 feet) wide at the upper part, and .28 m (.92 feet) thick. Owing both to the weight of the stele, at 1,000 k (2,204 lbs.), and to its excellent state of conservation, excavators believed that the Baal Stele had not been moved after the destruction of the city, and that originally it had been erected very near where it was uncovered in 1932 CE (Figure 3.1).[120]

On the face of the stele, in bas-relief (more precisely, in champlevé), a standing Baal-Hadad is represented, striding forward while wearing a horned helmet-crown, and brandishing in his raised right hand a mace, while in his left hand he holds a vertical lance (this lance is sometimes interpreted as lightning, as a stalk

Figure 3.1 Baal Stele © www.BibleLandPictures.com / Alamy Stock Photo

of grain, or as both simultaneously), its tip pointed toward the ground. In the field behind Baal, between the lance and the left advancing leg of the divinity, stands on a pedestal or altar a small person dressed in a long tunic (this figure is most commonly thought to be a king of Ugarit).

The forward movement of Baal is rendered skillfully, and Baal looks powerful, elegant, and full of life. The stele is clearly reminiscent of Egyptian style and composition; the artist of this stele seems to have been formed by the school of Egyptian art, in that the stele keeps tightly to the traditional compositional formulas of head and body-below-the-waist in profile view; chest in ¾ view.[121] The composition of this stele is clearly patterned after Pharaonic images of power and dominance; in particular, the posture of the figure of the deity in the Baal Stele is nearly identical to the 'smiting' posture on the palette of Egyptian Pharaoh Narmer, first Pharaoh of unified Egypt, and founder of the First Egyptian Dynasty in the end of the fourth millennium BCE (ca. 3000 BCE) (Figure 3.2).

Based upon its find-spot and elements of Baal's dress, hairstyle, and beard, the stele has been dated to sometime between the 15th and 13th centuries BCE.[122]

Figure 3.2 Narmer Palette © Art Collection 2 / Alamy Stock Photo

Ugarit was under the direct political control of Egypt ca. 1400–1350 BCE, and then under the control of the Hittite Empire ca. 1350–1200 BCE; however, both cultures over a long span of time influenced Ugaritic culture, and several material remains excavated from Ugarit consisted of Egyptian objects with hieroglyphic inscriptions from the middle Bronze Age (1800–1600 BCE).[123]

The composition of the Baal Stele demonstrates evidence of Egyptian political influence in that it employs a widespread and influential image of power and domination, using Pharaonic registers. However, it is also an excellent example of the functioning of a common pool of ancient Near Eastern figures, narratives, and motifs in practice: the Baal Stele utilizes an influential Egyptian motif of power (or perhaps it simply was an *ubiquitous* motif of power, as sharp distinctions such as 'Egyptian' and 'Levantine' may reflect modern perspectives more than contemporaneous ones) to represent Baal-Hadad, the Levantine storm-god, but it does so in a way that reflects a Levantine geographical and cultural environment.

Among the Levantine elements of the Baal Stele are Baal's horned helmet-crown, which also references Baal *as* a bull, as well as his visage, hairstyle, beard, and short tunic, each of which represents a unique Syrian style different from that of the Narmer Palette, for instance.[124] Baal's weapons also are different: whereas Narmer wields a mace in his right hand and subdues an enemy in his left, Baal strikes with a mace in his right hand, but his left holds a lance/lightning bolt/stalk of wheat in the left. Most commentators agree that the lightning-bolt lance is Baal's signature weapon, and that its appearance is accompanied by conceptions of agricultural fertility. Most further agree that this image represents Baal as understood from his narratives of kingship and defeat of enemies (such as Yamm) in the Baal Cycle, using the weapons that had been created for him for the task.[125]

Another aspect unique to both the Baal Cycle and the Levant as depicted on this stele is that of its geographical elements: Baal stands upon four mountains (many feel this represents Mt. Sapan and its four lower peaks, which can be seen while standing at Ugarit), as well as upon a representation of the sea, indicating that Baal is lord of the mountain and has dominion over the waters.[126] Finally, the Baal Stele is different from that of the Narmer Palette in terms of its background: the Palette details a victorious battle and many other Egyptian elements, whereas in the Baal Stele, the only figure in the background is likely that of an Ugaritic King, dressed in long priestly robes, indicating the figure's veneration of Baal, and perhaps also implying (or invoking) Baal's protection and/or divine approval.[127]

The Baal Stele is a marvelous example of the Levantine and ancient Near Eastern common pool in practice, in that it appropriates a compelling contemporary motif but does so in a way that reflects its own Levantine perspective. In employing 'Egyptian' motifs and images of power – to say nothing of a potential Egyptian commission for the work – the artist of this stele (and its patron/s) may also have intended to reflect both political influences and the exigencies of small-state political maneuvering, which were common to the coastal buffer state of Ugarit. Finally, this stele demonstrates the importance Baal-Hadad and his narratives within Levantine cultures, as well as geographical influences upon these narratives and motifs in the forms of continual regional needs involving rain for agriculture.

Part Four: The storm-god Baal-Hadad site – Baalbek

Finally, we examine in this chapter an important geographical site long associated with the storm-god Baal-Hadad: Baalbek, located in what is today modern Lebanon. Baalbek lies in the Beka'a Valley, long a fertile region and known during periods of Roman rule as a granary or "bread basket" of the Roman Empire.[128] The site of Baalbek is a natural center of the upper part of the Beka'a Valley, as it is located at the highest level of the land at the watershed between the sources of two important regional rivers, the Orontes (or al-'Asi) and the Litani (or Leontes) Rivers, and on the main ancient transportation road that runs parallel to the coast along the eastern side of the coastal ranges.[129] In addition to its logistical importance, this site is symbolically important, as well, as it links Baalbek with Mt. Sapan via the Orontes River, and thus combines both the mythic and the geographical in its physical location. The name of the sanctuary of Baalbek is unmistakably related to Baal, the figure for whom the site originally was built, the Western Semitic storm-god. The name 'Baalbek' most likely means 'Baal of the Beka'a', or 'Lord of the Beka'a'. Long the site of a shrine to Baal-Hadad, the site perhaps served as a religious center of the Beka'a, as excavations at the Roman-era great court of Jupiter there have revealed a tell which provides evidence of human life at the site going back at least to the early Bronze Age (ca. 2900–2300 BCE).[130]

The ruined Roman-era site one sees there presently was called Heliopolis and dedicated to the Roman god Jupiter Heliopolitanus, himself the equivalent of

Greek Zeus Heliopolitanus, whom, as we have seen, of course regionally was identified with Baal-Hadad. Note that representations of Jupiter Heliopolitanus include elements that are considered both related to Baal, such as the attendant bulls and the now-broken but originally raised right-arm posture of the figure, as well as the left arm, which likely held a bolt of lightning, and that it includes elements which are considered Greek, Roman, and Egyptian, as well.[131] Near the shrine to Jupiter Heliopolitanus, there were as well slightly less grand sanctuaries dedicated at the site to the Roman goddess Venus and to the god Bacchus.[132] The site was not completed until the fourth century CE, during which time religious focus at Heliopolis and within the Roman Empire as a whole had begun to swing between traditional Hellenistic paganism and various forms of Christianity. During the reign of Theodosius (379–395 CE), a basilica to St. Peter was erected in the place of the main altar, and the site seems to have been little used during the fifth and sixth centuries CE. Under Arab rule beginning in the eighth century CE the site again became known as Baalbek, the local Semitic-language name for the site.[133]

Location and situation of Baalbek and Mt. Sapan: Compelling geography

The site and environs of Baalbek, the preeminent shrine to the Syrian storm-god located in the fertile Beka'a valley, is rife with both geographical and religious influences. Intentionally built at the watershed between two of the most important rivers in the region, the site and temples at Baalbek literally and figuratively sit both *above* the rivers and at their source, representing, perhaps, the dominance of the storm-god over these rivers (Figure 3.3).

To the south flows the Litani River, a name which should be familiar to us now from the Semitic *ltn* root ('Lotan', or as in the biblical 'Leviathan'); its name likely derives from the regional sea monster of the same name. To the north flows the Orontes River, also known, from the Semitic *tnn* root, as the *Drakon*/Draco 'dragon' or Typhon River; this name of the river is associated with the Greek serpent monster Typhon, who was himself a Greek monster known as a dragon and related, as we have seen, to the figure of Yamm.[134]

What we see in the example of Baalbek is a site whose geography either inspired or reinforced religious concepts relating to the compelling narratives of Baal-Hadad, particularly concerning Baal's dominion over Yamm-nahar (a foe long identified among many cultures with both the Orontes and Litani Rivers) and over the other waters by which he fertilized the earth. We see as well in Baalbek a site whose geography is literally and symbolically linked, via the Orontes River, to the location of Mt. Sapan on the Levantine coast. The home of the storm-god, and a site unequalled in importance to the god, Mt. Sapan sits within five miles of the mouth of the Orontes River, which empties just to the north of Mt. Sapan, and which is visible from its slopes.[135]

Physically dominant over the landscape to such an extent that its height influences the weather patterns coming eastward from the Mediterranean, the

Figure 3.3 Map of Baalbek

commanding position of Mt. Sapan, manifestly the home of the storm-god and often simply conflated with and deified as Baal-Hadad, over all surrounding life and other physical features, would have been obvious. Mt. Sapan was linked through myth with the Orontes River, which is itself physically linked to the site of Baalbek. Intentionally constructed by ancient people at a site that sits above both rivers called *tnn*/*drakon*/Typhon and Litani – long regional names for the serpent god whom Baal-Hadad defeated – the site of Baalbek linked both the mythic and the geographical in its physical location, and underscored the dominance of Baal-Hadad over both his foes and the region's waters.

Part Five: Conclusion – The motifs of Baal-Hadad and the Levantine common pool

This chapter dedicated to geographically contextualizing the regional storm-god Baal Hadad has demonstrated that, as we will see regarding the other figures in this study, Baal-Hadad himself was influenced by contemporaneous religious, political, and, largely, geographical forces. As a figure, he was a product of the common pool of his time, and we have seen evidence of the common pool process in texts, images, and sites dedicated to Baal-Hadad. We have seen evidence regarding religious influences from physically and temporally proximate groups, such as the Mesopotamian myths of Marduk and Tiamaat, and of other influential and cosmogonic stories involving the narrative of a storm-god overcoming a sea monster and defeating the forces of chaos.

In these same tales, and in the contemporaneous iconographical representation of the Baal Stele, we also have seen evidence of political influences of the day, such as that of the Egyptian pharaonic motif of power and dominion employed in the stele. Itself a monument to the political setting of Ugarit, as a small state amid the larger, more powerful empires of the Hittites and the Egyptians of the second millennium BCE, the Baal Stele represents as much about the Western Semitic narrative of Baal Hadad as depicted in the Baal Cycle as it does about regional politics of the Late Bronze Age.

Finally, and importantly, we have seen in all three sources – textual, iconographical, and geographical sites – evidence of the influence of physical geography. The geological and meteorological setting of the Levant – and especially in the north, in the case of the storm-god Baal-Hadad – with its dramatic mountains, storms, rivers, and valleys, naturally influenced the religious concepts of people who lived there. From Baalbek, situated at the center of the sources of two important regional rivers, to Mt. Sapan, dominating both land and sea and rising dramatically from the water over a mile into the air, affecting regional weather patterns and representing the local epicenter of rainfall, these sites speak to the profound impact of the natural environment upon religious concepts.[136] These geographical influences may have been the impetus behind the narratives regarding Baal-Hadad, or perhaps they were used as corroborating evidence by people to confirm those narratives – or, perhaps, both, in a very long, ongoing process.

Geographical motifs of Baal-Hadad

What we see reflected by Baal-Hadad is a Canaanite and ancient Near Eastern religious environment in which water from rainfall was essential both to agricultural and human life, where gods and goddesses ruled the natural environment and helped to explain its perplexingly beautiful and callously harsh phenomena, and where the sagas of human life and political power were intertwined with the favor or disfavor of the storm-god – the most powerful deity in the region.

It is difficult to overestimate the influence of Baal-Hadad upon the religious traditions of regional groups thereafter. Baal-Hadad, as we have seen, did not disappear as a regional influence after the destruction of the Late Bronze Age world and cities such as Ugarit, but continued on much as before amid the Canaanite agricultural cultures of the Iron Age and throughout the Greek and Roman eras of the first millennium BCE, lasting even into the first centuries of the Common Era, as his cult gradually was subsumed by the cults to Zeus and Jupiter in the Levant.[137] Furthermore, compelling geographical motifs associated with Baal-Hadad, such as the defeat of the sea/serpent/dragon; smiting or vanquishing a foe; stormy theophanic imagery involving rain and storms and riding a chariot in the clouds; associations with Mt. Sapan and other mountains and high places; associations with fertility, fecundity, and the seasonal cycle; and regular disappearance and return; are also motifs upon which we see the other figures in our study draw: Elijah, St. George, and al-Khiḍr each come to be associated with these motifs as well. The persistence of these geographical motifs demonstrates their enduring impact (as well as the enduring needs of people that are reflected in those motifs) upon those living in the region, over a very long period of time.

Moving to Elijah

One of the motifs intrinsic to Baal-Hadad – association with mountains such as Mt. Sapan and other high places – was the motivation behind hundreds of shrines to Baal-Hadad which were built on mountains and high places throughout the region. Indeed, one of Baal's common epithets during the first millennium BCE was 'Baal Zubal', 'Prince Baal', who was 'Lord of the High Places'. Hebrew Bible writers, who, as we will see in Chapter Four, disdained the figure of Baal-Hadad and local shrines of the 'high places', condemned 'Baal Zubal', or 'Baal Zebul', by making a Hebrew pun on this title with the cleverly rhyming insult 'Baal Zebub', meaning "Lord of the Flies."[138] As we will see in Chapter Four, when we examine the figure of Elijah, a primary mission of the Prophet Elijah as depicted in the first-millennium-era BCE Books of Kings of the Hebrew Bible was to eradicate Baal worship – viewed as false when compared with that of the *true* Lord, Yahweh – from the environs of Israelite religion and political life in the southern Levant.

Notes

1 See also Chapter Two. Note that Aaron Tugendhaft published in 2018 a very similar introduction to the Baal Cycle in *Baal and the Politics of Poetry*, The Ancient World, edited by Seth Sanders (New York: Routledge, 2018). The introduction above is my own, however, and similar to that from my 2016 doctoral dissertation. See Erica Ferg Muhaisen, "Continuity and Contradistinction: A Geography of Religion Study of the Ancient Near Eastern Storm-God Baal-Hadad, Jewish Elijah, Christian St. George, and Muslim al-Khiḍr in the Eastern Mediterranean," PhD diss. (University of Denver, 2016).

2 For more on the discovery of Ugarit and its impact, see Mark S. Smith, *Untold Stories: The Bible and Ugaritic Studies in the Twentieth Century* (Peabody, MA: Hedrickson Publishers, 2001). See also Peter C. Craigie, *Ugarit and the Old Testament* (Grand Rapids, MI: Wm. B. Erdmans Publishing Company, 1983), 7–25. For a firsthand account of early discoveries, see C. F. Schaffer's "The Discovery of Ugarit," in *Hands on the Past*, ed. C.W. Ceram (New York: Knopf, 1966), 301–306. Note that archaeological work at this site is ongoing, although it has been interrupted most recently by the Syrian war.

3 Robert Miller questions whether one could argue that there was a "Canaanite" culture or mythology extant at Ugarit, on the grounds that a 15th-century BCE use of the Akkadian term for the geographical territory *Canaan* (*ki-'ā-ni*) appears to refer to "Syria in general"; that Egypt would not have considered Ugarit to be a part of Canaan during the 14th-century BCE (rather, it would be a part of the territory it designated "Amurru"); and on the grounds that Ugarit is "quite far to the north" of the indigenous, non-Israelite population of Palestine in the 12th century CE. See Robert D. Miller II. *The Dragon, the Mountain, and the Nations: An Old Testament Myth, Its Origins, and Its Afterlives* (Winona Lake, IN: Eisenbrauns, 2018), 95–96. Questions about the various names given by outsiders to the territory in and around Ugarit aside, because the mythological picture presented by the textual remains at Ugarit corresponds with general knowledge about and definitions for 'Canaanite' mythology, and because Daniel Schwemer and other scholars do use the term Canaanite to refer to the mythology espoused in the Baal Cycle and the other literature found at Ugarit, so will this book. See Daniel Schwemer, "The Storm-Gods of the Ancient Near East: Summary, Synthesis, Recent Studies Part One," *Journal of Ancient Near Eastern Religions* 7, no. 2 (2007): 158. Also, in the absence of suggesting other terminology, even Miller himself uses the term 'Canaanite' to describe the region and mythology of Ugarit – see Miller, *The Dragon, the Mountain, and the Nations*, 117 and 119. Finally, although this hardly need be said, the religion and mythology of Ugarit and wider Canaanite belief are of course important on their own as a topic of study, and not solely for the ways in which they relate to the Hebrew Bible.

4 The Biblical perspective is that of the dominance of the religious viewpoints espoused; as we will see, especially in Chapter Four, the opposite was the case. See also Schwemer for how the importance of Ba'lu continued into the Iron Age cultures of Syro-Palestine and South Anatolia. "The Storm-Gods of the Ancient Near East: Summary, Synthesis, Recent Studies Part Two," *Journal of Ancient Near Eastern Religions* 8, no. 1 (2008): 15–16.

5 Margurite Yon, *The City of Ugarit at Tell Ras Shamra* (Winona Lake, IN: Eisenbrauns, 2006), 16. Based upon the archaeological finds at Ras Shamra-Ugarit, estimates of the dates of construction of the Temples of Baal and Dagān are during the end of the Middle Bronze Age or at the beginning of the Late Bronze Age (c. 17th to 15th centuries BCE). On the equation of Dagān, as the father of Baal, with the supreme god El or *'Ilu*, see Schwemer, "In the later Ugaritic myths the storm-god Ba'lu carries the petrified epithet "Son of Dagān", which must continue older North Syrian traditions, because on the level of mythological action 'Ilu was seen as the father of Ba'lu and the father of the younger generation of gods in general. The model for this filiation is surely the generational sequence Kumarbi-Teššub in Hurrian mythology, as Kumarbi was equated with Dagān in Upper Mesopotamia and on the Middle Euphrates." Schwemer, "The Storm-Gods of the Ancient Near East Part One," 156.

6 Craigie, *Ugarit*, 35–36.

7 Craigie, 28.

8 Schwemer, "The Storm-Gods of the Ancient Near East Part One," 121, 125, 158–159.

9 Alberto R. W. Green, *The Storm-god in the Ancient Near East* [Biblical and Judaic Studies from the University of California San Diego, edited by William Henry Propp, vol. 8.] (Winona Lake, IN: Eisenbrauns, 2003), 2. Note that this text has

been critiqued by Daniel Schwemer on the bases of methodology, philology, and, in particular, on Green's interpretation of images. See Schwemer, "The Storm-Gods of the Ancient Near East," Part One and Part Two (on the topic of iconography see Schwemer, Part One, 137, and Part Two, 31–36). Some useful critique aside, Green's text, like the work of Daniel Schwemer, largely remains a useful scholarly contribution to the study of the storm-god in the Ancient Near East. See also Daniel Schwemer, *Die Wettergottgestalten Mesopotamiens und Nordsyriens im Zeitalter der Keilschriftkulturen: Materialien und Studien nach derb schriftlichen Quellen* (Wiesbaden, 2001). Because the work of Green and Schwemer constitute the most important and comprehensive recent studies of the ANE storm-god, disagreements in their work, where pertinent, will be noted here.

10 Eric Nels Ortlund, *Theophany and Chaoskampf: The Interpretation of Theophanic Imagery in the Baal Epic, Isaiah, and the Twelve*, Gorgias Ugaritic Studies 5 (Piscataway, NJ: Gorgias Press, 2010), 267. Ortlund notes that the theophanic imagery which attends and describes Yahweh in the Hebrew Bible is largely mythic (referring to regional myths involving a defeat of chaos, themselves also influenced by meteorological phenomena) rather than metaphorical (a "contrived, figurative relation between two unrelated entities"). See also Alberto R. W. Green, who furthermore argues that to a certain degree, the Storm-god concept evolved into the foundation for modern conceptions of God (Green, *The Storm-God*, 1).

11 Schwemer, "The Storm-Gods of the Ancient Near East Part One," 121.

12 Green, *Storm-God*, 6. "In the cultural and religious evolutions of any region, certain inherent geographical and climatological factors contribute substantially to the local conception of a deity," 9. See also Schwemer, "The relative significance and sphere of activities of the individual storm-gods was dependent, among other things, on the climatic conditions in the individual regions." "The Storm-Gods of the Ancient Near East Part One," 129–130. Green notes that the varied forms and functions of the various semi-divine attendants constitute a key element of difference between manifestations of the Storm-god in different regions, 2, although see also Schwemer, "The Storm-Gods of the Ancient Near East Part Two," 31–36, who disagrees on the topic of iconography and in particular with Green's conclusions about semi-divine attendants.

13 See Daniel Ogden, *The Legend of Seleucus: Kingship, Narrative and Mythmaking in the Ancient World* (Cambridge, UK: Cambridge University Press, 2017), 117–118; and "The Zeus and Typhon in question were the Greek reflexes of a more ancient and indigenous storm-god-and-dragon pair," 173. See also Schwemer, "The Storm-Gods of the Ancient Near East Part Two," 26; as well as Miller, *The Dragon, the Mountain, and the Nations*, 121, 150, 227, 229, 231, and 232.

14 Green, *Storm-God*, 12–13.

15 Schwemer, "The Storm-Gods of the Ancient Near East Part One," 125.

16 Green, 11–12; see also 282–283.

17 Schwemer, "The Storm-Gods of the Ancient Near East Part One," 133.

18 Schwemer, 130–131.

19 Schwemer, 130.

20 Schwemer, 124.

21 Schwemer, 135.

22 Schwemer, 153.

23 Green, *Storm-God*, 166–169, quoting E. M. Lane, *Arabic-English Lexicon* (New York: Ungar, 1955–56), 2882. See also the entry for *hdd*, Hans Wehr, *A Dictionary of Modern Written Arabic*, ed. J. Milton Cowan, 4th ed. (Ithaca, NY: Spoken Language Services, Inc., with permission of Otto Harrassowitz, Wiesbaden, Germany, 1994), 1197. See also Schwemer, "The Storm-Gods of the Ancient Near East Part One," 135.

24 Schwemer, "The Storm-Gods of the Ancient Near East Part One," 130, as well as Part Two, p. 13: "Not explicitly attested in the texts is the worship of Baʻlu as protective

deity of sea-faring. The great significance of sea-trade for the city of Ugarit, the role of Ba'lu as victor over Yammu and the monsters of the sea, the discovery of stone anchors as votive gifts in the area of the Ba'lu temple (as in other sanctuaries on the Syro-Palestinian coast too), as well as the probable function of the Ba'lu temple which rises high above the city as an orientation point (and light-house?) for sailors make it plausible, however, that Ba'lu was ascribed this function, too." For more on stone anchors, Schwemer quotes "H. Frost, "Anchors Sacred and Profane. Ugarit-Ras Shamra, 1986; the stone anchors revised and compared", in: *Arts et industries de la pierre*, ed. M. Yon, RSOu 6 Paris 1991, 355–408.

25 Green, *Storm-god*, 173–175. Also, Schwemer, "The Storm-Gods of the Ancient Near East Part Two," 8–9.

26 Wehr, *Arabic-English Dictionary*, 82. Note also here that *ba'lī* / بعلي means "*unirrigated* land or plants," emphasis added.

27 Throughout the second half of the second millennium BCE and the first millennium BCE, Baal-Hadad often was named the patron deity of particular cities, inspiring local epithets of Baal-Hadad that linked him with those cities (e.g. Baal of Tyre, Baal of Aleppo). These names do not refer to separate deities, but should instead be considered multiple manifestations of Baal-Hadad as associated with a particular locality. See Hassan S. Haddad, "Baal-Hadad: A Study of the Syrian Storm-god" (PhD Dissertation, University of Chicago, 1960), 46. See also Spencer Allen, *The Splintered Divine: A Study of Ištar, Baal, and Yahweh Divine Names and Divine Multiplicity in the Ancient Near East*, Studies in Ancient Near Eastern Records 5 (Munich: De Gruyter, 2015). See also Schwemer, "The Storm-Gods of the Ancient Near East Part Two," 15–16.

28 Schwemer, "The Storm-Gods of the Ancient Near East Part Two," 15.

29 Greene, *Storm-god*, 165–166. See also Miller, *The Dragon, the Mountain, and the Nations*, 120–121. For a detailed discussion of *Ba'al* and *Ba'alšamêm/ Ba'alšamīm* (a regional name for Hadad that takes over during the Persian period) in the first millennia BCE, see Schwemer, "The Storm-Gods of the Ancient Near East Part Two," 15–16.

30 Green, 285. See also Deut 33:2, where Yahweh is described as having "come from Sinai," and is associated with the regions of Seir (identified with biblical Edom, the region southeast of the Dead Sea where the Arabian Peninsula meets the continent of Asia and forms the Jordan Rift Valley) and with Mt. Paran, which most commentators locate somewhere within the Sinai Peninsula.

31 Miller says "The Baal story was probably known to average Israelites more than any of the other myths explored in this book." *The Dragon, the Mountain, and the Nations*, 123, 145, 149.

32 Schwemer, "The Storm-Gods of the Ancient Near East Part One," 121, 125 and "Part Two," 26. See Miller, *The Dragon, the Mountain, and the Nations*, 155–156, for a discussion of whether Yahweh should be understood as a weather god.

33 Green, *Storm-God*, 285. For mythical characteristics of Baal attributed to Yahweh, such as riding on the clouds and thundering with a mighty voice, see also Deuteronomy 33:26, and Psalm 68:4, 68:33, and 104:3.

34 Miller, *The Dragon, the Mountain, and the Nations*, 97.

35 See Mark S. Smith, *The Ugaritic Baal Cycle Volume I: Introduction with Text, Translation and Commentary of KTU 1.1–1.2* [Supplements to Vestus Testamentum , vol. 55.] (Leiden: Brill, 1994), 1–20. See also Mark S. Smith, and Wayne T. Pitard, *The Ugaritic Baal Cycle Volume II: Introduction with Text, Translation and Commentary of KTU/CAT 1.3–1.4* [Supplements to Vestus Testamentum, vol. 114.] (Leiden: Brill, 2009), 9–10. Smith and Pitard argue that the three major episodes of the Baal Cycle are divided as follows: (1) the conflict between Baal and Yamm, which ends at Baal's victory banquet in *CAT* 1.3 I, or at the cessation of hostilities in 1.3 II; (2) the quest

for Baal's palace (1.3 III–1.4 VII); and (3) the conflict between Baal and Mot (1.4 VIII–1.6 VI). Because these sections do not correspond to the beginnings or ends of the tablets, Smith and Pitard argue strongly for considering the tablets as an organic whole. The authors note as well that there is disagreement within the field of Ugaritic studies about whether tablets 1 and 2 (*CAT* 1.1 and 1.2) represent multiple versions of the same story, but that there is little doubt that the conflict between Baal and Yamm detailed in those tablets was a major part of the Baal Cycle, particularly if one agrees with their argument that the episode of conflict between Baal and Yamm is not concluded until tablet 3 (*CAT* 1.3 I or II). Note also that the ancient name of the Baal Cycle is unknown, but the modern name 'Baal Cycle' is derived from the superscription to *CAT* 1.6 I 1, '*lb'l*', 'concerning Baal'. Smith, *Baal Cycle Vol. I,* xxii, 3n.

36 Mark S. Smith, "The Baal Cycle," in *Ugaritic Narrative Poetry* [Society of Biblical Literature Writings from the Ancient World Series, edited by Simon B. Parker, vol. 9.] (Atlanta: Society of Biblical Literature Scholars Press, 1997), 81. See also Smith, *Baal Cycle Vol. I,* 29–60, "According to many scholars, the Baal Cycle enjoyed a long oral history prior to its commitment to writing. The dates proposed for the terminus a quo of the Baal Cycle range from the third millennium down to the middle of the second millennium," (Smith, 29), on the basis of contemporary political records and cultural influences, and linguistic evidence. See also Green, who argues that "the theological conceptions of the Ugaritic pantheon and the nature and function of Baal in particular were probably well established as early as the third millennium BCE" (Green, *Storm-god*, 176.) See also Miller, *The Dragon, the Mountain, and the Nations*, 97, 105.

37 Smith, *Baal Cycle Vol. II*, 7–8. See also Miller who dates the tablets to 1350 BCE, *The Dragon, the Mountain, and the Nations*, 97. Aaron Tugendhaft, relying on the 2014 work of Dennis Pardee, dates the tablets to the late 13th century BCE in *Baal and the Politics of Poetry*, 30. Daniel Ogden dates the tablets to the 14th century BCE in *The Legend of Seleucus: Kingship, Narrative and Mythmaking in the Ancient World*, 119. Accordingly, I date the tablets to sometime between the 14th and 12th centuries BCE; approximately 1350–1190/85 BCE. For my purposes, however, the exact date of the tablets is not overly important, given that "according to many scholars, the Baal Cycle enjoyed a long oral history prior to its commitment to writing." Based on contemporaneous political records and cultural influences, and on the basis of linguistic evidence, "The dates proposed for the terminus a quo of the Baal Cycle range from the third millennium down to the middle of the second millennium [BCE]," Smith, *Baal Cycle Vol. I*, 29.

38 Yon, *City of Ugarit*, 22.

39 Smith, *Baal Cycle Vol. II*, 9.

40 Smith, *Baal Cycle Vol. I*, xxiv–xxv. Quote from xxv.

41 Note also that in this synopsis I am summarizing Mark S. Smith's translation of the Baal Cycle in *The Ugaritic Baal Cycle Vols. 1 and 2* for the episodes on tablets *CAT* 1.1–1.4, as well as from Smith's chapter titled "The Baal Cycle" in *Ugaritic Narrative Poetry*, for the episodes encompassing tablets *CAT* 1.5–1.6.

42 *CAT* 1.2 II 45–47.

43 CAT 1.3 III 20-31.

44 The figures *tnn* and *ltn* appear in the biblical text. See Isaiah 27:1, where *ltn*, often rendered in English as 'Leviathan', is described as the 'fleeing' 'serpent' (or 'snake'), and as the 'twisted' (or 'coiled') 'serpent' (or 'snake'). *tnn* 'dragon' is in this Biblical passage identified with *ltn*/Leviathan and described as "the dragon [or monster] that is in the sea." The whole passage reads, "In that day, the Lord [lit. 'Yahweh'], with his severe sword, great and strong, will punish *ltn* ('Leviathan') the fleeing serpent/snake, *ltn* ('Leviathan') the twisted serpent/snake, and he will kill the *tnn* ('dragon') that is in the sea." Cf. Psalm 74:13, "You split the sea by your strength; you broke the heads

of the *tanānīn* ('dragons') on the waters," and Revelation 13:1, "Then I stood on the sand of the sea, and I saw a beast rising up out of the sea; having seven heads and ten horns, and on his horns ten crowns, and on his heads a blasphemous name." Note that in Revelation 13:1, the 'beast of the sea' is described as having 'seven heads', as is *ltn*/*tnn* in the Baal Cycle. The commonalities between these texts appear to be instances of employing pervasive Levantine and ancient Near Eastern motifs involving the defeat of a sea dragon or serpent. These motifs are employed in multiple ways not only in the Biblical text but also in the Baal Cycle itself, where both Baal (*CAT* 1.2 IV 1–27 and *CAT* 1.5 I 1–4) and Anat (*CAT* 1.3 III 38–42) are described as having battled a figure associated with these motifs.

45 *CAT* 1.4 IV 43–*CAT* 1.4 V 9.

46 *CAT* 1.5 I 1–8. See also above, n. 43 for Biblical and other contemporary references to the motif of a sea serpent/dragon/monster referred to as *ltn* or *tnn*, pervasive throughout the Levant and ancient Near East.

47 *CAT* 1.5 V 1–26.

48 *CAT* 1.5 V 17–19; it is useful to recall that Baal often was portrayed iconographically as and understood *as* a bull.

49 *CAT* 1.5 VI 23–25. We see here a clear reference to the seasonal patterns and the summer, when Baal is "dead", and the rains do not come.

50 This episode at *CAT* 1.6 II 33–37 is also widely believed to reference seasonal and agricultural patterns, as Anat treats Mot as grain being harvested. See below.

51 *CAT* 1.6 III 1–21.

52 Smith, *Baal Cycle Vol. II*, 5 and 56.

53 Smith, *Baal Cycle Vol. II*, 56.

54 *Smith, Baal Cycle, Vol. I*, xxiv. See also Aaron Tugendhaft, who argues that pivotal content in the Baal Cycle is contemporaneous political commentary, in *Baal and the Politics of Poetry*, The Ancient World, edited by Seth Sanders (New York: Routledge, 2018).

55 Miller, *The Dragon, the Mountain, and the Nations*, 28. Note that this motif and my theme will have continuing resonance for the subsequent figure of St. George; see Chapter Five, 161–162; 178.

56 Miller, *The Dragon, the Mountain, and the Nations*, 32.

57 Miller, *The Dragon, the Mountain, and the Nations*, 11. However, see also Daniel Ogden, *The Legend of Seleucus: Kingship, Narrative and Mythmaking in the Ancient World* (Cambridge, UK: Cambridge University Press, 2017), who argues that the oldest version of the myths involving "battles between thunderbolt-wielding storm-gods and their opponents at Mt. Kasios," is the Ugaritic-Canaanite myth of Baal-Hadad vs. Yamm and Litan, which he dates to the 14th century BCE, followed in the 13th century and before by the Hurrian myth of Teššub vs. Hedammu, followed by the 13th century BCE Hittite myth of Tarḫunna vs. Illuyanka, followed by Strabo's ca. 24 CE Greek myth of Zeus vs. the *drakon* Typhon, who becomes the Orontes River, 119.

58 Miller, *The Dragon, the Mountain, and the Nations*, 67.

59 Schwemer, "The Storm-Gods of the Ancient Near East Part Two," 27.

60 Norman C. Habel, *Yahweh Versus Baal: A Conflict of Religious Cultures* (New York: Brookman Associates, 1964), 53.

61 Miller, *The Dragon, the Mountain, and the Nations*, 124–125, and Schwemer, "The Storm-Gods of the Ancient Near East Part Two," 26–27.

62 Smith, *Baal Cycle Vol. I*, 113; see also 224n.

63 Miller, *The Dragon, the Mountain, and the Nations*, 107.

64 Miller, *The Dragon, the Mountain, and the Nations*, 110 and 123.

65 See also Chapter Two, 26–27.

66 Robin Lane Fox, *Travelling Heroes: In the Epic Age of Homer* (New York: Vantage Books, 2010), 354. See also 351–355.

67 See also Fox, 243, "In the Near East, just as in Greece, landscapes were interpreted through myths."

68 M. Sioutas, T. Renko, W. Szilagyi, A.G. Keul, "Waterspout climatology over the Central-Eastern Mediterranean" COMECAP 2014 e-book of proceedings, Vol 3 (2014): 154–158. Although, the authors note that "observation of occurrence may strongly be biased by population density," 156. Informal accounts from Naval Officers and other seafarers throughout history confirm the infrequency of waterspouts on the open ocean. Of course, this as well could be impacted by the sheer size of the ocean.

69 https://www.nationalgeographic.org/encyclopedia/waterspout/

70 Haddad, "Study of Syrian Storm-god," 126–127, quoting a tenth-century CE Arabic work by Murūj al-Dhahab Mas'udi.

71 Haddad, "Study of Syrian Storm-god," 130–132. For more about the Hittite myths of Illuyanka, see also Haddad, 118–121. See also Oya Pancaroğlu, "The Itinerant Dragon-Slayer: Forging Paths of Image and Identity in Medieval Anatolia," *Gesta* 43, no. 2 (2004): 151–164. Note also that "Yajuj and Majuj" in Islamic traditions equates with the biblical land of "Gog and Magog," and reference to this location in Arabic and Islamic idiom generally implies a land "in the east" or "to the north."

72 See also Ortlund, *Theophany and Chaoskampf*, 8n.

73 See above, 25–26. See above, Chapter Three, 65–67.

74 This event took place on July 20, 2018 at Gelendzhikskaya Bukhta ("Gelendzhik Bay") along the Black Sea, in the Krasnodar region of Russia. A similar waterspout-event, contacting a fishing vessel, took place earlier in the week and farther out at sea on July 16, 2018. https://www.abc.net.au/news/2018-07-23/waterspout-captivates-russian-beachgoers/10024696

75 See above 68n and Chapter Two, 26–27.

76 See Chapter Two, 27–28. See also below, Chapter Three, 70–71; 80–83.

77 See Gertrude Lowthian Bell, *Syria: The Desert and the Sown*, (New York: Tauris Parke Paperbacks, 2016. First published London: William Heinemann, 1907), 309. See also Chapter Three.

78 BBC News, 20 November 2018. https://www.bbc.com/news/world-europe-46281048

79 See the account of Claude de la Sengle (1494–1557 CE), Grand Master of the Order of St. John, http://www.islalocalcouncil.com/promseng.htm#claude.

80 Andrea De Giorgi, *Ancient Antioch: From the Seleucid Era to the Islamic Conquest* (Cambridge, UK: Cambridge University Press, 2016), 40.

81 De Giorgi, *Ancient Antioch*, 42, referencing J. Weulersse, "In the 1930s, Weulersse took measurements of the river levels using three stations along its course. His project succeeded in demonstrating the Orontes' unpredictable behavior and its susceptibility to sudden, abrupt flow changes in response to rainfall increase, especially upstream in the territory that now corresponds to modern Syria." J. Weulersse, *L'Oronte: Etude de Fleuve* (Paris, 1940), 35, italics added.

82 Ogden, *The Legend of Seleucus*, 124, quoting John Malalas, *Chronicle* 37–38.

83 Habel, *Yahweh Versus Baal*, 73–76. Note that the title "Cloudrider" is also applied to Yahweh (Psalm 68:4), as well as to Zeus, "*kelainephēs*," "the one in a black cloud" (Iliad 2:412, 6:267, 15:46, 21:520), (Smith, *Baal Cycle Vol. I*, 123 9n.)

84 Miller, The Dragon, the Mountain, and the Nations, 288, quoting Ernst Jentsch, "On the Psychology of the Uncanny (1906)," repr. *Angelaki: Journal of the Theoretical Humanities* 2 (1997): 11.

85 Green, *Storm-God*, 195.

86 See also Aaron Tugendhaft, who argues that pivotal content in the Baal Cycle is contemporaneous political commentary, in *Baal and the Politics of Poetry*. Tugendhaft argues that the Baal Cycle's "noncosmogonic employment of the topos of divine battle against the sea … is consistent with the poem's representation of political rank as unstable and ambitious." 79. I see no reason not to agree that the Baal Cycle is not cosmogonic, and also that its authors could reflect in their writing – even argue for – "political rank as unstable and ambitious." However, the "noncosmogonic

employment of the topos of divine battle against the sea," as we have seen, is neither, in and of itself, unusual, nor unprecedented. Tugendhaft argues that "the latter half of the thirteenth century was tumultuous for the Hittite empire. Both internal and external developments put pressure on traditional conceptions of politics and the divine – leading, eventually, to unprecedented claims about the Hittite sovereign's own divinity. I want to suggest that the innovative royal Hittite claims to divinity and the Baal Cycle's questioning of politics' divine foundation were two sides of the same coin. Both reflect a breakdown of traditional norms, though one arose at the seat of Hittite imperial power whereas the other took shape at the periphery. Ilimilku's poem provides a glimpse of politics as seen from the edge of an anxious empire." 127–128. In my estimation, this *Baal Cycle* poem certainly could and does "provide a glimpse of politics as seen from the edge of an anxious empire," but that may be because the political situation of Ugarit, whether independent or subsumed by larger empires, *always* was that of a small state maneuvering among the greater political and military powers of the day. Tugendhaft argues that "lacking any solid evidence that the tablets we possess record a poem that was passed on without significant alteration for centuries, I believe it is most prudent to begin studying these unique documents in the context in which they were found." Although, Tugendhaft himself admits that "Though I make use of contextual evidence from the late thirteenth century, I never take the poem to be a roman à clef. The Baal Cycle speaks about the kind of things that happen in Bronze Age politics, not particular political events. *The wisdom the poem displays could have been acquired earlier in Ugarit's history*. Even so, I believe the late thirteenth century provides the most compelling context for the poem's production." 30, emphasis added. I agree, of course, with Tugendhaft's deft and extended argument that texts function like artifacts that can tell us a great deal about the societies in which they were produced, and also that the *Baal Cycle* tells us a great deal about the political experience of Ugarit and of "politics as seen from the edge of an anxious empire." However, the *Baal Cycle* tablets clearly share elements in common with narratives older than the late 13th century BCE – specifically, the pivotal motif of a younger god having to fight against other rivals for kingship. See Schwemer, Part One, 155–156, and Part Two, 12, 24, and 27.

87 Smith, *Baal Cycle Vol. I*, 122–23. See also Chapter Two. Note that in the Hebrew Bible, 'Zaphon', as a location, is so influential as to also mean simply 'north'; see Ezekiel 47:17.

88 Smith, *Baal Cycle, Vol. I*, 123, referencing Apollodorus, Bibl. I, 5, 3.7f; cf. *Iliad* 2:78f.; Hesiod, *Theogony*, 820f. See also Chapter Two, 28. See also below, Chapter Three, 80–83.

89 Smith, *Baal Cycle Vol. I*, 123. For the reference to rainfall amounts, see N. Hunt, "Mount Saphon in Myth and Fact" in *Phoenicia in the Bible; Proceedings of the Conference held at the University of Leuven on the 15th and 16th of March 1990*, E. Lipiński, ed (Leuven: Departement Oriëntalistiek/Utigeverji Peeters), 103–105. See also Haddad, "Study of Syrian Storm-god," and "The Holy Mountain," 86–104, and Robin Lane Fox, *Travelling Heroes*, "A Travelling Mountain," 242–258; esp. 243–244 for a description of Mt. Sapan. See also Chapter Two, 28. See also below, Chapter Three, 80–83.

90 Daniel Ogden, *The Legend of Seleucus: Kingship, Narrative and Mythmaking in the Ancient World* (Cambridge, UK: Cambridge University Press, 2017), 117–118. See also Ogden's magnificent chart of typological layers of this storm-god-defeats-dragon myth at Mt. Sapan, 119.

91 Miller, *The Dragon, the Mountain, and the Nations*, 227. See this reference as well for a comprehensive list of the many accounts of Zeus battling Typhon.

92 Ogden, 123, quoting Strabo C750-1.

93 Mt. Haimos is Haemus Mons, a Balkan Mountain range whose name likely is related to the original Thracian word *saimon*, meaning a 'mountain ridge'. In Greek, '*haema*' means 'blood', and '*haimon*' means 'bloody'. Thus, the name of the Haemus Mons

range is linked to the narrative of the mountain range having become bloody with Typhon's blood during his battle with Zeus.

94 Apollodorus 1.6.3, cited in Arthur Bernard Cook. *Zeus: A Study in Ancient Religion, Vol. ii, Zeus God of the Dark Sky (Thunder and Lightning)*," Part i, "Text and Notes" (Cambridge, UK: University of Cambridge Press, 1925), 448–449. Robert Miller (and others) point out that this narrative shares several elements in common with the Hittite Illuyanka myth. See *The Dragon, the Mountain, and the Nations*, 229–230.

95 Fox, *Travelling Heroes*, 246. See also Jona Lendering, "Seleucia-in-Pieria," www.livius.org/place/seleucia-in-pieria for later additional associations between Mt. Kasios and Mt. Olympus.

96 Fox, 280. See also Fox's description of Thessalonian Greek officers of Alexander the Great who reported during their fourth-century BCE visit to Armenia that they had discovered Armenian monuments which had been built in honor of the Greek hero, Jason. However, recent investigations have explained these 'Jason memorials' by the local word for the holy places sited on hill-tops, which western Iranians had long called '*ayezana*'. To "imaginative Greek ears, these *ay-ez-ana* sounded just like 'Jasonia', especially when so much else [such as the Armenians' style of dress] had appeared to derive from Jason's visit" (176, quoting P. Bernard, "Les Origines thessaliennes de l'Arménie vues par deux historiens thessaliens de la génération d'Alexandre," in P. Briant (ed.), *Topoi supplément*, 1:131–216.).

97 For stories about myths or tales that rely on community notions of a distant, more splendid past (for eighth-century Greeks, this may have been reflected in tales and stories that originated in late Bronze-Age Mycenaean culture) see Fox, *Travelling Heroes*, 33–34.

98 Fox, *Travelling Heroes*, 266–267; and Fox, 33–34. See Chapter Two, 26–29; see also below, Chapter Three, 80–83.

99 Fox, 266. See also Miller, *The Dragon, the Mountain, and the Nations*, 106 and 231.

100 Fox, *Travelling Heroes*, 39–40, 317.

101 Fox, 246, 266, and 298.

102 Fox, 113, quoting Gertrude Bell, "Notes on a Journey Through Cilicia and Lycaonia, Part II," (*Rev. Arch.*, 1906) 7–36. However, this quote actually can be found in Gertrude Lowthian Bell, *Syria: The Desert and the Sown*, 309.

103 Fox, *Travelling Heroes*, 298.

104 Seleucia, originally called Seleucia-Pieria, was founded by Seleucus Nicator as a port and harbor for the inland city of Antioch, which was named in honor of Seleucus' father, Antiochus. Macedonian Greeks renamed the Bay of Seleucus (Bay of Antioch) "Seleucia-Pieria," because it reminded them of the landscape of the region of Pieria, a district in their Macedonian homeland, which also consisted of a region between the sea and a mountain range; specifically, that of Mt. Olympus. Antioch, the city further inland for which Seleucia functioned as a port, had a population that consisted of Macedonian colonists, Greeks from the existing surrounding villages, and numerous native Syrians; among them many Jews. Antioch remained the capital of the successive Seleucid kings, and, after 64 BCE, Pompey made Antioch the capital of the new Roman province of Syria. Accordingly, for centuries Antioch benefited from the favors of many Greek and Roman rulers and their allies. For more, see Jona Lendering, "Seleucia-in-Pieria." As we will see in Chapter Five, Antioch, along with Alexandria, another Macedonian Greek city founded as a result of Alexander's regional conquests, also became an important center of Christianity. Antioch suffered from devastating earthquakes in 184 BCE, 37 CE, and 115 CE.

105 Appian, *Syrian Wars*, 58.

106 Haddad, "Study of Syrian Storm-god," 54–56. Haddad quotes on p. 56 Malalas from his *Chronicles*, Bk. VIII (Transl. Spinka and Downey, Chicago, 1940), 13. See also Elizabeth Jeffreys and Roger Scott, *The Chronicle of John Malalas*, Byzantina Australiensia 4 (Melbourne, Australia: Australian Association for Byzantine Studies,

1986), Book VIII, 105. Haddad notes as well that April 23 is still celebrated throughout the Levant as St. George's day; furthermore, this celebration date is also observed among regional Muslim communities for the figure al-Khiḍr. For more on Seleucus' sacrifice to Zeus at Mt. Kasios, see also Fox, *Travelling Heroes*, 246–247, and Ogden, *The Legend of Seleucus*, 100–101.

107 Michael Blömer, "Religious Continuity? The Evidence from Doliche," in *Religious Identities in the Levant from Alexander to Muhammed: Continuity and Change*, eds. Michael Blömer, Achim Lichtenberger, and Rubina Raja. Contextualizing the Sacred 4, Elizabeth Frood and Rubina Raja, editors (Turnhout, Belgium: Brepols, 2015), 129–130.

108 Blömer, 129–130.

109 Blömer, 135. See also Fox, 280, who argues that: "The neo-Hittite weather-god had an active shrine and cult up in the mountains of Syrian Commagene at ancient Doliche, modern Tell Dülük. Not even a venturesome Euboean went up so far north and discovered it. The cult persisted, ignored by the great waves of Alexander and Graeco-Roman history, but it was then encountered by Roman soldiers, perhaps first by soldiers serving in the region in the 70s AD. Soldiers, then and later, helped to spread the cult. They identified this weather-god as Jupiter "Dolichenus," giving him an adjective of place."

110 Fox, *Travelling Heroes*, 246–250.

111 Fox, 250.

112 Smith, *Baal Cycle Vol. I*, 18. Smith notes here as well that Baal's combat with Mot reflects elements of the narrative of warrior combat evident between Gilgamesh and Enkidu in the Epic of Gilgamesh.

113 *CAT* 1.6 II 33–37.

114 See Chapter Two, 26–29, for information about regional weather patterns.

115 Smith, *Baal Cycle Vol. II*, 57.

116 Smith, *Baal Cycle Vol. I*, xxvi. Israelite religion of course also had other sources of influence, such as religious beliefs and motifs representing southern religious influences (Arabian and Egyptian among them), but the West Semitic religious literature must certainly be counted among them in importance.

117 El is often the name used for God in the Hebrew Bible, especially in the older and poetic texts. See, among other references, Deuteronomy 33:2, 33:26 and Psalm 68:4, 68:33, and 104:3.

118 Smith, *The Baal Cycle Vol. I*, xxvi–xxvii. Claims involving Common Era texts of Christians, Rabbinical texts, the Qur'ān, and other regional religious texts are my own as will be advanced in this project, but these claims arguably do not violate the spirit of Smith's assertions.

119 Smith, "The Baal Cycle," 85–86. Claims involving Islam are my own, but, again, perhaps not unjustifiable in the spirit of Smith's comments. Among the aims of this chapter has been to highlight that the Baal Cycle itself was a product of the religious, political, and geographical influences of its time. Therefore, while figures, narratives, and motifs from the cycle can be argued to be among the strongest direct influences upon subsequent regional religious traditions, the Baal Cycle should not be understood as a prototype in the sense of being an *original*, because, as a text that was influenced by the figures, narratives, and motifs of its own time, it too equally was subject to the same processes of influence, and the same persistent compelling Levantine needs, as were those texts of subsequent religious traditions.

120 Claude F. Schaeffer, "La Stèle du 'Ba'al au Foudre' de Ras-Shamra (Musée du Louvre)," *Monuments et Mémoires* 34, (1934):1–2. [1–18] This article, written by the head of operations at Ras Shamra during the initial seasons of excavation, remains the most authoritative article about the Baal Stele. The stele is today located in The Louvre Museum in Paris.

121 While it was the conclusion of excavator Claude Schaeffer that the stele artist had been trained in the Egyptian style and that the limestone block for the stele could have come

from a quarry near Ras Shamra, it is not clear whether this artist actually was Egyptian or simply had been trained in that style, or even where in fact the stele originally was created (e.g., Ugarit, Egypt, or another locale). In the early 1200s BCE the Pharaoh Merneptah responded to a letter from the king of Ugarit about the king's request to send a sculptor from Egypt so that the king may erect a statue of Pharaoh Merneptah in front of the temple to Baal (Cline, Eric. *1177 B.C.: The Year Civilization Collapsed.* Princeton, NJ: Princeton University Press, 2014, 107–108), so we know that at least in some contemporary instances in Ugarit, sculptors were requisitioned from afar.

122 Schaeffer, "Baal Stèle," 18.

123 Yon, *City of Ugarit*, 16.

124 Schaeffer, "Baal Stèle," 3–7.

125 Schaeffer, "Baal Stèle," 8–9.

126 Schaeffer, "Baal Stèle," 10. See also Miller, *The Dragon, the Mountain, and the Nations*, 110.

127 Schaeffer, "Baal Stèle," 11.

128 Ragette Friedrich, *Baalbek* (Park Ridge, NJ: Noyes Press, 1980), 13. Friedrich notes that the Beka'a (Ar., بقاع 'stagnant' or 'lingering') Valley was named for the stagnant waters that collected there before the valley was drained and irrigated. In Latin this region was known as Coele-Syria ('hollow' Syria) for its location between two mountain ranges.

129 See also Chapter Two, 27–30. See also Chapter Three, 80–83.

130 Fredrich, *Baalbek*, 16.

131 The statute to Jupiter Heliopolitanus that was located in the sanctuary of Jupiter is now gone, but we know of its description from the fifth-century writer Macrobius, who called the god 'Zeus Heliopolitanus', and who described the statue as made of gold, beardless, holding in his right raised hand a whip, like a charioteer, and in his left a thunderbolt with ears of corn. The best-preserved representation of Jupiter Heliopolitanus is from Baalbek and now located in the Louvre Museum in Paris. *Iovi Optimo Maximo Heliopolitano*, 'Jupiter the Most High and the Great of Heliopolis' is depicted wearing a huge *calathos*, a symbol of divinity, on his head, and displays a winged sun disc on his chest, which is a possible reference to the Egyptian god of Heliopolis. His hairstyle, visage, and dress are Roman in character, and he is clad in seven reliefs representing the seven planets of Roman astrology: Helios the sun god, Selene the moon goddess, Mars, Mercury, Jupiter, Venus, and Saturn. Ragette, *Baalbek*, 20–21.

132 Lina Murr Nehme, *Phoenician Baalbek: Visiting the Temples of Roman Epoch* (Beirut: Aleph et Taw, 2011), 7–9. Nehme notes that the Roman 'Temple of Bacchus' at Baalbek was superimposed upon that of the Greek goddess Atargatis. Atargatis regionally was known as the consort of Hadad and she probably represented a local fusion of the older Bronze-Age goddesses Asherah (/Athirat), Anat, and Astarte. Nehme notes as well that the Roman 'Temple of Venus', the third and smallest temple at the site, likely was imposed upon an older temple dedicated locally to the Greek figure Adonis. Later Latin inscriptions referred to the deity inside this third temple as 'Mercury', but Nehme and other archaeologists argue that it would not be logical for the Roman god Mercury to have been a part of a local triad comprising Baal and Atargatis at a time when the Greek figure "Adonis, on the contrary, had the most temples built in Phoenicia [i.e., Syria and coastal Canaan], after Baal and Atargatis." Soon after its completion, the 'Temple of Venus' became a Christian church dedicated to St. Barbara, which it remained through the 19th century (71.). See Also Schwemer, *The Storm-Gods of the Ancient Near East*, Part One, 161, and Part Two, 13–14.

133 Ragette, *Baalbek*, 72.

134 See also Chapter Two, 29.

135 See also Chapter Two, 27–29.

136 See also Grehan, *Twilight of the Saints*, 207.

137 As we have seen, Baal-Hadad was worshipped at sites across the Levant throughout the first millennium, and these sites continued in syncretic manner during a period of Greek and Roman rule into the first centuries of the Common Era. Narratives and sites originally dedicated to Baal-Hadad continued for over six hundred years after Alexander the Great under regional Greek and Roman rule. See also the example of the Nabatean shrine complex at Khirbet et-Tannur, which was in regular use from the second century BCE until being destroyed by earthquake in 363 CE, and was "dedicated to a storm god [variously identified as both Hadad and as a Nabatean deity named Qōs, and reflecting elements of the attributes of the supreme deities of the surrounding cultures, such as Zeus and the Egyptian god Serapis 69, 196 and 225] and his female consort, identified with Atargatis, who ensured good crops and herds in an agricultural area through the provision of rain, water, fertility, and good fortune, helped by the heavenly bodies." Judith S. McKenzie, ed., *The Nabatean Temple at Khirbet et-Tannur, Jordan: Volume 1 – Architecture and Religion* (Boston, MA: American Schools of Oriental Research, 2013), 231. Khirbet et-Tannur is important for this study as a site because it demonstrates the continuation (in a cultural sense) of the figure Baal-Hadad and of the continuing importance among regional inhabitants (in this case, the southern Levant) of the figure of a Storm-god who was associated with rain, water, fertility, and good fortune. This site also demonstrates the continuation of Edomite and other older, Iron-Age ritual burnt-offerings cult practice into the Common Era, long after they were presumed to have ended. Finally, the site of Khirbet et-Tannur is important to this study because the figures of the god and goddess consort at Khirbet et-Tannur themselves demonstrate geographical contextualization, being drawn in part from a contemporary pool of compelling religious figures (Hadad and Zeus among them), and being affected by the political and geographical circumstances of the southern Levant during the first centuries of the common era.

138 See "Ba'al Zebub" by Hebrew Bible writers in 2 Kings 1:2, 1:6, and 1:16. This name became 'Beelzebub' in the New Testament as a name for the devil (see MT 10:25, 12:24, 12:27; MK 3:22, and LK 11:15 and 11:19). 'Beelzebub', or 'Beealzebub', or the 'Lord of the Flies' has persisted for approximately the past 2,500 years as a name for the devil in Western Christian cultural imagination. See also Chapter Four, 113–116.

4 The Hebrew Bible and Elijah

Part One: Introduction

The iconic contest on Mount Carmel between the prophet Elijah and the prophets of Baal is arguably among the more memorable narratives in the Hebrew Bible. Indeed, because the Hebrew Bible can in part be characterized by its account of struggle to expurgate the 'foreign' deities of the ancient world, as well as by its account of struggle to promote the exclusive worship of the god YHWH (Yahweh), Elijah's contest on Mt. Carmel is emblematic of a greater project of the Hebrew Bible.[1] What the Elijah contest-narrative example further demonstrates is that the Elijah episode, and the Hebrew Bible, more generally – contrary to its internal ideology involving a narrative of the regional dominance of Yahweh – takes place in an environment consisting of *multiple* gods, and one in which Baal-Hadad was the most prominent.[2]

As mentioned above in Chapter Three, Yahweh in many respects was presented in the Hebrew Bible as an alternative to the regionally dominant god Baal, in that Yahweh regularly was depicted within the text as imbued with certain compelling qualities and powers that already were associated in the Levant with Baal-Hadad, such as Baal's stormy theophanic language, the motif of a conflict with a sea serpent or dragon, and Mount Sapan/Zaphon.[3] Unlike Baal-Hadad, however, and unlike other ancient Near Eastern narratives involving other gods, for that matter, Yahweh was presented in the Hebrew Bible as a god who acts within and controls events in *human* history, albeit clearly described from a later vantage point in time.[4] That is, a major distinguishing feature of Yahweh as compared to other gods of the time was his presentation by Hebrew Bible authors as taking an interest in a particular people – a people who agreed to hold him – Yahweh – above all other gods.

However, this people often fell short of their task, betraying Yahweh repeatedly by worshipping other gods. According to the narrative, that dereliction led to Yahweh's punishment of his people, and to their suffering and ultimately repentance, upon which time Yahweh saved them by commissioning a righteous leader from among them to lead them to triumph against their current adversaries. A basic sequence involving human history which runs throughout the Hebrew Bible is "covenant, promise, apostasy, repentance, and redemption," and thus although the historical narratives in the Hebrew Bible are presented as accounts of actual history, in reality the main thrust of the message largely is a didactic lesson in theology: worshipping gods other than Yahweh leads to destruction.[5]

Within the Hebrew Bible narrative, Yahweh was assisted in his aims by his prophets, such as Elijah, whose general mission was to warn of impending destruction to those people who did not worship Yahweh in the correct manner, as well as to portend good fortune to those who *did* worship Yahweh in the proper manner and place. Because of his zealous mission to eradicate regional Baal worship, Elijah was among the most striking prophets in the Hebrew Bible. Elijah intentionally was portrayed by authors as similar to Moses, arguably the original and most important prophet in the Hebrew Bible who had advocated for the correct and exclusive worship of Yahweh. However, as we will see in this chapter, as a result of his Hebrew Bible narratives, the figure of Elijah also became associatively linked with important regional geographical motifs of Baal-Hadad, such as control of the rain, and disappearance into the stormy sky via a celestial chariot.

Within the Hebrew Bible, *Yahweh* of course was the figure whom authors presented as an actual divine alternative to Baal-Hadad; Elijah's powers were possible only through the power and action of the god Yahweh. However, as we will see, Elijah's fight against Baal worship was so intimate that, in demonstrating the futility of Baal worship, Elijah himself narratively was imbued with the kinds of compelling motifs and characteristics – such as the ability to control the weather in the forms of rain and drought, among several other storm-god motifs – that already had been associated with Baal-Hadad within wider Levantine culture. Ultimately, this chapter argues that Elijah comes to function as an *antithetical alternative* to Baal-Hadad.

Elijah: Geographical contextualization

In order to contextualize Elijah, this chapter will begin with an overview of both the Hebrew Bible and specifically the Books of Kings in which the Elijah Cycle appears (as does the Cycle of narratives involving Elijah's assistant, Elisha). The major work of the chapter begins next in an analysis of the Elijah narratives in the Books of Kings.[6] Because the Elijah narratives became the canonical source-narratives within Judaism involving the prophet Elijah, they thus can be considered, from the perspective of later history, the format in which the prophet Elijah 'emerged'. We will investigate the Elijah narratives within the Hebrew Bible text for evidence of contemporaneous religious, political, and geographical influences. In this chapter we investigate, as well, common images of Elijah. Interestingly, this leads us into a discussion of the later Christian Saint Elias, with whom there are of course many images associated, and which have been derived from the narratives of the Hebrew Bible account, as well.

Additionally, this chapter examines, as well, an important geographical site associated with Elijah: Mount Carmel, on the coast of the southern Levant in modern-day Israel. Mount Carmel is the purported location of Elijah's contest with the prophets of Baal, and where cult sites dedicated not only to Elijah, but also to Baal-Hadad, long have existed. This chapter uses the information derived from the geographical-contextualization analysis of Elijah texts, images (and also lack thereof), and sites to investigate both what that data reflects about the religious tradition of Judaism, and what the figure Elijah contributed back to a regional common pool of compelling figures, narratives, and motifs.

Finally, this chapter will end with an overview of Rabbinic- and Christian-era Elijah, as Elijah remained an enormously popular figure in both canonical and agrarian religion long into the first and second millennia CE in the Near East, and even up to the present day. Elijah emerged in an environment that was dominated by Baal worship, and, as a figure representing a religious tradition that came to understand itself, in part, in contradistinction to other ancient Near Eastern religious traditions, Elijah represented a challenge to Baal from a competing religious perspective. Furthermore, this chapter underscores the ways in which Baal and other Canaanite deities continued, well into the early centuries of the Common Era, to be a part of religious life for regional inhabitants throughout the Greek and Roman periods,[7] existing alongside Jewish – and, later, Christian – notions of the regionally popular figure Elijah.

Part Two: The Hebrew Bible tradition in context

The Hebrew Bible is a collection of legend, law, poetry, prophecy, philosophy, and history, mostly composed in Hebrew and Aramaic, and consisting of textual and oral traditions that originated throughout the Levant and ancient Near East at various times during the first millennium CE, all stitched together as the result of long processes of collection, writing, editing, copying, and revising. The Hebrew Bible is the central scripture of the religious tradition known as Judaism, and as such it also forms the first part of the Christian canon. The Hebrew Bible or التورة *al-taurat* likewise has been adopted as the earliest scripture of the Qur'ān's scriptural tradition, and thus the Hebrew Bible has exercised an enormous textual influence upon the religious traditions of Judaism, Christianity, and Islam.[8]

The narrative of the Hebrew Bible

At the heart of the Hebrew Bible is a tale that describes the history of the people called Israel, and their continuing relationship with God (a god who was earliest named 'El' – related to the Semitic root for god, '*il*- – in the text). The narrative begins with human creation and continues through the fate of a single family – that of Abraham, whom God chose as progenitor of the people who would come to follow God's commands. Abraham's descendants, the patriarchs, lived in the land of Canaan where Abraham had been called from Ur, but eventually left there to seek shelter in Egypt during a time of great famine. The people of Israel became enslaved in Egypt, however, and the god of Israel then selected Moses as an intermediary to liberate the people from Egypt, and in order to reveal thereby the god of Israel's awesome power against the pharaoh of Egypt, who was at that time the most powerful human ruler on earth. In a memorable sequence of events, the God of Israel led his people out of Egypt and into the wilderness of Sinai, where God revealed his identity to his followers as YHWH, Yahweh. At Sinai, and through Moses, Yahweh then gave the people a code of law with which properly to guide their lives and community. The foundation of this law code was the command to worship no god other than Yahweh.

The Hebrew Bible then narrates the next several centuries of the history of Abraham's descendants, through the narratives of the conquest of Canaan and the establishment of a kingdom under King David and of a central temple dedicated to Yahweh at Jerusalem under David's son, Solomon. Soon after the death of Solomon, however, the Hebrew Bible recounts that ten northern tribes seceded from the united monarchy and forced the creation of two rival kingdoms: Israel, in the north, and Judah, in the south.

For the next 200 years, the rulers and people of Israel – of Yahweh – lived in two separate kingdoms and repeatedly lapsed into idolatry and the lure of foreign gods. Eventually, Yahweh sent outside invaders, such as the Arameans of Syria, to punish the idolatrous and unfaithful people of the northern kingdom of Israel (presented by later Hebrew Bible authors as irretrievably sinful). Ultimately, using the mighty Assyrian Empire, Yahweh destroyed the northern kingdom and exiled its inhabitants, and about one century later, Yahweh sent the Babylonian Empire to destroy and exile the southern kingdom of Judah.

While in exile, the tale of the Hebrew Bible narrative recounted both the suffering and repentance of the people, and Yahweh's eventual salvation of his people under the liberating auspices of the Persian Empire. Henceforth, some of the people of Yahweh's community returned from exile to Jerusalem and dedicated themselves to the reconstruction of the Temple. This Jerusalem-based, second-Temple, post-exile community zealously became dedicated to the worship of Yahweh alone, and became committed to the precise fulfillment of the regulations as outlined in the sacred texts.[9]

The structure of the Hebrew Bible in Jewish tradition

The Hebrew Bible itself consists of 39 books traditionally divided into three main parts: the Torah, the Prophets (*neviim*), and the Writings (*khetuvim*), and is also known by the acronym *Ta|na|kh*, which describes those three parts. The Torah, alternatively known as the first five books of Moses, or the *Pentateuch*, in Greek, is comprised of the books Genesis, Exodus, Leviticus, Numbers, and Deuteronomy. Generally speaking, these books narrate the history of the people of Israel from the creation of the world through Moses' farewell to the Israelite community at Sinai.

The division known as the 'Prophets' is divided into two main groups of scriptures: the Former Prophets, Joshua, Judges, 1 and 2 Samuel, and 1 and 2 Kings, which narrate the story of the people of Israel from their conquest of Canaan, through their defeat and exile by the Assyrian and Babylonian empires. The Latter Prophets includes the oracles, social teachings and messianic expectations of inspired peoples living from the mid-eighth century BCE through the end of the fifth century BCE.

The division known as the 'Writings' is a collection of homilies, poems, prayers, proverbs, and psalms that represent the most powerful emotional expressions of the Israelite community. These writings are the products of an ongoing process of composition that lasted hundreds of years, with a few originating from the late monarchic period and destruction of Jerusalem in 586 BCE, and most coming from the Persian and Hellenistic periods, between the fifth to the second centuries BCE.[10]

The main historical works of the Hebrew Bible are in the Torah or the 'Pentateuch', and in the Former Prophets, which narrate the history of the Israelite people from origin through the destruction of the Jerusalem Temple. Biblical scholars generally agree that the first four books of the Pentateuch are not a seamless composition, but a mosaic of different sources – usually identified as J (promoting the god Yahweh and concerned with the territory around Judah), E (promoting the god El – pl. Elohim – and concerned with the territory and tribes of the north), and P (meaning 'Priestly' and referring to those passages that deal with ritual matters). Each of these sources was written under different historical circumstances and to promote different viewpoints. However, the final book of the Pentateuch, Deuteronomy, is a different case altogether. Its terminology is distinctive and unique from the J, E, and P sources, and "contains an uncompromising condemnation of worship of other gods, a new view of God as completely transcendent, and the absolute prohibition of the sacrificial worship of the god of Israel in any place but the Temple in Jerusalem."[11]

The impact of the book of Deuteronomy upon the overall emphasis and message of the Hebrew Bible was significant. Bible scholars since the mid-20th century CE have recognized that the language, theological message, and connected narrative of the books subsequent to Deuteronomy – Joshua, Judges, 1 and 2 Samuel, and 1 and 2 Kings – indicate that the books clearly were linked, and thus these seven books have come to be known as the Deuteronomistic History (DH). The DH narrates the history of the people of Israel from the conquest through exile, and the theological thrust of this history expresses the ideology of a religious movement that originated – according to the text itself – in Judah in the seventh century BCE, and in particular during the reign of the reformist King Josiah.[12] Because the DH narrates the bulk of the historical-ideological core of the Hebrew Bible, it can be said, therefore, also to express the main didactic themes of the Hebrew Bible. Among the most prominent of the themes of the DH is the message that Yahweh was dominant over all 'foreign' gods, and that worshipping gods other than Yahweh leads to destruction. Accordingly, Yahweh must be worshipped exclusively, and in the proper manner.[13] However, a great amount of evidence within the Hebrew Bible text belies the central claims made therein about the dominance of Yahweh over all 'foreign' gods. That is, were Yahweh's contemporaneous dominance over all 'foreign' gods actually the case, there would not have been a need in the first place for the command to worship Yahweh exclusively.

Canaanite deities in the Hebrew Bible

Several Canaanite deities appear in the Hebrew Bible; some, as we will see, more prominently than others.[14] The gods El, Athirat/Asherah, Baal-Hadad, Dagon, and

Astarte; Anat; astral deities, such as the sun, moon, and Venus; and deities of the underworld, Mot, Resheph, Molech, and the Rephaim – gods and goddesses known to us from the Ugaritic texts – form the narrative backdrop against and within which Israelite religion developed.

El

As opposed to Yahweh, referred to in the Hebrew Bible as a god from the south (Deut 33:2), El in the Hebrew Bible frequently was associated with people and places in the north.[15] The god named El in the Hebrew Bible was referred to by several of the titles known already for the older Canaanite El from the Ugaritic texts, such as El-Shaddai ('god of the field'), El-Olam ('god of the world'), El-Bethel ('god of the house of El'), and El-Elyon ('god most high').[16] 'El', in Ancient Hebrew, as '*ilu*, in Ugaritic – also a northwest Semitic language – in fact was simply a form of the grammatical basis for the word 'god' within northwest Semitic languages.[17] As we saw in Chapter Three, Canaanite El sat at the head of the Ugaritic pantheon. Eventually, in a long and complicated historical process attested in the Hebrew Bible text, El and Yahweh – originally separate deities, both powerful and important among Israelite communities – became equated.[18] As the supreme deity of the Hebrew Bible, Yahweh likewise became represented in the text as sharing several traits with the venerable El; among them, Yahweh as an aged god (Job 36:26), Yahweh as wise (Gen 3:5), Yahweh as creator (Ps 102:25), and Yahweh as seated at the head of a heavenly court or pantheon (Ps 89:6–7).

Athirat/Asherah

Athirat of the Ugaritic texts, whom we saw in Chapter Three as the wife or the consort of the supreme god, El, also appears in the Hebrew Bible, where her name usually is transliterated as 'Asherah'. There are 41 references to Asherah in the text, and a remarkable incidence of Asherah's cult referenced throughout the DH. Scholarly consensus contends that, although this role was not retained in the Hebrew Bible texts, Asherah probably functioned among early Israelite communities in a similar manner as she did among Canaanite communities: as a consort of the supreme god (in this case, Yahweh).[19] Asherah most frequently was referenced by name in the Hebrew Bible as an abominated foreign god, or by reference to 'Asherah poles' wooden objects linked to her cult. Other than Baal, with whom frequently she is paired in the text, Asherah is the most-frequently-referenced foreign god. The common pairing of Asherah with Baal in the DH (such as in the Elijah contest on Mt. Carmel) may have been a way of discrediting the Asherah cults. That is because perhaps no god, from the perspective of the Hebrew Bible authors, was as reviled as was the god Baal.

Baal

When reading the Hebrew Bible, or the 'Old Testament', it becomes clear that it was the Baal cult which provided the greatest and most enduring threat

> to the development of exclusive Yahweh worship within ancient Israel. The fact that the Israelites were settled among the Canaanites, for whom the worship of Baal was so important, and that Palestine is a land utterly dependent for its fertility upon the rain, which was held to be Baal's special realm of influence, accounts for the tempting nature of this cult, as well as the strength of Old Testament polemic against it.[20]

Baal-Hadad, as we saw in Chapter Three, was the primary deity of the Levant during the second and first millennia BCE. Baal worship was so ubiquitous that peoples in particular localities associated manifestations of Baal with individual cities and mountain areas, such as Baal of Tyre, Baal of Aleppo, Baal of Ugarit, and Baal Sapan. Baal also became known in different eras regionally by particular titles, such as Baal-Shamem (Baal of the Heavens).[21] All of these titles for Baal, or, as in case of the Hebrew Bible narrative, the reference to 'Baals' in the plural, should be thought of as referring back to the dominant deity in the region, the Canaanite god of Storms and therefore of plant, animal, and human fertility and fecundity, Baal-Hadad.[22]

The name Baal is found 58 times in the Hebrew Bible, and a reference to 'Baals' 19 times. All refer to the storm-god Hadad, and most references were associated with particular place-name manifestations of the deity, such as Baal-Gad, Baal-Hamon, Baal-Hazor, Baal-Hermon, Baal-Peor, Baal-Tamar, and Baal-Zephon (a cult location in Egypt and which was modeled on Sapan, the mountain location in Syria),[23] among very many others. The text even mentions a 'Baal-Berith', that is, 'Baal of the Covenant', a Canaanite god with a temple at Shechem (mentioned Judg 9:4 and Judg 8:33).[24]

Many human names in the Hebrew Bible also were associated with the epithet Baal, such as Jerub-Baal, Ethbaal, and even names which conflate Yahweh and Baal, including Bealiah (2 Chron 12:6, one of David's warriors), and Yehobaal, a name found on a seventh-century seal. The names Bealiah and Yehobaal seem to mean respectively 'Baal is Yahweh' and 'Yahweh is Baal'; indeed, that Yahweh at some point in time was equated by people with Baal is clearly referenced by the entire context of Hosea 2.[25]

Baal worship in the Levant, throughout the entire first millennium BCE, was tenacious. Such is the power of the Biblical narrative, however, that we have come to understand the people called Israel as a people associated exclusively with the worship of the god Yahweh, and specifically with the doctrine of monotheism. Indeed, common wisdom suggests that the ancient Israelites entirely were dedicated to Yahweh as early as the time of the Exodus narrative, which, according to textual internal dating, took place in around 1250 BCE. To the contrary, however, and as the Hebrew Bible text itself demonstrates, Baal worship remained common – indeed, dominant – throughout the First-Temple period and into the Second-Temple period. The concept of monolatry (the worship of one god without denial of the existence of other gods) – let alone monotheism (the doctrine that there is only one god) – took a very long time to develop.

Moreover, Baal worship – to say nothing of the worship of other deities – remained *commonplace* during the first millennium BCE, even within the Jerusalem Temple itself. According to the DH, the temple in Jerusalem purportedly had been dedicated solely to Yahweh first by King Solomon, and then again re-dedicated to Yahweh by the eighth/seventh-century Judahite king, Hezekiah. To the contrary, however, we see in the Hebrew Bible account of the puritanical religious reform movement of Judahite king Josiah, ca. 639–609 BCE, vivid evidence of the extent of Baal worship within Jerusalem and its Temple and throughout the surrounding countryside.

Josiah was praised in the Hebrew Bible even more highly than had been King David before him, in having been described, "He did what was right in the sight of [Yahweh] and walked in all the way of his father David; he did not turn aside to the right or to the left" (2 Kings 22:1–2; cf. 2 Kings 23:25). After having been informed that the high priest of the Jerusalem Temple, Hilkiah, had uncovered a 'lost' document within the Temple, called the Book of the Law (widely considered by scholars to be a precursor document to the reformist book Deuteronomy), Josiah and his subjects embarked upon the making of a public covenant before Yahweh to worship Yahweh alone and to keep the commandments of Yahweh as written in the Book of the Law (2 Kings 22:3–23:3). Covenant or oath ceremonies to specific *rulers* were not uncommon in the seventh-century BCE, but Josiah's covenant ceremony to a specific god, Yahweh (and the Yahweh-covenant ceremonies referenced in the Hebrew Bible as attributable to Kings Solomon and Hezekiah), may have been a unique occurrence in th ancient Near East.[26]

As a concomitant part of the re-dedication of the Jerusalem Temple to Yahweh, Josiah commanded Hilkiah and all the priests to bring *out* of the Temple "all the vessels made for Baal, for Asherah, and for all the host of heaven [i.e., other gods]," burning them outside of Jerusalem (2 Kings 23:4). He deposed the idolatrous priests of the cities of Judah who previously had been ordered by Judahite kings to "make offerings to Baal, to the sun, the moon, the constellations, and all the host of the heavens [i.e., other gods]. He brought out the image of Asherah from the house of the LORD [that is, the Temple of Yahweh at Jerusalem]," then burned it outside of Jerusalem, beat it to dust, and threw the dust upon the graves of the "common people" (2 Kings 23:5). Indeed, the list of "idolatrous" practices King Josiah outlawed during his day, such as mediums, wizards, *teraphim* [household gods], idols, fertility cults, multiple gods, and all the altars to Baal on the "high places" which had been established throughout the land, is quite extensive (2 Kings 23:6–25).

But even Josiah's extensive reforms were not enough. Immediately upon the death of Josiah, Josiah's successor was recorded in the biblical text as having "done what was evil in the sight of YHWH, just as all his ancestors had done" (2 Kings 23:37). Indeed, the four successive kings following Josiah were recorded as having returned to the previous idolatrous ways, indicating that, even from the perspective of the Hebrew Bible, Baal worship (and the worship of gods other than Yahweh) continued to dominate in the region as late as the sixth century BCE. Baal worship continued in the region for longer even than that. It remained so popular, in fact, that Seleucid ruler Antiochus Epiphanes IV incited the riots known today as "Maccabean" when, in 168 BCE, he re-dedicated the Jerusalem Temple to Zeus Olympios. Zeus Olympios, as we have seen in Chapter Three, himself was a regional Hellenistic form of Baal.[27]

Astarte and Anat

Astarte, a consort of Baal-Hadad in the Ugaritic texts, was attested in the Hebrew Bible under the scribal distortion "Ashtoreth" or "Ashtaroth," meaning 'abomination' or 'shame' (1 Kings 11:5). Astarte became a popular regional goddess throughout the Mediterranean during the first millennium BCE, at cult locations such as Tyre, Sidon, Carthage, Cyprus, Italy, Malta, Spain, and Greece. Anat, a fellow goddess-consort of Baal familiar to us from the Baal Cycle, also was mentioned in the Hebrew Bible, although indirectly, through place-name associations, such as Beth Anot (Josh 15:59) and Beth Anat, among others. Throughout the wider Levantine culture of the first millennium BCE, Astarte figured more prominently within the region as the wife or consort of Baal than did Anat. However, a Greco-Syrian goddess called Atargatis – herself a conflation of Canaanite Astarte and Anat, and perhaps others – became popular in Syria during the Hellenistic and Roman periods. Atargatis was the goddess known most prominently as Hadad's consort into the Common Era.[28]

The fates of Canaanite deities in the Hebrew Bible and within regional history

As we have seen in the Hebrew Bible text, the prevalence of worship of other deities among ancient Israelite and Judahite communities was frequent during pre-exilic history. Even the admonitions made in Ezra and Nehemiah of the *post-exile* Jewish communities to "keep apart" – with varying levels of success – from the local populations, would seem to indicate that the mixed local religious environment continued on much as it had in earlier eras.[29]

Indeed, local peoples in the region continued to worship the Canaanite deities – and oftentimes their Hellenistic counterparts – throughout the final centuries of the first millennium BCE and into the early centuries of the Common Era. Even within the texts of Jewish – and later Christian – communities, Canaanite deities left a kind of 'afterglow'; particularly, as we will see in Jewish and Christian Common-Era texts involving the figure of Baal, in the realm of the demonic or apocalyptic.

In conclusion, this analysis of the Hebrew Bible text and the Canaanite gods and goddesses of the Levant highlights for us twin distinctive features of the Hebrew Bible: an argument for monolatry in an environment of multiple gods, and an argument for monolatry involving the god of the people of Israel – Yahweh – who acts within human history.[30] Both of these features are displayed prominently in the Books of Kings, where the Elijah narratives are located.

Part Three: Elijah text: The Elijah (and Elisha) Cycles in the Book of Kings

Introduction: The Books of Kings

The Books of Kings, as the setting for the Elijah Cycle, can be understood as a narrative ideological history of Israel during its monarchical period, from the reign of King David through the destruction of the Jerusalem Temple in 586 BCE and the beginning of the Babylonian exile. The text tells us that because of King David's dedication to Yahweh, he was able to establish a "united" kingdom, but that David's territory quickly became separated into competing northern and southern kingdoms, in part through the apostasy of other gods as introduced by his son Solomon's marriages to foreign wives (1 Kings 11–13). Over the next few centuries, and due to the repeatedly idolatrous behavior of Israelites and Judahites, Yahweh used the Assyrian and Babylonian empires to destroy both kingdoms (2 Kings 17–25).

Like the other books of the Hebrew Bible, the Books of Kings are the result of long processes of collecting, editing, writing, and revising both historical documents and oral traditions like the Elijah and Elisha cycles. Clear moments in composition and editing of the Books of Kings are identifiable as early as the reigns of Hezekiah (727–698 BCE) and Josiah (639–609 BCE), and final revisions were made to these books sometime after the exile of 586 BCE.[31]

The Books of Kings can be thought of as literature that is narrative, historiographical, and didactic. The plot of Kings can be summarized as the attempt that Israel makes (or, more often, fails to make), under its monarchy, to live as the people of God (i.e., of Yahweh) in Canaan – the 'promised' land – and how that god deals with their successes and failures. The Books of Kings also are books of historiographical literature, in that they tell a political history. However, that political history is told in order to reveal thereby the religious failure of the peoples of the northern and southern kingdoms: as a result of their apostasy to Yahweh, these people lost their national autonomy and became the lowly exiles of brutal empires.

Finally, the Books of Kings are didactic literature, in that they seek to teach several lessons, all of which are related to the single idea that the worship of gods other than Yahweh leads to destruction. First, *Yahweh* is God (and the other gods are not); as such, Yahweh controls both nature, and history. Second, Yahweh demands exclusive worship; as such, both the content of his worship and place of his worship are of essential importance. Third, because Yahweh defines true faith, he also judges and punishes wrongdoers. However, because Yahweh is merciful to those who worship him, he has as yet left open to the wretched exiles a path to redemption through the descendants of the house of David in the southern Kingdom of Judah, whom Yahweh favored – provided, of course, that those descendants emulate David's example, and worship Yahweh alone.

The Elijah and Elisha cycles

Among the more memorable prophets in the Hebrew Bible who embody the message that the worship of Gods other than Yahweh leads to destruction is the striking figure of Elijah. Renowned for his illustrious exploits, the major unifying theme that ties together Elijah's individual episodes in the Books of Kings is Elijah's defiant opposition to Baal worship.[32]

The Elijah and Elisha cycles, located at 1 Kings 17–19, 21, and 2 Kings 1–8, most probably originate in oral stories that later were incorporated in writing into the Books of Kings. Although the stories as they appear now are the products of a long period of development, many of the episodes have retained both a short anecdotal form and specific morphological and lexical features, particularly in quoted speech, that suggest a Northern dialect of ancient Hebrew, and thus bear markings of original orality.[33] Incorporated into the Books of Kings by Biblical authors and set in the ninth century BCE during the reigns of the infamous and idolatrous King Ahab and Queen Jezebel of the Omri dynasty in the northern kingdom of Israel, Elijah's primary mission – and that of his successor, Elisha – was the defiant opposition of Baal worship, and promotion of the exclusive worship of Yahweh.

In 1 Kings 17 we first encounter Elijah in the Hebrew Bible text. He is introduced as Elijah the Tishbite, a resident of Gilead,[34] and by his very name, אליהו 'eli-yahu' ('my god is Yahweh'), we know that he is operating in a multi-god environment. Furthermore, we see in the figure of Elijah an example of that multi-god environment in practice, as Elijah's name effectively blends both 'El' (albeit as a noun rather than as a proper noun) and 'Yahweh'. Theophoric names were not uncommon for figures in the Hebrew Bible; prior to the accounts of the monarchical period, theophoric names including the name 'El' were frequent, whereas explicitly Yahwistic names from that time seem to have been rare.[35] In the Books of Kings, personal names involving the god Yahweh are common; particularly for the kings of the southern Kingdom of Judah.

As we saw above, personal names involving the name Baal also were prevalent in the world recounted by the Books of Kings, and so these theophoric names also reflect a cultural pattern of the day: an environment characterized by the worship of multiple deities. Therefore, the theophoric names recorded in the Hebrew Bible text can be said conceptually to function as *relational antonyms*: they represent concepts that make sense primarily in the presence of opposing ideas; in this instance, they are names that make sense in the presence of opposing gods. Elijah's very name, 'my god is YHWH', signals a strong argument about the supremacy of Yahweh in opposition to other contemporaneous gods, and among whom Baal was the region's most prominent.

Baal worship did not dominate the environment of the Books of Kings without reason. As we saw above in Chapters Two and Three, the worship of Baal was so important to the inhabitants of the region because it is a land – particularly in the dry southern Levant and in the environs described in the Hebrew Bible – that utterly is dependent for its fertility upon the rain. Without enough rain, crops perished in drought and people starved and died. Because rain, fertility, and fecundity were believed to be within Baal's particular realm of influence, Baal was the primary god for most people. Yahweh, as a competing god, would have been viable to regional peoples as an alternative to Baal to the extent to which Yahweh came to resemble those most compelling aspects of Baal-Hadad, such as his control of nature, and particularly of rain.

Throughout the Hebrew Bible, Yahweh was depicted as revealing himself at times in a theophany of storm and extreme meteorological manifestations. Moreover, a major a theme running throughout the Books of Kings was that only Yahweh, the *true* god of nature, could perform the powers attributed to Baal-Hadad. In the Books of Kings, and through the narrative of the prophet Elijah, Yahweh was revealed as the god who controlled specific occurrences of both drought and rain, and did so not only to punish the idolatrous Israelites and Judahites, but also to demonstrate that worshipping Yahweh the to the exclusion of all other gods resulted in plenty and abundance (see Lev 26).

However, as we will see below, Elijah himself became an enormously compelling figure within the subsequent religious traditions of the Hebrew Bible, and within wider regional culture, both because of his iconic role as a defender of *true* faith – epitomized by his quintessential defeat of the prophets of Baal – and because Elijah became linked, through his narratives, to some of the most compelling powers associated with Baal-Hadad, such as the ability to control rain and drought, and his vivid translation into heaven via a celestial storm and chariot (albeit all only made possible through the power of Yahweh).

(1) Elijah and the Great Drought (1 Kings 17:1–24)
Elijah's struggle with the Omride house of the northern kingdom of Israel – particularly with the derided biblical figures of King Ahab and his Queen, Jezebel – primarily concerns Elijah's fight to rid the northern royal house of its idolatries.

The account opens abruptly, with Elijah, the prophet of Yahweh, introduced as having announced to King Ahab that, "by the life of Yahweh, God of Israel, whom I serve, there will be no dew or rain these years, except by my word" (17:1). After causing (through Yahweh) a drought throughout the land – and a drought which was laid partly in punishment for the idolatry of Ahab's house – Yahweh informed Elijah that he needed to leave and hide from the powerful Ahab in the Wadi Cherith, east of the Jordan River. Despite the existence of drought throughout the land and having sought refuge in a desert, Yahweh, through Ravens, miraculously fed Elijah both bread and meat in both the morning and evening (extravagant plenty for drought conditions). After a while, the wadi dried up because of the drought, and Yahweh then told Elijah to go to Zarephath of Sidon (outside of the territory of Israel and into Canaanite territory), and to stay with and be fed by a widow living there. Elijah met the widow (who, as a widow, would have been located within the poorest and lowest social class of the time) gathering sticks near the entrance of the town, and called to her to bring him water and bread. The widow responded that she had only a small amount of oil and flour remaining, and that she in fact was engaged in gathering firewood to bake one last bit of bread for herself and her son before they starved to death. Elijah proclaimed that if she would feed themselves and him as he asked, Yahweh would see to it that her stores of oil and flour would not give out until such time as Yahweh again returned rain to the land. The widow did as Elijah had bid her and baked him bread and gave him water, and her oil and flour stores did not fail. Sometime afterward, the widow's son "had no breath left in him" (17:17) because he had apparently died of starvation brought on by the drought. The widow railed against Elijah for having been part of the cause of her son's death, and Elijah responded for her to give him her son. Elijah took the boy upstairs to the room in which Elijah had been staying, performed a miraculous posture over the child, and prayed to Yahweh to "let the child's life return to its body" (17:21). Yahweh heard Elijah's call, and the child's life returned to his body. Elijah then returned the boy to his mother, and the widow proclaimed that Elijah was indeed a "man of God, and the word of YHWH in your mouth is true" (17:23).

(2) Contest on Mount Carmel (1 Kings 18:1–46)
The contest on Mount Carmel is arguably the most iconic of Elijah's narratives. Set three years into the drought which Elijah had proclaimed, when famine had become severe, and the land and people were starving, Yahweh announced to Elijah that Elijah should present himself to King Ahab, "so that I [YHWH] may give rain on the face of the earth" (18:1). Ahab spoke with his servant, Obadiah (who secretly feared Yahweh and who previously had saved 100 prophets of Yahweh during Queen Jezebel's murderous campaign against them, by having hid them in a cave), and Ahab said to Obadiah, "come, let us go through the land to all of the springs of water and to all the wadis. Perhaps we shall find some grass to keep the horses and mules alive…" (18:5). They split up to search, and Elijah came upon Obadiah while the latter was alone. Obadiah greeted Elijah respectfully and Elijah informed him to announce to Ahab that he had arrived. Obadiah revealed his mortal fear of telling Ahab, because Ahab long had searched fruitlessly for Elijah in all the surrounding kingdoms, and because Obadiah was afraid that Elijah might disappear, "the spirit of YHWH will carry you to somewhere I do not know" (18:12), and Ahab would then kill Obadiah in anger. Elijah promised not to leave, Obadiah announced Elijah to Ahab, and Ahab went to meet Elijah. Upon seeing Elijah, King Ahab asked him whether it really was he, Elijah, the troubler of Israel. Elijah responded that *he* was not the troubler of Israel; Ahab and the entire Omride royal line were responsible for the drought, by virtue of having abandoned Yahweh's commands, and having followed the Baals. Accordingly, Elijah asked Ahab to gather the entire community of the northern kingdom at Mount Carmel, including the "four hundred and fifty prophets of Baal and the four hundred prophets of Asherah who eat at Jezebel's table" (18:19). Once on Mt. Carmel and in order to set the dramatic scene before the contest, Elijah pointedly asked the assembly: how long will you go on wavering between two opinions? If Yahweh is god, follow Yahweh. If Baal, follow Baal. Tellingly, the people remained silent. This sets up the contest scene: Elijah and the prophets of Baal each will set up an altar, cut up a bull (an exalted sacrificial animal), but not set fire to the offering, as was the usual custom. Instead, each side would call upon their god to answer them by fire, and the god who answered would be considered God. The prophets of Baal called upon Baal repeatedly, but nothing happened; eventually, Elijah mocked them and Baal. They, and Baal himself, had proven futile. Now Elijah's turn, Elijah set up the altar and placed the offering, and then asked the assembly to pour water upon the offering and

altar several times (thus increasing the coming miracle). Elijah called once upon Yahweh and asked him to "let it be known today that you are God in Israel" (18:36). Yahweh answered immediately with fire which descended from the sky and consumed not only the offering and all parts of the altar, but the water as well. The assembly then fell to the ground, proclaiming that Yahweh is God. Elijah ordered the assembly to seize the prophets of Baal; all were taken down into the Wadi Kishon and he slaughtered them there. Elijah then informed Ahab that roaring rain was coming, and that he should therefore go eat and drink. Elijah went up to the top of Mount Carmel, got into a miraculous prayer position, apparently praying for rain, and told his attendant to go up and look out to the sea. The attendant went but reported back that he saw nothing. This happened seven times, but on the seventh time, the servant returned with the report that there was a "cloud as small as a man's hand rising from the sea [meaning the Mediterranean Sea]" (18:44). Elijah told his attendant to report to Ahab that Ahab should immediately hitch his chariot, lest his return be thwarted by the rain. The skies grew dark with clouds and wind, and there was a heavy rain. Elijah was inspired by the spirit of Yahweh and ran in front of Ahab's chariot all the long way back to the Jezreel Valley.

(3) Journey to Mount Horeb (1 Kings 19:1–21)
Ahab told Jezebel about how Elijah had killed the prophets of Baal by the sword, and Jezebel vowed in revenge to do all that and more to Elijah. Elijah fled for his life to Beer-sheba in the southernmost reaches of Judah, journeying alone a day even beyond there into the steppe. Exhausted, Elijah sat under a broom tree and prayed for Yahweh to take his life. An angel came to Elijah with a cake of bread and flask of water, bidding him to eat and regain strength. The angel brought food a second time, and Elijah walked by the strength of that food for 40 days and 40 nights to the mountain of God, called Horeb.[36] On Mt. Horeb, Elijah went into a cave and spent the night. The word of Yahweh came to him, asking Elijah what he was doing. Elijah repeated his complaint of having been persecuted for having been most zealous for Yahweh, despite the Israelites' abandonment of their covenant with Yahweh and destruction of Yahweh's altars. Yahweh told Elijah to go out and stand on the mountain before Yahweh, where Yahweh would appear to Elijah as a theophany of storm: wind, earthquakes, and fire, and informing Elijah that while Yahweh was associated with each of those phenomena, he was not *in* them. Elijah covered his face in front of the divine and went to the cave's entrance. There, Yahweh told Elijah to go toward the wilderness of Damascus, where he was to go and anoint Hazael as king over Aram, and to anoint Jehu son of Nimshi as king over Israel, and to anoint Elisha son of Shaphat of Abelmeholah as prophet in Elijah's place. Yahweh then swore the destruction of many through the fulfillment of his plan (which was to destroy entirely the house of Jeroboam I, ca. 931–909 BCE, and the entire northern kingdom, Jeroboam having introduced and first committed apostasy; see 1 Kings 14), and declared "I will leave seven thousand in Israel, every knee that has not bent to Baal and every mouth that has not kissed him" (19:18).

Elijah left to find Elisha, who was planting in his fields with 12 teams of oxen. Elijah went to Elisha and threw his cloak over him; Elisha understood that Elijah was bidding him to come with him, said goodbye to his family, slaughtered one yoke of oxen and used the wood of the harnesses for a bonfire with which to boil the meat, and give it to the people. Then Elisha rose and followed Elijah and became his servant.

(4) Naboth's Vineyard (1 Kings 21:1–29)
Naboth the Jezreelite had a vineyard in Jezreel next to the palace of Ahab, king of Samaria, and Ahab wanted it for his own. Ahab told him that he would either give Naboth a better vineyard in its place, or the value of it in silver. Naboth refused, saying, "Far be it from me by YHWH that I should sell my ancestral inheritance to you" (21:3). Incensed, Ahab returned home and retreated to his room to sulk. Upon learning that the cause of Ahab's distress was Naboth's refusal to sell Ahab his vineyard, Jezebel told Ahab not to be upset, because she had hatched an underhanded scheme. Jezebel wrote, in Ahab's name, to the elders of Naboth's town and told them to proclaim a fast (a sign that the town had fallen out of grace)[37] and to seat Naboth at the head of the assembly there. She then plotted to have two corrupt men publicly accuse Naboth of having "cursed God and king" (21:10, fitting the theme of a fast-worthy transgression), which would thus inspire the assembly to stone Naboth to death. Jezebel's plan successfully was carried out, and she happily announced to Ahab that he could take possession of Naboth's vineyard because Naboth was dead. At the same time, the word of Yahweh came to Elijah: go up to meet Ahab in Samaria, who had taken possession of Naboth's vineyard, and tell him that "Thus said YHWH: in the place where the dogs licked the blood of Naboth, the dogs shall lick your blood, even yours!" (21:19). Elijah found Ahab and reported to him Yahweh's decree, telling Ahab that Yahweh said that "because you have given yourself over to doing what displeases YHWH… [causing Israel to sin]," Yahweh would destroy Ahab's line, just as he had the House of Jeroboam and the house of Baasha (21:20–22). Furthermore, Yahweh vowed to punish Jezebel for her role in the plot and decreed that dogs would devour her. Yahweh decreed that "there was no one like Ahab who had given himself over to doing what displeased YHWH, whom Jezebel his wife instigated. He acted abominably by following the idols, just as the Amorites had done, whom YHWH had dispossessed before the Israelites" (19:25). Upon hearing the news, Ahab tore his garments and fasted in shame. Yahweh was moved by this act of repentant piety, and informed Elijah that thus Yahweh would not bring disaster upon the house of Ahab in Ahab's own days, but in those of his son.

(5) Elijah and Ahaziah (2 Kings 1:2–18)
Ahaziah, son of Ahab, succeeded to the throne of the northern kingdom (Ahab had been killed in battle by the army of Aram-Damascus under Ben-Hadad at Ramoth-Gilead; his death and burial were described in 1 Kings 22:1–38, and dogs had licked his blood just as Yahweh had decreed). It happened that Ahaziah fell through the lattice in the upper chamber of his palace at Samaria

and was injured. Accordingly, he sent messengers to go see Baal-zebub, god of Ekron, in order to inquire of him whether Ahaziah would recover from his injuries. An angel of Yahweh then spoke to Elijah the Tishbite, and told Elijah to meet Ahaziah's messengers and ask them, "'Is it for lack of a god in Israel that you are going to inquire of Baal-zebub, the god of Ekron?' Therefore, thus says YHWH, 'You shall not leave the bed you are upon, for you shall certainly die!'" (1:3–4). Returning early to Ahaziah, the messengers relayed Elijah's message. Ahaziah asked after the appearance of the man who had met them, and they replied that the man was "'a hairy man, girt with a leather belt around his waist'. And [Ahaziah] then said, 'It is Elijah the Tishbite'" (1:7–8). So, Ahaziah sent a delegation of 50 of his military company to meet Elijah. The officer climbed up the hilltop where Elijah had been sitting, and said to him, "O Man of God, the king orders, 'Come down!'" But Elijah replied and spoke to the officer of fifty, "And if I am a man of God, let fire [i.e., lightning] descend from heaven and consume you and your company of fifty." Whereupon fire descended from heaven and consumed him and his company of fifty" (1:9–10). Ahaziah sent up another officer and company of 50, and again Elijah replied that if he indeed was a man of God, let fire descend from heaven and consume the man and his company, whereupon an awesome fire descended from heaven and consumed them all. A third officer and 50 were sent up to Elijah, and this wise officer begged for his and his company's lives, "Indeed, fire descended from heaven and consumed the first two officers of fifty and their companies, so now value my life" (1:14). The angel of Yahweh then spoke to Elijah and told him not be afraid of this third man, and to go down and speak with the king. Upon meeting with Ahaziah, Elijah said, "'Thus' says YHWH, 'Since you sent messengers to inquire of Baal-zebub, the god of Ekron, as if there were no god in Israel to consult his word, therefore, you shall not leave the bed you are upon, for you shall certainly die,'" and so Ahaziah died in accordance with Yahweh's word, and was succeeded by his brother, Jehoram.

(6) Translation into heaven and the succession of Elisha (2 Kings 2:1–18)
This narrative represents Elijah's final episode in the Hebrew Bible. It opens with the phrase, "now when YHWH was about to take Elijah up to heaven in a storm," Elijah and Elisha were headed to Beth-el from Gilgal; thence to Jericho, and thence to the Jordan River. Thrice Elijah bade Elisha stay where he was, and thrice Elisha refused to leave his master's side. Upon arriving at the Jordan River, where Elijah and Elisha could see 50 Sons of the Prophets watching them from the opposite riverbank, Elijah took his mantle, rolled it up, struck the waters, and the river parted in two (2:8). As they crossed to dry land, Elijah asked Elisha what he could do for Elisha "'before I am taken from you'" (2:9). Elisha responded that he wished "'a double share of your spirit would belong to me'," [i.e., a son's inheritance] and Elijah replied portentously that "'if you see me being taken from you, you will have it; and if not, it will not be'" (2:10). As they continued walking and talking, "fiery chariots with fiery horses appeared and separated them one from the other,

and Elijah went up to heaven in the storm. All the while, Elisha looked on and kept shouting, 'My father, my father! The chariots of Israel and its horsemen!' And he saw [Elijah] no more. Then he took hold of his garments and rent them in two" (2:11–12). Afterward, Elisha picked up Elijah's mantle, which had fallen from Elijah as he was being taken up to heaven in the storm and went back and stood by the bank of the Jordan. Using Elijah's mantle, as he made to strike the waters, Elisha asked, "Where, indeed, is YHWH, God of Elijah?' When he struck the waters, they parted in two, and Elisha crossed over" (2:14). On the other side, the Sons of the Prophets who were at Jericho saw Elisha, and they said "'Elijah's spirit has come to rest upon Elisha.' So, they went to meet him and bowed down to the ground before him" (2:15). Thinking that perhaps "YHWH's wind has carried [Elijah] and thrown him against one of the mountains or into one of the ravines," the 50 Sons of the Prophets offered to search for Elijah. Elisha was pressed into accepting their offer, and the 50 men searched for three days and were unable to find Elijah anywhere. Reporting their failure to Elisha, who had been staying in Jericho, Elisha replied, "Didn't I tell you, 'do not go'?" (2:18).

Religious, political, and geographical contexts of the narratives

The overarching message within the six Elijah narratives in the Books of Kings mirrors that of the larger message of the Hebrew Bible: the worship of gods other than Yahweh leads to destruction, whereas the worship of Yahweh, to the exclusion of all other gods, leads to plenty and abundance. Elijah in the Hebrew Bible is, accordingly, a prophet of Yahweh who operates both in opposition to regional Baal worship, and in the service of Yahweh's mission of dominance.

Religious context

Yahweh is God

Clearly, the message about Yahweh that emerges from the narratives is that Yahweh is the *true* god in the region, despite the prevalence of Baal worship and the multiple-gods environment in which the Elijah narratives unfolded. Unlike the limited abilities of those other gods, however, Yahweh emerged in these narratives as a god not only of nature, but also a god of powerful miracles, and even as the god of *human* history, as well. In each of the six Elijah narratives except the Vineyard narrative, Yahweh controls natural geological and climatological phenomena, such as rain (and drought), storms, wind, earthquakes, fire, and lightning.

Yahweh also was capable of miraculous acts: in the Widow and Journey to Horeb narratives, Yahweh clearly has the power of miraculously feeding Elijah and others, and of bringing a boy back to life. In Yahweh's commission to Elijah on Mt. Horeb in the Horeb narrative, we see not only Yahweh's aims to strike blows at Baal worship in the region, but also Yahweh's plans to use the Israelite

Jehu and the Aramean king Ben-hadad to decimate the idolatrous northern dynasties, as well. In the Vineyard narrative, we see Yahweh's chilling vow to destroy Ahab and Jezebel, as well as their lineage after them.

Overall, we see Yahweh depicted in these narratives as so powerful that he was dominant even within Baal's own territory. In the narrative of the Widow, Elijah performed Yahweh's miracles in the widow's town of Zerephath, a Canaanite/ Phoenician town. In the Baal narrative, we see Yahweh and Elijah defeat Baal and his prophets on Mount Carmel, which, as we will see, was all the more significant because Mt. Carmel was another mountain long considered Baal's own.[38] And finally, in the Ahaziah narrative, we see Yahweh, through Elijah, intercept and disabuse the messengers heading to consult 'Baal-zebub' (which was a Hebrew-Bible derogatory epithet for Baal-Hadad)[39] in the Canaanite city of Ekron.

Yahweh punishes those who transgress his law

The category of those who transgress Yahweh's law largely is consonant in the Hebrew Bible with those who do not worship Yahweh exclusively. In the Widow narrative and our very introduction to the figure of Elijah, the drought Elijah caused was punishment from Yahweh for the north because of the previous apostasies of northern kings. That drought situation continued into the Baal narrative, where the context was its third crushing year.

Punishment of those who transgress Yahweh's law by not worshipping Yahweh exclusively also was a theme existing in the Baal narrative, when, in punishment from Yahweh, Elijah and the assembled crowd slaughtered the 450 priests of Baal. In the Horeb narrative, Yahweh's commission to Elijah was geared to punish and destroy both the house of Jeroboam (and all subsequent northern kings), as well as all those who had ever knelt to or kissed Baal. Some of Yahweh's greatest vitriol, however, was reserved for King Ahab and Queen Jezebel in the Vineyard narrative.

In this episode we see the full 'depravity' of Ahab and Jezebel on display. They were willing to commit or, in the case of Ahab, to sanction murder in order unlawfully to obtain property, and Yahweh vowed the destruction of Ahab and Jezebel as much for committing these sins against the law as for having given over to idolatry (1 Kings 21:25–26). Jezebel had been a reviled figure throughout the Elijah narratives, but we see her in the Naboth narrative as the authors had intended: not only as an instigator of idolatry, but as beyond the pale of the law. Indeed, Jezebel's very name in the Hebrew text – איזבל, ay-zbl, "where is the prince?" may indicate her idolatrous nature, as this apparently was a contemporaneous call of Baal's distraught human subjects while Baal was in the underworld.[40]

Throughout the Vineyard narrative, the message of the narrator is clear: Yahweh punishes those who transgress his law, as well as those who do not worship him exclusively. However, for those who demonstrate true repentance and remorse, such as even the irredeemable figure of Ahab, Yahweh can be merciful.

In the Ahaziah narrative, we see the unravelling of the house of Ahab as the delayed punishment foreordained by Yahweh. Ahaziah ruled for only two years before dying of an accident at the palace. However, from the perspective of the narrator, Ahaziah's real transgression was his act of seeking assistance from a god other than Yahweh; in this case, Ahaziah sent messengers to inquire about his fate from the god "Baal-zebub," of Ekron. Clearly identifiable as the Canaanite deity Baal-Hadad both by his name and by the town where his shrine was located, this narrative demonstrates that Ahaziah considered Baal attractive-enough as a deity to have compelled Ahaziah to send messengers from Samaria, where several shrines and prophets to Yahweh already were located, in order to consult Baal at a shrine within a neighboring Philistine city. This act incensed Yahweh, who, in punishment, foreordained Ahaziah's death forthwith.

Within this account, narrators referred to Baal as 'Baal-zebub'. As we saw above, in Chapter Three, Baal frequently was referenced in Ugaritic texts as '*zbl b'l arṣ*'; 'prince Baal of the land'. Thus, scholarly consensus on this issue is that Baal-zebul, 'Baal the prince', a contemporaneous epithet for Baal, was deliberately distorted by the narrator(s) of Kings into the polemical name 'Baal-zebub' (Heb. בעל זבוב, *Baal-zĕbûb*) meaning 'Baal' or 'lord' 'of the flies'.[41] This is not unlike distortions of the name '*bōšet*', 'shame' for Baal, and 'Ashtoreth' (with the vowels of *bōšet*) for Astarte.[42]

John Day points out that, subsequently, the name Baal-zebul was attested in New Testament (NT) sources, as well. In Mt 10:25, 12:24 and 12:27; Mk 3:22; and Lk 11:15, 18–19, 'Beelzebul' was used as the name of the 'Prince of Demons'; i.e., Satan. The original Greek reading of this name in almost all extant manuscripts was Βεελζεβούλ. The reading 'Beelzebub' is found later in the Vulgate and Peshiṭta, and, Day argues, apparently was an attempt to make the NT demonic name agree with the name of the god of Ekron, Baal-zebub, in 2 Kings 1:2. Furthermore, it is perhaps unsurprising that the name Baal-zebul had become by the time of NT usage a name for the 'Prince of the Demons' (cf. *zbl* as 'prince'), because "the name of the leading god [Baal], when abominated, naturally became transformed [Beelzebul] into that of the leading demon, [Satan]."[43] The idea that pagan gods are demons is also found in Deut 32:17; Ps 105:37; Bar. 4:7; and Ps 95:5 (in the Septuagint), as well as in 1 Cor 10:20 and Rev 9:20 of the NT. The 'Prince of Demons' usages in the books of Matthew, Mark, and Luke, moreover, attests to at least one first-century CE meaning of this name involving the god Baal, and would perhaps have been quite appropriate in an environment in which the 'pagan' god Baal/Zeus had remained popular among surrounding populations.[44]

Finally, in the Ahaziah narrative, Yahweh relented and did not send down "fire from heaven" upon the third officer and his company, but only because that officer had fallen on his knees before Elijah and had acknowledged what Yahweh's power had wrought upon the first two companies of soldiers (2 Kings 1:13–15). Again, narrators show us in this example that sincere acknowledgement of Yahweh as the most powerful god results in Yahweh's favor, and the opposite results of course in death and destruction.

Worship of Yahweh alone results in Yahweh's favor upon the believer

This is particularly significant because it is a clear message in every one of the Elijah narratives. In the Widow narrative, the woman was rewarded for her faith in Yahweh – as demonstrated by her initial acquiescence to Elijah's requests – with the miracles of her oil and flour stores not failing, and of her son being brought back to life. In the Baal narrative, the people were rewarded with heavy rains and an end to the drought for their unambiguous faith in Yahweh, as demonstrated at the end of the contest between Elijah and the Prophets of Baal. Elijah himself was favored by Yahweh as demonstrated by Yahweh's protection and care evident throughout the narratives, such as Yahweh miraculously feeding Elijah in the Widow narrative using birds and a humble widow (both unlikely contemporaneous sources of food), and through an angel in the Horeb narrative. In the Vineyard narrative, as we saw above, Ahab was favored (but not forgiven) for his sincere repentance by Yahweh's vow to postpone his destruction of Ahab's house until the time of Ahab's son, and in the Ahaziah narrative, the life of the third (and wise) soldier was spared by Yahweh in reward for that soldier's clear acknowledgement of Yahweh's supremacy. Finally, Elisha's service to Yahweh was, in the Chariot narrative, clearly rewarded through Elisha's having seen Elijah's departure, and thus in Elisha's succession and acquisition of Elijah's office (i.e., his mantle).

Themes regarding Elijah

Elijah's mission is defiant opposition to Baal worship

The theme that links Elijah's overarching mission in all the narratives is defiant opposition to Baal worship undertaken in defense of the true God, Yahweh. Among other examples, this theme is evident in the widow narrative as Elijah worked miracles in Baal's territory; in the Baal narrative as Elijah literally worked in defense of Yahweh against Baal's prophets; in Yahweh's commission to Elijah in the Horeb narrative; in the Vineyard and Ahaziah narratives as Elijah condemned the Baal-worshiping Ahab and his family; and in the Chariot narrative as Elijah was succeeded by Elisha and thus Elijah's mission was continued.

In defiantly opposing Baal worship, however, Elijah also became associated with certain supernatural events, such as ceasing and causing the rains. This may have resulted in Elijah being perceived in popular culture as himself associated with rain and storms, such as the popular regional folktale which suggests that thunder is caused by Elijah riding around the heavens in his chariot. Furthermore, Elijah's disappearance into the sky via Yahweh's fiery chariot in the storm sparked tales of Elijah's immortality. This event underscored for later hearers or readers the miraculous nature of Elijah himself (having been spectacularly translated into heaven), and specifically did not say that Elijah was dead; just "taken away" (2 Kings 2:9) up to heaven in a storm (2:1; 2:11), by Yahweh (2:1). Even the Sons of the Prophets, who witnessed the event from the other side of the river, did not believe that Elijah was dead, and sent a search party for him (2:16–18). This disappearance came to have enormous theological implications, as we will see, upon the figure of Elijah as 'always present' and perennially available to guide the community in the proper fulfillment of the law.

Elijah is like Moses

Throughout the Horeb and Chariot narratives, the author(s) of these tales intentionally has imbued Elijah with motifs and narratives related to Moses from the Hebrew Bible.[45] Himself the quintessential representation of both polemic against idolatry, and the exclusive and proper worship of Yahweh, it is fitting that the narrator(s) of this passage intentionally would weave into the Elijah narratives rich allusions to the towering figure of Moses.[46] In addition to the similarity of their missions on behalf of Yahweh, allusions to Moses in Elijah's narratives can be found in Elijah's journey of 40 days and 40 nights to reach the mountain of god (1 Kings 19:8), where Moses had spent "forty days and forty nights" receiving the Law (Exod 24:18).[47] Similarly, on Mt. Horeb, Elijah stayed in a cave there (1 Kings 19:8) and was bidden to come out as Yahweh passed by, just as Moses had stood "in the crevice of a rock" for a similar theophanic appearance of Yahweh on Mt. Sinai (Exod 33:22). Elijah covered his face with his cloak (1 Kings 19:13) in front of Yahweh's theophany (1 Kings 19:11), just as Moses had hid his own face at the burning bush (Exod 3:6), both of which reactions were not uncommon responses in the ancient Near East when 'meeting' the divine. Even Yahweh's appearance at Sinai in thunder and fire was echoed in Elijah's theophanic experience of the divine (1 Kings 19:11–12). Finally, when we meet the figure of Elisha in the Horeb narrative, we see another similarity with Moses; the presence of a faithful servant who becomes his successor. Joshua son of Nun was a servant of Moses for years before being appointed Moses' successor (Exod 33:11, Num 11:28, Josh 1:1).[48]

In the Chariot narrative, Elijah used his rolled-up mantle; i.e., his office and status as a Prophet in the service of Yahweh, to part the Jordan River, much as Moses had parted the sea (Exod 14:21). Also in this narrative, Elisha succeeded Elijah, just as Joshua son of Nun had succeeded Moses (Josh 1:1–9). However, unlike Moses, Elijah in the Chariot narrative did not die. Moses had died and was buried, albeit under mysterious circumstances (Deut 34:5–6), whereas Elijah was taken up into the sky in a storm in Yahweh's fiery chariot. Utilizing this image, Elijah's followers invested him with the quality of eternal life; a quality that surpassed even Moses. This produced enormous interest in Elijah in the centuries afterward, in both canonical and agrarian religious circles, because Elijah became associated both with the defense of true faith and with the quality of being immortal.[49]

Elisha is Elijah's rightful successor

After having assumed Elijah's mantle – figuratively, Elijah's prophetic office – in the Chariot narrative, Elisha, as Elijah's rightful successor, went on in 2 Kings both to fulfill prophesies made by Elijah and to engage in prophecies and miracles in a manner already patterned in the narrative by Elijah, such as miracles involving water, oil, flour, a woman, and the revivification of her dead son. Elisha also was associated in his narratives with motifs involving both Mt. Carmel (2 Kings 2:25 and 4:25) and famine. As opposed to Elijah, however, Elisha *did* die (2 Kings 13:20), and in fact his bones produced the miracle of bringing a dead body back to life and it standing on its own feet (2 Kings 13:21).

Elijah's commission at Mt. Horeb by Yahweh ultimately was fulfilled by Elisha: Elisha anointed Jehu in 2 Kings 9:1–13 and met with Hazael in Damascus in 2 Kings 8:8–15 in order to forecast Hazael's rise to the Aramean throne. Even though it was Elisha who fulfilled these prophecies of Yahweh, their fulfillment had been set in motion by Elijah, who had appointed Elisha as his servant. In that way, Elijah's mission ultimately was a success. However, it seems that whatever victory could be claimed for Yahweh by the Elijah and Elisha narratives was limited: according to the accounts in Kings, and as we have seen above, Baal worship continued in both the north and south long after the prophetic missions of Elijah and Elisha, and lasted on even through the destruction of both kingdoms.

Political context

Various political powers of the day

These narratives also demonstrate evidence of contemporaneous political, military, and legal contexts. In these accounts, we see the political and military machinations of the northern kingdom of Israel, the southern kingdom of Judah, of Canaanites, Phoenicians, Philistines, Arameans, and Assyrians (not to mention the contemporaneous Babylonians and Egyptians within the larger accounts of 1 and 2 Kings, as well). We see evidence of the wars between Israel and Aram-Damascus under Ben-hadad at Ramoth-Gilead (1 Kings 22:1–38) and in the fact that Ahaziah succeeded his father Ahab in the Ahaziah narrative. However, we also see in the narratives evidence that interactions between these contemporaneous kingdoms were not always bellicose: the account of Ahaziah's messengers sent to consult the god Baal (-zebub) at the shrine in Ekron, while presented in the narrative as an act that was abominable, did not seem to have been anomalous. Also, we see fairly free movement for both Elijah and Elisha throughout Israel and Judah in the Horeb and Chariot narratives. This indicates perhaps that interactions between peoples of various kingdoms were not uncommon, and perhaps even that contemporaneous peoples were more integrated than generally is presumed.

In the Vineyard narrative, we can see the legal workings of the northern kingdom. The operation of the judicial system in ancient Israel is evident in the norms of criminal trials (1 Kings 21:11–13), biblical-era property transfer rights (1 Kings 21: 15–16), and even inheritance laws (1 Kings 21:3).

Geographical context

In the Elijah narratives, we see plentiful evidence of the contemporaneous geographical context, as well. The dominant picture that emerges from these narratives is one of an agricultural society where drought was not uncommon, and where mountain-tops were prominent religious spaces.[50]

In the Widow and Baal narratives, we see the clear context of drought. Droughts of three years in length were and are not-uncommon for the region,[51] and we see the setting of a severe, three-year-long drought in the case of the Baal narrative. Also in the Baal narrative, we see both rain and storms and their necessity to life. Upon Elijah's successful contest with the prophets of Baal – and especially upon the assembled community's declaration that *Yahweh* was the true God – Elijah ascended to the near-summit of Mt. Carmel to pray for rain. His unnamed assistant at that time went up to the summit to finally see a small cloud rising from the sea, which led to dark skies, and heavy rains. We also see the stormy theophany of Yahweh in both the Horeb and Chariot narratives. Finally, in the Baal and Ahaziah narratives, we see lightning, as well: Elijah calls down "fire" from the sky in both cases: in the former, this lightning consumed the offering and even the entire altar; in the Ahaziah narrative, fire engulfed two separate companies of fifty officers each. These "fire from heaven" narratives underscored Yahweh as a sky god who could wield lightning at-will upon his foes. Despite differences in language (i.e., several modern languages differentiate between fire and lightning as conceptually distinct), most scholars agree that 'fire from heaven' referred to lightning. Given that lightning reaches temperatures of around 53,000 degrees Fahrenheit and is several times hotter even than a large bonfire, which reaches temperatures of around 3,000 degrees Fahrenheit, and given that a lightning strike can set alight that which it hits, it is easy to see how one might naturally have presumed that lightning was a strike of 'fire', sent from the sky.

Agricultural setting

The severe drought of both the Widow and Baal narratives highlights the contemporaneous agricultural setting: the miracle of the widow's flour stores not failing was all the greater in a drought context, as was the precious water used to drench the altar in the Baal narrative. In the Horeb narrative, Elijah found Elisha engaged in plowing his fields with several teams of oxen. While Elisha's oxen indicated his wealth, farming and agricultural life would have been the most common economic activity for all class levels, and remained so in the region up through the 20th century CE.[52] In the Vineyard narrative, Ahab coveted Naboth's vineyard for his own vegetable garden and perhaps not without good reason: the Jezreel Valley near Carmel long was known for its rich and fertile agricultural land.

High places

High places figure prominently in both the Elijah narratives and in the Hebrew Bible more generally, as the locations for shrines or as the places where God is found.[53] In the Baal narrative, Mt. Carmel is the setting for Elijah's contest, and, as we will see below, Elijah's victory there was made all the more prominent by the fact that Mt. Carmel was Baal's mountain. In the Horeb narrative, Mt. Horeb/

Mt. Sinai are the setting of the story and the place where Yahweh addressed both Moses and, later, Elijah. In the Ahaziah narrative, Ahaziah's soldiers found Elijah sitting on a hilltop, which is the area from which Elijah called down fire/lightning from the sky (just as he did from Mt. Carmel in the Baal narrative). Finally, in the Chariot narrative, Elijah disappeared "into the heavens"; that is, high into the stormy sky in Yahweh's fiery chariot.[54]

Elijah texts: Conclusion

We see in the themes above regarding the Elijah (and Elisha) narratives in the Books of Kings two main strands of religious influences. First, the narratives take place in an environment of multiple gods; and, thus, of what we might think of today as multiple religious traditions – in particular, the narratives take place in an environment that is largely dominated by Canaanite religious figures and practices, and among which worship of the god Baal was the most prevalent. Second, one repeatedly encounters the theological message that is emblematic of both the religious reform movements of the seventh century BCE under Judahite kings Hezekiah and Josiah, and of the DH itself: having gods other than Yahweh leads to destruction.

'Destruction', from the historical perspective of these textual narratives, took the form of aggressive and expansionist political powers of the day, such as the Arameans, Assyrians, Babylonians, Egyptians, and Canaanites, of whom one sees ample evidence within the Books of Kings generally and the Elijah narratives specifically. However, the books of the DH were composed, compiled, edited and revised over a long span of time, with decisive moments of composition probably taking place during the reformist reign of Josiah in 639–609 BCE, and during and after the exile in 586 BCE. Because the events of the Elijah and Elisha narratives, in particular, were set in the ninth-century BCE northern kingdom of Israel, the narratives cannot be said to be accurate and contemporaneous representations of historical reality, as is claimed within them. Rather, these histories are theological arguments written at a later point in time and primarily from a southern perspective, to explain *why* the northern and southern kingdoms had been destroyed: the Israelites and Judahites had sinned against Yahweh by revering other gods and by following the statutes of the other nations, whom YHWH had dispossessed before the Israelites (2 Kings 17:7–8) …

> and made offerings there, at all the high places, as the nations whom YHWH exiled before them; and did evil things, angering YHWH, and worshipped idols, about which YHWH had said to them, 'Do not do this thing!' YHWH even warned Israel and Judah by every prophet and seer, 'Turn back from your evil ways and keep my commands and statutes, in accord with all the Law which I commanded your ancestors, and which I sent to you through my servants, the prophets'. But they did not listen. … they went after emptiness and became empty themselves, and after the fashion of the neighboring nations which YHWH had commanded them not to imitate. They abandoned

> all the commands of YHWH their God; they made themselves molten images – two calves; they made a pole of Asherah; they bowed down to all the heavenly host [i.e., several gods]; they worshipped Baal, they passed their sons and their daughters through fire; they practiced divination and sorcery; they gave themselves up to doing what was displeasing to YHWH, making him angry. YHWH was very angry with Israel, and he removed them from his sight; only the tribe of Judah was left. But even Judah did not keep the commands of YHWH, their God; they followed the statutes practiced by the Israelites. Thus, YHWH spurned all the seed of Israel; he afflicted them by handing them over to plunderers, until he rid himself of them.
>
> (2 Kings 17:7–20)

Then, describing the fall of Jerusalem and Judah, "He [Judahite King Zedekiah] did what was displeasing to YHWH, just as Jehoiakim [his predecessor] had done. Because of YHWH's wrath did [the Babylonian Empire siege and destroy Jerusalem], until he [YHWH] had rid himself of them (2 Kings 24:19–20).

Thus, the theological argument that developed, worshipping gods other than Yahweh leads to destruction, was part of a theological reform movement designed in part to differentiate the followers of Yahweh from other nearby peoples (cf. Exod 33:16). From the perspective of the DH, other nearby peoples seem not to have been religiously distinguishable from one other, which explained, perhaps, those people's indiscriminate destruction. Therefore, an exclusive devotion to Yahweh alone, and to the nature and place of Yahweh's worship, were centrally important to the religious reforms of Josiah and the wider DH.[55] Such was certainly the focus of the Jewish community that developed in Jerusalem in the new Persian province of Yehud following the period of exile:

> one of the main functions of the priestly elite in post-exilic Jerusalem – beyond the conduct of the renewed sacrifices and purification rituals – was the continuing production of literature and scripture to bind the community together and determine its norms against the peoples all around.[56]

Part Four: Rabbinic-era, Christian-tradition, and Islamic-tradition Elijah

Rabbinic-era Elijah, as well as Elijah in the Christian and Islamic traditions, comes to be understood in both canonical and agrarian religious practices in ways that both are drawn from and different from the Elijah of the Hebrew Bible. In general, in later Jewish traditions, Elijah became known as an enigmatic figure who helps to ensure that the law properly is being followed, and thus who helps to keep the Jewish community on a straight path. Because of Elijah's wondrous translation by fiery chariot into the storm, Elijah has been thought of as one of the very few figures in Jewish tradition who did not die. Enoch, in Gen 5:24, was the only other figure in the Hebrew Bible to have been "taken by God," and thus stories of Enoch's immortality abounded as well, but Elijah is the only Biblical personality of whom it intriguingly was said that he "ascended to heaven in a storm."[57] Because of that, Elijah developed a reputation in all subsequent communities – Jewish, Christian, and Muslim – as a figure who effectively was immortal, and, as such, who can appear and disappear at will.

In the Hebrew Bible, Elijah's final appearance takes place in the book of 2 Chronicles 21:12–15, where a letter, sent in Elijah's name and addressed to King Jehoram of Judah (851–843 BCE), announced that Jehoram had led the people of Judah astray in the same idolatrous manner in which the people of Israel had been led astray, and predicted for Jehoram a painful death. In Jewish tradition and in the Hebrew Bible, 2 Chronicles traditionally is counted among the final four books of the Tanakh. However, in the Septuagint (LXX), a Greek translation of the Tanakh/Hebrew Bible undertaken in Alexandria during the Ptolemaic period, between the fourth and second centuries BCE, and named after the purported '70' scholars who worked on the project, the books of the Hebrew Bible were arranged to end with the 12 'Latter Prophets'. Thus, in the LXX, and in subsequent Christian biblical traditions, the final book of the Hebrew Bible or 'Old Testament' is the book of Malachi. That also is where, from the perspective of the LXX and subsequent Christian traditions, the final reference to Elijah is located. In Malachi 4:1–6, an immanent day of reckoning is described, when all the "arrogant and evildoers will be stubble,'' but, for those who revere Yahweh, "the sun of righteousness shall rise." Admonishing his followers, Yahweh says,

> Remember the teaching of my servant Moses, and the statutes and ordinances that I commanded him at Horeb for all Israel. Lo, I will send you the prophet Elijah before the great and terrible day of YHWH comes. He will turn the hearts of parents to their children and the hearts of children to their parents, so that I will not come and strike the land with a curse. (Malachi 4:4–6)

Accordingly, Elijah takes on, for later Jewish and Christian communities, the dual roles of harbinger of the messiah, and harbinger of the eschaton (the end of days).

Elijah's role in rabbinic Judaism

Elijah is an enigmatic and popular figure in Judaism. From his account in the Hebrew Bible, he was known as a zealous and uncompromising prophet for the proper worship of Yahweh. However, Elijah's role in both later canonical Judaism and in agrarian religious practice came mostly from his character in rabbinic literature, including in the Talmud and in folklore.[58] Rabbinic Elijah is partly angelic and partly human; mysterious, and only loosely resembling the Hebrew Bible Elijah. He can connect humankind to God, serving as a supernatural mediator. He teaches wisdom, rabbinic values, and ethical standards; he gives advice, and often comes unpredictably, without warning, to address problems. Because Elijah in the Hebrew Bible did not die, like an ordinary mortal, but instead was 'taken up into the storm', later Rabbis considered Elijah free to travel throughout the world, between heaven and earth, appearing to people at will.[59] The traditions of Rabbinic Elijah derived both from oral storytelling and midrash, and, as such, they allow us to compare Elijah with other mediators between God and humanity in both Judaism and in other religious traditions of the same era. Jews and non-Jews naturally shared stories, even though they may not have shared technical law or scriptural interpretation. "Traditions of supernatural mediators, whether gods, saints, or angels, entertained and inspired the interacting oral cultures of antiquity."[60] Accordingly, Elijah in the Rabbinic era also seems to have to acquired traits that resembled the contemporaneous Greek god, Hermes, and may suggest a kind of "competitive cultural borrowing" common in antiquity.[61]

Elijah's roles within the Babylonian Talmud can be divided into four main areas: as a teacher of rabbinic wisdom, as an ethical model, as a rescuer in times of trouble, and as a mediator of heavenly wisdom. Stories involving Elijah in medieval and later periods tend to portray Elijah as affirming faith in God's mysterious justice. Elijah in the Jewish traditions of the middle ages and later became "probably the most popular hero of Jewish folklore,"[62] fulfilling the role of overseeing every circumcision ceremony and playing a role in every Passover Seder dinner. Enigmatic as later Elijah may be, in his tasks involving the circumcision ceremonies and Seder meal, we see Elijah in both canonical and agrarian religious contexts as continuing to fulfill an important role that we saw of him in the Hebrew Bible: ensuring correct community adherence to the laws of Yahweh.

Elijah in Christianity

Due primarily to the role of Elijah as a harbinger of the Messiah and of the eschaton – as understood from the Book of Malachi – within early Christian tradition, both Jesus Christ and John the Baptist were associated in NT texts with Elijah. John the Baptist in particular was depicted as looking and living as "wild as Elijah," and of performing his ministry in the areas around the Jordan River, which was the location of Elijah's translation into the sky in 2 Kings (Mk 1:6 and Mt 3:4). The NT records Elijah and Moses as having been present together at the transfiguration of Jesus in Mk 15:53–56 and in Mt 27:46–49 (see also later Figure 6.2). Christian theological opinion came to espouse the idea that, because of the roles of Moses as the protector of the law and of Elijah as the protector of Messiah, and especially because of the references made to Moses and Elijah in Malachai 4:4–6, Elijah and Moses would thus have been present at the transfiguration of Jesus in order to affirm Jesus as the proper Messiah.[63] In this way, Elijah remained an important and hugely compelling figure within early Christian traditions – and many other contemporaneous religious traditions – of the Common Era. Elijah as a figure was so popular among early Christians that he became known as a saint – St. Elias – rather than simply as a figure from Hebrew Bible narrative lore, as we will see below.

Finally, the figure Elijah even proved useful in some instances of converting Slavic pagan tribes to Christianity. Particularly influential in a Slavic setting, and by virtue of Elijah's having bested the prophets of Baal, controlled the rain, and been translated into the sky in a fiery chariot in a storm, Slavic Christian proselytizers of the Middle Ages identified Elijah with various pagan sky- and storm-gods.

Elijah and Perun, the pre-existing Slavic god of storms, became difficult to separate in Russian Christian traditions; Russian peasants prayed to Elijah for rain and associated Elijah with the qualities for which Perun had been known. Because of the tenacity of the Perun cult, involving the god of thunder and storms, the Christian 'saint', Elijah, who also could call down fire from heaven, functioned among Slavic communities as a usefully analogous "storm-god" figure to that of Perun.[64]

Elijah in Islam

The identity of Elijah within Islamic traditions – in particular, when *named as Elijah* ('*Ilyās*') in the Qur'ān – is drawn primarily from Hebrew Bible accounts of Elijah.

> And indeed, Elias was from among the messengers, when he said to his people, "Will you not fear [Allāh]? Do you call upon Baal and leave the best of creators – Allāh, your lord, and the lord of your first fathers?" And they denied him, so they indeed will be brought [for punishment], except the chosen servants of Allāh. And we left for him [favorable mention] among the later generations, "Peace be upon Elias." Indeed, we thus reward the doers of good. Indeed, he was among our believing servants. (Q. 37:123–132; see also 6:85.)

In Islamic traditions, and, particularly, when named as Elijah ('*Ilyās*') in the Qur'ān, Elijah functions much as he does in his role within the Hebrew Bible: as a zealous prophet against Baal worship and for the worship of God (named in the Qur'ān 'Allāh'; i.e., the [one and only] God, and derived etymologically from the Semitic root for god, '*il*-). It should be noted, however, that despite this clear Hebrew Bible role for Elijah as outlined in the Qur'ān, Common-Era tales involving the popular figures of Elijah and Moses that were beloved among religious communities of Christians and Jews also were popular in sixth- and seventh-century Arabia, which we will see on vivid display in Chapter Six.

Part Five: Elijah image: Judaic traditions and Christian Saint Elias

Common images of Elijah in the Judaic tradition are somewhat rare, but not at all unknown. The circumscription of images relating to Elijah is the result of a tradition of aniconism that gradually developed in Israelite and later Jewish tradition,[65] stemming from the Second Commandment of the Law, which Yahweh revealed to Moses at Mt. Sinai/Horeb,

> You shall not make for yourself an idol, or any likeness, whether in the form of anything that is in heaven above, or on the earth beneath, or in the water under the earth. You shall not bow down to them or worship them; for I YHWH am a jealous God…
>
> (Deut. 5:8–9)

This command naturally can seem to arise from the first law, "I am YHWH your God, who brought you out of the land of Egypt, out of the house of slavery; you shall have no other gods before [or besides] me" (Deut. 5:7; see also Exod 20:1–5, the Hebrew text of which differs slightly).

From a biblical perspective, and especially that of the DH, it seems that the use or existence of idols easily could have been incorporated into (or could have been representative of) the worship of other gods, thus blurring the lines dangerously between the contemporaneous cult of Yahweh and the cults of all other gods, including Baal (see 1 Kings 12:25–32 and Hosea 2). The classic formulation of this image ban likely emerged during or after the exilic period. Thus, in keeping with Deuteronomistic religious reforms that distinguished followers of Yahweh from the followers of other gods, the followers of Yahweh strictly were admonished against the creation of idols: representations or likenesses, carvings or engravings, molten images or statues cast from metal, copies, patterns, likenesses, or similitudes of Yahweh or of any other deity. This tradition of figural aniconism, with respect to the representation of deity(ies), impacted the acceptability of figural images within some later traditions of Judaism.

However, images of Elijah among Jewish communities were not, by any means, unknown, and in some eras, they became quite commonplace. Evidence from the third-century CE community at the synagogue at Dura-Europos, located in modern-day Syria near the Euphrates River and along what then was the Roman-Parthian border, boasted several images of Elijah that were drawn from his Hebrew Bible narratives. Paintings illustrating scenes from Elijah's mission lined the walls of the synagogue, including The Failure of the Sacrifice to Baal (Figure 4.1), which was on the south wall, Elijah multiplying the Widow's Oil and Meal (south wall), Elijah Reviving the Widow's Son (west wall), and the Sacrifice of Elijah on Mount Carmel (south wall), which was painted in contradistinction to the unsuccessful sacrifice to Baal.[66]

Note in Figure 4.1 the small priest hiding underneath the altar to Baal, as well as the snake that bites and kills that priest, all of which represent extra-biblical elements from an apocryphal tale about this Elijah narrative, and which developed during the first few centuries of the Common Era. Note as well the somber priests of Baal, whose sacrifice has failed. One final interesting element of this image can be seen in the dress of the priests of Baal, which is patterned on the dress of third-century CE Syrians rather than that of ninth-century BCE Israelites. These painting elements demonstrate geographical contextualization in action: reference to compelling narratives in a way that reflects the culture, temporal context, and needs of the group doing the referencing.

Saint Elias

The Prophet Elijah, a kind of 'Second Moses' in the Hebrew Bible, and the defender of the 'true' god against false gods, became a very important NT figure within the Christian scriptural tradition as well. Elijah, written and pronounced in Aramaic, Greek, Latin, and Arabic as '*Ilyās*' or 'Elias' or 'Eliā', is often called,

Figure 4.1 Failure of the Sacrifice to Baal – Dura Europos Synagogue © The Picture Art Collection/Alamy Stock Photo

as a Christian saint, مار الياس 'Mar' Elias, or Ἅγιος Ηλίας, 'Hagios' Elias ('saint' Elias). Elijah's feast day in both Eastern and Western Christian traditions is July 20. Because Elijah did not die, but was instead translated into heaven, this date may have been related to an agricultural date for a festival involving Elijah rather than recalling a death/birthdate (as in the case of most Christian saints' festivals).

The earliest iconographical representations of Elijah in the Christian tradition involved his depiction as a prophet who defended the Law; in this portrayal, Elijah holds a scroll representing his role. This has remained a popular motif of Elijah, although most subsequent depictions and icons of Saint Elias began to emphasize his many associations with miracles; in particular, his having been fed in the desert by ravens, his defeat of the Prophets of Baal, and his miraculous disappearance. Almost all iconographical representations of Elijah emphasize the important feature of his mantle, and of his wild and ascetic appearance.

Political influences evident in the images of Saint Elias exist primarily within the realm of and implications surrounding the depiction of Elijah with attendants. Geographical influences often are evident in the inclusion of geographical features in the background, which tend to reflect 1) compelling geographical features from the Hebrew Bible story, 2) the geography of the artist, or 3) the geography of the location for which the image is displayed. Interestingly, and irrespective of the time of production, iconographical representations of Saint Elias tend to reflect religious influences drawn primarily from Elijah's role in the Hebrew Bible or directly from elements of his narratives therein, rather than agrarian-religious stories about and conceptions of Elijah. This reflects, perhaps, the 'stabilizing' power of texts,[67] as images of Elijah depict him long after the time when his canonical identity already had been established.

Part Six: Elijah site – Mount Carmel

'Mount Carmel' is made up of a coastal range of mountains and hills that, starting at what is the modern city of Haifa, extend for about 24 miles southeast from the Mediterranean Sea. Composed primarily of hard limestone which formed about 55 million years ago, this range runs between 5 and 8 miles wide throughout, and is pocketed by several caves.[68] The designation 'Mount Carmel' can refer to the entire range, to a 12-mile northwest section of the range, or, often, simply to the headland at the northwest end of the range (Figure 4.2).

This headland is called Mt. Carmel, הר הכרמל, in Hebrew, جبل الكرمل, *Jebl al-Karmel*, in Arabic, or جبل مار الياس, Mt. Saint Elias. Appearing as a sharply pointed cape or promontory along an otherwise-smooth coastline that extends all the way south to Egypt, this headland long has been a navigation point for mariners. It also is the site traditionally associated with Elijah's contest against the prophets of Baal (1 Kings 18:1–46). The Carmel Range physically splits the territory to the north and to the south of it. Although a narrow beach runs along the seashore, international foot traffic for millennia usually stayed to the north of the range, crossing into or out from the interior plains via passes near Yokneam and Megiddo, with access to the sea north of Mt. Carmel. This geographical divide created by the Carmel Mountains also caused a natural boundary or border region; indeed, in the setting of the Books of Kings, Mount Carmel formed the southern border of the kingdom of Tyre (see Figure 4.2), and thus often was considered a part of Phoenician or Canaanite territory.

The word 'Karm', 'כֶּרֶם ' in Hebrew means 'garden', 'vineyard', or 'orchard', and Karm-el 'כרמל' literally means 'El's Vineyard'/'god's vineyard'. The name likely reflects the fertile environs of Mt. Carmel, which catch the westerly breezes and moisture from the sea. Forests grow in the area, and olives, grains, and vineyards long have been cultivated there.

The caves of Carmel became famous during the biblical era as the hideouts for thieves and bandits, but these caves also were the site of some of the first human and humanoid habitation in the region.[69] Material cultural remains in the caves include artistic products like animal-head tool handles and beads dating from 150,000 to 10,000 BCE. Recent archaeological excavations at the site have returned evidence so far of human settlements dating from the Iron Age, although the paucity of these sources may indicate either that settlement was not encouraged during that time, or that the denser forests and maquis may have impeded human settlement. Excavations at the site also have returned coins dating from the time of Constantine through the late Roman Era, from the Byzantine period, and from Umayyad, 'Abbasid and Mamluk rule.[70]

The religious significance of Mt. Carmel as a 'high place' in the Canaanite fashion,[71] and one located along the sea coast, is well attested in extra-biblical

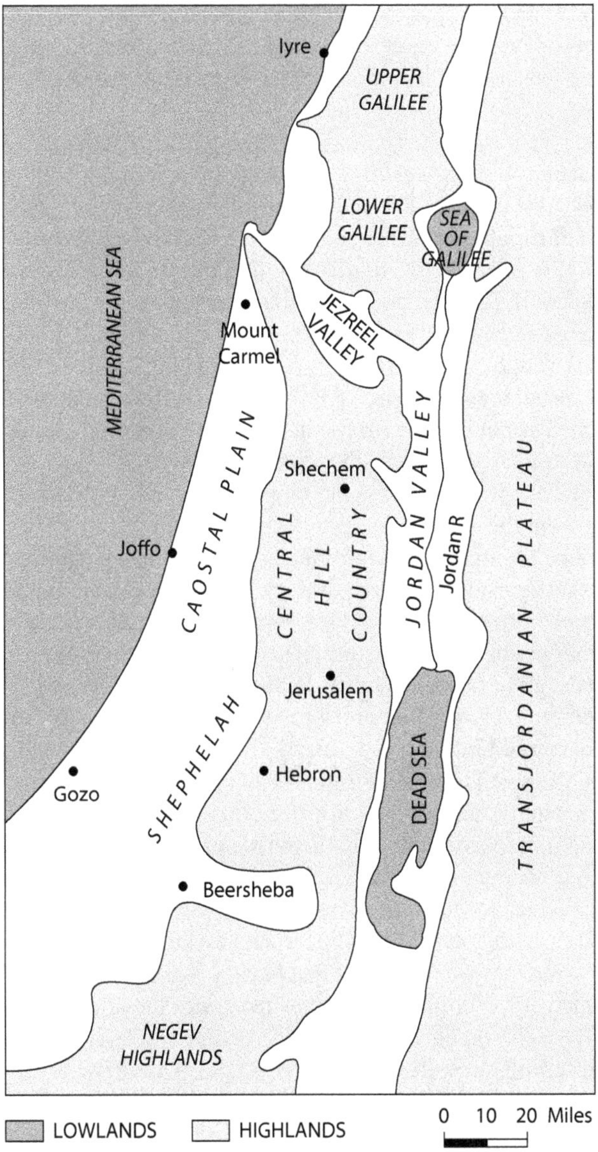

Figure 4.2 Map of the Mount Carmel region

sources. Mt. Carmel appears as '*Roš Qadeš*', 'Holy Head[land]', in the records of Egyptian Pharaoh Thutmose III (1490–1436 BCE). Assyrian sources from the ninth century BCE indicate that Carmel was a sacred mountain, and dedicated to Baal.[72] These sources indicate not only the religious significance of the mountain, but also help to explain the choice of this site by biblical writers (or by those who first circulated the oral Elijah and Elisha tales that were associated with Mt. Carmel in 1 Kings 18 and 2 Kings 2:25 and 4:25) as the site of the famous contest between Elijah and the 450 prophets of Baal. As the extra-biblical evidence attests, Elijah's defeat of Baal and his prophets was all the more impressive because it took place *on Baal's own ground.*[73]

Despite the drama of the Hebrew Bible contest, however, the text itself tells us that Baal worship continued at 'high places' throughout the area, as did the worship of Yahweh, and other gods besides. The site afterward also became strongly associated with the figure of Elijah; hence one name for Mt. Carmel also became Mt. Saint Elias. In the 12th century CE, a Roman Catholic monastery and 'Carmelite' religious order were founded and later rebuilt on the site of the purported battle, and the area became known as well within Arabic and Islamic tradition as المحرّكه *al-maharrakah*, the 'site of burning', referring to the dramatic fire Yahweh sent to consume the altar and offering. All the same, Baal worship itself continued the site of Mount Carmel into the first centuries of the Common Era, as associated with Greek and Roman presence in the region.[74]

In 1952, M. Avi-Yonah found in the Carmelite monastery on Mount Carmel a marble fragment dating from the early third century CE in the shape of the toes and fore-part of a right foot on a plinth. Using the size of the toes as an estimate, he suggested that the figure would have been twice life-size. The plinth under the sole of the right foot was inscribed in two lines of Greek, reading: "(Dedicated) to [Zeus] Heliopolitan, (god of) Carmel (by) Gaius Iulius Eutychas, colonist (of) Caesarea." That god of Carmel had been identified at least as early as the second century CE, and probably earlier, with Zeus Heliopolitanus (or Iupiter Heliopolitanus in the Roman tradition).

As we saw throughout Chapter Three, Zeus/Iupiter Heliopolitanus was one of the best-known gods of antiquity, and for whom there remain scores of figural representations and hundreds of inscriptions over the whole of the former Roman Empire. In the Hellenic and Romanized Near East, Zeus/Iupiter Heliopolitanus was identified with (Baal-) Hadad. Macrobius Ambrosius Theodosius, a Roman philosopher and writer living in around the year 400 CE and best known under simply the title 'Macrobius', wrote of the emperor Trajan having consulted an oracle of Zeus at the Baalbek sanctuary, "for god, whom they reverence the highest and the greatest, they have given the name of Hadad," "deo enim, quem summum maximumque venerantur, *Adad* nomen dederunt."[75] Of course, Adad/Hadad was the local Syrian name for Baal, the storm-god. Thus did the veneration of Baal at Mount Carmel continue long into the first centuries of the Common Era, just as it had at Baalbek and other places throughout the Levant. Avi-Yonah claims that it was a wave of polytheistic religiosity, coinciding with the regional popularity of the mostly finished temples at Baalbek, which had moved a wealthy patrician of Caesarea to erect a statue to his ancestral god.[76]

As Christianity became popular in the region during the first several centuries of the Common Era, the veneration of Canaanite and Hellenized Syrian gods and goddesses began to wane. By the mid-20th century CE, all that had remained of the once double-life-sized statue of Hadad/Zeus on Mount Carmel was a fragment of his foot, then stored in the mountain's Christian monastery dedicated to Elijah.

Part Seven: Elijah and the Levantine common pool

What Elijah texts, images, and sites reflect about ancient Israelite tradition

What we see *reflected* in the figure of Elijah is a religious environment that was dominated by multiple gods and goddesses, mostly Canaanite, and Baal-Hadad preeminent among them. This was because Baal-Hadad, the regional god of storms, long remained dominant in a religious environment in which water from rainfall was essential to human agricultural life.

What we see *represented* by the figure Elijah, however, is an example of a main theme running throughout the Hebrew Bible: Yahweh is the supreme god; there are no other gods before Yahweh. Therefore, worship of gods other than Yahweh leads to destruction. Because Yahweh is the supreme god, Yahweh does not act like other gods; he is jealous, and his followers must act in specific ways in specific places around him. They must also zealously be dedicated to Yahweh, who will reward them. That kind of behavior was modeled in prophets like Elijah (and, of course, Moses). Pious human worshippers of Yahweh, we learn from the example of Elijah in the Hebrew Bible, should in fact be *like* Elijah: single-minded and uncompromising in their dedication to Yahweh.

The canonical religion we see revealed by the figure Elijah is a religious tradition that is single-minded and exclusivist about its desire to distinguish itself from among other groups. It reflects the perspective of a small kingdom(s) and minority religious tradition attempting to exist and to thrive among the larger and more powerful players in the region. As such, the religious tradition revealed in the Hebrew text and revealed by the Prophet Elijah is single-minded and exclusivist about its desire to differentiate itself from other groups; in part, because the narratives took place in an environment of mixture and of heterogeneous peoples.

Amid the upheaval of the regional history of the Israelites and the Judahites over and against the larger powers of the day, as their religious tradition(s) became 'Judaism', during the late-first millennium BCE, the Hebrew Bible texts became the anchoring and central element of Jewish narrative history.[77] Thus, for all subsequent traditions which come to associate with the Hebrew Bible, such as Christianity and Islam, the texts of this tradition came to have an enormously formative impact on the narratives and figures within Christianity and Islam, as well. As Elijah in the Hebrew Bible became canonized in text and popularized in narrative, the compelling figure of the prophet Elijah became a fixture of regional culture, and within those later religious traditions, such as Christianity and Islam, which emerged out of the textual traditions of the Hebrew Bible.

The figure Elijah and a Levantine common pool of figures, narratives, and geographical motifs

What Elijah takes from *the common pool*

Baal-Hadad is the figure with whom Elijah forever is associatively linked, in that Elijah's mission in the Hebrew Bible was to eradicate Baal worship. Moreover,

Elijah also became associated with the regional narrative and motif of defeating and vanquishing a foe, often depicted underfoot.[78] In his quest to eradicate Baal worship, Elijah became associatively linked with the geographical motifs of the power to control rain, storms, and lightning. Because of his mysterious disappearance and translation into the heavens, Elijah also became linked with the regional motifs of disappearance and return, as well as with being a celestial chariot-rider who *causes* the sound of thunder. In these ways, Elijah came to function as an *antithetical alternative* to Baal-Hadad: Elijah was *not* Baal-Hadad – his mission was against Baal, in fact – but, as a figure engaged in Baal-worship eradication, and who thereby also became associatively linked with some of Baal's most compelling geographical motifs, the figure of Elijah also effectively came to function in the region as an *antithetical alternative* to Baal-Hadad.

What Elijah contributes* to *the common pool

Compelling new elements associated with Elijah and which he contributed *back to* the common pool include Elijah's role as a defender par excellence – of course, alongside Moses – of the 'true' god, against idolatry and polytheism. Elijah became associated with several compelling motifs, as well: miracle stories around drought, being fed by widows and ravens, ensuring unfailing flour and oil stocks, the bringing back to life of a child, the iconic contest on Mount Carmel with Baal, with fire/lightning and the killing of 'false' prophets; associations with Mount Sinai/Horeb (again like Moses); with the maligned figures of Jezebel and Ahab and the false god Baal-zebub, with fire from the sky which can descend and consume foes; with fiery chariots of god, and with being taken up into the heavens in a fiery storm.

Elijah, the zealous and memorable Hebrew Bible prophet of Yahweh, is emblematic of a larger project of the Hebrew Bible: the move to distinguish between 'true' and 'false' gods, and the differentiation between followers of Yahweh, and followers of any other god. Later religious traditions, such as Christianity and Islam, which continued within the lineage of the Hebrew Bible, also participated in the legacy of this exclusivity project, which we will see in Chapters Five and Six. For that reason, Elijah has remained enormously important, within the subsequent religious traditions of Christianity and Islam, as a figure who defends *true* faith. Furthermore, as we will see, an understanding of the figure of Elijah is essential to a proper historical understanding of the wider phenomenon involving both St. George and al-Khiḍr, as well. This is despite the fact that, due to long-term changing demographic factors in the region, and in particular due to several modern political factors, Elijah in the Levant – from a contemporary 20th- and 21st-century perspective – is not as prevalent of a figure there as he once was.

Moving to the figure of Saint George

Elijah remained an enormously influential figure within the religious culture of the Eastern Mediterranean; in particular, among agricultural communities, because of his associations with rain and storms. As we will see in Chapter Five, several compelling motifs and narratives of Elijah from the Hebrew Bible – in particular, the narratives of Elijah as the impassioned eradicator of false worship, and as a miracle-worker for a widow and her son – also intentionally were employed in the hagiography of St. George. In the earliest hagiographical account of the life of St. George, we see direct allusions to Elijah: St. George, closely following the model of Elijah from the Hebrew Bible, was depicted as the defender of 'true' religion – that is, *Christianity* – against the many pagan gods of the Roman world.

Notes

1 Leah Bronner, *The Stories of Elijah and Elisha: As Polemics Against Baal Worship*, Pretoria Oriental Series, A. Van Selms, ed. Vol. VI (Leiden: E.J. Brill, 1968), 1.

2 John Day, *Yahweh and the Gods and Goddesses of Canaan*, Journal for the Study of the Old Testament Supplement Series 265, David Clines and Philip Davies, eds. (Sheffield, UK: Sheffield University Press, 2000), 70.

3 Green, *The Storm God*, 285. See also Chapter Three. See also Day, *Yahweh and the Gods and Goddesses of Canaan*, 91–106. See also Chapter Three.

4 This evaluation is representative of most historical accounts within the Hebrew Bible. These 'historical accounts' are not contemporaneous eyewitnesses to historical events, but, rather, are theological interpretations of historical events, created centuries after the events they described. See Israel Finkelstein and Neil Asher Silberman, *The Bible Unearthed: Archaeology's New Vision of Ancient Israel and the Origin of its Sacred Texts* (New York: Simon and Schuster, 2001), 120.

5 Finkelstein and Silberman, 121–122. This message is, moreover, emblematic of the larger aim of the final forms of the books which comprise the Deuteronomistic History.

6 The English translation of these books that will be used herein is based on the Masoretic Text (MT), and primarily made by Mordechai Cogan and Hayim Tadmor See Cogan, *1 Kings*. See also Mordechai Cogan and Hayim Tadmor, *II Kings: A New Translation with Translation and Commentary*, The Anchor Bible Series, William Foxwell Albright and David Noel Friedman, eds., Vol. 10 (New York: Doubleday, 1988).

7 See also Sergio Ribichini, "Beliefs and Religious Life," in *The Phoenicians*, Sabatino Moscati, ed. (New York: Rizzoli, 1999), 120–152.

8 Finkelstein and Silberman, *The Bible Unearthed*, 6. Furthermore, the Hebrew and Christian Bibles are directly and indirectly most frequently referenced within the Qur'ān as a conjoined scriptural tradition under the term '*al-kitab*', 'the book' or 'the scripture', which is understood, where not abrogated by the Qur'ān, as forming the scriptural foundation of a tradition which also includes the Qur'ān. The Qur'ān is considered, of course, within the text, to be the *complete* '"book" of truth', in contradistinction to the Hebrew and Christian Bibles. See Q. 3:3–4. While Qur'ānic reference to the Hebrew or Christian bibles is made most frequently by reference to the term '*al-kitāb*', on a couple of occasions, the Hebrew Bible and Christian Bible are mentioned directly by the respective titles '*al-taurat*' (the Torah) and '*al-injīl*' (the Gospel(s)).

9 This overview of the central narrative of the Hebrew Bible was adapted from Finkelstein and Silberman, *The Bible Unearthed*, 8–10.

10 This overview of the structure of the Hebrew Bible has been adapted from Finkelstein and Silberman, *The Bible Unearthed*, 5–7.

11 Finkelstein and Silberman, *The Bible Unearthed*, 13.

12 Finkelstein and Silberman, 13–14. See also the account of Josiah's reforms in 2 Kings 22:1–23:30.

13 See also Bronner, *The Stories of Elijah and Elisha*, 1. Lev 26: 1–46 offers a good example of this Hebrew Bible perspective.

14 Many other gods appear in the text as well, such as the Mesopotamian god Tammuz (Ezek 8:14), but unfortunately there is not space here to examine textual references to all contemporaneous divinities. For an interesting discussion involving the translation of Levantine Tammuz worship into Greek culture in the form of the figure Adonis (so named, according to this argument, because Greek-speakers heard and misunderstood the cry of 'Adonai!', 'my lord!', as the *name* for the seasonally disappearing god Tammuz, thus calling him in Greek 'Adonis'), see Fox, *Travelling Heroes*, 227–242.
15 Deut 33:2; see also Chapter Three, 59, 30n.
16 Day, *Yahweh and the Gods and Goddesses of Canaan*, 16.
17 The northwest Semitic word for 'god' itself was likely derived from the archaic Proto-Semitic bilateral root *'il-*, meaning 'god' or 'deity'.
18 Day, *Yahweh and the Gods and Goddesses of Canaan*, 17. For traits of El appropriated by Yahweh, see 17–24.
19 Day, 59–60.
20 Day, *Yahweh and the Gods and Goddesses of Canaan*, 70. For an archaeological understanding of Israelite history as emerging naturally from within Canaanite culture, over and against textual claims of conquest and settlement, see also Finkelstein and Silberman, *The Bible Unearthed*, 97–122.
21 See also Chapter Three, 58, 27n.
22 Day, *Yahweh and the Gods and Goddesses of Canaan*, 68. See also Spencer Allen, *The Splintered Divine: A Study of Ištar, Baal, and Yahweh Divine Names and Divine Multiplicity in the Ancient Near East*, Studies in Ancient Near Eastern Records 5 (Munich: De Gruyter, 2015). See Also Schwemer, "The Storm-Gods of the Ancient Near East: Part One and Part Two," Part One, 124; Part Two, 15–16. See also Chapter Three, 58, 27n.
23 See Chapter Three, 58, 27n.
24 Day, *Yahweh and the Gods and Goddesses of Canaan*, 68–69.
25 Day, 72. The seal reference comes from N. Avigad, 'Hebrew Seals and Sealings and their Significance for Biblical Research', in J.A. Emerton (ed.), *Congress Volume*, Jerusalem 1986 (VTSup, 40; Leiden: E.J. Brill, 1988), 7–16 (8–9).
26 See Mordechai Cogan and Hayim Tadmor, *II Kings: A New Translation with Translation and Commentary*, The Anchor Bible Series, William Foxwell Albright and David Noel Friedman, eds., Vol. 10 (New York: Doubleday, 1988), 296–297.
27 Day, *Yahweh and the Gods and Goddesses of Canaan*, 71. The reference was to Baal-Shamem, Baal of the Heavens. See also Chapter Three, 71–75, for more on Greek and Roman cults to Baal-Zeus and Jupiter.
28 Day, *Yahweh and the Gods and Goddesses of Canaan*, 128–131. Note also that Atargatis was the Syrian goddess mostly likely worshipped at the so-called 'Temple of Bacchus' at Baalbek, alongside her consort Baal-Hadad (see above, Chapter Three). See also Schwemer, *Part One*, 161, and *Part Two*, 13–14.
29 Day, 232.
30 Day, 233.
31 This introduction is drawn in part from the introduction to the Books of Kings in Michael D. Coogan, ed. *The New Oxford Annotated Bible: New Revised Standard Version with the Apocrypha*. 3rd ed. (Oxford: Oxford University Press, 2001), 487–489.
32 Cogan, *1 Kings*, 430.
33 Cogan, *1 Kings*, 92.
34 We are told in the Septuagint that Elijah is a *tšbi* (although it is unclear what location or concept is referenced by that term); an outsider who is residing in Gilead, located east of the Jordan River, in modern-day Jordan. In the Masoretic Text, *tšbi* is not described as a place-name. No town of 'Tishbe in Gilad' is attested in ancient sources, although a "Thisbe in Galilee (of the Tribe of Naphtali) is mentioned in Tob. 1:2, and this toponym may have influenced the present gloss specifying Tishbe in

Gilead" (see Cogan, *1 Kings*, 424–425). There also is a morphological and root-letter similarity between '*tšb*' and Teššub/'Teshub', the name of Hurro-Hittite Storm-god. Teshub was worshipped in many places, among them Aleppo, in Syria. In the Hittite-Levantine boundary locales such as Syria, Teshub often was identified or conflated with the Storm-god Adad/Hadad. (See Chapter Three, 57, 15n. See also Schwemer, Part One, 159, and Part Two, 12.) Of course, the morphological, root-letter, and locale similarities between '*tšb*' and 'Teshub' simply may be coincidental. Moreover, Hurrian was not a Semitic language.

35 Day, *Yahweh and the Gods and Goddesses of Canaan*, 16–17.

36 Mt. Horeb, also called Mt. Sinai, also was the mountain location of the prophet Moses' previous theophanic meetings with Yahweh, including the episode of the burning bush (Exod 3:1), and in relaying to Moses the covenant law Exod (31:18). Mount Horeb, in the Sinai, known as the mountain of Yahweh, is in part why Yahweh was identified as a god from the south.

37 Cogan, *1 Kings*, 479.

38 See also Chapter Four, 126–128.

39 See Chapter Three, 84, 138n.

40 Jo Ann Hackett, "Jezebel," in The Oxford Guide to People and Places of the Bible, eds. Bruce M. Metzger and Michael D. Coogan, (Oxford: Oxford University Press, 2001), 78–79. Hackett also notes that 'Jezebel' later becomes an insulting epithet for a woman and is also used in Rev 2:20 for a prophet of whom the author apparently disapproves. Conversely, Jezebel's name may have been aimed to mock her: איזבל, 'ay-zbl', might have been intentionally shortened version of אביזבל, 'abi-zbl', meaning of the Sidonian princess, 'my father is a prince'. 'אי' is a negation that occurs in Phoenician inscriptions, however, and 'זבל' in both Hebrew and Ugaritic can mean 'dominion and rule'. Thus, Jezebel's name as recorded in the Hebrew Bible, איזבל, 'ay-zbl', could also have been an intentional distortion of the name of Ahab's Queen from Sidon: 'not-dominion/not-rule'; i.e., 'not-queen'; see Bronner, *The Stories of Elijah and Elisha*, 9–11.

41 Day, *Yahweh and the Gods and Goddesses of Canaan*, 80. See also Cogan, *II Kings*, 25. See also Chapter Three, 84.

42 Day, *Yahweh and the Gods and Goddesses of Canaan*, 80.

43 Day, 80.

44 Day, 232. See also Chapter Three, 57. See also Chapter Five, 140.

45 Cogan, *1 Kings*, 456.

46 Although, the anti-idolatrous nature of Moses himself is not without question. See Amy L. Balogh, *Moses Among the Idols: Mediators of the Divine in the Ancient Near East* (Lexington/Fortress Press, 2018) for an interesting discussion of Moses as intentionally portrayed within the Hebrew Bible as himself analogous to an idol.

47 For more on the association in the Hebrew Bible of Mt. Horeb with Mt. Sinai, see 36n. above.

48 Cogan, *1 Kings*, 455.

49 Cogan, *II Kings*, 33–35, in particular, 33.

50 Cf. Chapter Three on Mt. Sapan and other 'high places', 70–71; 80–83.

51 See Chapter Two, 26–29.

52 See Chapter Two, 24–35.

53 Cf. Chapter Three on Mt. Sapan and other 'high places', 70–71; 80–83.

54 Cf. Chapter Three, Baal as the 'Cloudrider', 69, 83n.

55 See Finkelstein and Silberman, *The Bible Unearthed*, 246–250, for an argument about the eighth- and seventh-century BCE religious reform movements in the kingdom of Judah following the destruction of the northern kingdom. See also Frank Moore Cross, *Canaanite Myth and Hebrew Epic: Essays in the History of the Religion of Israel* (Cambridge, MA: Harvard University Press, 1973), 274–288, and Bruce Halpern and D. Vanderhooft, "The Editions of Kings in the 7th–6th Centuries B.C.E." *Hebrew Union College Annual* 62: 179–244.

56 Finkelstein and Silberman, *The Bible Unearthed*, 310.
57 Cogan, *1 Kings*, 34–35.
58 Kristen H. Lindbeck, *Elijah and the Rabbis: Story and Theology* (New York: Columbia University Press, 2010), ix.
59 Lindbeck, ix–xii.
60 Lindbeck, xvi.
61 Lindbeck, xvi.
62 Lindbeck, 146.
63 We will see Moses and Elijah prominently associated as well in Chapter Six, 216–223.
64 Cherry Gilchrist, *Russian Magic: Living Folk Traditions of an Enchanted Landscape* (Wheaton, IL: Quest Books, 2009) 82. See also Mike Dixon-Kennedy, ed., "Perun," *Encyclopedia of Russian and Slavic Myth and Legend* (Santa Barbara, CA: ABC-CLIO, 1998), 218. See also Miller, *The Dragon, the Mountain, and the Nations*, "Slavic and Baltic Examples," 36–38.
65 Ryan Bonfiglio, "Images and the Image-Ban in the Hebrew Bible and Israelite Religion," *Oxford Biblical Studies Online*, notes, drawing in part upon the work of Tryggve N.D. Mettinger, *No Graven Image: Israelite Aniconism in its Ancient Near Eastern Context* (University Park, PA: Eisenbrauns, 2013 [1995]) "thus, rather than reflecting a general aversion to figurative imagery, Israelite aniconism is best understood as a strategy of replacement in which certain visual depictions of the deity [iconic depictions; those that were intended to capture or copy a deity's appearance in naturalistic manner, anthropomorphic or otherwise] are prohibited and/or destroyed in favor of rival iconographies [iconographies that were aniconic]." Thus, although a tradition of aniconism gradually developed, "religion in ancient Israel was routinely expressed and mediated through images and visual culture."
66 See these images and analysis of them in Bezalel Narkiss, "'Living the Dead Became': The Prophet Elijah as a Holy Image in Early Jewish Art," in *Byzantine East, Latin West: Art-Historical Studies in Honor of Kurt Weitzmann*, Christopher Moss and Katherine Kiefer, eds. (Princeton, NJ: Princeton University Press, 1995) 75–80.
67 See Chapter One, 11, 43n. and 44n.
68 Much of the background information in this section is drawn from Henry O. Thompson, "Mount Carmel," in *The Anchor Bible Dictionary*, Vol. 1, ed. by David Noel Freedman (New York: Doubleday, 1992), 874–875. See also Chapter Two, 31, 22n.
69 Henry O. Thompson, 874–875.
70 Shimon Dar, *Rural Settlements on Mount Carmel in Antiquity*, (Oxford, UK: Archaeopress Archaeology, 2014) 158–163; 174.
71 Cf. Chapter Three on Mt. Sapan and other 'high places'.
72 Thompson, "Mount Carmel," 875.
73 Thompson, 875, emphasis added.
74 See also Chapter Three, 71–75, esp. 75, 111n. See also Chapter Seven, 244–248.
75 Macrobius, *Saturnalia*, 1, 23, 10, emphasis mine.
76 M. Avi-Yonah, "Mount Carmel and the God of Baalbek," 119 and 124. The name 'Gaius Iulius' indicated that the patron's Roman citizenship had extended to the time of the Iulio-Claudian dynasty or even back to the time of Augustus; hence Avi-Yonah's description of the patron.
77 Finkelstein and Silberman, *The Bible Unearthed*, 301, 316–317.
78 Note: Later-developed "vanquishing" posture in the iconography of St. Elias may also reflect the influence and popularity of regional depictions of Ss. Theodore, Demetrius, and George as much as it does the Biblical narrative.

5 Early Christianity and Saint George

Part One: Introduction and historical backgrounds of Christianity

In 332 BCE, Alexander III of Macedon (the 'Great') conquered much of the Near East. The culture he brought with him, and that which remained behind him through his generals and their successive Ptolemaic and Seleucid kingdoms, is known today as 'Hellenism'. This legacy of Greek, and, later, Roman culture, influenced, and, in many cases, gradually blended with local Near Eastern cultural and religious traditions. Indeed, two of the region's most important cities founded after Alexander's conquests were Antioch, near coastal Syria, along the Orontes River near Mount Kasios, and Alexandria, a port city along the Egyptian coast near the western tributary branches of the Nile River.[1] Together with Rome, these cities later came to form the centers of political and cultural life in the Roman Empire. Within the first few centuries of the Common Era, they joined Jerusalem as the preeminent Christian cities of the East. One primary legacy of Hellenism, therefore, was that this backdrop constituted the political and cultural milieu within which Christianity formed.

Accordingly, Christian figures, like St. George, naturally were a product of multiple contemporaneous influences, which we will see in this chapter. Textually, St. George intimately was related to the towering biblical figure of Elijah, who had offered the model of a victorious fight between true and false gods. In legend and eventually in image, as we will see, St. George and the communities who venerated him came to identify in him several features that also had been associated with the storm-god Baal-Hadad and with Levantine Zeus and Jupiter, such as a feast day on April 23, storms, lightning, fecundity, and the image and narrative of the vanquishing of a serpent, dragon, or human foe, albeit in Roman-era dress and equestrian setting. These compelling geographical motifs also came to be applied to St. George, who evolved over several centuries into the figure known and beloved throughout the Mediterranean today.

This chapter gives an overview of the historical and religious background of the rise of Christianity, of which St. George was a product. It then examines St. George's earliest text: the Syriac-language *Acts of Saint George*, ca. 600 CE, which formed the basis for all subsequent hagiographical accounts of St. George, and which is our earliest-known and most-complete witness to the original Greek narrative (ca. 450 CE). The chapter then examines the early Christian iconographical tradition as it arose and was distinguished from Hellenistic and Roman iconographical practices, in order to understand the iconographical representations of St. George. This section investigates how St. George's imagery changed over time, and what those changes reveal. Throughout these analyses, the textual and iconographical sources are analyzed for contemporaneous religious, political, and geographical evidence from both canonical and agrarian religious sources that helps to contextualize St. George's emergence and evolution in the Near East.

The development of Christianity from Judaism

Exilic and post-Exilic Jewish communities from the second half of the first millennium BCE were spread around the Mediterranean basin, with centers in Jerusalem, Galilee, Babylon, and eventually Alexandria, Antioch, and Rome. A majority of those in Jewish communities lived in the Levant and among what we might think of as a diverse religious milieu. By the time of Jesus of Nazareth, the Jewish population centers in the Eastern Mediterranean – Jerusalem, Galilee, Antioch, Syria, and Alexandria – had

> been under 'Greek' influence for over 300 years, so one can with complete justification designate all Judaism of the first and second century after Christ as 'Hellenistic'; i.e., stamped in various ways by the transmission of Hellenistic civilization and by the conflict involved.[2]

Thus, after the fourth century BCE, Jewish communities had adopted some Greek practices and customs of 'Hellenism', while preserving various forms of 'Jewishness'.[3]

Roman political and military control over the region began in 63 BCE, after the Roman general Pompey took over control of Jerusalem. Caesarea became the capital of the Roman province Judaea from 6 to 41 CE, when local governance was entrusted to the non-Jewish Idumaeans of the region, which served to aggravate tensions that had existed since the time of the mid-second-century 'Maccabean' revolts.[4] As Roman political control grew during the last half of the first century BCE, even sharper distinctions between 'Jewish' identity and practice were provoked.

By the time of the birth of Jesus of Nazareth, and certainly by the time of the Roman-Jewish wars of 70 CE, there were many divisions within 'Judaism', including major groups known as Sadducees, Pharisees, Essenes, Zealots, and Sicarians. Connected generally through their uses of the books of the Hebrew Bible, and, in various ways, through beliefs, practices, and ethnic communities, Jewish communities of the first century CE used a variety of languages in religious practice, including Hebrew, Aramaic, and Greek, depending upon the group.[5] What we now consider the religion of 'Judaism' was thus neither defined nor unified during the first century CE. Jewish communities, moreover, existed within and among the mixed religious impulses of the day, at the time when a subset of one of those Jewish communities began to adopt particular practices and beliefs in remembrance of a contentious rabbi from the region of Galilee.

The earliest Jewish followers of Jesus of Nazareth did not distinguish themselves from most Jews of the day. The career and teachings of Jesus of Nazareth had harmonized with a messianic religious and political current long evident in Jewish thought since the internal upheavals initiated by the fourth century BCE Macedonian conquests. The earliest followers of Jesus primarily had in him hopes of messianic deliverance, rather than those of religious reform. Martin Hengel argues that the conflict between the messianic Jewish movement and the majority Jewish groups of the first century CE who did not join this movement involved disputes not over the central religious concerns of Judaism (theological belief, hope, and practice), but "the relation between messianic redemption and the traditional validity of the Temple and Torah."[6]

The primary religious setting for the earliest followers of Jesus was thus the various forms of Judaism of the day. As such, it is important to recall that early 'Christians' largely were indistinguishable as a Jewish sect during the first century CE. In Acts 24:5, during the description of the trial of Paul, Tertullus, the rhetorical prosecutor from Jerusalem chosen by the high priest Ananias, spoke of the Jewish "sect/heresy of the Nazarenes," "τε τῆς τῶν Ναζωραίων αἵρέσεος"; 'Nazarenes' being an appellation derived from Jesus' origin in the town of Nazareth. Even contemporaneous first-century CE Roman historians such as Pliny the Younger and Publius Tacitus referred to the beliefs of early Christians as a "*superstito*" which had begun in Judaea, thus indicating the movement's Jewish origins.[7]

Indeed, many scholars argue that, because of the "overwhelmingly Jewish substratum in the earliest Christian texts," and the fact that a vast majority of New Testament authors were Jewish Christians, most of the books of the Christian New Testament should be considered among the most important sources for *Judaism* of the first century, along with, of course, the writings of Josephus, Philo, the Qumran Library, and the early rabbinic tradition.[8]

Gradually, however, this group did come to see itself as something different from a majority of Jews of the day. "Without separating itself from 'Judaism', either by form of worship or by creed, this community would nonetheless adopt certain new practices, reported by Acts 2:42 and 4:32, including rituals, communal meal, prayers, and communal living."[9]

As early as the first century CE, there were, in at least some places, such as the early community in Antioch (Acts 11:26), Christians who called themselves as such and who were recognizable as not-Jews. At this early date, and even into the fourth century CE, it is not possible to speak of "Christianity and Judaism as fully formed, bounded, and separate entities and identities," but it does seem that there were "at least some Christians who were not Jews, and, of course, many Jews who were not Christians."[10] Indeed, Daniel Boyarin cogently argues that the processes of Christian distinction of 'Christianity' as something that was *not* Judaism, as evidenced in the aims of heresiological writers beginning in the second century CE, created both Christianity, and, to an extent, Judaism.

Boyarin's thesis is that Christian heresiologists, beginning in the mid-second century and lasting throughout the ante-Nicene period – and, in response, their Jewish counterparts, the rabbis of the Tannaitic period – "named [one another] 'Judaizers' or '*minīm*', respectively, and attempted to declare their beliefs and practices, their very identities, as out of bounds."[11] As a result, the diverging beliefs and practices of groups of Jews and Christians of the second and third centuries became transformed into the 'religions' of Judaism and Christianity through discourses of orthodoxy and heresy, and that is a perspective as well that is adopted in this project.[12]

A secondary component of Boyarin's argument about the discursive formation of Christianity and Judaism, however, is that while Christianity was created as a 'religion' through this distinction process, Judaism was not. In Boyarin's view, Christianity became a 'religion' consisting of beliefs and practices, defined by Orthodoxy(ies), which one could choose to hold, whereas Judaism cannot be considered a 'religion' in the same manner, because the rabbinical tradition ultimately determined that holding heterodox views in Judaism cannot make one an outsider.

While that theological formulation very well may be the case within Jewish community membership following the fifth–seventh centuries CE, the terms of Boyarin's argument that anticipate such a conclusion will not be adopted in this project. 'Judaism', as a tradition, may have been constructed in part through the heresiological dialogues of Christian and rabbinic writers of the second, third, and fourth centuries CE, but Boyarin presumes that Jewish beliefs and practices did not *themselves* emerge during the first millennium BCE from earlier religious frameworks in the Levant; namely, frameworks that were Israelite, Canaanite, Ancient Near Eastern, Egyptian, Sinaitic/Arabian, and, latterly, Hellenistic in orientation, as we saw in Chapters Three and Four.

Boyarin describes Judaism of the first century CE as an 'ethnicity', or 'cultural tradition' which was associated with a specific locality and related to itself in a 'fleshly' manner, but Boyarin perhaps begins his analysis of the construction of Judaism and Jewish identity at too late a date. As we have seen in Chapter Four, Israelite – and thus Jewish – religious identity and practices themselves were partly constructed through the discourses that surrounded the creation, compellation, redaction, and editing of the Hebrew Bible.

An orthodoxy/heresy text of the highest order, the Hebrew Bible demonstrates that Israelite religious identity was neither given, nor ethnic, nor associated with only one place, nor genetic, but, within an environment of variegated religious practices, came into being in contradistinction to practices and peoples that authors constructed, within the text, as heretical. As Jewish communities of the post-Exilic, Persian, and Hellenistic eras continued the production and maintenance of the Hebrew scriptures, and simultaneously reaffirmed their identities around these scriptures and associated practices, one could perhaps share Boyarin's assessments of the nature of 'Judaism' by the time of the first centuries CE. However, the perspective within this project is that "Jewish" religion, identity, and practices came into being in significant part through the heresiological discourses of the Hebrew Bible, and that Christian and rabbinic heresiological writings of the second and third centuries CE distinguished between and thus began to construct Christianity as a separate 'religion' from Judaism, and simultaneously to articulate Judaism in a different way; i.e., in contradistinction to Christianity.

General religion in the Levant during the first centuries of the Common Era

Most people of the region in this era – indeed, during most eras before the modern period, as was argued in Chapter Two – were in general less religiously distinct from one another than we tend today to presume or to project upon them. Accounts from the first centuries of the Common Era and throughout the first millennium evince less sharp-cut religious identities among people, and more indistinction and overlap.[13]

A vast majority of peoples living in the first several centuries of the Common Era seem to have been less concerned with orthodoxy or orthopraxy, and more interested in which gods and practices were effective. Within the Levant there existed a religious mix of various forms of Judaism, various forms of Christianity, Greek and Eastern mystery cults, magic, astrology, polytheisms, stories of divine men ('θείοι ἄνδρες') and their miraculous deeds, and popular Hellenic philosophy, amid much more.[14]

Most people of the time seem to have been fluent in a kind of "religious Koine," a common religious language of the period, to use Martin Hengel's term.[15] Beliefs and practices that accompanied the average person throughout the day, not just on special festivals or anniversaries, involved the more peripheral, 'unofficial' parts of religion: magic and superstition. Canonical religion, on the other hand, was separate and often accompanied by official shrines and representatives, but "a most important characteristic, shared by both the official and the unofficial, was the considerable degree of homogeneity of belief that developed over time, at least among the urbanized population."[16]

One account of religious conversion dating from the first third of the fourth century CE, around the time of Constantine, demonstrates the high degree of intermingling of beliefs to be found. It involved a conversion account of a prominent Jew named Josephus from Tiberias and Scythopolis in the Roman province of Syria-Palaestina (Judaea). The account is memorable because it

> shows the intermingling in the cities that was so noteworthy: non-Christian festivals are attended by people of every religious persuasion, quite openly, while on the other hand non-Christians are aware of Christianity especially as a healing power, and may invoke it on that account. The selection also contains material on magic, especially as it was practiced among the Jews.[17]

Thus, while this chapter, and the book, more generally, refers to communities and identities that are 'Jewish', 'Christian', 'Polytheistic', etc., it will be understood throughout that religious categorization was blurred rather than rigid for most laypeople in the region, for most periods in history, up to the 20th century CE.[18]

Zeus/Jupiter

Zeus (and Jupiter), whom we have seen in preceding chapters, was by far the most frequently revered religious god or figure in the Levant during the Greek and Roman eras. According to frequency of mentions in Latin and Greek epigraphic inscriptions, Zeus, among Greeks, and Jupiter, among Romans, both considered the supreme deity, were invoked at least 2.5 times as often as any other deity.[19] Since the time of the first Greek settlements in the region, Zeus also had been associated with – and likely was partly derived from – the figure of the storm-god.[20] Thus it is that cults and shrines to Zeus-Baal, or to Zeus-Hadad, or to simply to Zeus or Jupiter of a particular locale in the Levant, came to subsume Baal worship in the region and to remain popular and even dominant throughout the first centuries of the Common Era. Sometimes, cults simply to Baal remained, known from the Roman writer Marcus Minucius Felix's list of gods and goddesses: Felix listed "Ba'al" as the god "among the Chaldeans" as late as the second to third century CE.[21]

One shrine dedicated to "Zeus Baetocaece" (in Syria) lasted for some 500 years, from ca. 293–261 BCE to 260 CE, and an altar in Dura-Europos, dating to the early third century CE, was found inscribed in Greek and dedicated "To the ancestral God, Zeus Betylos, of those by the Orontes [River], Diphilanos, soldier of the Legion IV Scythica Antoniniana, has offered [this altar] in fulfillment of a prayer."[22]

Earlier Canaanite beliefs about Baal-Hadad remained a part of local Greek and Roman cults to Zeus and to Jupiter. Ramsay MacMullen argues that the kind of worship that changed 'labels' was "in fact very little changed from their form as it had been before Greek or Roman conquest."[23] Fergus Millar, on the other hand, contends that it is difficult to say whether

> rural temples [and altars] built in classical forms, whose known worshippers used Greek when they put up inscriptions, did or did not embody older local traditions and forms of belief… [however] it must nonetheless be significant that such hypothetical older traditions could now be expressed in Greek forms.[24]

Indeed, this book argues that such longevity of 'expression' reflects continuing regional needs and beliefs.

Languages

Because Aramaic was the language of administration associated with the Persian Empire and with the era of Persian political domination over much of the Near East (ca. 550–332 BCE), Aramaic gradually became the common language of the general population throughout the Levant. After Alexander, Greek also became a language used in commerce and by the Greek and erudite populations; thus, many among the regional population learned to understand Greek.[25] Some Jewish communities also began to read the scriptures of the Hebrew Bible in Greek, while others continued to read them in Hebrew. The Letters of Paul and all of the Gospels in the New Testament were written in Greek, thus indicating the degree of contemporaneous Hellenistic intercultural diffusion.[26] Into the first centuries of the Common Era, Latin also became a language in use in the region, and Syriac, a first-century CE Syrian dialect of Aramaic, "was the only language which emerged [from the region] for the first time in this period, developed as a vehicle for literature, both pagan and Christian, and has remained a Christian language to this day."[27]

The rise of Christianity and development of the New Testament

Early Christian communities

As we saw above, the earliest 'Christians' did not separate from Jewish worship or practice, but they did begin to distinguish themselves by adopting certain new practices and rituals (Acts 2:42 and 4:32). An early Christian community began to develop in Jerusalem following the crucifixion of Jesus of Nazareth, but that community was curtailed when Jerusalem fell to the Roman army in 70 CE. With the loss of the community at Jerusalem, the growing Christian community at Antioch became preeminent in the region.

Early Christian communities met at house churches at least once per week; in the beginning, on the Sabbath, but eventually on Sunday. The liturgy presented at these meetings was like that of the synagogue, including prayer, reading of scriptures, a sermon, chants, but also with invocations of the 'Holy Spirit'. These assemblies would conclude with a common meal, including ceremonies of breaking bread and blessing the cup, similar to the events recounted of the Last Supper. Little by little, eucharistic theology developed, including these elements and those outlined in the *Didache*, 'Teaching', a text composed at the end of the first century CE in Syria that addressed ethics, rituals, such as baptism and a eucharistic meal, and church organization.[28]

Over the course of approximately the second through fourth centuries CE in the region, Christianity touched all social classes. The last group of elite Romans, both polytheistic and Christian, was born in the late fourth century CE into a "world in which most people believed that the pagan religious order of the past few millennia would continue indefinitely."[29] Indeed, the world of the fourth century CE was "full of gods, temples, churches, and synagogues, whether fully functioning, recycled, looted, vandalized, or abandoned."[30] As late as the late fourth century CE, long after the council at Nicaea, elite polytheistic Romans remained "oblivious to the establishment by Constantine's sons of the formal Christian domination of what was becoming a formally Christian empire."[31]

Development of the Christian New Testament

The 27 books of the Christian New Testament detail the life and ministry of Jesus the 'Christ', as well as the teachings of Christianity (through the letters of Paul to early churches), and the history of the apostolic followers of Jesus. A final book, Revelation, consists of a series of apocalyptic prophesies involving the ultimate success of Christianity, the return and final battles involving Jesus, and the renewal of the cosmos – heaven and earth – with the heavenly Jerusalem descending to that new earth.[32] Like the books that comprise the Hebrew Bible canon (not established until the first centuries of the Common Era), it took several centuries (and many omissions) to establish the 'canon' of the 27 books of the Christian Bible.

Early Christian communities gathered in house churches to read the scriptures, but different communities used different scriptures.[33] As early as the time of Eusebius (ca. 263–339 CE), it was clear that debates over the canon had not been resolved, as they would remain, even within proto-orthodox circles, some 200 years after the last of the books of the New Testament had been produced. Eusebius categorized a list of books that were 'recognized', 'disputed', and 'spurious'.[34]

Eusebius' list, and its ambiguities, continued in practice after him. The most famous of the lists of accepted New Testament canonical scriptures, and that which became the standard among most subsequent Christian communities, was that of Athanasius, Bishop of Alexandria, in his 39th Festal Letter from Alexandria in 367 CE.[35] In it, Athanasius listed the 27 books of the Christian scriptures that usually are considered canonical today. Athanasius probably was also the first to use the term canon κανών for reference to a closed body of sacred scripture. Even so,

> there was never a time in either the fourth or fifth centuries when the whole church adopted as scripture all the 27 books of the NT and those books alone… many Christians continued in practice to reject parts of the greater church's canon long after there was a general recognition of it.[36]

Christianity, as we have seen, did not 'triumph' after the Council of Nicaea, which is a common but erroneous way of characterizing Christian history. Rather, the growth of multiple Christian communities and orthodoxies was gradual, not given. As late as the sixth century CE, the polytheistic population of the Levant remained numerous.[37]

Martyrs and martyrdom in Christianity

The Roman Empire was overall quite tolerant in matters of religion, as any large empire must be. Multiple religious groups and orientations existed relatively freely alongside Roman state religion. Until the middle of the third century CE, persecutions against Christians and Jews remained sporadic, and it was often the lifestyle of Christians that invited official hostility. From a Roman state perspective, Christians were not objectionable because of their beliefs and practices, but because of their claims that some gods were false, for which Christians often were called 'atheists'.[38]

A first well-documented persecution targeted Christians at Bithynia in Asia Minor in 112 CE. From the authorities' point of view, these persecutions could be explained because Christians "refused to render to the [Roman state] gods, to whom the Empire supposedly owed its prosperity."[39] Pliny the Younger, then-governor of the Province, wrote to Emperor Trajan about his concerns over Trajan's actions toward the Christians at Bithynia, and their correspondence established a sort of effective jurisprudence that would be applied in the legal actions against Christians until the time of Emperor Decius in 250 CE. The general practice was to condemn Christians who identified themselves as such – and, usually, only the clergy: bishops, priests, and deacons – but not to prosecute them unless they officially were denounced by non-anonymous accusers. Also, they commonly pardoned those who ultimately agreed to sacrifice to the gods.[40]

Various martyrdoms took place during the second and third centuries, throughout Asia Minor, in Alexandria, and in Syria-Palestine. These, however, were sporadic, limited in nature, and seemed to follow the legal framework established in the Pliny-Trajan correspondence. Under Emperor Decius (249–251 CE), the persecution of Christians took a new turn, because, in that case, prosecution was instigated by imperial edict. The edict, requiring all inhabitants of the empire to express their piety or devotion to the gods by participating in a sacrifice and praying for the salvation of the empire, was intended to induce a public demonstration of loyalty, and was not at first directed primarily against Christians. Persecution of Christians became the reality during this campaign, however, causing dread and creating numerous martyrs among the Christian communities of the empire.

The most memorable – and final – persecution of Christians was undertaken by the Emperor Diocletian in 303 CE. It outlined the destruction of churches and scriptures, and the forfeiture of all honorary titular posts and privileges of upper-class Christians, the imprisonment of heads of churches, and the compulsion, upon pain of physical threat, for all to make a sacrifice. In the eastern part of the Empire (i.e., the Eastern Mediterranean), the persecution was particularly violent and long-lasting; most Christian 'martyrs' were created during this campaign of persecutions. Constantine's Toleration Edict in March 313 CE put an end to official Roman persecution of the Christian population, and, although various additional 'martyrdoms' of Christians took place thereafter, it was not in an official Roman capacity.

The experience of martyrdom, however, had left its mark upon Christianity: imitation of the suffering and death of Jesus already had informed Christian perspectives, and was reinforced – and reenacted – by a long and visceral history of martyrdom among Christians.[41] Furthermore, in many cases, martyrdom bolstered the Christian community: not all Christians were targeted or had to be martyred in order to benefit from the prestige and notoriety of martyrdom, and martyrdom provided a kind of authenticity of religious belief which proved attractive to many converts: many observers were persuaded by the veracity of a faith for which one was willing to die. Finally, martyrdom left another enduring legacy among the Christian world: sainthood. While early 'saints' in Christianity came from many venues, by far the most common and established path to sainthood and to the veneration of one's earthly remains was martyrdom.[42] Along with the legacy of martyrdom, the religious and political background of the rise of Christianity in the Eastern Mediterranean formed the environment in which the figure St. George the μεγαλομάρτυρ 'great martyr' arose in the early fourth century CE.

Introduction to St. George and his cult

The fantastical and beloved figure of St. George is often placed into a category of saints termed 'Byzantine warrior saints'. These figures, as the name indicates, were saints who originated in the eastern part of the Roman Empire, and who also were warriors. This category of saint was first investigated by Hippolyte Delehaye in 1909 in *Les légendes grecques des saints militaires*. George, the 'exemplar' warrior saint, was classified by Delehaye in the category of *état-major*, or major warrior saints. Along with Ss. Theodore Tiron/Theodore Stratelates, Demetrius, Procopius, and Mercurius, St. George long was considered preeminent among the major warrior saints, and his cult remains outstanding even until this day.[43]

The term 'warrior saints', however, originates much earlier than Delehaye's investigation. This category of saints was said to have been executed, for refusing to renounce their Christian faith, during the third and early-fourth-centuries CE – especially during the final campaign of imperial persecutions (ca. 303–313 CE).[44] 'Warrior saints' or 'martial saints', however, hardly were distinguishable from general martyrs. For that reason, it is important that St. George be understood both in the context of 'warrior saints', and from within the general category of martyrs, whose basic characteristics he shared.

The essential characteristic of a martyr was his or her witness of faith and perseverance unto death; accordingly, Eusebius began to popularize the term "athlete" "ἄθλητής" to this act of endurance.[45] The *Acts* of martyrs, including that of the warrior saint, George, belong to the realm of epic hagiographical literature.[46]

A second characteristic of saints – one of the more compelling, in terms of cult generation and promulgation – was that of the intercessory power attributed to saints for the benefit the living. This doctrine, which developed alongside a contemporaneous cult of relics, was formulated by Origen (d. 254 CE), who anchored this belief in a passage from II Maccabees (15:11–16). As the practice of invoking saints as intercessors grew (certainly, this type of belief had contemporary parallels and antecedents among other religious communities) the Christian doctrine of intercession became more fully developed by Gregory of Nyssa (d. 394) in his *Encomium* of Saint Theodore Tiron. "Saints were believed to be able to perform all sorts of services for men," and "the office of warrior saints would become more particularly that of protection against the inroads of demons and human enemies."[47]

Despite the dearth of historical evidence for the person of St. George – indeed, this lack of evidence has been cited throughout history by those who began, as early as the sixth century CE, to claim St. George as a spurious saint – 'George' undeniably became a popular figure, with an enormously influential cult, from an early date.

Etymological origins of the name 'George'

George's name is another of his interesting aspects, and one that ties his cult closely both to nature and to the figure of the storm-god. The name George, 'Γεωργιός' (georgios), comes from the Greek word 'γεωργός' (georgós), meaning farmer, or, more precisely, one who cultivated the land. Γεωργός, 'farmer', is composed of two parts: 'γε', meaning 'earth', and 'εργον', meaning work, labor, or toil. Thus, the name Γεωργιός is related to γεωργια (georgia), agriculture. While there are ample references to γεωργοι (georgoi) 'farmers' throughout Greek and Latin literature, γεωργός was not used in early literature as a proper name, but only as the noun for a category of person who cultivated the land.[48] The proper name Γεωργιός, 'George', began to emerge in the Common Era, as can be seen in Aelios Herodianos' third-century CE list of theophoric names, including: "Georgios, Demetrios, and Ammonios ...."[49] When the Greek suffix *-ιος* is added to a noun, it creates the meaning of 'pertaining to', 'belonging to', or indicates an origin. 'Demetrios' is thus a Greek male name meaning 'belonging to/devoted to Demeter', the Greek goddess of grain, while 'Ammonios' meant 'belonging to/devoted to Ammon', the Greek form of the popular Egyptian deity 'Amun'. 'Georgios' in this list perhaps meant 'belonging to/devoted to Zeus Georgos'; that is, to 'Ζεύς Γεωργός', the well-attested Athenian god of farmland and crops,[50] and about whom we will see more below. While the proper name Γεωργιός, 'George', emerged in the third century CE, it only became a widespread given name during the fifth and sixth centuries CE, once it had become popularized by the Christian cult to the saint 'George'.[51]

Oftentimes the name of a saint corresponded not to their 'original' proper name, but to their function or mission. For instance, the name 'Peter' from St. Peter ("Simon Peter") comes from the Greek word for rock, 'πέτρα' '*pétra*'. In Matthew 16:18, Jesus is reported to have said, "κἀγὼ δέ σοι λέγω ὅτι σὺ εἶ Πέτρος, καὶ ἐπὶ ταύτῃ τῇ πέτρᾳ οἰκοδομήσω μου τὴν ἐκκλησίαν...". "I say to you that you are Peter ('Πέτρος'), and upon this rock ('πέτρᾳ'), I will build my church... ."[52]

Another example of this phenomenon, in a slightly different formulation, comes from St. Lucy. The English name 'Lucy' is derived from the Latin name 'Lucia'. 'Lucia', as a proper name, shares a Latin root, *lucis*, with the word for light, 'lux'. Both 'Lucia' and 'lux' are related to the verb *lūcēre*, 'to be visible'. Lucia was reported to have been martyred in 304 CE in Syracuse as a result of Emperor Diocletian's final campaign, and later medieval accounts of her legend began to recount that 'Lucy's' eyes also were gouged out as a torture prior to her death. Accordingly, St. Lucy became during the medieval era a saint of 'vision', perhaps due to medieval creative word-association with her name. Lucy often was depicted in later iconography as holding her eyes, and she remains known as the patron saint of the blind or those with vision problems.

St. 'George', Γεωργιός, thus may have been the name given to the cult of the figure who was venerated by agricultural communities. Such explanation certainly aligns with the agricultural traits for which George also is known, such as his associations with fertility, fecundity, and rain. Likewise, St. 'George', Γεωργός could have been the name given to the *Christian* saint 'George' – in what may have been a Christianized version of a local Levantine cult already dedicated to 'Zeus Georgos', "Zeus the Farmer/land cultivator."[53] Hasan Haddad argued that,

> One can surmise that, in urban centers such as Antioch, it was applied to the Baal or Zeus worshipped in the shrines of the countryside by the peasantry, possibly called *Zeus Georgeus* or *Belus Georgeus* ... This Baal or Zeus of the country folks is almost certain to be the origin of St. George.

Allaire Stallsmith noted that "Greek Epithets also expressed the deity's local connection, whether geographical or genealogical, and the aspect of his personality or function manifested in a particular cult. ... Cult inscriptions employ such functional titles as Zeus *Georgos* (Farmer) or Ge *Kourotrophos* (Nurse) to make it clear what role the deity is filling in a particular ritual situation.[54] In "New Inscriptions from Lividia" (a town in central Greece), Jean Jannoray likewise observed that the role and function of 'Zeus Georgos' was one "presid[ing] over the eternal cycle of the vegetal world, where life constantly follows death."[55]

The title 'Zeus Georgos' is attested not only in Eastern Mediterranean textual sources, but also in archaeological remains. In a study of excavations of sixth-century BCE – second-century CE votive offerings from the Sanctuary of Demeter and Kore on Acrocorinth (upper Corinth), names of 'sacrificial cakes' include "*ναστός* (nastos): a cone-shaped cake with raisins, almonds, and honey sauce inside, offered to Zeus Georgos and Men."[56]

The first centuries of the Common Era are replete with examples of Greek and Roman Gods who became transformed into *saints* in the Christian tradition. Other late-third- to early-fourth-century 'Byzantine warrior saints' cults, such as to Ss. 'Demetrius', and 'Mercurius', likely at least partly came into being when contemporaneous cults to the gods Demeter and Mercury (/Greek: Hermes), respectively, began to wane, and cults to the Christian martyrs began to rise. Hans Kloft argues that after the cult of Demeter began to diminish during the fourth century CE, the rites and roles of the goddess gradually were transferred, at least in part, onto the figure and cult of 'St. Demetrius'.[57]

Γεωργός 'Georgos' – later, Γεωργιός, 'George' – functioned as a saint for 'farmer' and agricultural communities, and the motifs with which he earliest was associated – even in text – were – rain, greenness, fertility, fecundity, lightning, a feast day of April 23, and, especially, the defeat of a serpent or dragon. All of these data points together suggest that the very early cult of St. George was quite likely to have originated in – or at least overlapped with, or perhaps offered an alternative to – local cults to Zeus-Baal or Zeus-Georgos, and later to have been defined, in an explanatory Christian capacity, by the extraordinary accounts of the martyr-warrior, St. George.

The cult of St. George

Most hagiographers have based their arguments about the authenticity of St. George not upon any historical evidence for "George's" life, of which there is none for an historical person, but upon the ample evidence of his cult, which can be dated in terms of architectural remains to the early sixth century CE.

The earliest-recorded and longest-continuing sanctuary to St. George was located at Lydda (Diospolis) in Palestine (modern-day Lod, Israel), and built around his purported remains. In about 530 CE, the pilgrim Theodosius wrote "In Diospolim, ubi sanctus Georgius martyrizatus est; ibi et corpus eius est et multa miracula fiunt," "In Diospolis, where the martyr Saint George is; there his body is and many miracles are worked."[58] In this early period, as we will see, George was not quite as popular, regionally, as was St. Theodore Tiron/Theodore Stratelates, although the cult of St. George had spread rapidly to Constantinople, where at least nine churches were dedicated to him.

In addition to the sanctuary at Lydda, there also was a church outside of Jerusalem that was dedicated to St. George and may have been constructed as early as the late fourth century CE.[59] The Porta San Sebastiano in Rome was put under the protection of St. George by Belisarius in 527 CE, and George's ubiquitous relics reached as far west as southern France, where Gregory of Tours (538–594 CE) possessed one as well.[60] There also was a Byzantine church dedicated in the early sixth century CE to St. George at Madaba, Jordan.[61] Finally, a church at Ezra (Zorava) in Syria dating from 514 to 515 CE and apparently still in use during the 19th century CE, was, founded, according to its inscription, upon relics of St. George, who "appeared to [the church's patron] not in sleep but in reality." Built apparently upon the site of a destroyed pagan temple, which were of course still common in Syria in the sixth century CE, the beginning of its inscription – a fitting tribute, as we will see, to St. George – reads,

> A house of God has replaced the dwelling of demons. The light of salvation has shone in a place which darkness previously covered. Where sacrifices were made to idols, there now are choirs of angels. Where God was provoked, now God is appeased.[62]

The several fantastical stories which surround the *Acts* of St. George, as we will see, have multiple sources of influence, some of which can be identified. Like the genre of hagiographical literature in general, the *Acts* are less accounts of history than they are, of course, arguments made to valorize martyrdom and Christian theologies. The *Acts* of 'St. George' describes his origin as a Roman citizen of material wealth and military importance from Cappadocia, and states that, during the terrifying persecutions of the emperor 'Dadianus' (later authors refer instead to Diocletian ca. 284–305 CE), George presented himself willingly to testify to his belief in the Christian god and to be martyred, in order to oppose the false gods of the Emperor, and to convince others to believe in the Christian god.

Part Two: Saint George text: *Acts of Saint George*

History of the text

The *Acts of St. George* originally was written in Greek in the early fifth century CE, and may have originated in the region of Cappadocia in Asia Minor under a milieu of various influences; among them, Persian, Greek, and Christian.[63]

The oldest form of the fifth-century CE Greek text survives today in fragments, which are preserved in Vienna.[64] The Syriac version of the *Acts* was translated from the Greek version in around the middle of the fifth century CE, a few decades after the original Greek manuscript was composed.[65] The oldest surviving mostly complete copy of the *Acts*, and that which will be used in this project, is a Syriac manuscript, written around the year 600 CE. It is preserved at the British Library, Add. 17205, and written in the Estrangelo script of Syriac, the earliest Syriac liturgical script.[66]

This Syriac manuscript, Brit. Mus. Add. 17205, is missing ½ a leaf at the beginning, 2 leaves after folio (f.) 26, nine or ten leaves after f. 27, and a leaf after f. 28. F. 23–26 are torn at the top, and f. 28 is torn at the bottom.[67] The English translation used here, unless otherwise indicated, is rephrased from E. W. Brooks' 1925 publication.[68] Brooks supplied the content from the leaves missing in Add. 17205 with that from an 11th-century Syriac Sertā-script manuscript, Brit. Mus. Add. 14734, which preserved substantially the same text of the earlier Syriac version, Add. 17205.[69]

Summary of the text

The appended summary has been broken into arbitrary episodes that are inspired by the headings from Kiraz' text, but which are not original either to the Syriac text or to Brooks' translation. The text below is faithful to Brooks' 1925 translation (or, where indicated, my own).

> **Introduction**
> In the power of our Lord Jesus Christ we begin to write the martyrdom of the illustrious George and of Antonius the General and of Alexandra the Queen who were martyred and crowned (their prayer be with us. Amen!)
>
> **King Dadianus**
> When the churches of Christ were standing, winter storms were roused by the kings in every country, and with threats they seized the preachers of truth, and brought them to worship fiends, and forced them to sacrifice. At that time Satan instigated the king of the Persians whose name was Dadianus (and he had four evil counsellors his associates); and, having seated himself upon his judgement-seat (βῆμα), he wrote letters running thus. "Since a report has reached us, and has penetrated to our ears that the peoples are worshipping him whom Mary bore, and not worshipping Apollo and Heracles, but him whom the Jews scourged with rods and fastened to a tree, therefore I have written to your high mightinesses, in order that we may stamp out the thing that has happened." When the letters had been sent to all the kings in all the world, many kings and peoples set out and came to him, so that even his capital city was not large enough to hold them.
>
> On the next day the king seated himself upon his judgement-seat, and ordered all the instruments of torture to be set before them, frying-pans

and bronze cauldrons and sharp points, and elaborate fetters, and irons, and instruments to cut out tongues, and forcipes to pull out teeth, and hooks to bend the neck, and spits with tortures of every kind. And, when they had brought them before him, the asp-serpent Dadianus the king began to say: "If so be I find rebellious men who are acting contrary to the worship of the gods, I will destroy the towers of their bodies, and strip off the skin of their heads, and extract their brain while they are alive, and tear out the pupils of their eyes, and cut away their feet from their anklebones, and saw asunder the soles of their feet, and extract their bowels, and what remains I will throw to the dogs." And, while everyone was standing in astonishment, then those who were intending to be martyred greatly trembled and shrank at the sight of the tortures (for everyone was anxiously thinking to remove from himself the burden of the pains), so that for three months none dared to say "I am a Christian," except

George confronts Dadianus

this minister[/servant] of righteousness whose light shone between the height and the depth, who came from a Cappadocian family, and served in his rank as a tribune (τριβοῦνος) and, when he had finished his time of service in that rank, after amassing much gold, betook himself to Dadianus the king in order to serve as a count (κόμης). And, when he saw that Christ was being insulted and demons were being praised before him, he distributed all that he possessed, gold or silver, and gave it to the poor and needy; and, having stripped himself of his clothes, he stood before he king, crying and saying "I am a Christian, but your threats, king, are idle, and name not those who are gods; but let gods who did not make heaven and earth perish from the earth [Jer. X, 11]. For I worship one true God, with his Son and his Holy Spirit, one Trinity and one Godhead without division." The king looked at him and said to him, "You have deceived[/insulted] me, proud George, haste therefore to entreat the gods, who know how to forgive an offense in those that transgress. Come up therefore and sacrifice to them; and know that Apollo stretched out the heavens and Heracles laid the foundations of the earth, and Serapion and Posidon they it was who restrained the sea that it should not pass its limit. But Christ of whom you speak the Jews scourged with rods, and hung upon a tree. But who made any of the things that are seen?" Looking at him [George], Magnetius the general (στρα τηλάτης) said to him: "From what city do you come, and whence came you hither, and what is your name?" The blessed man said to him: "As to my first name, I am a Christian. But, if you inquire as among men, I am called George (γεωργός)." After these things the king said to him: "Come up and sacrifice, lest you die an evil death." George answered and said to him: "Get thee behind me, Satan. Thou art an offense to me." [Matt 16:23].

Dadianus Tortures George

Then the king ordered him to be hung on a piece of wood and scraped. And, when the king saw that his limbs had been loosened and his blood was running down upon the ground, he ordered them to take him down and thrown him on his belly. And he ordered a wheel to be made like a saw, and long nails to be fixed to it like meat-forks, and that there should be wedges at its sides, and spits around it like a catapult (?). This resolved, and the structure of it was completed like the work of a craftsman; above it looked like a sword and below it shone like knives. And he ordered them to place the saint on top of the wheel. When the blessed man came to that place, and saw the wheel prepared, he thought to himself, and was seized with a great trembling saying, "I shall never escape from these inflictions." And again he repented in his mind, and said "Why, my soul, have you had these thoughts? Consider the lot that has come to you, and know that Christ your Lord was hanged between two robbers." Then the vigorous combatant (ἀθλητής) ran with joy and mounted the wheel, saying: "Christ, in thy hands I place my self" [Luke 23:46]. And he was cruelly caught among the teeth of the wheel, and among the spits, and his limbs were cut into ten pieces. And Dadianus the king lifted up his voice, and the king of Egypt, and king Traquillinus, with Magnetius the general, saying, "You know, peoples, that there are no other gods besides Apollo and Heracles and among females great is Artemis the goddess of the Ephesians [Acts 19:34]. Where then is George's god whom the Jews tortured? Wherefore did he not come and rescue his friend from my hands?" Then the king ordered them to throw the blessed man into an unused pit; and they placed a great stone over the mouth of the pit. Now it was suppertime and at the tenth hour there was great fear, so that the mountains were shaken; and darkness was spread over the earth and a cloud of fire, and the likeness of a chariot of fire; and our Lord Jesus appeared above the chariot, and suddenly a company of angels by the mouth of the pit. And our Lord said to Gabriel: "To thee I say, angel of my covenant (διαθήκη), go down into this pit and bring up thence for me my bondman George; because he said 'I shall not escape from these tortures', that they many confess me and believe that I am the God of Abraham and of Isaac and of Israel." And, when he came up from the pit, our Lord took him by the hand, and said to him: "This is the hand that fashioned the first man". That it is which resuscitated thee." And he breathed into his face and filled him with the Holy Spirit. And our Savior gave him a greeting and said to him: "Go and put Dadianus the king and all the kings his fellows to shame, and utter thereupon a cry of praise." And our Lord ascended to heaven and all his angels.

George confronts Dadianus again

Then the blessed George went and sought for the kings and found them in the idols' house. And he stood before the king, and said to him: Know you me, king Dadianus? The king looked at him and said to him "Who are you?" The blessed man said to him: "I for my part am George who was cut on the wheel. Wherefore did you insult Christ and say 'He cannot save you from my hands? Lo! You see that it was he who brought me to life from among the dead." And the king looked at him and said "It is himself." Magnetius said "It is very like him." The saint said: "I myself am in truth George whom you shut in the pit." And Antoninus the general on seeing that George had come to life and risen from among the dead believed on God himself and all his troops (τάξις). And, when king Dadianus saw that many people had believed on God, the king ordered them to be put to death in a desert place outside the city; and they divided them into ten companies; and they completed their martyrdom with a good confession. But as to the holy George the king ordered him to go to prison, 'until I consider how to destroy him and make havoc of his fair boyhood'. Then Satan put it into the king's heart, and he made an iron shoe, and put it on the saint's feet, and nailed them inside it; and the nails, because they were long, penetrated and extended above the soles of his feet, and the blood was flowing cruelly; and, since he was unable to bear the shoe, he entered the city at a slow walk. But the impious man when he saw him laughed and said to him: "What is it, George? Why are you not running? Recognize the lot that has fallen to you." Then the blessed man said: "'Why art thou agitated, my soul' [Ps 42:6] and why art thou grieved? Know that Christ thy Lord was stretched upon a tree." And again the blessed man prayed and said: "Lord my God, leave me not nor depart from me." And the same hour Michael the archangel appeared to him carrying some dew in his closed hand and sprinkling it on his feet; and suffered no more from the pains. And, having come and stood before the king: "Tell me the names of your gods since you said to me that Apollo stretched out the heaven, and Heracles planted the earth firmly, and Athena diffused the sunlight; but they made none of the things that are seen. Know therefore that it is not the gods who made creation, but they are futile images. But I have many sheep to choose from this flock, and to bring into the fold of our Lord and our God [John 10:16]. But, since you have told me the names of your gods, I also will tell you the names of the just men. Tell me, King; which seems to you the worthier by comparison, Simon the chief of apostles, or Posidon the chief of brigands (ληστής)? Samuel the chosen prophet, or Actaeon the madman? Moses who led the people forty years, and gave manna to the children of Israel, or N q ṭ ['Antaeus'] and Heracles the profligates? Tell me which of these you choose, the sagacity of the martyrs and the love of the confessors, or the striving of the possessed persons or the hostility of the priests? Mary who gave birth to God in our manhood, or Jezebel the slayer of God's prophets? [1 Kings 18:4; M has 'Artemis the slayer of her lover'.] But I see that your gods are mad persons [DMV has 'demons'] in whom there is no profit." Then the unjust king ordered him to be beaten with thongs; and the blessed man was beaten until all his body was torn to pieces.

Magnetius asks for a miracle

But, after he had been beaten, Magnetius said to him: "I ask a sign of you. If you show it to me, I will believe on your God. Lo! There are here fourteen kings' seats, and each seat has in it planks of wood, some of fruit-bearing trees, and some of trees that do not bear fruit. If you pray and they are broken up again, and those that are of trees that do not bear fruit bloom and stand up without fruit, and those that are of fruit-bearing trees give fruit, I will believe on your God." The blessed George says to him: "Not for your sake will I do this, but for the sake of the bystanders I will pray before God." And he knelt and prayed so that the air (ἀήρ) was disturbed and the earth trembled, and there was a great terror, and terrific lightnings appeared on the earth, and upon the fourteen seats; and the planks were broken up and the trees took root; and those that were fruit-trees showed themselves with fruit, and those that were without fruit showed themselves without fruit. And, when king Dadianus saw it, he said: "Great art though, god Apollo, who showest thy power even in dry wood. Nay, by my lord the sun and the seventy-two gods, you shall not escape from my hands, O George." And he ordered that he should go to prison 'until I contrive of a method of putting him to death'.

Traquillinus asks for a second miracle

King Traquillinus says to him: I also wish to ask George for a certain sign. And they sent and he fetched him from the prison and set him before him. And the king said to him: "We have here a coffin hewn out of rock, and the age of the persons buried in it no man knows. If then your prayer is heard, pray that these corpses may rise, and we will believe on your God." George says to them: "Bring these bones up for me here." And, when the king had gone and opened that coffin, and they found no bone solid in it, since they had become dust from the lapse of time, George says to them, "Collect that dust and bring it here." And the blessed man, having taken that dust, set it before the Lord; and he looked to heaven and prayed and said: "Lord All-holder, who are not dissolved [DMV "passest not away and"], clad in victory, eternal Light, Lord of all, to thee I call, Maker, Good Hope Jesus Christ King of kings, grant me this request that I may show the devisers of evil things Dadianus the king and the seventy kings who are with him that thou only the Lord God, who weighedst the mountains in a scale, and settest the weight of the hills in a balance, and driedst the Sea of Papyrus [Sc. The Red Sea], which men could not dam, and formedst created things by thy nod, and madest the ages by thy grace, now also, Lord, look on thy people, and on the flock of thine inheritance, which thou redeemedst through thy beloved Son our Lord Jesus Christ, suffer it not to be scattered by the hands of unjust men, because thou carest for all thy created things for ever and ever Amen and Amen!" And, when he had finished his prayer and said 'Amen!', there was a violent disturbance of the air (ἀήρ), and flashes of terrific lightning were seen, and shone upon the whole of the place in which that dust lay, and souls of men and of women and of children rose, two hundred bodies. And, when the king and his associates saw the thing that had happened, and that which had actually been done, then one of the kings called to one of those who had risen from among the dead, and asked him and said to him: "What is your name?" And he that had been resuscitated said to him: "Yubla." The king says to him: "How long is it that you have been dead?" Yubla says: Two hundred years more or less we have been in *Sheol*." The king says to him: "Did you worship Christ, or Apollo?" Yubla says to him: "We for our part did not know Christ, but worshipped idols. And when we died angels carried and brought us to a river of fire, and there we were till today, so that not even on the first day of the week had we relaxation, because we had not been wont to observe the first day with the fear of the living God." Then afterwards those who had been resuscitated looked at the holy George, and cried with a loud voice and said to him: "We beseech you, sir, bondman of our Lord Jesus Christ, have mercy upon us, since we were lying in great misery. Give us the mark of our Lord Jesus Christ, since we were resuscitated through your prayers and came up out of that bitter distress; and now, sir, help our souls and give us the mark of our Lord's baptism, that we may not again see that burning abyss." The blessed man, seeing that they had believed with their whole heart, asked for water, and no one gave it him; and he struck that place with his foot; and much water came out from it; and he baptized them in the name of the Father and the Son and the Holy Spirit. And, when he has finished his prayer, he said to them: "In the name of our Lord Jesus Christ you go to the Paradise of God." And no one saw them again from that hour. Then king Dadianus said to his fellow-kings: "Did I not tell you that this man is a sorcerer? And he has raised an appearance of fiends before us, saying 'I have raised the dead'. But for my part I know how I will put an end to this race (γένος) of Galilaeans."

George and the widow

And he commanded the ministers of iniquity, "Seek for me a poor widow woman, and confine this man in her house, in order to disgrace him, that he may be a laughing-stock to those who know him, and to those who love him, when he is imprisoned there, until I devise a method of putting him to death." And, when the illustrious man had gone to that widow's dwelling, he said to her: "Give me bread to eat since I am hungry." That woman says to him: "I have no bread in my house." The holy George says to her: "Of what religion are you?" She says to him: "Of that of Apollo." The blessed man answered and said to her: "That is why you have no bread in your house." Then that woman formed in her heart the plan of going out to one of her neighbors and asking for bread and setting it before this man. And, when she had gone out to ask, the illustrious George stood up in prayer, and leaned upon a pillar that was in the house, and at the same moment the tree brought forth and produced leaves and branches, and it rose to a height of fifteen cubits above the roof. And Michael appeared to him, giving him food from heaven; and he ate, and refreshed himself and became joyful. And, when that woman came to her house, and saw that that tree had sent forth shoots and sprouted, and the table covered with delicacies, she fell down before the saint's feet from her fear crying and saying: "The God of the Christians has come to me in the body." But the holy George took hold of her and raised her up and said to her: "Rise, woman, I am not the God of the Christians as you think, but I am a bondman of Jesus Christ." That woman says to him: "Sir, if I have found favor in your eyes [Gen. 18:3], let your handmaid speak before you. Lo! There is a boy in my house who is deaf and blind and withered. If then, sir, my son is healed by your prayer, I also will believe on your God." The blessed man says to her, "Bring him here to me." And, when she had brought him to him, he said, "Boy, our Lord Jesus Christ heal thee." And he breathed into his face, and there fell from his eyes as it were scales [Acts 9:18]; and the same hour he saw. His mother says: "Sir, let him hear with his ears and walk with his feet." The saint says to her: "Keep him for me till I shall call him for the work that will be required by me; and he shall hear with his ears and walk with his feet and come to me, and he shall to me a minister of speech." And that woman was silent and dared not answer him another word, because his face (πρόσωπον) was bright like the sun [Acts 6:15; CDMV 'as of an angel'; common description of interaction with the divine in the ANE world].

St. George is asked to sacrifice to the gods

And the next day king Dadianus rose up and the seventy kings who were with him, and they saw that that tree where George was lodging had grown and was looking out fifteen cubits above the roof; and they all marveled, and they say: "The Galilean lodged there." And then he sent after him and brought him to the palace. And, when he came, he was singing and saying: "Thou, Lord, be not far from me. *El, El,* remain for my help" [Ps 22:20]. And, when he came in before the king, Magnetius said to Dadianus the king: "This race (γένος) of Christians is stubborn. Let us rather cajole this man by blandishment, and by soft words, that he may come to do our will and that he may recognize what is right." And the king began to entreat the saint and say to him: "By the sun our god and the victory of all the gods, if you listen to me, George, I will give you much property and make you second in my kingdom. Come up therefore and sacrifice; and after my death I will make you sit on my throne, putting on the crown of my kingdom." The saint says to him: "Now you have spoken well. But wherefore said you not these things to me before? For now, you have been torturing me seven years; and where shall I go and seek the ill usage of all this time?" The king says to the saint: "Forgive me this offense; since I am as your father; and know that you shall surely reign after me." The illustrious man says to him: "Where are your gods? I will sacrifice to them." When the king heard this announcement, he rejoiced with very great joy; and he ordered a crier to go up and stand in a high place, and cry and say: "Come near and see the Galilean initiate, who lo! Today will come to the sacrifice of the gods." But, when that widow woman heard the voice of the crier, she suddenly picked up her son, and ran to the illustrious man crying with a loud voice saying: "O George, who gave to the blind the power of seeing and to the lame also the power of walking, and cleanse the lepers and cast out demons, and heal the sick, are you even now coming to sacrifice to the vain Apollo?" but, the holy George looked at her, and she trembled with a great trembling and he said to her: "Put your son down out of your arms." And, when she had put her son down, the blessed man said to him: "Rise, boy, and come to me, and you shall be to me a minister of speech." And the same hour he rose and ran to him and made obeisance to him. The saint says to him before all the people: "To you I say, boy, go into this temple (ναός) and say to Apollo: 'Come out at once for the bondman of our Lord Jesus Christ is standing outside and waiting for you." And, when that boy came into the temple, he said to that idol: "To you I say, dumb idol and vain chattel, come out thence quickly for the bondman of God Most High is standing outside and waiting for you." And the demon who lived in that image cried and said thus: "Out upon thee, Nazarene, since thou hast drawn all men to thee, and hast now sent thy bondman George against me." The blessed many says to that demon: "Are you the god of the pagans?"; the demon who lived in that image cried and said to him: The god of the pagans I am not, but one of the captains of the hosts of the enemy." The holy George says: "Wherefore lead you man astray from the fear of the living God?" That demon said: "By the hell of fire that is prepared for me, if I had been able, I would have ruined you also, and would have led you astray and not spared." George, says to him: "Come see your place"; and he struck the ground with his foot, and a great chasm was laid bare; and the holy George said to him: "Foul demon, go down into this abyss, until the day of your torment." And he sealed that place, and it was not known. And he ran and went to into the temple and overthrew the idols of Zeus and Heracles; and he cried with a loud voice and said: "Away with you, dead idols, for I indeed am the bondman of Jesus Christ who is God over all" [the actual destruction of the idols is omitted]. When the priests of sin saw what the illustrious man had done, they arrested him and put him in bonds and brought him before the king: and they told the king what he had done to their gods. And the king said: "Did you not promise me to sacrifice to Apollo?"; the illustrious man says: "To me gods who deceive are no gods. Bring them to me here; and by the boast of the Christians I will not leave one of them till the evening that I will not break to pieces." The king says: "Did you not promise me to sacrifice to Apollo?" George says a second time: "Bring them to me here; and I for my part will sacrifice to them before you." The king says: "I for my part heard that you buried them in the abyss of Sheol alive; and now wherefore do you wheedle me?" And, when the king saw that he was mocking him, he ordered that he should go to prison 'till I consider by what death to put an end to him'.

Queen Alexandra

And, when the king came into his palace, he repeated to the queen all that he had done in prison. And the queen said to him: "O king, keep your hands off the bondman of the living God, and let him go where he wishes." The king says to her: "Be not deceived, queen Alexandra, nor be enticed into the error of the Christians; since they will not be able to escape from my hands until they worship my gods." The queen says: "Foul-smelling man and shedder of blood, most unrighteous of all man, if you seek to eat blood and flesh, receive your portion with that of your father Satan." Then the king ordered that she should be hanged on the wood and they should scrape her. But she while being scraped looked to heaven and said: "Have mercy on me, my Lord, because I sinned against thee, the hope of the Christians." And the king ordered George to come. And when he came and the queen saw him, she cried and said: "O combatant (ἀθλητής) of Christ, give me the mark of baptism, that I too may enter Christ's mansion." George says to her: "Fear not, queen Alexandra, nor be afraid in the matter of baptism; for you may be baptized and cleaned in your blood." Then again the abominable man ordered them to take the blessed woman down from the stake, and flog her with new cords until her flesh should be torn by the flowing of her blood.

The next day the king sat on his judgement-seat and wrote in the book of the kingdom thus. "Hear me, kings of the earth, and multitude of people who surround me. Alexandra the queen, who deserted the gods and believed on him whom the Jews crucified in Jerusalem [rest of sentence missing]. Hear therefore, all ye kings, because I am innocent of her blood." The same hour the abominable man commanded, and her sentence (ἀπόφασις) was given. And, while they were bringing the blessed woman out of her palace, and she was going along the street to be crowned for Christ's sake, she stood in the midst of the road, and cried with a loud voice and said: "Our Lord Jesus Christ, see that I am now leaving my palace for thy name's sake, and I did not shut my doors; and thou also, my Lord, shut not the door in the face of thine handmaid." And she bowed her neck and was crowned [martyred], in the month of Nisan [April] on the eighth of it (may her memory be for a blessing Amen!).

The martyrdom of St. George

After these things the king called George and said to him: "Lo! You led the queen also astray, to destroy her out of this life. But now know that I will not endure your sorcery; but now also I grant your own petition [/sentence]." And the king lifted up his voice before all the peoples and said: "As for George the Christian initiate who would not sacrifice to Apollo, after all these tortures, I give a sentence (ἀπόφασις) against him of death. Know therefore, all ye kings, that this man chose death for himself; who for the long space of seven years refused to sacrifice to the gods. But from this time I give order that he be beheaded by the sword, and fear be aroused so that no man commit any presumptuous act against the gods." And, while they were holding the saint, the king ordered that he should go outside the city to the place where Alexandra the queen was crowned. Then the saint requested those who were leading him and said: "I pray you, my brethren, give me a little space to pray to God, for whose sake I am being sacrificed today, and to ask grace of him for myself, and for all sinners who are like me." These Romans say to him: "Pray as you wish." Then the blessed man looked to heaven; and he knelt and said thus: "Lord God, hear me because many are standing and seeking to take my body, and my body and bones are not sufficient for all the world, Lord God, grant me this petition that whoever shall be in torture or in fear or have a terrifying dream and remember my name shall have what is good, and evil hateful visions shall depart from him. Lord God, grant to my name and to my bones that everyone who shall be engaged in a dangerous lawsuit and remembers me shall come out of his suit without danger and without harm. Lord my God, grant me this favor, that when clouds are gathered together and men remember me in that country there shall not be there burning heat or hail. Lord God, bestow on me this favor that, whoever shall make mention of George or make an oblation and remember the day of his contest (ἀγών), there shall not be in his house one that is leprous, nor shall a stammerer and a blind man be born in it, nor one that is palsied and one that is blind, nor one that is driven by a demon; and mention not their sins, because thou art a merciful God, and remember that they are flesh and blood and have mercy on them for my name's sake." And the Lord spoke with him from a cloud, saying to him: "Come now, George, good and strenuous soldier [2 Tim 2:3], to the paradise of rest. Come rest from thy labor in the country of delights. But as to the favor that you asked of me, by myself I swear to thee that everyone who shall be in much distress and remembers my name and thine shall be delivered from all his distresses, and I will not mention their sins; for I am a God of the penitent." And, after the voice that spoke with him ceased, the holy George prayed again, and said: "Our Lord Jesus Christ, King of all the ages, send the fire which thou sentest in the days of Elijah the prophet, and it devoured the captain of fifty and the fifty who were with him, and let it devour the kings who believed not in the signs which they saw done through me." And the same hour lightning came down from heaven like fire, and devoured the seventy kings, and not one of them escaped. But the blessed man looked to heaven, and made the seal of Christ on his face, and he was crowned by the sword, making a good confession. And in that same great contest (ἀγών) many perished, men and women without number from the terror of the lightning; and everyone believed in the living God. And the illustrious George the bondman of Christ was crowned on the twenty-third of the month of Nisan [April], on the preparation at the seventh hour.

Ending

And I Pasicrates, a bondman of the same Mar George, was attached to my lord, and wrote all these things from beginning to end.

The martyrdom of the illustrious George and those with him who were martyred and crowned in the days of Dadianus the king is ended. Glory to the Father and to the Son and to the Holy Spirit, now and always, forever and ever. Amen!

Textual analysis: Competitive religious environment

Mixed religious milieu

The *Acts* depicts the mixed religious context of the day. We see the presence of Christians, Roman state polytheism, and even sorcery and magic: King Dadianus refers to George as a "sorcerer" in both the Magnetius episode and in the episode of George's final martyrdom. Through King Dadianus' derisory tone, it is clear that sorcery and magic are considered false, but also that 'sorcerers' who could produce magical feats were a part of the paradigm of the day.

Roman state polytheism

State polytheism was a dominant religious tradition within the Roman Empire and was based upon the concept that a multitude of gods ruled over the celestial and meteorological phenomena, and over the human realm. As such, these gods needed to be recognized and honored through the regular act of sacrifice. From the statements in the text of King Dadianus, we see that the god Apollo was the sun god who "stretched out the heavens," and Heracles "laid the foundations of the earth," and Serapion and Posidon "restrained the sea such that it should not pass its limit." In addition to Apollo and Heracles, against whom, says King Dadianus in the first episode where he tortured George, no other gods can compare, "among females [gods] great is Artemis the goddess of the Ephesians."

We learn furthermore that the gods were worshipped in temple(s) (ναός), and that these gods demanded regular indebted acknowledgment in the form of sacrifice. However, as we saw in Dadianus' speech in the initial episode where George confronted Dadianus, the gods would forgive a person for the transgression of ignoring the duty to sacrifice, provided that that person eventually made amends through a sacrificial offering.

Roman views of Christianity

Through this glimpse into Roman state polytheism in the text, we can also see reflected in the text contemporaneous Roman views of Christianity. In the Traquillinus Miracle episode and in the section where George is asked to sacrifice to the gods, we see that Romans referred to Christians of the day as a "race (γένος) of Galilaeans," reiterating the contention that Christians were a sect originally from Judaea and underscoring their Jewish origins.

Second, we learn from an analysis of this text that Roman state perspective derided Christian beliefs as absurd. Rather than worshipping the gods, who were plainly worthy because of their celestial power to have "made the things that are seen," the Christians worshipped a god who, in Christians' own estimation, was born of a human woman, "Mary," and whom the Jews – a nearly powerless people within the empire – had "scourged with rods and hung upon a tree."

Imperial Christianity: Trinitarianism and the biblical tradition

We see also in the text a reflection of the author's(s') contemporaneous Christianity, one that was colored by the debates of the day and which espoused a perspective that could be called post-Nicene. Two main strands of Christian thought, involving the nature of God and the biblical tradition of Christians, are evident here.

Trinitarianism

Within this text, the Christian god is clearly identified as the same god of the biblical (Hebrew) Scriptures. In the section where George feigned acquiescence in sacrificing to the gods, he referenced Psalm 22:20 as he cried, "Thou, Lord, be not far from me, *El*, *El*, remain for my help." Jesus in the first confrontation episode called Gabriel the "angel of *my covenant*" (διαθήκη) and declared that George's brave actions would convince people to "confess me and believe that I am the God of Abraham and of Isaac and of Israel"; i.e., the biblical God.

However, in a manner quite different from that described of God in the Hebrew Scriptures, God in the Christian conception revealed by this narrative is Trinitarian in nature. George declared to King Dadianus upon presenting himself that he worshipped "one true God, with his Son and his Holy Spirit, one Trinity and one Godhead without division." Jesus was furthermore referred to in the text as both "the living God," and God "in the flesh," which aligned with a contemporaneous Imperial Christian position regarding Jesus following the Council of Nicaea: Jesus was *homoousios*, (ὁμοούσιος) or "of the same being" with God the Father, and, thus, both fully human and fully divine.[70] In example, Jesus in the narrative later breathed into George's face the "Holy Spirit," in order to revive George, and thus demonstrating Jesus' combined divine and human natures in the person of Jesus.

Biblical tradition

In order to underscore religious positions in the narrative, or biblically to substantiate certain claims, the *Acts* employed several references to both the Hebrew Bible and New Testament texts. From the Hebrew Bible are references to Psalms 42:5 and 22:20, Jeremiah 10:11 and Genesis 18:3, and from the New Testament are references to Matthew 16:23, Luke 23:46, John 10:16, and Acts 9:18 and 6:15. This selection of texts from the New Testament aligns with the post-Athanasian composition of "accepted" scriptures and further situates the *Acts* within a particular period of time. Indeed, both the Christological and Trinitarian beliefs reflected in this text, as well as the frequent references to canonical Christian scriptures, contextualize this text within an Imperial Christian tradition post-fourth century CE.[71]

General themes

The overarching message of this text is that the god of the Christians is *God*. George performed several miracles in order to convince people of the power and veracity of the Christian god, including miraculously enduring excruciating tortures and performing astounding feats. All the miracles adhered to a clear theme: the Christian god is the true God, because he is the most powerful, controlling both life and death. The Christian god can bring the dead to life – thus recalling a Christian notion of resurrection – and can, likewise, destroy his enemies. Accordingly, beyond that central message, there are two others related, and which likewise recall the Elijah narrative from the Hebrew Bible: the worship of other gods leads to destruction, and worship of the Christian god leads to God's favor upon the believer.

The worship of other gods leads to destruction

The *Acts* presents other gods as not only false, but as idols and demons who intend to lead people astray. In the episode where George feigned sacrificing to the gods in order to confront the 'demon' inside of the Apollo idol, George demanded of him, "Wherefore lead you men astray from the fear of the living God?" "By the hell of fire that is prepared for me," replied the demon, "if I had been able, I would have ruined you also, and would have led you astray and not spared."

The destructive result of worshipping these 'demons' is on display in the episode where St. George revived two hundred people from a state of dust in the rock coffin: when George questioned Yubla, recently resuscitated from dust in the coffin, George asked Yubla, "Did you worship Christ, or Apollo?" and Yubla's answers was,

> We for our part did not known Christ, but worshipped idols. And when we died angels carried us and brought us to a river of fire, and there we were till today, so that not even on the first day of the week [i.e., Sunday, the Christian day of worship] had we relaxation, because we had not been wont to observe the first day with the with the fear of the living God.

Worship of the Christian god leads to God's favor on the believer

George was referred to as the "bondman," or servant, of the Christian god six times in the text. Thus, when we see George saved repeatedly or favored by God in some way, we understand the clear message: God favors those who confess that the Christian god *alone* is the true God. In the Queen Alexandra episode, this message was also clear. While Alexandra was being tortured, she cried, "Have mercy on me, my Lord, because I sinned against thee, the hope of the Christians." In the next scene, when George arrived, she called to him, "O athlete (ἀθλητής) of Christ, give me the mark of baptism, that I too may enter Christ's mansion." George replied," Fear not, queen Alexandra, nor be afraid in the matter of baptism; for you may be baptized and cleaned in your blood." Just before being martyred, Alexandra called aloud, "Our Lord Jesus Christ, see that I am now leaving my palace for thy name's sake, and I did not shut my doors; and thou also, my Lord, shut not the door in the face of thine handmaid." In response, the text tells us, Alexandra received from the Christian god the crown of martyrdom.

Alexandra's anxiety around baptism, as well as that of Yubla, the resuscitated man from among the rock-coffin dead, further demonstrate that receiving the Christian ritual of baptism – and, thus, indicating the supremacy of the Christian god – resulted in everlasting life in God's favor. Afterlife in God's favor was described as "the country of delights," and the extreme opposite of "the burning abyss" that, Yubla declared, was the fate of all those who do not possess "the mark of our Lord's baptism."

A final means by which, in the text, worship of the Christian god lead to favor upon the believer, was through the intercession of Christian saints. In Pasicrates' introduction to the George narrative, he declared, "In the power of our Lord Jesus Christ we begin to write the martyrdom of the illustrious George and of Antoninus the General and of Alexandra the Queen who were martyred and crowned (*their prayer be with us*. Amen!)." George verified this power just before his own final martyrdom, in his lengthy prayer and request to God that all those who remember, mention, or make an oblation to George shall be free from torture, fear, terrifying dreams, dangerous lawsuits, heat, hail, physical ailments, demons, and even their own sins. Thus, when one recalls the Christian saints, one will be rewarded by the Christian god.

King Dadianus as serpent and April 23: Motifs related to the storm-god

King Dadianus as serpent

St. George, as we will see, was well known for the valorous act of vanquishing a dragon. In the extant iconography, however, George seems not to have been associated with this motif before the sixth century CE. In the *Acts*, the earliest text associated with George, we also do not read an account of George vanquishing a dragon. However, an interesting parallel component in the narrative is located early on. King Dadianus was introduced in the text as George's chief opponent: a bloodthirsty tyrant who was responsible, along with Satan, for a cruel campaign of torture upon Christians. Referred to as "the asp-serpent Dadianus the king," Dadianus threatened explicit tortures upon those "rebellious men who are acting contrary to the worship of the gods." This call challenged George, who confronted and ultimately defeated Dadianus.

In the Syriac version of the *Acts*, the word translated as 'asp-serpent' 'ܚܘܘܐ', 'ḥewwā', most nearly means 'serpent or 'snake'. Later tenth-century CE Greek versions provide there 'δράκων',[72] 'dragon', and thus it seems that the terms 'serpent', 'snake', and 'dragon' had conceptual overlap between Greek and Syriac, just as the Ugaritic and Hebrew terms '*ltn*' 'snake', and '*tnn*', 'dragon', had had conceptual overlap in the registers of the Baal Cycle and in the Hebrew Bible.[73]

In the *Acts*, we thus witness an allegorical slaying of the 'dragon' or 'serpent', when George, the *Acts*' protagonist, ultimately defeats the antagonist King Dadianus. In naming Dadianus as the 'asp-serpent', the author(s) of the *Acts* explicitly employed a popular regional motif earlier associated with the storm-gods Baal-Hadad and Zeus.

April 23

Moreover, the *Acts* recounts that St. George "was crowned [i.e., martyred] on the twenty-third of the month of Nisan [April]." This established George's feast day, as Christian saints were and are celebrated on the day they had been martyred. Perhaps as a consequence both of this detail in the *Acts*, and of existing 'Georgic' cultic practice – it is, of course, impossible to say – April 23 eventually became the feast day of St. George in both the Eastern and Western Church calendars. The date of April 23 is itself related to regional agriculture. Known as the start of summer all over the Near East,

> Peasants consider their fruit trees safe from frost after that date. Tradition has it that snakes do not appear until the coming of St. George's Day. Horses and cattle are sent out to pasture about the same time. ... April 23 was considered an official day for summertime activities by government circles of the Ottoman Empire. On that dated some civil or military operations were carried out. The squadron that sailed to cruise the Aegean Sea started on that day; so was the departure of the horses of the imperial stables to the grazing grounds.[74]

As we saw above, in Chapter Three, Seleucus Nicator, successor to Alexander, in 300 BCE founded the city of Seleucia-in-Pieria near Antioch by making a sacrifice to Zeus-Kasios, on Mt. Kasios, on April 23.[75] This account comes to us from John Malalas, an Antiochene historian who lived long after the event described, during the first part of the sixth century, CE. Malalas was writing about earlier Greek events that first had been recorded by the Roman historian Tacitus, during the first century, CE, and Malalas apparently supplied the date of April 23. Whatever the historical veracity of Malalas' details about Seleucus' earlier sacrifice, what we can actually tell from Malalas' account and the *Acts*, together, is that, by the sixth century CE in the region, April 23 evidently had become a date associated not only with regional agriculture, but with both the storm-god Zeus, and with the cult of St. George, as well.

Whether the motifs of defeating a serpent or dragon, and the date of April 23, were employed in the *Acts* because they would resonate as 'powerful' motifs among wider culture, or because elements of the 'George' cult already had been associated, by the date of the text, with the local cults of Zeus – the application in the *Acts* of the serpent/dragon motif and that of April 23 helps us better to understand the ways in which the cult of St. George developed. In particular, the intentional inclusion of these elements helps us to see how the cult of St. George developed in explicit congruity with important aspects of the local cults to the storm-god.

Queen Alexandra

Tales about St. George also became later associated with the narrative of George saving a princess from the dragon.[76] In those narratives, St. George saved a princess – sometimes named 'Alexandra' – and this heroic act either inspired her father the king to convert his entire kingdom to Christianity, and/or George married the princess.[77] In the text of the *Acts*, Alexandra, who was the wife of King Dadianus, was not physically saved by St. George, but was instead inspired by George's example and mission to convert to Christianity and face martyrdom herself.[78] This may represent a spiritual "saving," but it was the same rescue enjoyed by the General Antoninus, who does not appear in later versions of the George narrative.

George's contest was not between religions, but between gods

George, we see clearly in the text, is the 'bondman' or servant/slave of Christ. In the service of Christ, George promotes the true God of the Christians in the face of the false polytheistic or 'pagan' gods. Indeed, George's mission is intended to convince people that only the Lord God Jesus Christ is God. When they are convinced, as we see in several of the episodes, it leads people to believe.

It is important to note that, throughout the narrative, people are led to "believe" or to "confess" that George's god – the god of the Christians – was the true god, and not that the 'tenets of Christianity' were correct above those of all others. Thus we see that this was a contest not between conceptions of 'religions', but between gods. The king asked Yubla, "Did you worship Christ, or Apollo?" And when George spoke with the widow, he asked her "Of what religion are you?" and her answer was "of that of Apollo." Among other potential observations, this indicates that contemporary peoples characterized their 'religious' identity in terms of which God they followed, rather than which 'religion' they followed.[79] It also reflects a contemporaneous historical reality; one in which the tenets of Christianity(ies) were still in the process of being constructed.

Certainly, throughout at least the first six centuries of the Common Era, the bulky theological apparatus of Christian doctrines, theologies, and rituals, variously defined, were still coming into being. Later Christians would come to identify themselves more with particular sectarian theologies[80] than they would by which 'god' they followed, but at the time when the *Acts* was written and the time to which it referred, Christian religious identification was different – and related to its own historical religious environment – involving a contest between multiple gods.

Themes regarding St. George

Who was St. George?

George in the *Acts* came from a Cappadocian family, served as a tribune in the army of Emperor Diocletian, was wealthy, fair, and young. After seeing "Christ being insulted, and demons being praised before him," George distributed his earthly belongings to others – communalism being a common practice among early Christians – and readily announced himself as a Christian to King Dadianus, despite the physical tortures to which he would be subjected and of which he was frightened. George's identity as a Christian, which, as we have seen, aligned with an Imperial or Nicene position, was strongly colored by his declaration that he was the 'bondman' of Christ; the second person of the Godhead.

Upon being questioned by King Dadianus about his identity, George replied, "As to my first name, I am a Christian. But, if you inquire as among men, I am called George (γεωργός)." This reply is interesting, as the author of the *Acts* seems to convey the idea that the man/martyr himself was an undifferentiated 'Christian' martyr. However, if one were to inquire "as among men," he was known, among them, as "Georgos." This detail in the *Acts* may further be evidence that 'George's' name functioned less as a given name than that it was associated with a figure with an agricultural cult – either a new agricultural cult, or one that already had been established, as in the case of cults to Zeus-Georgos.

Furthermore, we learn in this text that George *can eradicate demons*. In the episode where George pretended to sacrifice to the gods, George "struck the ground with his foot, and a great chasm was laid bare; and the holy George said to [the demon who inhabited the Apollo icon]: 'Foul demon, go down into this abyss, until the day of your torment'. And [then George] sealed the place, and it was not known." Moreover, we learn in George's final petition to God before martyrdom that prayer to George can protect one from demons. "Lord God," prayed George,

> bestow on me this favor that, whoever shall make mention of George or make an oblation and remember this day of his contest (ἀγών), there shall not be in his house one that is leprous, nor shall a stammerer and a blind man be born into it, no one that is palsied and one that is blind, nor one that is driven by a demon.

These attributes of George in the text indicate not only that George had the ability to eradicate demons, but also that there was a contemporaneous overlap between the concepts of illness and physical maladies and 'being driven by a demon', as we saw above in Chapter Two, "Levantine Agrarian Religion."[81]

Finally, we learn in the *Acts* that, because of the miracles God worked through George, George exhibited some traits of divine contact, himself. In the widow episode, after George's prayer had healed her son, George appeared to her with a "face (πρόσωπον) bright like sun."[82] This type of description in the ancient Near East and within the biblical tradition was common for identifying those who had had contact with the divine.[83] In Exodus 34, after Moses spoke with and received the Commandments from Yahweh on Mt. Sinai, the skin of Moses' face was described as having "shone" so brightly that Moses was forced to veil his face before others (Exod 34:35).[84]

In defense of the True *God: a Christian conception of God*

The mission of Elijah in the Hebrew Bible was defiant opposition to Baal worship in defense of the true God, Yahweh. Similarly, the mission of St. George in the *Acts* was a religious contest against the false gods of the Roman Empire and in defense of the true God, Jesus Christ. As we have seen, the earliest followers of Jesus were Jews, although a separate 'Christian' identity, built around the nature of Jesus Christ, gradually began to emerge from within and among these followers. Similarly, the Christian conception of God seems to have widened the nature of God as represented by the Hebrew scriptural tradition. Indeed, by the time of the *Acts*, Jesus was considered by Christians not only to have been a man from Judaea, but to be the second person of the Godhead and God's embodied 'son' – and, at the same time, the same as the God of the Hebrew Bible.[85] Whatever the apparent Christian widening or clarification of the nature of the God, George, in the *Acts*, clearly was depicted as defending the *true* God, just as Elijah had done before him in the Hebrew Bible account.

George is like Elijah

Additionally, in order patently to highlight George's association with Elijah, George was also purposely depicted as sharing several elements from Elijah's own narrative; namely, being engaged in an explicit religious contest, lodging with a widow, performing miracles for her involving sustenance, and healing that same widow's son.[86]

George engaged in a religious contest

In addition to the overarching context of the *Acts* as a religious contest narrative, George engaged in the text in several smaller direct contests, as well. Among them, in the episode where George confronted Dadianus for a second time, and after being relieved through the holy water of Michael the archangel of the pains of the iron shoes nailed to his feet, George posed the following confrontation to King Dadianus:

> Tell me, King: which seems to you the worthier by comparison, Simon the chief of apostles, or Posidon the chief of the brigands (ληστής)? Samuel the chosen prophet, or Actaeon the madman? Moses who led the people forty years, and gave manna to the children of Israel, N q ṭ ['Antaeus'] and Heracles the profligates? Tell me which of these you choose, the sagacity of the martyrs and the love of the confessors, or the striving of the possessed persons or the hostility of the priests? Mary who gave birth to God in our manhood, or Jezebel the slayer of God's prophets?[87] But I see that your gods are mad persons[88] in whom there is no profit.

In this way, among other examples, George was presented, like Elijah, as being involved in a direct confrontation and religious contest. Whereas Elijah's direct religious contest occurred in the Hebrew Bible account on Mt. Carmel (1 Kings 18), the *Acts* depicted George as engaged in several direct contests, such as in the episode of his challenge to and defeat of the 'demon' in the Apollo icon.

Lodged with a widow and performing miracles

George was also portrayed as very similar to Elijah in having been forced to lodge with a widow. In the *Acts*, Dadianus devised lodging with a lowly widow to humiliate George, but, like Elijah, George used this awkward social situation as a way to increase the value of his miracles performed there.[89] As had Elijah in his narrative, George first asked the woman for bread. When she replied that she had none and George learned that she was "of the [religion] of Apollo," George replied, "That is why you have no bread in your house." This is also like the Elijah narrative, in that the woman in Elijah narrative had no flour as a result of the famine that had been caused by Yahweh (through Elijah) in punishment for Baal worship in the north, which was the location of her town.

The woman in the George narrative then left to get George bread from a neighbor's house, and George produced two miracles: first, by simply leaning against it, he turned a pillar in the house into a living tree that sprang leaves and branches fifteen cubits (approx. 22.5 feet) above the widow's house. Second, Michael the archangel appeared to George and gave him "food from heaven" (cf. the ravens and the angel Gabriel feeding Elijah 'food from heaven'), which refreshed George and made him happy. When the widow returned to her home and saw the huge living tree and the table covered with delicacies, she fell before the saint in fear and exclaimed, "The God of the Christians has come to me in the body." George replied that he was "not the God of the Christians as you think, but I am a bondman (/servant) of Jesus Christ."

Healing the widow's son

The woman then begged George to heal her son, who was deaf, blind, and withered. If George could do that, she said, in return, "I also will believe on [sic] your God." George invoked the "Lord Jesus Christ to heal thee," breathed into the boy's face, and he was cured of blindness. Later in the narrative, George caused the boy to hear and to walk, even to the extent that the boy became to George a "minister of speech." Like the widow in the Elijah narrative, who, after Elijah had revived her son from death, had proclaimed that Elijah was indeed a "man of God, and the word of YHWH in your mouth is true" (1 Kings 17:23), the widow in George's *Acts* was moved to believe in the veracity of the Christian god after her own son miraculously was healed.

George can call fire/lightning from the sky

Finally, George can call down lightning from the sky which causes miraculous things, much as Elijah was described in the Books of Kings. George's prayers brought lightning which struck the fourteen wooden seats and caused them to become living trees again, and his lightning resurrected 200 people who had turned to dust in the rock coffin. Thus, we learn that George's God (and, by extension, George himself) has the power of life, whether agricultural or human.

In the final scene, George called down fire from heaven to devour the 70 kings, and to cause thereby "everyone to believe in the living God." George prayed,

> Our Lord Jesus Christ, King of all the ages, send the fire which thou sent in the days of Elijah the prophet, and it devoured the captain of fifty and the fifty who were with him [2 Kings 1: 9–10], and let it devour the kings who believed not in the signs which they saw done through me.' And the same hour lightning came down from heaven like fire, and devoured the seventy kings, and not one of them escaped.

Thus, we learn that George's god – and, by extension, even George himself, like Elijah – also has the power of death.

Political themes

Roman religious campaign against Christians

The text contains several references to its contemporary political environment. The context of the narrative is plainly a religious campaign on the part of the Roman state undertaken against Christians in the empire. The account closed with the line, "The martyrdom of the illustrious George and those with him who were martyred and crowned in the days of Dadianus the king is ended."[90] As we saw above, two explicit campaigns against the Christians in general – not simply targeting the clergy or the prosperity of the Roman state – took place in the third and fourth centuries, under the emperors Decius (r. 249–251 CE) and Diocletian (r. 284–305 CE). Of the two, Diocletian's was the longer, and most sources date George's purported martyrdom to the early fourth century, during Diocletian's campaign against the Christians.[91] The *Acts* names this king "Dadianus," and suggests that he was the king of the Persians, although later versions of the *Acts* record the name of the persecuting king as Diocletian.[92]

Imperial persecution was a threat to the Christian community

We see also from this text that contemporaneous Christians were afraid for their community's survival, reminding us that while we know the outcome of the persecutions and of Constantine's Toleration Edict just a few short years later, the perspective of contemporary Christians – and even of the *Acts* itself – was that the Christian community might indeed be 'stamped out', as 'Satan' suggested in the opening of the narrative. During the miracle episode when St. George revived the bodies of those in the rock coffin, George prayed to God to complete the miracle of their resurrection. "Lord, look on thy people, and on the flock of thine inheritance, which thou redeemedst through thy beloved Son our Lord Jesus Christ, *suffer it not to be scattered by the hands of unjust men…*"

Christian valorization of the martyrdom experience

Because torture was a potential experience for Christians, we also see in the text a message of valorization of martyrdom and praise for martyrs. Thus, George and Queen Alexandra both vocalize their fear of torture, and George inspires himself by recalling several times the tortures endured by Jesus. Martyrs in the text were referred to as 'athletes' or 'combatants' (ἀθλητής), and their brutal contest (ἀγών) led to the 'crown' of martyrdom.

Christians acted in defiance of Roman law

The text demonstrates furthermore a Roman legal perspective on the punishments: Christians were choosing to refuse the order to sacrifice – willfully ignoring Roman law – and thus those Christians' punishment was not a form of persecution, but one of prosecution. Indeed, it was hoped that the gruesome deaths endured by martyrs might guide other Christians to the light. In the episode of George's final martyrdom, king Dadianus announced,

> As for George the Christian initiate who would not sacrifice to Apollo, after all these tortures, I give a sentence against him of death. Know therefore, all ye kings, that this man *chose* death for himself; who for the long space of seven years refused to sacrifice to the gods. But from this time I give order that he be beheaded by the sword, and fear be aroused so that no man commit any presumptuous act against the gods.

Indeed, in the episode where King Dadianus put Queen Alexandra to death, he announced to all, "Here therefore, all ye kings, because I am innocent of her blood." That is, Queen Alexandra was put to death because she chose to commit offenses against the gods, not because Dadianus himself persecuted her.

Geographical themes: Agricultural and meteorological phenomena

In the *Acts*, several of George's miracles have agricultural and meteorological aspects. In the miracle where George resuscitates the people from the rock coffin and is asked by them for baptism, George was refused his request for water, and so he struck his foot against the ground, and a spring gushed forth.[93]

George in the *Acts* furthermore regularly performed miracles that involved turning dead wood into living, flourishing trees. In the Magnetius episode, George's prayers called down lightning which struck the 14 king's seats and caused them to take root and grow into full trees – some fruit-bearing and some not, depending on which type of tree the wood had originally come from. In the Widow narrative, George's touch caused a pillar in the home to turn back into a living tree 15 cubits tall.

The *Acts* also included direct references to weather phenomena. The raging campaign against the Christians was described as a tempestuous winter storm, "When the Churches of Christ were standing, winter storms were roused by the kings in every country, and with threats they seized the preachers of truth, and brought them to worship fiends, and forced them to sacrifice." 'Severe winter storms' is a notable reference because it reflects the Eastern Mediterranean meteorological environment in which the *Acts* was composed.

The *Acts* moreover includes stormy theophanic imagery. Jesus Christ appeared and "there was a great fear, so that the mountains were shaken; and darkness was spread over the earth and a cloud of fire, and the likeness of a chariot of fire; and our Lord Jesus appeared above the chariot…." God in the final martyrdom episode, in response to George's last prayer, replied and spoke to George "from a cloud." Finally, George's prayer, the means by which he caused his miracles, created disturbances in the air, as well as earthquakes, and, of course, lightning. These references demonstrate a continuing regional understanding of God as associated with storms and meteorological imagery.

St. George text: Conclusion

George, in the *Acts*, was depicted as engaged in a contest much like that of Elijah from the Hebrew Bible: George represented the "true" god in face of the false Roman gods. Thus, the *Acts*, to a certain extent, is a heresiological text, in that it constructed categories of true and false gods, and that it did so at a time of competitive religious environment. Accordingly, the *Acts* also reflects a great deal about Roman state polytheism and about contemporaneous Christians regarding Christology, the nature of the Christian god, and the nature of Christian religious identity.

In performing similar miracles and being associated with specific narratives, such as with the widow and her son, George clearly was patterned for his audience on the Elijah narratives from the Hebrew Bible account. Elijah was at that time in the region a very popular biblical figure upon whom to draw for narratives and motifs regarding a contest between competing gods. In employing these similar motifs and narratives of Elijah, the author(s) of the *Acts* thus intended George to appear a good deal like Elijah, but during Roman and Christian context. At the same time, motifs such as defeating a dragon and the agricultural date of April 23 also were intentionally employed in the text, perhaps reflecting elements of an already-extant cult to 'George'. Accordingly, we see in the *Acts* the resonance of the biblical Elijah stories among regional religious communities at that time, as well as the resonance of regional dragon and agricultural motifs, both of which as now applied to a figure of Christian orientation.

Part Three: St. George icons

Antecedents and development of the St. George Icon tradition

Demons, in antiquity, were believed to be supernatural beings who could exercise their powers for the good or ill of humans, but who did so most often for evil purposes. In order to placate and/or repel demons, amulets, on which written characters and symbols were inscribed, could be worn or used by a human subject to thwart demons' evil intentions.[94] Apotropaic amulets, which we saw above, in Chapter Two, "Levantine agrarian religion," and which long existed throughout the Mediterranean, were condemned during the first centuries of the Common Era by Christian writers and councils. Canon 36 of the Council of Laodicea in the late fourth century decreed that Christian priests and clerics could not be "magicians, enchanters, or astrologers," and the contemporary *Apostolic Constitutions* refused admission to baptism to those who made amulets (περιάμμαατα).[95]

Despite that, communities of both Christians and Jews regularly used amulets, and eventually Christian amulets began officially to supplant 'pagan' amulets for use among the Christian community. Cappadocian Church Father Gregory Nazianzus wrote that the Trinity was "the great and good *phylacterion*" (amulet or charm as a safeguard against danger), and Gregory of Nyssa's sister Macrina wore an iron cross, described as a phylacterion, as well as a ring with a fragment of the wood from Christ's cross.[96]

The Jewish cult of Solomon was popular among Jews, Christians, and pagans throughout the first centuries of the Common Era, perhaps even as late as the seventh century CE. Solomon was said to have had both medical knowledge and power over demons, concepts which, as we have seen in this chapter and in Chapter Two on Levantine Agrarian Religion, closely were related in the classical world. In the first century CE, Josephus wrote about Solomon's God-granted knowledge of the art used against demons and incantations which relieve illnesses, and the ca. third century CE *Testament of Solomon*, a Judaeo-Christian apocryphal text, reported that the archangel Michael had given Solomon a seal ring which he could use to exercise power over demons, listing the names of demons who were responsible for specific maladies.[97]

This regional cult of Solomon gave rise to a very popular amulet-type of Solomon, on which one face has incised a figure in armor on horseback. He holds a spear which is pointed downwards towards a prostrate naked female figure with long hair. Solomon is identified by the legend 'ΣΟΛΟΜΩΝ', and the obverse side says 'ΣΦΡΑΓΙΣ ΘΕΟΥ', 'seal of god'. The female demon is evidently Abyzou/Obyzouth, listed in the *Testament of Solomon* as known to strangle newborn babies at birth. Recall also that this notion involving a female demon was commonplace in agrarian religious contexts, where we see her also as 'Lilith' or 'al-Qarīna'.[98] Christopher Walters argues that "this was the original iconographical type, called 'Holy Riders', from which derived that of warrior saints killing a dragon, obnoxious beast or a persecutor," but notes that such type also has antecedents in both classical and Egyptian art.[99]

In Christian iconography, argues Walters, protective Holy Riders progressively assumed the identity of warrior saints, such as Ss. George and Theodore, which will be the perspective adopted here as well. However, this book argues that the iconographical type of the Holy Rider who kills a dragon, beast, or human persecutor is a prime example of a long-lived compelling motif from the Near Eastern common pool: one which, in being associated with the narrative of the defeat of a dragon or serpent, also had ties to the Eastern Mediterranean narrative of the storm-god Baal-Hadad.

Development of Christian iconography

In addition to pictorial and written amulets, people living early in the Common Era also used images of the gods as protectors in their personal and home shrines.[100] Despite apparent image prohibitions in the Hebrew Scriptures, a ban on images was not universally observed by Jewish communities, as we saw reflected in the frescoes at the synagogue at Dura Europos, in Syria.[101]

Like their polytheistic – and some Jewish – contemporaries, Christian communities also used images in religious practice, a trait that was reported during the fourth century by Eusebius, Bishop of Caesarea in Palestine: "I have examined images of his apostles Paul and Peter, and indeed of Christ himself, preserved in color paintings; which is understandable, since the ancients used to honor saviors freely in this way following their pagan custom." A few images of the "saviors" honored in pagan homes during the first two centuries of the Common Era have survived, and this practice seems to have informed the Christian icon tradition.[102]

One example of such an image is the icon of *Suchos and Isis*, ca. 200 CE, discovered in a house in Fayum, Egypt. The gods, heads ringed by halos, sit in a cushioned double throne, holding the symbols of their fertility, and gaze with wide eyes directly at the viewer. The frame of the icon was equipped with a sliding lid, allowing the viewer to activate or to conceal the divine presence, if the gaze became too intense.[103]

Domestic worship of the gods involved not only worship of fertility gods who could ensure the health and growth of the family, but also the private worship of military gods, who could protect one in this life and the next. Heron was a popular military god venerated in Syria, and a wood-panel image of him with an anonymous military god from ca. 200 CE confirms his protective status. In that image, both figures, with haloes like rings of fire around their heads, are dressed as soldiers, and Heron, on the right, carries a spear and displays a frightening gorgon's head on his curiass. The companion military god wields a double-headed axe and a spear with a cobra wound around it, and a small female figure in the bottom left corner may represent the owner of the icon.[104] The figures in this image do not enact a story, but instead are posed statically, to engage the viewer through their powerful gaze.[105]

Early Christian icons continued in the traditions of pagan images and imperial Roman artworks. An icon of Christ and St. Menas, from the ruined St. Apollo monastery at Bawît, Egypt, shows Christ and St. Menas in a posture and with features quite similar to those of the pagan iconography above from Syria and Egypt. The squat, full-body figures stand in front of a background that perhaps indicated the Nile landscape, engaging the viewer with their exaggerated eyes and gaze.[106] The Christ figure holds a copy of the Gospels, and St. Menas carries a scroll that perhaps represented the Order of his monastery. The date of this icon is disputed, but most likely originated between the sixth and eighth centuries CE.[107]

Other early icons exhibited elements of Roman portraiture painting, such as the sixth-century icon of St. Peter, located at St. Catherine's monastery in Sinai. In this icon, Peter is dressed and posed like a classical orator in the half-length format of Roman portraits, while exhibiting the symbols of his Christian apostolic identity, including keys and the cross of martyrdom. Matthews argues that the Byzantine icon tradition which ultimately developed represented a fusion of the 'pagan' icon genre with Roman secular portraiture, in part to distinguish the Christian iconographic tradition from that of pagan iconography.[108]

George icons

These contemporary iconographical influences were brought to bear upon the early images of St. George, himself a figure of multiple influences. St. George, as Christopher Walter argues, "had all the characteristics of a warrior saint, but also readily assimilated those of other saints and deities who were receiving cult in the regions where devotion to him developed."[109] Thus, argues Walters, St. George ought not be understood as a reincarnation of pre-Christian divinities with which he shares characteristics (among them, Walters suggests, Tammuz, Adonis, Mithra, and Horus, who, on horseback, speared a crocodile representation of the god Setekh), but argues instead that "osmosis" led ultimately to St. George "replacing them in folklore and popular devotion."[110] What Walters calls "osmosis" this book understands as an absorption and application – continuation, even – of compelling regional and geographical motifs. Among those motifs – applied to other warrior saints as well, such as St. Theodore Tiron – was that of the holy rider who vanquished a human or dragon foe, as we will see.

An ecclesiastical tradition of painted Christian icons began probably early in the fourth century, after the advent of Constantine's Toleration Edict and the subsequent legalization of Christianity in the Roman Empire, as well as the imperial Council at Nicaea.[111] Produced sporadically in the fourth century, the number of Christian icons increased during the fifth century, and by the "sixth century the cult of images was firmly established."[112] While few icons remain from the sixth century, and none from earlier centuries, there is textual evidence of Christian icons, both from the fourth-century writings of Bishop Eusebius of Caesarea in Palestine (see above), and from a ca. 600 CE text, *Life of Theodore of Sykeon*, written by Theodore's disciple, George. In the text, Theodore was described as a great devotee of St. George, and one whom George had saved from an illness at age 14, by torturing and banishing the demon who had caused Theodore's malady.[113] Furthermore, the *Life of Theodore* mentions two instances of contemporary icon usage: first, the icons of Ss. Cosmas and Damian, reportedly which had hung above Theodore's bed; second, Theodore's grandmother, Elpidia, to whom St. George had once appeared. Elpidia's vision was of a young man, "exceedingly handsome with shining clothes and curly hair gleaming like gold." Elpidia had no difficulty in identifying the vision as St. George, "for he closely resembled his portrait."[114] Thus, we see that an iconographical tradition of St. George existed at least as early as the sixth century, and perhaps earlier.

The earliest extant icon of St. George is most likely the icon of the *Enthroned Virgin between Soldier Saints* at the St. Catherine Monastery at Sinai. Founded by decree of the Byzantine Emperor Justinian I (r. 527–565 CE) on the locally purported site in Sinai of Moses' encounter with the burning bush, the monastery at Sinai benefitted from several centuries of imperial patronage. The icon collection at St. Catherine's is remarkable not only because it has been in existence since the time of Justinian, but also because it contains early icons from the periods before and during the tumultuous era in Byzantine ecclesiastical history known as Iconoclasm, or Εἰκονοομαχία, a series of conflicts, between 726–842 CE, over the acceptability of icon usage in Christian practice, and during which time most Byzantine icons were destroyed. Owing to its remote location in the Sinai Peninsula, far from Constantinople, icons within the monastery were spared, and continued to be produced.

The *Enthroned Virgin between Soldier Saints* icon dates from the sixth century, and displays the Virgin wearing Byzantine royal purple tunic and shoes, seated on a throne and flanked by two unnamed soldier saints, whom most scholars identify as St. Theodore, on the left, and St. George, on the right.[115] George in this icon is depicted, like Theodore, in the ceremonial garb of the imperial guard. He is young and handsome, with blonde curly hair, wearing a light grey tunic with dark purple borders and roundels over the shoulder and knee. Over George's right shoulder, his lavender chlamys is held together by a bow fibula – as is the chlamys of his companion, St. Theodore – a feature that dates the icon to the sixth century CE. Both George and Theodore carry crosses of martyrdom and gaze widely at the viewer.[116]

Another icon of George, also dating from the sixth century, was uncovered at the ruined North Church in the Monastery of St. Apollo in Bawît, Egypt. In this icon, George was represented full-length, beardless, and with curled blonde hair in a circle around his head, wearing a curiass underneath his chlamys, and with a sword girded to his left side. In Chapel 18, there was also an icon of St. George, in bust form, with similar features and accompanied by an identifying inscription.[117]

What we see from these early icons of St. George is that he was identified, at least as early as the sixth century CE, as a youthful military saint, features which certainly align with his description in the fifth-century CE text of the *Acts*. Another narrative feature with which St. George is early identified in iconography is his combat with a dragon or serpent. Nicole Thierry dates to the sixth–seventh century an iconographical representation of St. George vanquishing a dragon at the St. George rupestrian (cave) church in Zindanönü, Cappadocia, although the state of preservation of the Zindanönü icons is quite poor.[118]

There is, however, a series of terracotta icons, recovered in 1985 from outside the walls of a fortress known as Viničko Kale, near the town of Vinica, Macedonia, on which George is identified by name and depicted as killing a dragon. On this icon, St. George stands to the right of St. Christopher, holding up his shield with his right hand. Both saints spear a serpent with a human head, and though neither saint wears military uniform, both have military attributes. Because the text is inscribed in Latin, Walters dates this icon to a time when the region still was under the ecclesiastical jurisdiction of Rome; i.e., sometime before Leo III brought the region under the jurisdiction of Constantinople in 733 CE.[119]

Other dragon-slayers

Among the Viničko Kale Terracottas was also an icon of St. Theodore spearing the dragon, with the inscription 'Theodorus Draco'. Theodore was associated in text as early as 754 CE with the legend of slaying a dragon.[120] Theodore also was depicted in a ninth- to tenth-century icon at St. Catherine's Monastery in Sinai as vanquishing a dragon, alongside George, who was represented in the same posture, but vanquishing a human foe rather than a dragon. Theodore and George also were twice depicted as together slaying two serpents twisted around a tree on two churches in Cappadocia, from the Yilani Kılıse 'Snake Church', ca. 11th century. Walters notes that this composition "recalls in both style and iconography early Oriental models." This icon from the Yilani Kılıse in Cappadocia stylistically is quite similar to the Hittite-era bas-relief from the

Gate of Lions in Malatya from the 12th or 11th century BCE, which depicts the Hittite storm-god and his son attacking a coiling serpent.[121] Thus, both Ss. George and Theodore were associated with the killing of a dragon, but Walters suggests that this association was both earlier and more widespread for Theodore than it was for George, who eventually began to supplant or to be conflated with Theodore in this role.

Walters is doubtless correct that, of the two saints, George ultimately became the more popular and the more frequently associated with the legend of slaying dragon, especially in later centuries. However, both George and Theodore iconographically were associated from an early date with the dragon, and, if the dating of the George icon at the St. George Church in Zindanönü, Cappadocia is correct, the earliest witness to this legend in iconography is George, not Theodore.

In any event, the issue of dating is moot, as iconographical representations of riders on horseback spearing a fallen enemy or dragon long predate both St. George and St. Theodore: see the Solomon Holy Rider amulet-type, as well as the first- to second-century CE Roman carving of Sextus Valerius Genalis spearing a fallen enemy. Instead, this iconographical composition should be understood as a compelling regional motif; an ubiquitous image of power employed in different circumstances, like that of the smiting posture shared by figures in both the Egyptian Narmer Palette (see Figure 3.2) the Baal Stele (see Figure 3.1).

Rescue of a princess

Another textual and iconographical legend for which St. George is known is the rescue of a princess from the dragon. While this has become the modern legend and image for which St. George is known, the textual narrative of George rescuing a princess currently has not been found before that of a Georgian manuscript dating from the 11th century CE.[122] This princess-rescue legend was greatly popularized through the publication in 13th-century Italy of Jacobus de Voragine's *Legenda Aurea*,[123] a collection of hagiographies which, in the West, remain paradigmatic today. The earliest-extant iconographical type of this princess-rescue legend also comes from Georgia, at Pavnisi, dated ca. 1158 CE.

Walters notes the similarities between the legend of George rescuing a princess from a dragon and the earlier Perseus and Andromeda myths,

> Perseus rescued Andromeda from a sea monster at Joppa, which is close to Lydda [the location of an early shrine to St. George at Diospolis], although it was not at Lydda that the apocryphal account of the rescue originated. Moreover, since the gap in time is so great and since there is no literary *filière* between the two prodigies, a direct connection between them is hard to establish.[124]

This book, however, argues that the similarities in the princess-rescue-from-a-sea-monster stories between the St. George legend and that of Perseus and

Andromeda can be explained by the adoption of this compelling regional motif – in both narratives. Indeed, as we saw in Chapter Two, the Perseus-Andromeda myth may itself have linkages to the earlier regional tale of Astarte and the Sea.[125] Moreover, the *Acts* also involves a queen – Alexandra – who is not saved physically by St. George but is saved spiritually through his mission. Thus, we see that while the earliest-extant textual story of George rescuing the princess dates to the 11th century, associations between George and a queen are not without antecedents in even his earliest text.

Warrior saints as protectors

By virtue of their military qualities, warrior saints imparted an important protective status for those who venerated and invoked them.[126] In his *De Sancto Theodoro,* from the late fourth century, Gregory of Nyssa attributed to St. Theodore Tiron "protection from demons, curing maladies, and occasionally saving lives."[127] Saving lives took place in a number of ways – protection from demons and the curing of maladies foremost among them – but military saints also were believed to provide assistance in battle, to triumph over unjust rulers, and to rescue those in need.

Assistance in battle

Among the warrior saints, George was known to intervene most frequently in battle. He was said to have intervened in a battle to save the life of Domnitziolus, nephew of the Byzantine Emperor Phocas (602–610 CE), and there is a *Canon* composed by George Skylitzes in which George's aid was requested to help the Imperial army variously to gain victory over the Scythians, Persians, and barbarians.[128] George helped not only the Byzantines, however, as he was invoked both by Serbian kings, and adopted by the English and French Crusaders during their 11th- and 12th-century campaigns in the Levant. In 1348, English King Edward III put his Order of the Garter under the banner of St. George, thus establishing George as the patron saint of England and displacing thereby Ss. Paul and Peter.[129]

Triumph over unjust rulers

Like St. George, fellow warrior saint Demetrius eventually became associated with the narrative of defeating an unjust ruler. St. Demetrius was believed to have successfully defended the city of Thessaloniki in the early 13th century from the Bulgarian king Ivan Kalojan, just as "Ss. George Sergius, Theodore, and Mercurius were reputed in their time to have disposed of other persecutors and enemies."[130] St. George's principal adversary in legend was the Emperor Diocletian, who is often identified as the human foe depicted in George iconography in place of the dragon.[131]

Rescue: Pillion rider

George's interventions to rescue people also were associated with his military status. One interesting iconographical association with St. George is that of the pillion rider, the small figure who accompanied not only George but also sometimes Theodore and Demetrius in iconographical representation. Earliest associated with the icon of the Rescue of the Youth of Mytilene, ca. 1250 CE, who was said to have been a captive of Saracens (Muslims) on the island of Crete and to have been rescued in the very act of offering drink to his captors, the youth was carried back to his family in Mytilene, across the Aegean sea, by St. George (Figure 5.1).

This iconographical theme involving St. George became more frequent in the Eastern Mediterranean and Asia Minor after the Turkish conquests and into the Ottoman Era. During these time periods, the youth was depicted as a Christian servant in the court of the Sultan, but this motif was often employed as a component of the George icon in any region where Christians constituted a minority of the population, such as in Greece and Eastern Europe.[132]

However, the iconographical type involving a pillion rider was original neither to St. George nor to warrior saints in general. Existing at least since Sassanian-era, artworks depicted Sassanian king Bahram V (r. 420–438 CE), who was challenged to feats of archery by his favorite young lyre player, the slave girl Azadeh. In the instance of the St. George and the rescue of the youth of Mytilene icon, we witness a compelling regional motif of the young-captive pillion rider being applied to the iconographical narratives of warrior saints, who were known as protectors. This protective iconographical motif was especially apropos of St. George, the martyr-warrior saint who had defeated a pagan tyrant, vanquished a dragon, rescued a princess, and ultimately became the most popular saint in the Eastern Mediterranean.

Part Four: Conclusion: St. George and the Levantine common pool

What St. George texts, images, and sites reflect about Christian tradition

What we see reflected in the figure of George is a mixed religious environment that was both cooperative and competitive. We see communities of Jews, Christians, Roman polytheists/'pagans', Jewish-Christians, and various categorizations between these. The religious environment of the first several centuries of the Common Era, as is characteristic of much of agrarian religion, was dominated by general belief in demons, saints, magic, and icons, alongside growing cadres of 'orthodoxies' in religious organization, all of which we can see reflected in St. George texts and iconography.

What the figure of St. George – himself, as we have seen, comprised of multiple religious influences – represents about early Christianity is a religious movement identified with biblical tradition and simultaneously differentiating from Jewish identity and practices. We see in early Christianity a religious tradition that, like that of Judaism and by virtue of its association with the biblical tradition and Hebrew Scriptures, is differentiated from the polytheistic traditions of the Hellenized world.

Figure 5.1 St. George and the rescue of the youth of Mytilene © World History Archive / Alamy Stock Photo

From the *Acts*, we can glean an emerging Christian conception of God as the same as the biblical God, but with an expanded or clarified description: Trinitarian in nature, and, in accordance with a contemporary Imperial Christian position regarding Jesus following the Council of Nicaea, incorporating Jesus as the second person of the Trinity; at once human and divine, in separate measure.

St. George and the Levantine common pool

In the *Acts*, we see St. George as clearly associated with Elijah from the biblical tradition. George, like Elijah, was depicted as a religious contest figure par excellence who represented the 'true' god in face of the false gods – in George's case, the false gods were Roman. In performing similar miracles and being associated with specific narratives, such as with the widow and her son, George in the *Acts* was clearly patterned for his audience on the widely popular Elijah narratives from the Hebrew Bible account.

We also see in George's very name, Γεωργός 'Georgos', his function, as a saint or cult figure for 'farmer' and agricultural communities. The motifs with which he earliest was associated, even in text: rain, greenness, fertility, fecundity, lightning, feast day of April 23, and, especially, the defeat of a serpent of dragon, suggest that the very early cult of St. George likely originated in – or at least overlapped with, or perhaps offered an alternative to – local cults in the Levant to Zeus-Baal or Zeus-Georgos, as they existed during the early centuries of the Common Era.

An important motif from the Levantine common pool which became associated early-on with St. George was that of the Holy Rider who defeated a human foe, dragon, or serpent. Employed by numerous Roman, Jewish, and Christian figures, this ubiquitous motif of power was applied to the figure of St. George not only in iconography, but also in text: in the *Acts*, George's author deliberately named George's antagonist a "serpent," or "dragon," positioning St. George, who was ultimately victorious, as vanquishing a figurative dragon, as well. Significantly, therefore, not only the earliest iconographical evidence, from the sixth to eighth centuries CE, but also the textual evidence of the *Acts*, from the mid-fifth century CE, demonstrates that George was from his earliest extant evidence associated with the vanquishing of a dragon. Association with a dragon, therefore, appears to be an original element of the figure of St. George, and related to motifs native to his Eastern Mediterranean place of origin, rather than being, as often is claimed, a "western medieval accretion" to the legend of St. George.[133]

What the figure of St. George contributes to *the common pool*

St. George became known as a brave and faithful Christian martyr who endured numerous evils and ultimately triumphed in the religious contest against false gods. As such, St. George was forever afterward associated by people with the figure of Elijah, who, to their minds, also had defended the true God.

George became known as a powerful protector who could rescue princesses and captives of all kinds; a great savior who also could vanquish both demons and dragons.[134] 'Green' George furthermore was a powerful agricultural figure, associated regionally with lightning, storms, rain, and crops.

Conclusion

A popular, powerful figure, St. George became, over the succeeding centuries, the most pervasive saint in the Eastern Mediterranean, as well as the saint most readily identified with the defeat of a dragon. Even under Islamic rule, beginning in the seventh to eighth century CE, George remained a popular and venerated figure. During the Ottoman era in the Levant, beginning in 1517 CE, Christian church building often was curtailed, except in the case of churches dedicated to St. George.[135] Muslims in the Levant, as we will see, greatly respected St. George, and came to identify him with the Qur'ānic figure al-Khiḍr.

Partly because of the regional popularity of St. George among Christian communities, and partly because of Ottoman support for him, today, more churches, shrines, and monasteries are dedicated to St. George than to any other saint, and are second in number only to the universally beloved figure of Mary.[136] St. George sites in the Levant are located either at churches which display George icons, or at sites throughout Syria, Lebanon, Israel, and Palestine, where George is reputed to have lived, worked miracles, or to have defeated the dragon. Unsurprisingly, given the influence of geography on the development of these narratives and motifs, the numerous sites throughout the Levant purported to be the location of George's battle with the dragon often are associated with rivers, caves, and subterranean water.[137]

Moving to the figure of al-Khiḍr

In the 600s and 700s CE, when the figure al-Khiḍr emerged in Qur'ānic and exegetical/*tafsīr* sources, St. George was a contemporaneous figure. During that time period, as we have seen, St. George was a popular figure, but not as differentiated from other saints and gods in the Levant as later he would become. Furthermore, his cult locations were established at sites throughout the Eastern Mediterranean, and not in the Arabian Peninsula, where the Qur'ān emerged.[138]

When the figure al-Khiḍr emerged in text during the seventh century in Arabia, it was amid a late antique religious environment. The biblical tradition, and extra-biblical lore, as we will see – along with the more-memorable biblical figures, like Elijah – comprised the bulk of the late antique religious environment within which the Qur'ān and its narratives and figures developed. Tellingly, as we will see, the earliest textual references and associations to al-Khiḍr and another figure in the early Islamic literature of both *tafsīr* and *hadīth* always were to Elijah.

Notes

1 For more on the city of Antioch, see above, Chapter Three, 74, 104n. See also Wayne A. Meeks and Robert L. Wilken, *Jews and Christians in Antioch in the First Four Centuries of the Common Era*. Society of Biblical Literature Sources for Biblical Study, 13. Missoula, Mont.: Scholars (1978).

2 Martin Hengel, "The Beginning of Christianity as a Jewish-Messianic and Universalistic Movement," in *The Beginnings of Christianity: A Collection of Articles*, Jack Pastor and Menachem Mor, Eds. (Jerusalem: Yad Ben-Zvi Press, 2005), 87.

3 Canivet, "Context of the Mediterranean Civilizations," 51.

4 On Caesarea, see Lee I. Levine, *Caesarea under Roman Rule*. Studies in Judaism in Late Antiquity, 7 (Leiden: Brill, 1975).

5 Canivet, "Context of the Mediterranean Civilizations," 51–53.

6 Hengel, "The Beginning of Christianity as a Jewish-Messianic and Universalistic Movement," 94. Note that Hengel's position on this matter is challenged by R. Horsley and J. Hanson, J, discussing popular movements at the time of Jesus. *Bandits, Prophets and Messiahs*, Trinity Press International, 1985. See also R. Horsley, "The Zealots: their Origin, Relationships and Importance in the Jewish Revolt," *NovT* 28 (1986): 159–182.

7 Hengel, 91.

8 Hengel, 88–90. See also Amy-Jill Levine, *Short Stories by Jesus: The Enigmatic Parables of a Controversial Rabbi*, (New York: HarperOne, 2014).

9 Canivet, "Context of the Mediterranean Civilizations," 54.

10 Daniel Boyarin, *Border Lines: The Partition of Judaeo-Christianity* (Philadelphia, PA: University of Pennsylvania Press, 2004), 6–7.

11 Boyarin, 2. See also See Robert C. Gregg, *Shared Stories, Rival Tellings: Early Encounters of Jews, Christians, and Muslims* (Oxford, UK: Oxford University Press, 2015), who argues that part of the development of canonical religion takes place through the work of tradition-specific commentators and exegetes, who "participated in each religion's development of its own distinctiveness in belief, worship, and thought, and, at the same time, contributed strongly to the differentiation and distance between the three faith communities [of the religious traditions of Judaism, Christianity, and Islam]," xiv. Additionally, Gregg argues that exegetically 'competitive' scripture interpretation, of shared narratives, between religious commentators, functioned as a "singularly powerful force in the early divergence between Christians, Jews, and Muslims, and in their separation into discrete, independent religious cultures," Gregg, 598.

12 Boyarin also notes, following the work of Robert A. Markus (who was himself partially following Arnaldo Momigliamo), that such Christian discursive practices also helped to construct 'paganism', because, as a varied group of cults and observances, "'paganism' never constituted a single coherent religious movement analogous to either Christianity or Judaism. It only existed in the minds and in the speech habits of late-fourth-century Christians." Robert A. Markus, *The End of Ancient Christianity* (Cambridge: Cambridge University Press, 1990), 28. This project adopts as well the perspective that discursive practices of the second, third, and fourth centuries CE contributed to constructing 'Paganism' as a religious formation.

13 For firsthand accounts from the period, see Ramsay MacMullen and Eugene N. Lane, Eds., *Paganism and Christianity 100–425: A Sourcebook* (Minneapolis, MN: Fortress Press, 1992). See also A. D. Lee, *Pagans and Christians in Late Antiquity: A Sourcebook* (New York: Routledge, 2000).

14 See James J. O'Donnell, *Pagans: The End of Traditional Religion and the Rise of Christianity* (New York: Ecco/HarperCollins 2015); Ramsay MacMullen, *Paganism in the Roman Empire* (New Haven, CT: Yale University Press, 1981); Helmut Koester, *Introduction to the New Testament, Vol. 1: History, Culture and Religion of the Hellenistic Age.* 2nd ed. (Berlin: de Gruyter, 1995).

15 O'Donnell, 87.

16 MacMullen and Lane, *Paganism and Christianity, 100–425*, 1.

17 MacMullen and Lane, 2. See also the translation of Epiphanius' account, *Panarion*, 30.4–12, in J. P. Migne, *Patrologia graeca* (Paris: Garnier, 1857–1891), 41, col. 109ff.; translation by MacMullen and Lane.

18 See Chapter Two, 37–50.

19 Ramsay MacMullen, *Paganism in the Roman Empire* (New Haven, CT: Yale University Press, 1981), 1–7. Note that the exception to the dominance of Jupiter among Roman provinces was in the African provinces. Of course, both Zeus and Jupiter were understood in varied ways among different groups during particular times and places. Likewise, characteristics of Zeus and of Jupiter in the Levant were fairly uniform and specific to that location. Furthermore, this data confirms

that in the Levant they were the gods most frequently mentioned in inscriptions. MacMullen, 5.

20 MacMullen, *Paganism in the Roman Empire*, 43–45. See also Chapter Three, 71–75.

21 MacMullen, 4, referencing Marcus Minucius Felix, *Octavius*, 6.1, ca. 160–250 CE.

22 Fergus Millar, *The Roman Near East, 31 BC – AD 377* (Cambridge, MA: Harvard University Press, 1993), 1–2. For more on the altar at Dura-Europos dedicated to "Zeus Betylos," see 532.

23 MacMullen, *Paganism in the Roman Empire*, 4.

24 Fergus Millar, *The Roman Near East*, 274. For more on the shrine/cult to Zeus Baetocaece, see pp. 270–274. See also MacMullen and Lane, *Paganism and Christianity 100–425*, 43–45. MacMullen and Lane also include the text of a first-century "Hymn to Zeus," 62–63.

25 Canivet, "Context of the Mediterranean Civilizations," 53.

26 Canivet, 51.

27 Fergus Millar, *The Roman Near East*, 521. The written language of Syriac first appeared in Edessa in the first century CE.

28 Canivet, "Context of the Mediterranean Civilizations," 60. See also in particular Jonathan A. Draper and Clayton N. Jefford, *The Didache: A Missing Piece of the Puzzle in Early Christianity* (Early Christianity and Its Literature, 14, Atlanta: SBL Press, 2015).

29 Edward J. Watts, *The Final Pagan Generation: Transformation of the Classical Heritage* (Oakland, CA: University of California Press, 2015).

30 Watts, Chapter One.

31 Watts, Chapter Three.

32 On the Book of Revelation, see Elaine Pagels, *Revelations: Visions, Prophecy & Politics in the book of Revelation* (New York: Viking, 2012).

33 See Wayne A. Meeks, *The First Urban Christians: The Social World of the Apostle Paul*. 2nd ed. (New Haven, CT: Yale University Press, 2003), 74–77.

34 On the subject of the formation of the Christian canon, see Lee Martin McDonald and James A. Sanders, eds., *The Canon Debate*, (Peabody, MA: Hendrickson Publishers, 2002). Relevant discussion is located at pp. 381–415; note in particular the work of Gregory A. Robbins. See also G. A. Robbins, "Eusebius' Lexicon of 'Canonicity'", Studia Patristica, Vol. XXV (1993), 134–141.

35 On the subject of Athanasius' Festal Letter, see David Brakke, "Canon Formation and Social Conflict in Fourth-Century Egypt: Athanasius of Alexandria's Thirty-Ninth Festal Letter," *Harvard Theological Review* 87 (1994): 395–419.

36 Lee Martin McDonald, *The Formation of the Christian Biblical Canon: Revised and Expanded Edition*. Peabody, MA: Hendrickson Publishers, 1995. See also Lee Martin McDonald, *The Biblical Canon: Its Origin, Transmission, and Authority* (Peabody, MA: Hendrickson Publishers, 2007). Note: also Tatian, Diatessaron, Syriac communities. Even during the Reformation, the books that were listed (and removed) from Protestant denominations' canons of the Bible indicate that the issue of canon was still not a 'closed' debate, as late as the 16th century, CE. Indeed, the issue of canon remains loosely open even today. It must, of course, as the notion of canon always is constructed anew by every community.

37 Maraval, "Christianity in the Middle East in the Second and Third Centuries," 80.

38 On the general topic of martyrdom in early Christianity, see W. H. C. Frend, *Martyrdom and Persecution in the Early Church*. Reprint (Grand Rapids, MI: Baker Book House, 1963/1980). See also Candida Moss, *The Myth of Persecution: How Early Christians Invented a Story of Martyrdom* (New York: HarperOne, 2013); Daniel Boyarin, *Dying for God: Martyrdom and the Making of Christianity and Judaism* (Palo Alto, CA: Stanford University Press 1999); Elizabeth Castelli, *Martyrdom and Memory: Early Christian Culture Making* (New York: Columbia University Press, 2007).

39 Canivet, 81.
40 Canivet, 80.
41 On early Christian 'reenactment' of Jesus' suffering and death, especially with respect to hagiographical practices, see Candida Moss, *The Other Christs: Imitating Jesus in Ancient Christian Ideologies of Martyrdom* (Oxford: Oxford University Press 2010).
42 See also Peter Brown, *The Cult of the Saints: Its Rise and Function in Latin Christianity* (Chicago: University of Chicago Press, 1981), as well as Candida Moss, *The Other Christs: Imitating Jesus in Ancient Christian Ideologies of Martyrdom.*
43 Christopher Walter, *Warrior Saints in Byzantine Art and Tradition* (Burlington, VT: Ashgate Publishing Company, 2003), 1, 109.
44 Walter, 4, 22–23.
45 Walter, 25.
46 That is, the *Acts* are less historical accounts than they are of course arguments made to valorize martyrdom and developing Christian theologies. See Candida Moss, *Ancient Christian Martyrdom: Diverse Practices, Theologies, and Traditions* (New Haven, CT: Yale University Press, 2012). See also Candida Moss, *The Other Christs: Imitating Jesus in Ancient Christian Ideologies of Martyrdom.*
47 Walter, 28–29.
48 Greek writers such as Plato, Aristophanes, Xenophon, Menander, and Aristotle, among many others, referenced *γεωργοι* as a category of persons who cultivated the land. Virgil's Latin *Georgica* described the contemporary smallholder farming economy in upper Italy. See Robin Osborne and Dominic Rathbone, "Farmers," in *Brill's New Pauly*. Hubert Cancik and Helmuth Schneider, eds. (Brill Online, 2015).
49 J.F. Boissonade, *Ηρωδιανου 'επιμερισμοι / Herodiani Partitiones* (E. Codd. Paris. London, 1819, Repr. Amsterdam: Hakkert, 1963), 172. See "Τὰ διὰ τοῦ *ιος*προπαροξύτονα ὀνόματα, κύριά τε καὶ ἐπίθετα, καὶ ἀπὸ τόπου λαμβανόμενα, διὰ τοῦ ἰῶτα γράφονται· κύρια μέν· οἷον· Γεώργιος· Δημήτριος· Ἀμμώνιος…." "And the names of the prophets, names, and statues, and the names of the people that are received by it, are written: chiefly, Georgios; Demetrios; Ammonios…."
50 Stella Georgoudi, "Sacrificing to the Gods: Ancient Evidence and Modern Interpretations," in *The Gods of Ancient Greece: Identities and Transformations*, Edinburgh Levantis Studies 5, Jan N. Bremmer and Andrew Erskine, eds. (Edinburgh, Scotland: Edinburgh University Press, 2010), 104, 42 n., referencing Franciszek Sokolowski, *Lois sacrées des cites grecques* (Paris: De Boccard, 1969), no. 52, 12–15 (Athens).
51 Hassan S. Haddad, "'Georgic' Cults and Saints of the Levant," *Numen*, vol. 16, Fasc. 1: 1969, 24.
52 Matt. 16:18.
53 Haddad, "Georgic Cults," 24, says the invocation of Zeus Georgos was made "in connection with the sacrifice of the 20th of the month of Maimekterion." Haddad cites the 'Georgos' article in Pauly-Wissowa, *Real-Encyclopädie der klassichen Altertumswissenschaft*, 1953.
54 Allaire B. Stallsmith, "The Name of Demeter Thesmophoros," *Greek, Roman, and Byzantine Studies* 48 (2008): 116, citing ancient sources in 7f.
55 Jean Jannoray. "Nouvelles Inscriptions de Lébadée," *Bulletin de Correspondance Hellénique*. Vol. 64–65, (1940): 36–59. "Tout de même, c'est un phallos qui représentait Hermès, personnification de la luxuriance féconde de la nature, au sommet du mont Cyllène; c'est par un phallos qu'était figuré Zeus Telesphoros, le génie qui mène à maturité, très proche parent de Zeus Meilichios. Gomme ces δαίμονες, comme Zeùs Trophonios, Zeus Oporeus ou Zeus Georgos, Zeus Meilichios préside à l'éternel cycle du monde végétal, où la vie succède sans cesse à la mort." "All the same, though, it is a phallos that represented Hermes, personification of luxuriance of nature, at the top of Mount Cyllene; it is through a phallos that Zeus Telesphoros, the genius who leads to maturity, was depicted, very close relative of Zeus Meilichios. Blur those δαίμονες,

like Zeùs Trophonios, Zeus Oporeus or Zeus Georgos, Zeus Meilichios presides over the eternal cycle of the vegetal world, where life constantly follows death." Jannoray, "Nouvelles Inscriptions de Lébadée," 54.

56 Allaire Brumfield, "Cakes in the Liknon: Votives from the Sanctuary of Demeter and Kore on Acrocorinth," *Hesperia: The Journal of the American School of Classical Studies at Athens*, Vol. 66, No. 1 (Jan.–Mar., 1997): 147–172. The Zeus Georgos reference is located on p. 170.

57 Hans Kloft, *Mysterienkulte der Antike: Götter, Menschen, Rituale* (Munich: Verlag C.H.Beck, 2010):

> "Der heliage Demetrius, Schutzheiliger der Bauern und Hirten, zugleich Beschutzer des Ackerbaus, schient, wie es Nilsson vermutet hat, zumindest teilweise das Erbe der machtigen paganen Muttergottheit angetreten zu haben." "The holy Demetrius, patron saint of farmers and shepherds, at the same time protector of agriculture, seems, as Nilsson suspected, to have at least partially inherited the powerful pagan Mother Goddess."
>
> Kloft, *Mysterienkulte der Antike*, 25.

58 Christopher Walter, *Warrior Saints*, 112, referencing Pierre Maraval, Ed., *Récits des premiers pèlerins chrétiens en Proche-Orient* (Paris, 1996). Walter further notes that while Christian pilgrimage accounts of the area from the period after Theodosius include references to St. George's sanctuary there, Saint Jerome (347–420 CE), son of Eusebius, in his *Letter* no. 106, mentions Lydda but not George, which may indicate an earliest possible date for the construction of this shrine as sometime between 420 and 530 CE.

59 Walter, 113, also citing Maraval, *Récits des premiers pèlerins chrétiens en Proche-Orient*.

60 Walter, 113, also citing Gregory's *Liber in gloria martyrum*, PL 71, 792–793.

61 The famous floor-mosaic map of Jerusalem is dated to 560 CE. See Herbert Donner, *The Mosaic Map of Madaba*. Palaestina Antiqua 7 (Kampen, Netherlands: Kok Pharos Publishing House, 1992).

62 Donner, 114, citing H. Leclerq, 'Ezra' (*DACL* 5), 1052–1056, and H.C. Butler, *Early Churches in Syria*, E. Baldwin Smith, ed., (reprinted in Amsterdam 1969), 122.

63 Cappadocia frequently was under Persian (Sasanian Empire, 224–651 CE) influence.

64 This introduction is generally adapted from George Anton Kiraz, *The Acts of St. George and the Story of his Father*, (Piscataway, NJ: Gorgias Press, 2009). The earliest Greek fragments were edited by Krumbacher and Erhard, 1911.

65 Kiraz, 2.

66 Kiraz, 2, quoting W. Wright, *Catalogue of the Syriac Manuscripts in the British Museum*, Part 3, p. 1087 (London: 1872, reprinted in Piscataway, NJ in 2002).

67 E. W. Brooks, *Acts of Saint George*, Analecta Georgiana vol. 8, George Anton Kiraz, Series Ed. (Piscataway, NJ: Gorgias Press, 2006, originally published in *Le Muséon*, vol. 38, 1925), 2 (orig., 68).

68 Brooks, *Acts of Saint George*.

69 Brooks, *Acts of Saint George*; see also Kiraz, *The Acts of St. George and the Story of his Father*, 2.

70 Christianity can be said to take on an 'imperial' character after the time when certain disputed theological positions within the wider community of Christians received imperial acknowledgment as veracious, and other theological positions did not. An early example is the disputed theological position concerning the homoousian nature of Jesus, the 'son' of God, to God the 'father', which became the official imperial position after the Council of Nicaea in 325 CE. See also Chapter Six, 193–195.

71 See above, 70n.

72 Kiraz, 4.

73 See Chapter Three, 62, 44n. There is of course the serpent/dragon motif in the Book of Revelation, chapters 12–13. The two (serpent/dragon) are equated in 12:9 explicitly. The ultimate defeat of the dragon/serpent is narrated in Revelation 20, where the angel "coming down from heaven," seizes and binds the dragon/serpent. The mythic tradition in Revelation can be traced, of course, as we saw above, to the Leviathan (from Hebrew: *ltn* 'the coiling one') and Behemoth traditions in the Hebrew Bible, and to multiple wider and older ANE cosmic enemy narratives, such as the Enuma Elish and the Gilgamesh Epic. On the topic of dragon imagery in the Book of Revelation, see also Elaine Pagels, *Revelations: Visions, Prophecy & Politics in the book of Revelation*, p. 24. See also the standard study of the dragon/serpent imagery in the Book of Revelation, Adela Yarbro Collins, *The Combat Myth in the Book of Revelation*, (Missoula, MT: Scholars Press, 1976).

74 Hasan S. Haddad, "'Georgic' Cults and Saints of the Levant," *Numen*, 16, Fasc. 1 (April 1969), 28.

75 See Chapter Three, 74–75.

76 See also references to the Perseus and Andromeda tales in Chapter Two, 42; Chapter Five, 174–175; and Chapter Seven, 250.

77 See Jacobus de Voragine, *The Golden Legend: Readings on the Saints*, 2 vols., William Granger Ryan, transl. (Princeton, NJ: Princeton University Press, 1993), 238–242.

78 See Kiraz, p. 10.

79 See also Chapter One, 8, 31n. See also Chapter Two, 39; 37–50.

80 See below in Chapter Six, 193–195.

81 Likewise, an account from the fourth century CE records the contemporary belief that "madness" was caused by demons. See Epiphanius' account in his *Panarion* of the Jew, Josephus, who drove a demon from a madman by sprinkling water, over which Josephus had made the sign of the cross, upon the man. MacMullen and Lane, *Paganism and Christianity, 100–425*, 6–7. See also the translation of Epiphanius' account, *Panarion*, 30.4–12, in J. P. Migne, *Patrologia graeca* (Paris: Garnier, 1857–1891), 41, col. 109ff.; translation by MacMullen and Lane. See also above, Chapter Two, 43–44.

82 Another recension of the *Acts*, CDMV, has "face *as of an angel*." Cf. Acts 6:15.

83 In both later Zoroastrian and Christian traditions, the 'shining face' from ancient Near Eastern traditions which indicated divine contact may have become represented in the form of a halo.

84 A 'shining' or 'bright' face was likewise associated with divine contact in neo-Babylonian culture as well. See Balogh, *Moses Among the Idols: Mediators of the Divine in the Ancient Near East*.

85 For more on the evolution of Jesus from the status of human to divine, see Bart D. Ehrman, *How Jesus Became God: The Exaltation of a Jewish Preacher from Galilee* (New York: HarperOne, 2015).

86 Of course, George in this text – characteristic of hagiographies from this time – is like *Christ*. He is presented in *imitatio Christi* as a 'Christ figure'. See Candida Moss, *The Other Christs*. However, once we accept that role for St. George as a given, we are able to see as well clear parallels in this text with the 1 and 2 Kings narratives of Elijah.

87 Cf. 1 Kings 18:4; recension M has "Artemis the slayer of her lover."

88 Recension DMV has "demons."

89 Cogan, *1 Kings*, 427.

90 My argument here is of course not that a text such as the *Acts* is historically accurate – indeed, I have argued the opposite. However, one of my greater arguments in this work is that texts, images, and sites function like artifacts that reflect a great deal about the societies in which they were produced. Thus, I quote this passage from the *Acts* not as a piece of historical evidence from a 'true' text, but as a piece of direct historical reference from a fifth-to-sixth century CE text whose narrative contents cannot be substantiated.

91 See the footnote above. Regarding the question of the veracity of this – and most – hagiographical literature, see as well Candida Moss, *Ancient Christian Martyrdom: Diverse Practices, Theologies, and Traditions* (New Haven, CT: Yale University Press, 2012), and *The Myth of Persecution: How Early Christians Invented a Story of Martyrdom* (New York: HarperOne, 2013).

92 See George Anton Kiraz, *The Acts of Saint George and the Story of his Father*, 1. Also, N. Thierry; description of Cappadocia under Persian influence. Note also that in ancient texts, the names of rulers sometimes intentionally were obscured for protection.

93 Note also that there is a similar Islamic motif employed of the baby Ishmael in the traditional Islamic story of Hajar and Isma'il (Hagar and Ishmael, in the biblical tradition), and involving the origin of the Zamzam well located in Mecca. Hajar could not at first find water for them to survive, but in some versions of the story, the baby Isma'il's foot kicked the ground and there a spring miraculously welled up. This is referenced not to claim direct linkages between the *Acts of St. George* and this *sīrah* literary narrative of Hajar and Isma'il, of course, but merely to point out that the narrative of a holy person striking their foot against the ground and a spring therefrom gushing forth may have been a compelling contemporaneous motif.

94 Walter, *Warrior Saints*, 33–38.

95 Walter, citing *Constitutiones apostolicae* 8 32, PG 1, 1128–1133.

96 Walter, citing *Life of St. Macrina* (*Bibliographica hagiographica graeca*, 1012), P. Maraval, ed. (Paris, 1971), 240; PG 45, 989. Note also that 'phylactery' continues to refer, in Judaism, to small black leather cubes worn during weekday morning prayers strapped to the head and left arm by orthodox male Jews and containing verses from Deuteronomy and Exodus. Among Christians, 'phylactery' continues to refer to a receptacle which contains a holy relic.

97 Walter, referencing the "Testament of Solomon," in *The Old Testament Pseudepigraphia*, BHG, 944–987.

98 See Chapter Two, Part Three, 42–43.

99 Walter, *Warrior Saints*, 36–38.

100 See Roman Household Shrines book. See also Thomas F. Matthews, *Byzantium: From Antiquity to the Renaissance* (New York: Harry N. Abrams, Incorporated: 1998), 45.

101 Kurt Weitzmann, *Studies in the Arts at Sinai: Essays by Kurt W. Weitzmann* (Princeton, NJ: Princeton University Press, 1982), 19. See also Chapter Four, 123–126.

102 Walter, *Warrior Saints*, 21. See also Matthews, *Byzantium*, 43–48.

103 Matthews, *Byzantium*, 46.

104 Matthews, *Byzantium*, 46.

105 Matthews, 47.

106 Matthews, 48.

107 The Louvre Museum, Paris, where the icon resides, dates it to the eighth century, while Matthews dates it to the sixth century, 48.

108 Matthews, *Byzantium*, 49–51.

109 Walter, *Warrior Saints*, 109.

110 Walter, 123.

111 Walter, 266–267.

112 Kurt Weitzmann, *The Monastery of Saint Catherine at Mount Sinai: The Icons. Volume One: From the Sixth to the Tenth Century* (Princeton, NJ: Princeton University Press, 1976), 5, quoting E. Kitzinger, "The Cult of Images in the Age Before Iconoclasm," D.O.P. VIII, 1954, 83ff.

113 Walter, *Warrior Saints*, 115–116. Referencing *Vie de Théodore de Sykeon* (Bibliographica hagiographica graeca, 1748), ed. A. J. Festugière, Brussles, Belgium, 1970), § 120, Greek text, pp. 96–97, translation pp. 100–101.

114 *Vie de Theodore*, § 32, p. 29 of the Greek text; pp. 31–32 of the translation.

115 Because the saints are unnamed, Walter identifies only Theodore Tiron and not George in this painting, arguing that George could also be St. Demetrius. However,

he does note that an 18th-century icon in the National Art Gallery of Sofia, Bulgaria, there is an icon of Theodore and George on horseback with exactly the same features, Walter, *Warrior Saints*, 124. Weitzmann, however, identifies the saints as Theodore and George on the basis of George's boyish, golden features and on the basis of the frequency of other named icons which combine Theodore and George, especially in consideration of the fact that Theodore is either not or infrequently paired with Demetrius. Most scholars also identify the saint on the right as George. Weitzmann, *Monastery of St. Catherine*, 18–20.

116 Weitzmann, *Monastery of St. Catherine*, 19.

117 Walter, *Byzantine Warrior Saints*, 124. Quoting J. Clédat, "Les fouilles exécutées à Baouît," in *Memoires de l'Institute d'Archéologie Orientale du Caire*, 12, 1904, pp. lxii-lxiii, 91.

118 Nicole Thierry, *Haut Moyen-Âge en Cappadoce: Les Églises de la Région de Çavuşin*, Vol. 2 (Paris: Librarie Orientaliste Paul Geuthner, 1994), photograph of icon pl. 156 a; drawing rendered on p. 302. Cf. Walter, who dates this icon to the latter half of the sixth century, *Warrior Saints*, 121.

119 Walter, *Warrior Saints*, 125.

120 Walter, *Warrior Saints*, 47–53. Theodore's *Passion* is located in *Bibliographica hagiograhica graeca* with *Auctarium*, 1764. The earliest manuscript copy of the *Passion* dates from a ninth-century manuscript, although the text dates itself to 754 CE.

121 Walter, 125, 99n. See also Chapter Three, p. 25.

122 This Georgian manuscript is located in the Patriarchal Library, Jerusalem, Cod. 2, ca. 11th century.

123 See de Voragine, *The Golden Legend: Readings on the Saints*, 2 vols., William Granger Ryan, transl. (Princeton, NJ: Princeton University Press, 1993).

124 Walter, *Warrior Saints*, 121–122.

125 See also Chapter Two, 42; and Chapter Seven, 250.

126 Cf. the protective qualities of pagan military gods, above.

127 Walter, Warrior Saints, 118, quoting Gregory of Nyssa, *De Sancto Theodoro* (*Bibliographica hagiographica graeca*), J. P. Cavarnos, ed., *Gregory of Nyssa, Sermons* II, 1 (Leiden/New York: 1990).

128 Ibid., 133. See also S. Pètridés, "Deux canons inédits de Georges Skylitzes," in *Vizantijskij Vremmenik* 10, 1903.

129 Walter, *Warrior Saints*, 132–134. See also P. Deschamps, "La légende de S. Georges et les combats de croisés dans les pientures murals du Moyen Age," *Monuments et Memoires*, (Fondation E. Piot, 44, 1950): 109–123, plates 12–15.

130 Walter, *Warrior Saints*, 93.

131 Walter, 129.

132 Walter, 130.

133 Samantha Riches, *St. George: Hero, Martyr and Myth* (Sutton Publishing Company, 1997). See also Chapter One, 5, 22n; Chapter Three, 65–70; Chapter Five, 161; Chapter Seven, 245–248.

134 Even into the early 20th century in the Levant, "mad" persons were chained to the churches of St. George, because it was believed that madness was caused by demons, who could be expurgated by St. George. See especially Chapter Two, 43–44.

135 Fieldwork interview with Greek Orthodox bishop (at Balamand University).

136 ARPOA stats, *Sur les Pas des Saints au Liban.* See also Chapter One. Note that Muslims also revere Mary, whom they call *Maryam*, and after whom the 19th *surah* of the Qur'ān is named.

137 See Chapter Two, 41, 77n.

138 See the various locations of shrines to St. George listed in John Wilkinson, *Jerusalem Pilgrims: Before the Crusades* (Warminster, England: Aris & Phillips Ltd., 1977).

6 The emergence of Islam and Al-Khiḍr

Part One: Introduction and the emergence of Islam in late antiquity

The late antique period in the Near East, ca. 200–750 CE, spanned an enormous series of transformations in regional political and social organization.[1] Generally considered the active transition period between the classical Roman era and the rise of classical Islam, the late antique era included the division of the Roman Empire into western and eastern halves, the political demise of the west and the ascendency of the eastern portion of the Empire – which now we designate 'Byzantium', but they did not – the growth and division of Christianities around the Mediterranean, and the proliferation of numerous other apocalyptic and prophetic religious movements within and among the contemporaneous extended Byzantine and Sasanian empires.

The Byzantine Emperor Justinian I (482–565 CE) could be considered perhaps the late antique figure *par excellence*, as his shadow falls long over the histories of both east and west. Justinian's legacy (r. 527–565 CE) includes the commission of still-extant monumental ecclesiastical buildings and works of art, the formal theological divisions of eastern Christianity, a revision of the Roman law code into the *Corpus Juris Civilis*, which remains to this day the basis of many western legal systems, and the ambitious re-extension of the empire, for a time, to the Atlantic Ocean. Considered alternatively the 'last Roman' and the 'first Byzantine', it is all the more astonishing to recall that the Byzantine Emperor Justinian was a contemporary of the prophet Muḥammad ibn 'Abd Allāh, the founding figure of the religious tradition of Islam.

Traditional Muslim accounts of Muḥammad date his birth to the year 570 CE, five years after the death of Justinian.[2] This proximity in time is illustrative of a larger point that will be highlighted throughout this chapter: the emergence of the Qur'ān and of the religious tradition of Islam, often depicted as a distinct break from and at variance with the political, religious, and social history of the Near East, arose instead as a movement in natural congruity with the social and intellectual currents of the late antique world.

In this chapter, we will examine the figure of al-Khiḍr, الخضر, known in Muslim tradition from the wisdom-literature narrative with which he is associated in the Qur'ān (Q 18:60–82), through his later naming in *tafsīr* 'exegesis'. Al- Khiḍr, a legendary figure whose name in Arabic means approximately 'the Green [One/Man]', has come to be understood in Islamic tradition as the wise, esoteric figure who taught Moses. This in turn has led over subsequent centuries to Khiḍr's associations with the mystical Muslim traditions of Sufism, which are built around esoteric knowledge and the sort of disciple-master teaching relationship displayed in Q 18:60–82. Khiḍr was associated in early Islamic literature with the biblical figure of Elijah, and, since at least the 11th century CE, he has been popularly associated with both of the figures Elijah and St. George in the Eastern Mediterranean.[3]

By examining al-Khiḍr's earliest appearances in text, both in the Qur'ān and in exegetical *tafsīr* literature, this chapter geographically contextualizes the Islamic figure of al-Khiḍr. Unlike the texts of Elijah and of St. George, however, the narrative in the Qur'ān linked to al-Khiḍr does not purport to be an historical account of events, but rather is an instance of wisdom literature, making it an account that is both outside of time and applicable in all times.[4] After geographically contextualizing the Khiḍr narrative, we compare it to a similar medieval rabbinical *al-faraj* 'delivery from a problem'/'consolation' literature narrative, involving nearly the same frame story, but with Elijah in the place of al-Khiḍr as the wise teacher. This section investigates both how these stories have influenced one another, as well as how they have influenced subsequent textual associations in Islam between al-Khiḍr and Elijah. Then, this chapter examines important images associated with al-Khiḍr, as well as what differences in those images – meditated by geographical place of origin – indicate. This chapter argues that the name 'al-Khiḍr' most likely was an epithet for the figure of late antique Elijah. But first, this chapter will give an historical introduction to the late antique social, religious, and political environment from within which the Qur'ān and its figures and narratives arose.

Arabian environs

Our account begins in the Arabian Peninsula, the location where the religious tradition of Islam has its earliest roots. Historically it has been difficult to define the location of Arabia and the Arabs, for not least of which reason that the Arab population, which originated within the center and north of the peninsula, traditionally was nomadic. Nomadism is probably the basis of the Arabic word 'Arab', عرب, as, from its earliest historical appearances in both biblical and Assyrian texts, the term refers to peoples of the Arabian and Syrian deserts who migrate seasonally with their animal flocks.[5] The term 'Arabia' in this project thus will refer both to the Arabian Peninsula surrounded by the Red Sea and the Persian Gulf, [6] and also to the desert regions on the dry side of the 200 mm (8 inches) isohyet in Mesopotamia and in the east of modern-day Syria, Jordan, and Iraq.[7] Arabia is a land mass of nearly 1.5 million square miles; slightly larger than India or Europe – encompassing a substantial area of the Near East.[8]

Arabian geography

Arabian geography can be divided into four distinct regions: a central high plateau area comprised of hard, rocky desert, surrounded by a series of three relatively softer and sometimes sand deserts. Starting in the north is the Syrian Desert, located between Mesopotamia and the Levant. South of there is the *Nafuḍ* Desert in the northern section of the Arabian Peninsula proper; below is the *Rub' al-Khālī*, the 'empty quarter', the world's largest contiguous sand desert, spread over most of the central-southern portion of the ax-blade of the peninsula.

The eastern section of the Peninsula contains no rivers but has been able to support sedentary populations and cities for several thousand years, thanks to its considerable groundwater reserves. This region runs the length of the eastern peninsula along the Persian or Arabian Gulf, through to the modern country of Oman. Because of its proximity to the larger Bronze Age cultures in southern Mesopotamia and Iran, and owing to its location between these lands and the copper mines of Oman, the eastern part of the peninsula, particularly the island of Bahrain and its surrounding mainland territory – called then Dilmun – were well known and prospered or suffered along with the fortunes of these larger territories.[9]

The southern portion of the Arabian Peninsula, roughly coincident with modern Yemen, was known to Roman-era geographers as 'Arabia Felix', 'fortunate Arabia'. Because of its geographical location, it receives monsoonal rains, making this the only large verdant area of the Arabian Peninsula. The southwest is able both to sustain agriculture, and, due to its flora – like that of eastern Africa, where the bushes which produce frankincense and myrrh grow – the south became during the first millennia BCE and CE the location of powerful kingdoms, such as Saba/'Sheba' and Ḥimyar, enriched through trade. Despite being surrounded by water, the only suitable port for docking along the coast of the entire peninsula is located at Aden (in modern-day Yemen),[10] bestowing the south a further advantage in trade: both the overland and water trade routes passed through the south.

A mountain range runs the length of the western portion of the peninsula and reaches its highest point in the south. The west is thus mountainous, especially toward the southwest, and generally inhospitable, save for areas with groundwater reserves and in some cases oases which have supported fixed communities, such as at Ṭā'if, Mecca, Yathrib/Medīna, Khaybār, and Taymā'.

Owing to the geographical diversity of the peninsula and the *natura maligna* nature of its desert environments, the regions and peoples of the peninsula largely were separated early in history, although gradually they began to integrate, beginning in the first millennium BCE. Eventually, the nomadic population from the west and especially the center/north, known as Arabs, began to dominate the peninsula. [11]

Arabian trade

Despite its largely inhospitable environs, the Arabian Peninsula is located between what historically were the larger, richer, and politically better-organized regions of India, Mesopotamia, Africa, and the Mediterranean. For most overland trade, and all seaborne trade, Arabia – mostly around the perimeter, but also on occasion through the deserts in the center – had to be engaged. This of course was true as well for military transport; there is an account of the Assyrian king Esarhaddon in 671 BCE thanking an Arab king for his assistance with camels and water skins in moving his army.[12]

Prized for its trade in and production of myrrh, frankincense, and other aromatics, but also as an essential station along the lucrative highway of silk trade, Arabia and its peoples thus were part of the part of the wider ambit of the Near Eastern world. While academic portrayals of the religious history of the Near East often present the religious and political cultures of the Near East as segmented and discrete, in fact, gods, stories, and what we might think of now as religious notions traveled freely wherever peoples came into contact. Trade routes ought thus to be thought of as currents of religious thought and contact as much as of material goods, and can help us to visualize the connected nature of Near Eastern religious communities (Figure 6.1).

Arabian religious communities

Both trade and the remoteness of the Arabian Peninsula were attractive to regional religious communities. This particularly was so for Christian communities after the Council of Chalcedon in 451 CE, when Arabia became an appealing location for sectarian missionizing. Located between the competing Byzantine and Sasanian Christian communities, Arabia represented expansionist potential for bishoprics.[13]

Arabian polytheism

What is known of internal Arabian religious life (outside of later Islamic historical accounts) comes to us primarily from the tens of thousands of rock inscriptions found throughout the peninsula.[14] Communities of Jews have existed in Arabia since the first millennium BCE. However, until about the fourth century CE, most inhabitants were polytheists. We know the names of many of their gods because the most common form of Arabian inscription was to invoke the gods in some way, usually petitioning the gods or thanking them.[15] For the most part, the gods seem in some instances to have been associated with specific geographical regions, and sometimes, as in the case of the popular goddess Allāt, to have been known and venerated throughout the Arabian Peninsula and in places around the northern Syrian Desert, at locations like Palmyra and Nabataea.[16]

In the western portion of the Peninsula, specifically in the region of the Ḥijāz, the location of the city of Mecca, deities in addition to Allāt seem to have been of local importance; namely, al-'Uzzā and Manāt (Q 16:16, 19:80, 22:72), named by Arab antiquarians, and goddesses that had been worshipped throughout the Syrian desert regions from at least half a millennium earlier.[17] In general, in Arabian polytheism, astral deities such as the sun, moon, and Venus/al-'Uzzā, among others, were worshipped. The Arabian gods, who often were the same as the polytheistic gods and goddesses of the wider Near East in late antiquity,[18] seem to have represented – much like gods everywhere – those forces which were important to people, but beyond their control, such as rain, fertility, health, love, and death.[19]

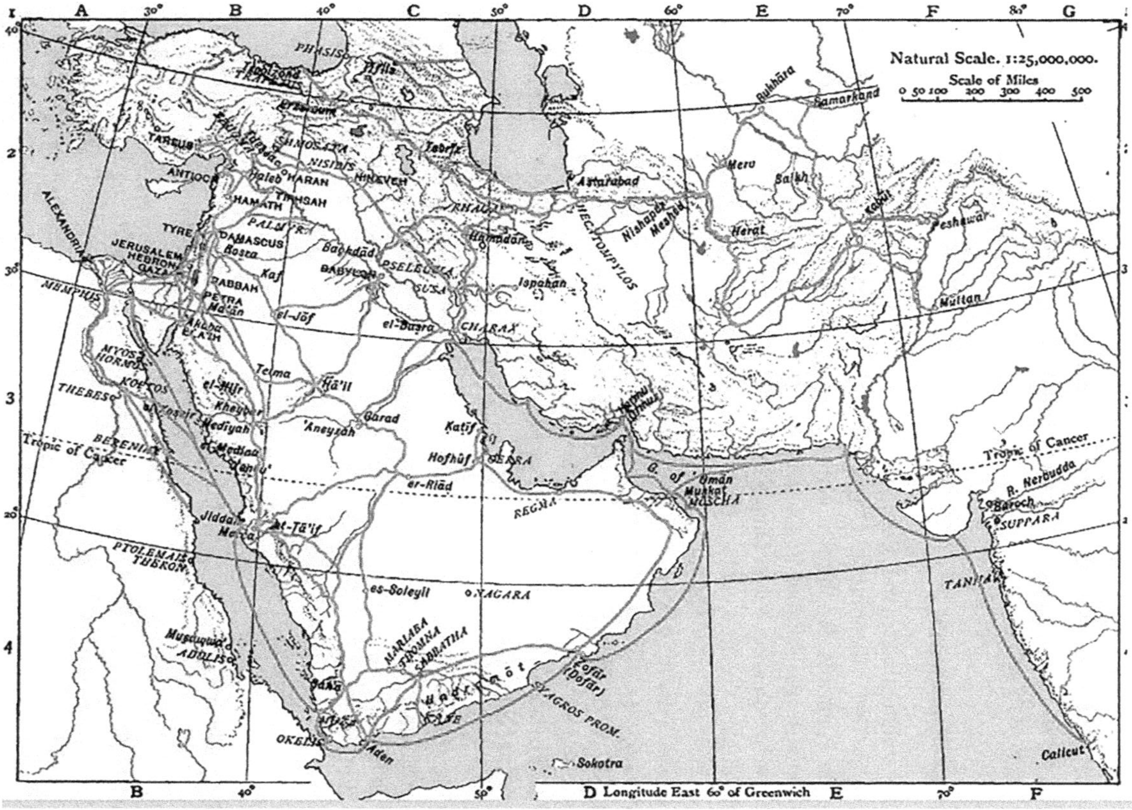

Figure 6.1 Map of Near Eastern trade routes

A particular feature of Arabian religious ritual and worship was that the gods were worshipped at local shrines, called *aḥrām* (sg., *ḥaram*). These *aḥrām* consisted of a definitively bound and marked sacred area with a shrine at the center. Usually, a single family or tribe served as the caretaker of the shrine, and within the territory of the *ḥaram*, violence was forbidden, making this a sacred space for all visitors to honor gods or to conduct business. Like the Arabian cities of Ṭā'if and Ṣan'ā', the city of Mecca, the traditional birthplace of Muḥammad, was just such a demarcated sanctuary city (and remains so to this day), with the shrine of the Ka'ba at its center.[20]

Arabian monotheism

Jewish communities in the Arabian Peninsula were attested as early as the second half of the first millennium BCE, especially in the northwest and in the south of the Arabian Peninsula. By the first centuries of the Common Era, there were fairly large Jewish communities in southern Arabia, particularly in the Ḥimyār region, where a Jewish king, Yūsuf Dhu Nawās, ruled during the early sixth century.[21]

By at least the third century CE, Christian communities had begun to be established in Arabia.[22] Indeed, during the fifth century and especially the sixth century, it became a matter of policy within the Roman/Byzantine empire to encourage conversion to Christianity in the Arabian Peninsula and in the Horn of Africa.[23] After the Council of Chalcedon in 451, sectarian Christian communities began to compete in Arabia for new territories and converts. Thus, by the sixth century, Christian communities were present throughout the peninsula.[24] At least with respect to south Arabian inscriptions,

> the speed and finality of the change in the religious phraseology in south Arabian inscriptions in the fourth century AD certainly suggests a revolution in the religious outlook of the ruling elite. References to the pagan deities of the ancient tradition disappeared almost completely in favor of mention of the one unique God, referred to as 'the Merciful' or simply as 'God' and usually qualified as 'Lord of Heaven' or 'Lord of Heaven and Earth'.[25]

That being said of the religious outlook of the ruling elite in the south following the fourth century CE, sizeable communities of those whose religious orientation was polytheistic in nature continued to exist throughout the Arabian Peninsula, which was not, of course, unlike the general religious situation of the greater Near East at that time. Traditional accounts of early Islamic history, written during the first two centuries after the death of Muḥammad, emphasize the presence of polytheist communities in Muḥammad's Arabian environment over and above contemporaneous Jewish or Christian communities. Given the legacy of those traditional accounts in shaping perceptions of the Arabian past, western scholars of Islam as well long accepted the validity of a primarily polytheistic orientation to Arabian religious composition in the sixth and seventh centuries, but that has begun to change in light of new research and perspectives.[26]

Given the abundant textual and material evidence for Arabian Jewish and Christian communities, as well as the documentary evidence for these communities from sources outside of the peninsula – to say nothing of the extensive evidence for the presence of these communities from within the text of the Qur'ān itself, as we will see – we likewise ought not presume the Arabian Peninsula religiously to have been substantially different in composition from other areas within the late antique Near East.[27] By the sixth–seventh century, communities of Jews and Christians (among, of course, many other religious groups) were established throughout the Mediterranean, Africa, the Near East, and central Asia, as they were in Arabia. Therefore, we briefly review next the status of majority religious communities in the Near East as they appeared in the late sixth and early seventh centuries, as this environment formed the religious milieu within which the Qur'ān and its narratives and figures took shape.

Religious currents in the late antique Near East

Throughout the late antique period, the major political powers of the Near East were the Roman-Byzantine Empire to the west of the Euphrates River, and the Sasanian Empire, to the east. All other regional polities – and their religious communities – fell within these two grand orbits. The Byzantines and Sasanians competed not only for territory, but for the control and taxation of luxury trade goods – silk, spices, and aromatics – which kept their interests intertwined with the Arabian Peninsula. Between the fourth and seventh centuries CE, the Byzantines and Sasanians were at war with one another seven times.[28]

Christian sectarianism and the Byzantine Empire

As we saw in Chapter Five, the Roman-Byzantine Empire became Christian in its imperial religious orientation throughout the fourth century CE, establishing Christianity as the official religion of the Empire toward the end of the century, and convening several church councils that were intended to develop an orthodox theology. Orthodoxy in Christianity thus was proclaimed through councils that declared specific theological doctrines to be correct and others to be heretical. Theological debates about the precise nature of Jesus (called Christology) evolved along with developments in orthodoxy.

Early mainline Christology was marked by belief in the humanity of Jesus, as apostolic Christianity focused upon the first three Gospels and the teachings of Paul. Alongside that belief, however, as we began to see in Chapter Five, a second foundation of mainline Christology was developing; one which began to assert the divinity of Jesus. This Christology was inspired by the Gospel of John, with its language about the 'Word' (a divine reality distinct from God the 'Father' in the Christian Trinity) becoming flesh, and, by as early as the 180s CE, Christians (and/or Jewish-Christians) who believed that Jesus only was a human were labeled heretics. However, this theology of the 'incarnation' raised vexing questions which theologians in subsequent centuries attempted to answer in different ways;

namely, just how was the divine 'Word' united with or incarnated with the human person of Jesus?[29]

The Council of Nicaea in 325 CE established the precedent of declaring that the 'Word' absolutely and completely was divine; of one substance (consubstantial, ὁμοούσιος) with God the Father. The outcome of Nicaea was reaffirmed later at the Council of Constantinople in 381, and, thereafter, mainline Christology became inseparable from a belief in the 'Word's' complete divinity. Subsequently, debate developed over the precise nature of and titles for Mary, the mother of Jesus.

In the first third of the fifth century, the Bishop Nestorius of Constantinople objected to the use of a specific title that had developed for Mary – Θεοτόκος, "Theotokos," 'God-bearer' – as he felt it imperiled heretically the human nature of Mary. Nestorius preferred instead the title Ξριστόκος, "Christokos," 'Christ-bearer," as this seemed a more appropriate title. The Council of Ephesus in 431 CE affirmed as orthodox the title for Mary of *Theotokos*, however, and eventually Nestorius was excommunicated, initiating the first of many sectarian divisions within Christianity (sectarianism becoming possible once an imperial orthodox position had become associated with particular theological positions, as at Nicaea in 325). Nestorius and his followers developed their Church where they had been offered refuge in Sasanian Persia, far from the reach of those in Byzantium who enforced an imperial orthodox position. Pejoratively termed by outsiders the 'Nestorian' church, members of this confession referred to it instead as the Church of the East.

Christological questions of exactly how the divine and human natures of Jesus were joined still festered, however. The main debates involved the questions of whether the divine and human natures of Jesus were dyophysite (two natures; and, if so, how those two natures were separated or combined), or, whether the divine and human aspects of Jesus were monophysite (one nature). In 451 CE, Emperor Marcian called the Council of Chalcedon to produce a theological statement that would end all uncertainty and dispute; it declared that Christ was "recognized in two natures," but balanced that position with the assertion that Christ also was "in one person and hypostasis."[30]

The "of two natures" formulation was a theological calamity for the bishops of Syria and Egypt, who felt that this formulation violated irretrievably the earlier position of Nicaea, which had clearly decreed that Christ was "of one substance" – homoousious with the Father.[31] The Council of Chalcedon in 451 thus had the effect of establishing a second sectarian division from imperial Christianity: the churches of Antioch (Syria) and of Alexandria (Egypt) rejected the Chalcedonian formulation and promulgated their own.

In the Antiochene and Alexandrian formulations, Christ was considered to have two natures, but which existed mixed in one nature or hypostasis – i.e., ὁμοούσιος (homoousious) with the Father (thus echoing the formulation of Nicaea). These sects are called Oriental (i.e., Eastern) Orthodoxies (i.e., theological positions are determined by councils), and are often mistakenly termed 'monophysite' traditions. In fact, these churches effectively accepted the 'dyophysite' – human and divine – natures of Jesus, but believed that these aspects existed in Jesus in only *one* mixed human-divine nature or hypostasis. For this reason, the correct theological designation with respect to the Oriental Orthodoxies, and the classification by which they identify themselves, is 'miaphysite'. These miaphysite churches also became known as the Syrian Orthodox and Coptic Orthodox churches. In the late antique period, these churches often were called 'Jacobite', after the miaphysite theological position followed Jacob Baradaeus, Bishop of Edessa in Syria from 543 until his death in 578 CE.

The Council of Chalcedon also had the effect of reaffirming an imperial orthodox theological position sanctioned by the Byzantine emperor. The 'Orthodox' view (that which imperially could be enforced) was the belief articulated at Chalcedon; i.e., that of the dyophysite nature of Jesus Christ: an understanding that *two* natures, or hypostases – human and divine – were *separately* related in the person of Jesus Christ. Churches that adhered to this theological position are called Eastern Orthodox, or Greek Orthodox, reflecting the language of imperial Christianity. These imperial orthodox churches became known during the late antique period as 'Melkite', i.e., 'belonging to the king', from the Syriac *malkāyā*, 'royalists'.

Thus, after the council of Chalcedon in 451 CE, and by the sixth to seventh century, the Christians of the Near East comprised several well-defined communities, each with its own theological interpretations. The Byzantine or imperial orthodox 'Melkite' Christians, whose liturgical language was Greek and sometimes Christian Palestinian Aramaic (CPA), or Syriac,[32] predominated in Anatolia, the Balkans, Greece, Palestine, and urban centers where imperial authority was strong. In Syria, Egypt, and Armenia, especially in non-urban areas, the 'Jacobite' miaphysite churches, whose liturgical languages were Syriac and Coptic, were predominant. In Persia and east of the Euphrates River, 'Nestorian' monophysite churches, whose liturgical language was Syriac, prevailed. The Christians who figured prominently in the Qur'ān, as we will see, and which literally surrounded and entered the Arabian Peninsula, were thus 'Chalcedonian' Melkites, and 'non-Chalcedonian' Jacobites and Nestorians.

Sasanian Empire and Zoroastrianism

To the east of the Euphrates River lay the Sasanian Empire (224–651 CE), which extended eastward to Afghanistan and Central Asia and had its capital at Ctesiphon (near modern-day Baghdad). The primary language of many within this large empire was Middle Persian (called پهلوی 'Pahlavi'). Alongside Zoroastrianism, several religious communities existed within the empire.

Large communities of Jews had existed in Persia since the 587/6 BCE Babylonian Exile. Indeed, it was in Persia, along the Euphrates and Tigris Rivers, where the Jewish academies were located, and the Babylonian Talmud was compiled, and mature ca. 600 CE. In addition, there were substantial communities of Christians, both Syrian miaphysites and so-called Nestorians; the seat of the Nestorian (or Church of the East) patriarch was at Ctesiphon. In addition to numerous smaller religious communities, there were also a substantial number of Buddhists in the eastern portion of the empire.

The largest religious tradition, however, and that which took on an imperial character in being identified with the Sasanian state, was Zoroastrianism. Zoroastrianism, named for its founding prophet, Zoroaster (زردشت *'zardosht'*), was a dualistic faith that conceived of the universe as the seat of a cosmic battle between the forces of good, epitomized by the god Ahura Mazda, and the forces of evil, epitomized by the god Ahrimān. The forces of good were symbolized by light – especially fire – and those of evil were symbolized by darkness. Zoroastrian rites involved both the sun, and fire temples, in which fires were continually kept burning by priests.[33] Several Zoroastrian ideas were absorbed into Jewish belief and doctrine (and thus into later Christianity and Islam), and also independently spread westward. Among the most prominent was the notion of 'dualism' (especially of heaven and hell, good versus evil, and light versus dark).[34]

Asceticism and apocalypticism

One characteristic feature of the late antique religious environment in general was an inclination toward asceticism. Christian hermits living in the Egyptian deserts emulated the ascetic lifestyle they believed Jesus had promoted, and monastic communities began during the third century in Egypt. Monasteries were established throughout the Near East during the fourth to sixth centuries; in particular, at Mar Saba, in Palestine, St. Simeon, in Syria, and Quartmin, in Mesopotamia.

Often, a famous hermit was the basis for the establishment of a monastic community, such as the stylite ('pillar saint'; i.e., an ascetic who lives atop a pillar or column), Simeon, in Syria. Frequently, famous ascetics around the Near East were visited by common people, in the hope that thereby they might attain some of the holy individual's sanctity. In general, a broader ascetic movement within Christianity during the fourth to sixth centuries "saw the articulation of a range of popular religious practices, including pilgrimages, processions, the worship of saints' shrines and relics, and the veneration of icons," which were practices that afforded laypersons tangible contact with the sacred.[35]

Another characterization of late antique religious communities was a growing sense of a coming 'apocalypse', i.e., predictions of the approaching cataclysmic end of the world. Apocalyptic traditions often involved notions of morality, catastrophic destruction, and an ensuing era when the righteous (variously defined) would be rewarded.[36]

Prophetic traditions and piety

Prophetic traditions – the social and religious lifestyle of "abiding by the teachings, ethics, and law of a divinely inspired or sanctioned leader" – could be considered the salient religious phenomenon of the Near East from at least the Bronze Age.[37] The multiple-religions environment and sectarianism of the Near East might best be understood as competing religious movements with one primary element in common: that of prophetic traditions.

Similar to, although not synonymous with, the growing mood of asceticism in the late antique Near East was the growth in religious movements involving pietistic orientations and practices. Most directly this can be seen in the reinterpretation of classical civic organization brought about through Christian governmental agents:

> Bishops replaced councilors in caring for the welfare of a city's inhabitants, churches and shrines overtook theatres and temples as the centres of communal life, monks and ascetics became the new heroes of the people, hagiographies and miracle stories dislodged secular writings as the most popular choice of literature, and icons and crosses triumphed as symbols of divine protection.[38]

Holy books

The late antique period also can be characterized by the compellation of and codification of holy books. Between the second and fifth centuries CE, authoritative Latin, Syriac, and other versions of the Hebrew scriptures and the New Testament were undertaken. During the Sasanian period, the books of the *Avesta*, the Zoroastrian scripture, were compiled in written form, as was the *Zand*, a commentary on the *Avesta*. From the fifth through seventh centuries, the Palestinian (*Yerushalmi*) and Babylonian (*Bavli*) Talmuds, representing the two main centers of rabbinic scholarship in Palestine and Mesopotamia, respectively, were completed.[39] Extensive commentaries on the materials gathered in the *Mishnah* (ca. 200 CE), and the first authoritative compilation of the law and lore of the rabbis, the Talmuds were the preeminent legalistic texts for Near Eastern and Mediterranean Jewish communities.[40] Religious communities in the late antique Near East thus came to be defined "as much as anything by the fact that they had their own codified holy books."[41]

The Qur'ān: A late antique religious text

The Qur'ān consists of just over 6,000 verses of 'recitation' (Q 75:17–18) of divine revelations written in Arabic, and mostly composed in *sāj*, the rhymed prose style characteristic of early Arabic poets (Q 68:41–42). Traditional Islamic history and mainstream scholarship date the period of revelation from 610–632 CE, and the codification of an official codex of the Qur'ān to the tenure of the Caliph 'Uthman, ca. 650 CE.[42] These dates may be revised in the near future, but for now they remain mainstream and it will be the perspective of this project as well that the Qur'ān reached its codified form in the second half of the seventh century CE.[43]

In the following sections, we will discuss Jews and Christians in the Qur'ān, as well as the Bible in the Qur'ān. We will also discuss features specific to the Qur'ān, such as its critiques of the Trinity and its own distinctive prophetology – exemplified by Muḥammad but embodied as well in the Qur'ānic figures of Abraham and of Moses – and how that prophetology accords with Qur'ānic notions of God. This information is important for an accurate understanding of the Qur'ān in its late antique environment, as well as it being a framework for arguments that shortly will be made shortly regarding the 'Khiḍr' narrative.

The Qur'ān is not arranged chronologically in the manner of some biblical books but consists rather of specific instances of revelation apparently compiled according to an external ordering scheme at a time after the instance of revelation. Several primary themes emerge from a reading of the Qur'ān. Above all, the Qur'ān imparts a message of strict monotheism, imploring its audience to recognize and be mindful of the Oneness of God (known as *tawḥīd*). From this distinct central notion, most other themes in the Qur'ān derive,[44] such as piety, righteous living, charity, a notion of the 'book' as God's word and apparently in relationship with the scriptures of the Jews and Christians, and a belief in the 'last day', reflecting both distinct notions of apocalypticism, and the potential for divine mercy beforehand.

The audience addressed in the Qur'ān is monotheistic, and a vast number of Qur'ānic revelations presume familiarity with biblical stories and lore. Furthermore, the Qur'ān infrequently addresses 'Muslims' in its audience, referring instead to Muḥammad and his followers as 'believers', *mu'minūn*. Both the words '*islām*' and '*muslim*' appear in the Qur'ān, but '*muslim*' occurs only 75 times, whereas '*mu'minūn*', believers, occurs nearly a thousand times.[45] Most scholars agree that, much like Christianity and Judaism (or any religious tradition, for that matter), 'Islam' emerged as a distinct religious tradition only gradually. That is the perspective of this book, as well, as is the notion that, like the exclusivist biblical traditions of Judaism and Christianity, 'Islam' emerged in part in a process of contradistinction from the polytheistic religious practices which long had characterized the Near East.

Christians and Jews in the Qur'ān

Perhaps the most fundamental evidence for the presence of Christians and Jews in the Qur'ān's audience is the knowledge it presumes on the part of its audience with respect to biblical narratives, figures, and lore. There are hardly any extended narratives or re-tellings of biblical stories; instead, there are allusions to narratives and to biblical characters. Sometimes, the Qur'ān comments on the characters or on the stories or gives additional details or interpretations.[46]

> The most basic thing one notices about the Qur'ān and its interface with the bible is the Islamic scripture's unspoken and pervasive confidence that its audience is thoroughly familiar with the stories of the biblical patriarchs and prophets, so familiar in fact that there is no need for even the most rudimentary form of introduction.[47]

The Qur'ān clearly presumes the presence of Arabic-speaking Jews as well in its audience. In the Qur'ān, this community are addressed about 30 times, by the reference 'Jews' (*'yahūdī'*, *'yahūd'*), by the verbal form of 'those who profess Judaism', *'hādū'*, and, when referencing the time of Moses or the revelation of the Torah, as 'Children of Israel', *'banū isrā'īl'*.[48]

There is evidence for Christians in the audience of the Qur'ān in at least four ways. First, the presence of non-Arabic vocabulary (mostly Syriac, as we will see) in the Qur'ān; second, the references made in the Qur'ān to contemporaneous extra-biblical Christian lore; third, the distinct criticism made of specific Christian doctrine and practice; particularly the notion of the Trinity, and, fourth, the direct reference to Christians, primarily as *'naṣārā'*, Nazarenes.[49]

Furthermore, Islamic tradition records peoples from these communities as important within early Islamic history. The *sīrah* biographical literature as well as the *ḥadīth* literary tradition include accounts of Muḥammad's interactions with several important Jewish tribes in Yathrib/Medina and with local Christians, as well. Figures such as Waraqah ibn Nawfal (purported to be a learned Christian relative of Muḥammad's first wife, Khadija), and Sergius Baḥîrâ, a Syrian monk who was said to have seen Muḥammad as a child and noticed his special nature, figure prominently in Islamic tradition. In Qur'ānic reference, however, rather than referring directly to Jews or Christians, the Qur'ān refers instead to these communities as "[People] 'of the Book'," or "Scripture People," or "Bible People," (*'ahl al-kitāb'*) 54 times,[50] indicating not only the contemporaneous presence of these communities, but in particular the Qur'ānic perspective that Jews and Christians possessed authoritative scriptures.

Another form of evidence for the existence of these communities within the Qur'ānic milieu comes from later Islamic historical writing. In particular, Muḥammad b. 'Abd Allāh al-Azraqī's *Akhbār Mecca*, which recalls the numerous Christian landmarks around Mecca and Medina, including the *masjid Maryam* (Mary's Church), the *mawqaf al-naṣārā* (Christian Station), and the icon of Mary said to have resided within the Ka'ba itself. Al-Azraqī' died in 865 CE, placing his lifetime long after the Qur'ānic period.[51] However, his account is nonetheless an important record of the contemporaneous ninth-century houses of Christian worship and architectural landmarks of Mecca and Medina, and it would seem unlikely that these Christian spaces newly were built in the historical heart of the Islamic world long after Islam had become an imperial power.

The Bible in the Qur'ān

Bible as Qur'ānic subtext

Judging by content, by far the most salient scriptures within the Qur'ān's milieu were the Hebrew Scriptures (Q 5:44) and rabbinic commentaries, as well as the Gospel traditions (5:47) and other New Testament books.[52] Extra-biblical lore, and so-called apocryphal books outside of the canons of Jews and Christians, also were important. Narratives and figures apparently external to the biblical tradition, such as from the *Epic of Gilgamesh*, may underlie portions of narratives in the Qur'ān;[53] however, the overwhelming religious subtext of the Qur'ān involves the canonical and extra-canonical biblical traditions of contemporaneous Jewish and Christian groups.

The Qur'ān also records several non-Arabic words, including those which have been shown ultimately to come from Akkadian, Ugaritic, Hebrew, Aramaic, Syriac, Ethiopic, and possibly Greek.[54] In passages in the Qur'ān which reference religious terminology; in particular, with respect to Christian thought and practice, there are a high incidence of words of a Syriac and Ge'ez background.[55] Given the composition of Christian religious communities in Arabia – Syriac-speakers in the Syrian Desert regions and wherever Jacobite communities existed throughout the Peninsula, and Ethiopian/Abyssinian (Axumite) communities, which had been present in the south at Najrān since at least the early sixth century, and whose liturgical language was Ge'ez – these linguistic origins of religious terms are natural, especially where contemporaneous Christian theological issues are referenced in the Qur'ān. Furthermore, the Qur'ān's environment intersected primarily with Syriac-language Christian communities, rather than with Greek-language communities, which largely were limited to the urbanized coastal areas of Syria and Palestine, such as at Antioch and Jerusalem.[56]

Overwhelmingly, foreign vocabulary in the Qur'ān has a Syriac origin – according to some estimates, by as much as 70% of the non-Arabic terminology.[57] Even the term 'Qur'ān' (Ar. 'recitation') may have been related early on to the Syriac word *qeryānā*, a 'lectionary', or portions of the Bible to be read aloud at a church service.[58] Recent research furthermore has demonstrated the linkages between Qur'ānic language narratives and Syriac-Christian narratives and concepts. An understanding of Syriac literature helps illuminate Qur'ānic language concerning the Trinity, the nature of Jesus, the narratives of Mary, the story of the Sleepers in the Cave (Q 18:9–26), the narrative of Dhū al-Qarnayn (Q 18:83–98), the *hūr 'īn* 'heavenly beings' in Q 56:22, and even the legal culture of the Qur'ān. [59] Indeed, "the probable background of the Christian biblical lore, both canonical and apocryphal, that one can find echoed, alluded to, or evoked in the Qur'ān … point to an Aramaic or Syriac provenance."[60] Even narratives from the Hebrew Bible and the stories of the older biblical figures like Abraham, Joseph, and Moses, as they are referenced and presented in the Qur'ān, may have a Syriac-language background.[61]

This research indicating the presence in the Qur'ān of the bible and its related lore, and of contemporary Jewish and Christian communities and their theological orientations and debates, is so pervasive that Gabriel Said Reynolds has suggested that the Bible could even be understood as the "subtext" of the Qur'ān.[62] Sidney Griffith similarly characterizes one role of the Qur'ān as a "kind of biblical commentary in Arabic, reacting to the Bible," although he furthermore clarifies that "the Islamic scripture is certainly larger in scope and purpose than its interface with the Bible, albeit that its divine message is presented as continuous with the earlier scriptures."[63]

Given the level of pre-Islamic writing in Arabic, as well as the lack of any examples of surviving pre-Islamic Arabic literature,[64] the mainstream conclusion within the field of Qur'ānic studies is that the biblical and extra-biblical lore present in the Qur'ān must have been spread orally in Arabic within the Arabian environment.[65] Communities of Arabian Jews and Christians would have accessed their scriptures in ecclesiastical or clerical contexts in liturgical language(s) (e.g., Syriac, Hebrew, Aramaic, and possibly Greek), and perhaps in oral Arabic translation, as well.[66]

Considering the nature of Qur'ānic discussion of the Bible and its religious communities, the Qur'ān seems to refer, as a part of its audience and environment, to those majority and 'mainstream' communities of Jews and Christians such as were spread throughout the greater Near East. "Judging by what the Islamic Scripture says about [Jews] and their religious usages by way of acceptance or criticism, and by what it evokes from their scripture traditions, [the Qur'ān] seems to have in mind Jews of the early seventh century."[67] Among Christians, the biblical, apocryphal, and ecclesiastical lore referenced in the Qur'ān "all had circulation in the so-called Melkite, Jacobite, and Nestorian Christian communities of the day," which thus indicates that the Christian scriptures and communities referenced in the Qur'ān reflected contemporaneous mainstream Near Eastern Christian communities.[68]

Qur'ānic corrections: Critiques of the Christian Trinity

As recent investigations underscore, the Qur'ān does not simply *reference* biblical material haphazardly; rather, figures and narratives are recollected in an essentially reformatory manner, in order to present thereby an alternative or 'corrected' position. "The Qur'ān means not to retell the biblical stories but to recall them and to recollect them within the corrective framework of its own discourse."[69]

In example, the Qur'ān is highly critical of the contemporaneous Christian notion of the Trinity, which it rejects unequivocally (Q 4:171, 5:72–78). The Qur'ān condemns in 5:73 the notion that 'God is the third of three', '*thālith thalāthatin*', a concept that was common in contemporaneous Syriac Christian homiletic texts in the adjectival form of '*tlîthāyâ*', meaning 'one of three', 'trinity', or 'triune'.[70] Indeed, in 5:75, the Qur'ān states,

> The Messiah, son of Mary, was only a messenger. Messengers have passed away before him. His mother was a truthful woman. They both ate food. See how We [i.e., God] make clear to them the signs, then see how deluded they are.

In this passage, the Qur'ān critiques not only the notion of the Trinity (i.e., through the assertion that Jesus the Messiah actually was a human messenger just like previous messengers), but also enters into Christian theological debates involving the nature of Mary. Explicitly referring to 'the Messiah' as the 'son of Mary', '*ibn marīam*', the Qur'ān pointedly aligns with the contemporaneous Nestorian rejection of the title for Mary of 'theotokos', 'God-bearer', a term which Jacobite and Melkite doctrine embraced, in favor of the title 'Christokos', 'Christ-bearer', as this latter title emphasized the human nature of Mary.[71]

Qur'ānic prophetology

As Sidney Griffith astutely has pointed out, what is notable about the biblical material in the Qur'ān is that it involves not so much the

> Bible per se, as it [does] well-known accounts of the Bible's principal dramatis personae: Adam, Noah, Abraham, Ishmael, Isaac, Jacob, Joseph, Moses, Aaron, Miriam [Maryam/Mary], David, Solomon, even Job and Jonah, along with Zachariah, John the Baptist, Mary, and 'Jesus, son of Mary', just to mention the major personalities.[72]

Large sections of the Bible are never mentioned in the Qur'ān, such as the letters of Paul, which were of great interest to contemporaneous Christian communities. This seems to be because what is presented in the Qur'ān is a version of prophetical history that is unique to the Qur'ān itself.

When the Prophets are recalled in the Qur'ān, rarely are they described in a detailed manner that quotes narratives from the Bible. Instead, the references in the Qur'ān are more akin to "paraphrases, allusions, and echoes," indicating that the Qur'ān's audience is expected to be familiar with the figure. Furthermore, the Qur'ān's selection of references to prophets, patriarchs, and narratives from the Bible is not random, but instead selected in accordance with the Qur'ān's distinctive prophetology.

> It envisions a series of 'messengers' and 'prophets' sent by God to warn human communities, which 'messengers' and 'prophets' God protects from the machinations of their adversaries. The Qur'ān recalls only such biblical stories as fit the paradigm of its prophetology, and it edits the narratives where necessary to fit the pattern.[73]

Recollections of prophetical figures are presented in a manner that culminates in the figure and prophetical career of Muḥammad, described as the "seal of the prophets,"[74] '*khātama al-nabīīn*' (Q 33:40); that is, the final prophet. As Griffith describes it,

> the pattern is always the same: the prophet/messenger arises within his own people (he is 'their brother' *akhūhum* Q 26:106, 124, 142, 161), he delivers his message, is discredited by his audience but is vindicated by the divine pains and hurt visited upon his adversaries, the retelling of which becomes a 'sign' for those who will believe.[75]

Differences between prophets in the Bible and Qur'ān

Prophets in the Hebrew Bible are expressly chosen and divinely inspired individuals who enter into the salvation-historical narrative at specific times and places to bear pietistic witness to notion that Yahweh is God, and to implore the community to whom they have been sent to do the same and to live in strict accordance with the spirit of Yahweh's revealed law. Prophets (both biblical and Qur'ānic) in the Qur'ān are the major figures of salvation history, and their role is to conduct God's unadulterated and unchanging messages to the community to whom they have been sent and of which they are a part. They face resistance from their communities (cf. Luke 4:24), members of whom also eventually distort the messages which have been brought to them, but God always supports the prophets' missions and vindicates them in their struggles.

Additionally, there are two distinct but overlapping categories of prophets in the Qur'ān, and for which exact parallels in the Bible do not exist. A prophet (*nābī*) is an individual sent by God to specific peoples to proclaim God's message, while a messenger (*rasūl*), a much more exclusive category of prophet, delivers to his people a divine revelation. The major messengers referenced in the Qur'ān (there are others) are Abraham, to whom was given/sent down the 'scrolls of Abraham' *ṣuḥuf ibrahīm* (Q 87:19),[76] Moses, to whom was given/sent down the Torah *al-tauwrat* (Q 53:36) David, to whom was given/sent down the Psalms *al-zabūr* (Q 4:163), Jesus, to whom was given/sent down the Gospels *al-injīl* (Q 57:27), and Muḥammad, the final prophet and messenger (Q 33:40) to whom was given/sent down the Qur'ān, the final (and perfected) revelation (Q 42:7).

Abraham, Moses, and Muḥammad in the Quran vis-à-vis strict monotheism

The two most prominent prophets in the Qur'ān are Abraham and Moses. Abraham was extremely important in the Qur'ānic prophetic scheme because he (together with Ishmael) had constructed the *ka'ba*, the House of God, *al-bayt* (Q 2:127–128), but primarily due to his role as the 'battler of idolatry' in defense of God/*Allāh*.[77] This tradition about Abraham is not mentioned in the Bible, but comes from a popular third- to fifth-century CE rabbinic *midrash* (*aggadic*/homiletic commentary) written in Aramaic on the book of Genesis, and which expounded upon the details of Abraham's life.[78] Like Abraham, Islamic tradition depicted Muḥammad as having destroyed the idols and idolatry that existed during Muḥammad's own generation (this time the idols were in the *ka'ba*), and having tried to bring people to faith in God, who was the author of the divine scriptures.[79] Furthermore, the 'faith of Abraham' *millāt ibrahīm* as referenced in the Qur'ān was associated with being neither a Jew nor a Christian, but a *ḥanīf*, a pious religious orientation identified both with pure monotheism (Q 3:67), with the prophet Abraham, and was "a state of being and a religion that coincide[d] with the message of Muḥammad."[80]

The prophet most often mentioned by name in the Qur'ān was Moses. Named 136 times, his life was described in detail and sometimes repeated in multiple *sūrahs*.[81] The focal point of Moses' message and

> his importance as a model for Muḥammad is clearly stated in the Moses section of *sūrah Ṭāhā* (Q 20:9–99): Moses said to Aaron and the Israelites after

> the incident with the golden calf (cf. Exod 32): "your god (*īlāh*) is only God (*Allāh*), there is no other god (*īlāh*) than he, he comprehends everything in knowledge" (Q 20:98); and God said immediately to Muḥammad, "Like this do We narrate to you reports of what has gone before, and We have brought you a recollection (*dhikran*) from Us" (Q 20:99).[82]

From this passage we glean four important points: first, the Qur'ānic conception of God (*Allāh*) was identified clearly with the God of the Hebrew Scriptures. Second, the Qur'ānic conception of God as exemplified in this verse is like that echoed in the creedal statement of later Islam, "لا إله إلا الله," *lā 'ilāha 'illā llāh*, 'there is no god but God'. Third, God in the Qur'ānic perception was not just a god/deity (*īlāh*), but apparently identified by the specific name of *Allāh*;[83] thus, God in the Qur'ān has at least some Arabian association, even linguistic, albeit that God (*Allāh*) as presented in the Qur'ān also was synonymous with the God of Moses. Fourth, Moses, to whom was sent the Torah, is paralleled in the figure of Muḥammad, who likewise was a messenger to whom a divine scripture was sent down.

The Torah was referred to by name in the Qur'ān 18 times. More than 12 times, the Torah was referred to as "the scripture We brought Moses" (Q 2:53 and 2:87); twice, the Torah was called *al-furqān* (Q 2:53 and 21:48),

> a term that is also used in reference to the Qur'ān itself (2:185 and 25:1) and is usually translated into English as 'criterion' or 'standard of judging' in the sense of something by means of which one distinguishes true from false, right from wrong… The term *al-furqān* occurs seven times in the Qur'ān, and it seems that it both echoes the Syriac term *purqānâ*, 'salvation', 'deliverance' (and possibly *paqdānâ*, 'command'), as well as reflecting an inner Arabic sense of 'separation', 'distinction'.[84]

In that way, Muḥammad was depicted in a manner parallel to Moses, who had brought a divine scripture which 'distinguished', as well as to Abraham, who, according to the later *sīrah* literature, had battled idolatry and established some of the most important rituals and sites named in the Qur'ān. Like Moses and Abraham before him, Muḥammad was presented in the Qur'ān as an exemplary prophet and messenger, and Muḥammad did so in large part by bringing a 'distinguishing' or 'separating' text. In that sense, the Qur'ān also can be understood as heresiological text, in that it created standards of 'true' and 'false' worship. Above all, the Qur'ān promoted a standard of strict monotheism that was presented in contradistinction both to contemporaneous polytheistic practices and communities, and to contemporaneous monotheistic communities and notions (such as the Christian conception of the Trinity) which were considered, in the Qur'ān, a tepid form of monotheism. El-Badawi argues that the Qur'ān's 'strict monotheism' was "a type of monotheism whose nature is anti-trinitarian, post-rabbinic, and apocalyptic."[85] Such is the perspective of this project, as well.

Version of the Qur'ān used in this study

The Qur'ānic references in this study are taken from the standardized version of the 1924 Cairo Codex (*muṣḥaf*). The Cairo *muṣḥaf* edition is linked to the specific reading *qīra'* of the Qur'ān associated with 'Asim (c. 744 CE).[86] The translations herein are drawn from the work of A. J. Droge, *The Qur'ān: A New Annotated Translation*,[87] or are specified as my own.

Part Two: al-Khiḍr Text: *Q 18:60–82*

Introduction

The narrative with which later exegetes/*mufassirūn* identify the figure of al-Khiḍr is located in the 18th *sūrah* of the Qur'ān, known as *Sūrah al-Kahf*, the 'Cave sūrah/chapter'. The 'Khiḍr' narrative of Q 18:60–82 in the Qur'ān falls into a category of narrative known generally as wisdom literature. It is a tale about the mysterious justice of God, understanding of which is beyond the grasp of ordinary humans. In this account, Moses was named as a seeker of knowledge, who sought knowledge from God's wise servant, identified in the Qur'ān by the anonymous title "a servant from [among] our servants" *'abdan min 'ibādinā'* (18:65). Accordingly, the account also falls into a category of narrative known as disciple-master didactic literature. As we will see, the 'servant' figure was earliest and most often identified in later exegetical literature or *tafsīr* as 'al-Khaḍir', 'the Green [One]', although other parallels for this figure have been suggested in scholarship; namely, the biblical prophet Elijah, the biblical figure Enoch, and the figure Utnapishtim from the *Epic of Gilgamesh*.[88] This section will argue that Elijah is most likely the source for the figure named 'al-Khiḍr'.

The narrative of 18:60–82 in the Qur'ān long has been thought to draw upon varied sources and influences.[89] Adding to the confusion of potential meanings behind and origins of this narrative are the traditions of related Islamic literature in the forms of *tafsīr* commentary and *hadīth* recollections. These later Arabic sources generally were written 100–200 (or more) years after the narratives of the Qur'ān were compiled, and in many cases these later explanatory sources can function more as literary creations than they do as contemporaneous witnesses to history.[90] Until very recently, scholarship on Qur'ānic passages has tended exclusively to rely upon the explanations of Arabic commentaries, despite the large gap in time between those commentaries and the Qur'ān. This is not to claim that the Arabic commentaries have no interpretive value; rather, it is to critique sole reliance upon them in attempting to discern the original meanings and references in Qur'ānic passages. The methodology of this project throughout has been to study the texts of each of these figures as "texts in their own historical context,"[91] to paraphrase Kevin Van Bladel on the topic, and this is an approach that, as we will see, helps to illuminate 'al-Khiḍr' in the narrative at 18:60–82, as well.

Accordingly, this analysis examines 18:60–82 by situating it within the context of the late antique world; from such a perspective, and considering recent research involving contemporaneous religious and literary influences, several concepts within the passage begin to make sense. This project moreover argues that the 'Moses and the Servant' narrative can only properly be understood when it is viewed in the context of *sūrah* 18 as a whole.[92] Such an argument is not commonly made about passages from the Qur'ān, which is a text regularly viewed as disjointed, and usually analyzed in discrete segments. In keeping with the larger argument of this book, however, such compartmentalization of analysis misses important connections among the whole that illuminate a more thorough understanding.

Therefore, this analysis of the Khiḍr text will make two main arguments: the first concerns the comprehensive nature of *Sūrah al-Kahf* and its uniform theological orientation. The second argument involves our suggestion here that the 'Moses and the Servant' narrative may have had a parallel in contemporaneous late antique literature (and which may have included the figure of Elijah in the role of the 'servant'), on the following six grounds: first, the unusual content of the narrative's extra-biblical Moses tale; second, on the basis that late antique texts underlie the other two primary narratives in this *sūrah*; third, on the grounds that wisdom literature and tales with a disciple-master didactic orientation were common in late antique literature; fourth, on the distinctive evidence that the early Arabic exegetical tradition identified the narrative's figure of the 'servant' as "al-Khaḍir," and who also was identified both with Elisha and Elijah, highly popular biblical figures in the late antique period; fifth, on the grounds that contemporaneous late antique literature was full of tales of Elijah as a wise teacher and guide; and, finally, sixth, on the basis that if indeed there had existed a contemporaneous text or tale involving Moses and Elijah with which the Qur'ān was in conversation, that too would not have been incongruous with late-antique literary topoi in which Moses and Elijah regularly were combined. Thus, this section will not claim to identify a contemporaneous Near Eastern text as the source of Q 18:60–82, but instead suggests, on the basis of the arguments outlined above and detailed below, that the existence of such a contemporaneous tale would not have been implausible.

Sūrah al-Kahf *Q 18 in late antique context*

Sūrah al-Kahf is distinguished by its three primary narratives: first, the 'Men of the Cave' (18:9–26); second, 'Moses and the Servant', which is the narrative where Khiḍr later was identified in exegesis/*tafsīr* as the 'servant' (18:60–82); and third, 'Dhū al-Qarnayn', the narrative about a figure regularly identified as Alexander the Great (18:83–98). *Sūrat al-Kahf* is distinctive not only for these stories, but also because at least two of them, the 'Men of the Cave' narrative and that of 'Dhū al-Qarnayn', have antecedents in Syriac Christian literature, and the details of those narratives in the Qur'ān thus are illuminated by an understanding of the stories in conversation with their Syriac parallels. The 'Moses and the Servant' narrative is remarkable because, as we will see, it is the only such account of Moses in either the Qur'ān or in the Bible, although this narrative also is illuminated by understanding it within the genres of both wisdom literature and disciple-master didactic literature, common both to contemporaneous rabbinic and Christian traditions.

The short tales and parables in the *sūrah* other than the three main narratives are comprised of exhortations to follow the divine guidance in the 'Book', *al-kitāb*, referring to the Qur'ān (18:1–3); anti-trinitarian polemic (18:3–8 and 110); encouragement to the prophet in his mission (18:27–29); warnings of a dire afterlife for those who disbelieve and of a paradise for those who believe (18:29–31 and 102–108); the parable of two men who shared abutting gardens: one man who was wealthy but impious, and the other man who was less fortunate in wealth and sons but truly pious, saying "what god pleases"; the garden of the former was buried in its own excess, and the audience was reminded that God is powerful over everything and that righteous deeds endure longer and are better in reward than is the "splendor of this present life," such as wealth and sons (Q 18:32–46); warnings against idolatry and *Iblīs*[93] and the *jinn*[94] (Q 18:50–51); apocalyptic judgment scenes (Q 18:47–49, 52–53, 99–101); a warning about disbelief and its consequences (Q 18:54–59), and a brief notice that if the sea were ink for God's words of revelation, the sea would give out before the words of God (Q 18:109).

These narratives and parables that accompany the longer passages are not random or disjointed insertions, however: they make sense in the larger structure of the *sūrah*. Carl Ernst has noted that *Sūrat al-Kahf* follows a particular pattern, characteristic of "middle and later Meccan Suras."[95] The intentional symmetry between the opening and closing eight verses of the chapter exemplifies ring composition, in that specific verses in that the introduction and the closing intentionally parallel one another, primarily around the themes of Qur'ānic revelation (18:1 and 18:109), apocalypticism (18:2, 8 and 18:102), anti-trinitarianism (18:4–5, 18:110), final judgment (18:103–108), and the Qur'ānic prophetology of Muḥammad (18:6 and 18:110).

Besides the parallelism of the introductory and closing sections, the remainder of the shorter narratives and parables in the chapter are located after the 'Men of the Cave' passage and before the 'Moses and the Servant' passage, indicating that the narratives of *Sūrah* 18 were located in specific places for specific purposes, rather than randomly bundled together. In addition to these structural elements, the entire *sūrah* has a specific theological orientation as well, which we will see below.

The 'Men of the Cave' Q 18:9–26

The narrative of the 'Men of the Cave' (Q 18:9–26) usually is identified with the Christian Syriac legend known as the 'Seven Sleepers of Ephesus'.[96] In that account, which first appeared in Syriac sources from the sixth century CE, the 'sleepers' were young men from Ephesus (in modern-day Turkey) who hid in a cave to avoid the persecutions of the notorious Roman Emperor Decius (r. 249–251 CE).[97] In the legend, they "fell asleep" in the cave for many years (i.e., God took their souls to heaven while their bodies remained in the cave).[98] They awoke during the reign of Emperor Theodosius II (408–450 CE), having remained there so long that the Empire and even the new Emperor himself had become Christian. However, during the reign of Theodosius II, some Christians had begun to question the veracity of bodily resurrection, asserting instead that only the soul was resurrected. Learning of the men in the cave, the Emperor hastened to see them, and they announced to the Emperor that they had been 'awoken' in order to demonstrate the truth of resurrection.

The Qur'ānic narrative counts the tale of the 'Companions of the Cave' among the marvels or signs '*ayāt*' of God. The men enter the cave because, as the Qur'ān recounts, the young men were God-fearing and had rejected the notion that their people had taken gods other than God, so God instructed them to take refuge in the cave. There they remained for 309 years, until God "raised them up" *ba'aṯnāhum* in order that the people of the city would know that God's promise *wa'd Allāh* (concerning bodily resurrection)[99] was true, and that there was no doubt about the [coming of the Last] Hour (Q 18:19–21).

Recent research into the Syriac sources of this story has helped to illuminate, among many other elements, one aspect of the Qur'ānic account that long troubled Islamic *mufassīrūn*; namely, how it could be that the Qur'ānic story references a dog, ("and their dog (lay) stretched out (with) its front paws at the door (of the cave)" Q 18:18), when dogs were known in Islamic tradition to be unclean. As Gabriel Said Reynolds has demonstrated, the 'dog' referenced in the Qur'ān makes sense in the light of Syriac literature and Christian tradition regarding this tale.[100] In the Syriac homily *mêmrê* of Jacob of Serugh (d. 521 CE) on this subject, Serugh described the 'sleepers' as "a flock" and as "blessed lambs" over whom God left a "'watcher' to be the guardian of [the 'sleepers''] limbs."[101] Not only could the 'watcher' be interpreted as a watch-dog or sheepdog according to the pastoral metaphor drawn by Serugh,[102] but, as the contemporaneous pilgrimage account of the Christian visitor Theodosius shows, by the year 530 CE, the city of Ephesus had become famous for being the location of "the seven sleeping brothers, and the dog 'Viricanus' at their feet."[103] The Qur'ān's account of the Christian legend of the 'Seven Sleepers' demonstrates "the ways in which the Qur'ān on the one hand removes the Christian frame of reference and on the other hand provides an Islamic, Qur'ānic horizon within which the legend takes on a whole new hermeneutical significance."[104]

'Dhū al-Qarnayn' Q 18:83–102

The main figure in the narrative of 'Dhū al-Qarnayn' is usually identified as the Macedonian Alexander III (the 'Great', ca. 356–323 BCE).[105] Kevin van Bladel (following the original work of both Theodor Nöldeke and G.J. Reinink) convincingly has demonstrated that the Syriac text titled *Neṣḥānâ dîleh d-Aleksandrôs*, "The Glorious Deeds of Alexander," ca. 630 CE, a manuscript uncovered by E.A. Wallis Budge in 1889 CE along with the Syriac version of the *Alexander Romance* of Pseudo-Callisthenes, and known in scholarship as the "Alexander Legend," is the source of the account of Dhū al-Qarnayn found at Q 18:83–102, of which the Qur'ānic version essentially is a retelling.[106]

Incorporating the research of G.J. Reinink, Van Bladel demonstrated that the Syriac *Alexander Legend* was written at the end of a long and difficult war between the 'Romans' and the Persians (603–630 CE), which turned out to be the final war between the Byzantine and Sasanian Empires. Most likely, the *Alexander Legend* was written in the year 630, the year during which the Emperor Heraclius finally had reversed the decade and more of Persian control over large parts of the Byzantine Empire, and the year in which Heraclius also had reportedly restored the relic of the True Cross to Jerusalem. Reinink and Van Bladel both argue that the *Alexander Legend* was an apocalypse, and a "piece of pro-Heraclian postwar propaganda," designed to reestablish Roman control over areas formerly under Persian control and to overcome the divisive Christological differences between Chalcedonian and non-Chalcedonian Christians in the empire, by equating the universally popular figure of Alexander with the Emperor Heraclius, and by ending the *Legend* with a "message of Byzantine Imperial eschatology: the prediction that one Byzantine emperor soon will establish a worldwide Christian rule which will be followed by the return of the Messiah."[107]

The events related in both the *Legend* and in Q 18:83–102 are given in precisely the same order, and almost every element in the Qur'ānic tale has a more-detailed counterpart in the *Legend.* Thus, if not directly, then by means of oral transmission, "a Syriac text quite current and important in the last years of Muḥammad's life was adapted for twenty verses of the Qur'ān."[108]

However, unlike the *Legend,* the Qur'ānic account does not include a final prophecy that declared the Romans eventually would defeat the Persians and establish a worldwide Christian rule lasting until the return of the Messiah. Instead, the Qur'ānic account ends with a warning from Dhū al-Qarnayn that God's judgment is imminent (98–102). The Qur'ānic account thus adapts this popular contemporaneous tale[109] by emphasizing its own message: "the Qur'ānic account puts more emphasis on the coming end of things and God's judgment and, not surprisingly, does not mention any expectation of a universal Christian empire for the Romans."[110]

Late antique references

In addition to the Syriac Christian tales of the *Seven Sleepers* and the *Alexander Legend* with which the Qur'ān is in conversation in the 'Men of the Cave' and the 'Dhū al-Qarnayn' narratives, respectively, there are several allusions in *sūrah* 18 to biblical passages and communities that help to illuminate the Qur'ān's common pool of figures, narratives, and motifs. In addition to references, through anti-trinitarian polemic, to contemporaneous forms of Christianity (Q 18:3–8 and 110), we see the presence of parables (Q 18:32–46), a popular genre of didactic narrative throughout the late antique period and on specific display in the biblical sayings attributed to Jesus.[111] We see also references to heaven, *firdaws* (Q 18:107), and to hell, *jahannam*/'Gehenna' (100, 106), and 'the fire' *nār* (Q 18:29), echoing dualistic, apocalyptic and eschatological beliefs current among biblical (particularly Christian) and wider Near Eastern registers. Finally, we see reflected of the Qur'ān's common pool of figures and motifs in this *sūrah* reference to the biblical figures 'Gog and Magog' (Q 18:94 cf. Ezekiel 38:2–3), to angels *malā'ikah* (Q 18:50), and, as an apocalyptic herald, a reference to "a blast on the trumpet" (Q 18:99 cf. Matt 24:31, 1 Cor 15:52, and 1 Thess 4:16); a reference repeated frequently in the Qur'ān (Q 6:73, 20:102, 39:68, 69:13, 74:8, and 78:18). There also is an episode in this *sūrah* in which God ordered the Angels to prostrate before Adam (Q 18:50), which, while not a part of the account in the book of *Genesis*, was a theme current in late antique Christian literature (cf. Heb 1:6, the *Life of Adam and Eve* 12:1–16:1, and the Syriac *Book of the Cave of Treasures* (2:22–25)).[112]

'Moses and the Servant' Q 18:60–82

The narrative of 'Moses and the Servant' begins about halfway through the *sūrah*, after the 'Men of the Cave' narrative and situated directly preceding the 'Dhū al-Qarnayn' narrative. It is 23 verses long, and is quoted here directly:

> (60) (Remember) when Moses said to his young man, "I shall not give up until I reach the junction of the two seas, or (else) I shall go on for a long time." (61) But when they reached the junction between them, they forgot their fish, (for) it took its way into the sea, slipping away/*tunneling*. (62) So when they had passed beyond (that place), he said to his young man, "Bring us our morning meal. We have indeed become weary from this journey of ours." (63) He said, "Did you see when we took refuge at the rock? Surely I forgot the fish – none other than Satan made me forget to remember it – and took its way into the sea – an amazing thing!" (64) He said, "That is what we were seeking!" So they returned, retracing their footsteps. (65) And they found a servant from [among] our servants whom we have given mercy and whom we have taught from our own knowledge. (66) Moses said to him, "Shall I follow you on (the condition) that you teach me some of what you have been taught (of) right (knowledge)?" (67) He said, "Surely you will not be able (to have) patience with me. (68) How could you have patience for what you cannot encompass in (your) awareness of it?" (69) He said, "You will find me, if God pleases, patient, and I shall not disobey you in any command." (70) He said, "If you follow (me), do not ask me about anything, until I mention it to you." (71) So they both set out (and continued on) until, when they sailed in the ship, he made a hole in it. He said, "Have you made a hole in it in order to drown its passengers? You have indeed done a dreadful thing!" (72) He said, "Did I not say, 'Surely you will not be able (to have) patience with me?'" (73) He said, "Do not take me to task for what I forgot, and do not burden me (with) hardship in my affair." (74) So they both set out (and continued on) until, when they met a young boy, he killed him. He said, "Have you killed an innocent person, other than (in retaliation) for a person? Certainly you have done a terrible thing!" (75) He said, "Did I not say to you, 'Surely you will not be able to have patience with me?'" (76) He said, "If I ask you about anything after this, do not keep me as a companion. You have had enough excuses from me." (77) So they both set out (and continued on) until, when they came to

the people of a town, they asked its people for food, but they refused to offer them hospitality. They both found in it a wall on the verge of collapse, and he set it up. He said, "If you had wished, you could indeed have taken a reward for that." (78) He said, "This is the parting between me and you. (Now) I shall inform you about the interpretation of what you were not able (to have) patience with. (79) As for the ship, it belonged to poor people working on the sea, and I wanted to damage it, (because) behind them (there) was a king seizing every ship by force. (80) As for the young boy, his parents were believers, and we feared that he would burden them both (with) insolent transgression and disbelief. (81) We wanted their Lord to give to them both in exchange (one) better than him in purity, and closer (to them) in affection. (82) As for the wall, it belonged to two orphan boys in the city, and underneath it was a treasure belonging to them both, (for) their father had been a righteous man. Your Lord wanted them both to reach their maturity and bring forth their treasure as a mercy from your Lord. I did not do it on my (own) command. That is the interpretation (of) what you were not able (to have) patience with."

Overview

This account details the narrative of Moses seeking a specific location, the 'meeting of the two seas' *majma' al-baḥrayn*, where Moses and his young servant boy *fatā[hu]* found there one of God's 'servants', "a servant from [among] our servants whom we have given mercy and whom we have taught from our own knowledge," *'abdan min 'ibādinā ātanāhu raḥmatan min 'indanā wa-'allamnāhu min ladunnā 'ilman*. Moses requested to be able to travel with this 'servant', in order that Moses might be able to learn some of the servant's divine knowledge. The servant reluctantly agreed and took Moses (now alone) on a journey involving three outrageous and seemingly unjust actions. From the beginning, Moses could not quiet his objections, and after Moses' third outburst the servant left, after having countenanced his actions as just. The servant furthermore declared that he did not perform the actions of his own accord *wa ma fa'alatuhu 'an amrī*, but, instead, the actions were God's own design.

Understanding 'Moses and the Servant'

Understanding the Qur'ānic narrative of 'Moses and the Servant' is challenging, particularly as no precise literary precedent for this tale has been identified. Exegetical and scholarly work on the narrative thus have interpreted it in various ways, from identifying it with the Alexander tales, to understanding it as a model for both disciple-master and esoteric knowledge. The latter interpretation probably has proven the most enduring for later Islamic tradition, and the enigmatic story for centuries has served as a model for both mystical and Sufistic practice. While such is the predominant and authentic interpretation of the tale for both Islamic tradition and Sufi orientation, I would like to propose here another understanding of this passage; in particular, as it concerns its late antique Qur'ānic context.

Unusual portrayal of Moses

The narrative of 18:60–82 regarding Moses does not come from biblical sources. Moses, as we have seen above, was a central figure in the Qur'ān, and mentioned far more frequently than any other biblical prophet. The Qur'ānic narratives of Moses, taken in the aggregate, presented Moses in a way that generally was similar to the biblical accounts, but with an added importance: Moses was presented in the Qur'ān as the prophet-messenger exemplar who defeated idolatry and delivered to his people God's words in the *taurat*; in that way, the Qur'ānic Moses also was an ideal model of prophethood for Muḥammad.

That makes the account at 18:60–82 even more noteworthy: in it, Moses was shown to be both lacking in knowledge, and impatient, neither of which are usual biblical descriptions of Moses. Indeed, subsequent secondary works about the Islamic prophets have tended to include additional sub-sections for understanding the 'Moses and the Servant' narrative.[113]

Exegetes as well worked to explain the account of Moses at 18:60–82. The exegetical explanation drawn from the Ubayy ibn Ka'b → Ibn 'Abbas → Sufyān ibn 'Uyayna narration reported in the *tafsīr* collection of al-Ṭabarī (d. 922 CE) explains that in response to a question from the Children of Israel, Moses had claimed to be the most learned of people, upon which event God rebuked Moses for not having ascribed Moses' knowledge to God. In response, God told Moses that there was at the 'confluence of the two seas' one of God's servants who possessed more knowledge than Moses. Moses asked God how he could meet this servant, and God then told Moses that the servant would turn up at the place where the [fish in a basket] is found to be missing.[114]

Brannon Wheeler argues that through exegetical commentary on the passage at 18:60–82 – in particular, through using the Ubayy ibn Ka'b narrative above to explain the hubris of Moses – Muslim exegetes had worked both to explain that Moses had failed because he would not admit that he was a mere human, and to demonstrate that Muḥammad, by contrast, was a prophet who *did* admit his humanity, and who acknowledged that the source of his knowledge was divine.[115] This book agrees with Wheeler's argument about the aims of Muslim exegesis, however, it argues that the Qur'ānic passage at 18:60–82 *itself* already promotes a similar message, in asserting that only God is the source of all wisdom, and, especially, by presenting as anonymous the identity of the 'servant'.

Similar to the ways in which the Syriac narratives of the Seven Sleepers and the Alexander Legend have been shown above to be compelling late antique narratives that were taken up and recast by the Qur'ān, and considering as well the unusual formalistic elements in 60–82 regarding the Moses figure, I detail the possibility below that 18:65–82, like the Seven Sleepers and the Alexander Legend, could have been drawn from a contemporaneous narrative of wisdom literature involving Moses; a narrative that, likewise, could have been recounted in the Qur'ān in order theologically to be recast. First, we will discuss aspects of the Moses/servant tale that have late antique parallels, then formalistic elements of the narrative itself, followed by contemporaneous instances of wisdom and disciple-master didactic literature, and, finally, later Arabic exegetical references involving the figure of al-Khiḍr.

Links to Alexander stories and cosmological notions in the late antique era

The opening verses of 18:60–82, specifically vv. 60–65, have been shown both to draw on the Alexander narratives, and upon cosmological and paradisiacal beliefs current in late antiquity. Working from the fourth- to fifth-century Recension β of the Alexander Romance, on the Babylonian Talmud (*Tamīd* 32a-32b), and on the *Alexander Song* (ca. 630–636), Tommaso Tesei has demonstrated that elements from the first five verses of this narrative, specifically, the memorable pericope of the escaping fish (vv. 61 and 63), can be traced to not only the *Alexander Song* but also to cosmological and paradisiacal notions current in the late antique world, and even earlier.[116] Tesei showed that the fish-escape episode in vv. 60–65 was related to the motif of the water or fountain of life from the earlier Alexander legends, in which a salted fish reanimated when it contacted the miraculous water. The motifs of the fish and of the water of life, Tesei argued, also were contemporaneous Christian symbols related to Christianity, baptism, and to the resurrection, which would explain why reference to the revivified fish pericope was omitted in the Talmudic accounts that otherwise followed the Alexander narrative.[117]

Tesei further demonstrated that the miraculous passage of the fish into the sea, marked in the Qur'ān by the Arabic adverbial term *saraban* (61), a tricky word that appears only once in this form in the text and is related by root *srb* to both *sarāb* ('mirage') in 24:39 and to *sarīb* ('to go forth or away'), can be understood as the accusative form of *sarab*, which means either 'tunnel' or 'subterranean excavation'. *Saraban*, used in the passage to describe the means by which the fish 'took its way into the sea', *fa-ttakhadha sabīlahu fi l-baḥr*, accordingly has been translated in various ways in the exegetical and scholarly literature in order to reconcile the "apparent discordance" between the meaning of the term *sarab* as "tunnel" or "subterranean passage," with the location of the sea to which it is linked.[118]

However, Tesei demonstrated that Christian thought from the first centuries of the Common Era, as evidenced in the writings of the historian Philostorgius (d. ca. 439 CE) and the prominent Syriac theologians Ephrem (d. ca. 373 CE) and Narasi (d. 502 CE), among many others, held that paradise was a physical space situated on the other side of the ocean encircling the earth, and that the four rivers which flowed from paradise (the Pishon, Gihon, Tigris, and Euphrates), passed under this ocean to reach the inhabited part of the world. This belief about the location and rivers of paradise stemmed from ancient Near Eastern cosmological notions, and was attested as well in the text in Genesis 2:10–14.[119]

When viewed in light of cosmological and paradisiacal notions contemporaneous in the late antique world, the Qur'ānic references, through its engagement with elements of the Alexander stories, both to the wondrous revivification of the fish (63) and to the fish's mysterious course *saraban* to the sea (61), make it highly likely that *saraban* in 18:61 "is meant to describe [a] subterranean passage under the sea that the fish takes once resurrected by the miraculous water of the paradisiacal rivers."[120] However, while the Qur'ān refers in vv. 60–65 to tales and concepts current in the late antique world, such as the fish being revived in the water of life, the Qur'ān does not include overtly Christian elements, such as those found in the *Alexander Song*. Instead, the narrative at vv. 60–65 introduces a wisdom literature tale; one presented from a distinctly Qur'ānic perspective.

Qur'ānic language

The narrative of 'Moses and the Servant' was introduced in the Qur'ān by the interjectory expression '*wa-idh*', '*idh*' being a characteristic signal for the start of an exposition about a narrative or figure of biblical or extra-biblical lore.[121] This is significant because the interjection '*wa-idh*' seems to have been used for narratives with which the Qur'ān's audience presumably was familiar, but which now would be addressed from a Qur'ānic perspective.[122] Moreover, as we have seen demonstrated above by Tommaso Tesei, the beginning of the narrative (vv. 60–65) at 18:60–82 was drawn in part from literature and concepts current in the late antique world. Thus, from the very start of this passage, we can identify a linguistic reference '*wa-idh*', which apparently underscores the pre-extant nature of the following Moses narrative (60), as well as evidence of contemporaneous narratives from the late antique world already woven into the 'Moses and the Servant' tale (vv. 60–65). These elements together suggest that the 'Moses and the Servant' narrative which followed may already have been familiar to the Qur'ān's audience.

Wisdom literature

The narrative at 18:60–82 can be understood as an instance of wisdom literature; engaging the topic of God's mysterious justice.[123] God's wisdom, the account clearly demonstrates, is unknowable to humans, who lack both the capacity and the patience *ṣabr* (a word mentioned seven times in 23 verses) to understand the divine plan. Later Islamic exegesis understands this narrative as more closely related to the topic of predestination, or *qadr*,[124] but in its late antique context, this account fits demonstrably into the genre of wisdom literature.

As Haim Schwarzbaum noted in his 1959 work on the Theodicean components of vv. 60–82, the disharmony between the concept of a God of justice and the evils that exist in a world where the righteous suffer and the wicked prosper "constitutes one of the most crucial and perplexing problems in the history of mankind."[125] Similar instances of Near Eastern wisdom literature, such as the biblical book of Job or even the Akkadian *Dialogue about Human Misery*, engage the question of why the righteous seem to suffer while the wicked prosper. The solution offered by these and similar narratives is that "a mortal is urged not to pry into God's unfathomable decrees and mysterious ways," because human capacity is too limited to understand the enigmatic ways – deep and inscrutable – of the divine.[126]

In a Talmudic account from the late antique era, Moses also was depicted as asking three things of God: first, he asked that the Divine Presence should rest upon Israel; second, he asked that the Divine Presence should not rest upon the idolaters; and, third, he asked that God should show him the ways of the Holy One, and it was granted to him. "Moses said before Him [i.e., God]: Lord of the

Universe, why is it that some righteous men prosper and others are in adversity, some wicked men prosper and others are in adversity?"[127] Thus we see that among rabbinic circles of the late antique world, not only did they engage, in various ways, the popular question of theodicy, but at least one contemporaneous narrative included the figure of Moses asking to understand God's mysterious ways.

Disciple-master didactic narrative

The disciple-master narrative structure reflected in 18:60–82 also was a common literary form in the late antique world. One of the most popular and widespread Christian texts of the first few centuries of the Common Era was the *Apophthegmata Patrum*, the *Sayings of the [Desert] Fathers*, a collection of more than 1,000 brief sayings of the monastic desert fathers, originating in Lower Egypt in the 330s to the 460s CE. Originally a Coptic oral tradition, the *Apophthegmata Patrum* was written first in Greek in the monasteries of Palestine during the late 400s CE. The *Sayings of the [Desert] Fathers*, sometimes short aphorisms, and sometimes a record of teaching episodes between younger monks and their elders, were extremely popular forms of parable and folk wisdom in late antiquity. As such, they were translated into several languages, including into Syriac during the early seventh century by Ânân Îshô, under the title the *Paradise of the Fathers*.

Rabbinic texts, especially as depicted in the Talmud, also were characterized by being didactic in nature. Consisting of stories involving the well-known rabbis and sages of the Common Era, Talmudic references often incorporated the motif of a disciple-master lesson. The Talmud in Babylonia was composed and redacted in Aramaic among the rabbinic academies located along the Euphrates and Tigris Rivers, during the first several centuries of the Common Era, and reached a final form in the early seventh century CE. Given the level of exchange and interaction between Jewish communities of the late antique era, one can adduce that Talmudic stories widely were shared, and with non-Jews.[128]

Recent research into the Babylonian Talmud demonstrates the shared literary elements between the literatures of the Aramaic-language Talmud and the Christian monastic *Sayings*, especially as used in the Syriac churches of the Sasanian Empire.[129] These elements indicate sometimes-nonpolemical Jewish-Christian literary relations in the late antique Persian Empire, and furthermore remind us that popular late antique sources that appear to stem from 'clear' 'Talmudic' or 'Syriac Christian' sources themselves may be related to other forms of Near Eastern contemporaneous religious literature.

The passage at 18:60–82 aligns with the genres of late antique wisdom literature and with the literary form of disciple-master instruction. As yet we have no evidence of a parallel contemporaneous late antique wisdom literature narrative involving Moses, but we can infer that neither the wisdom-literature format, nor the figure of Moses as involved in disciple-master instruction – as, for instance, in Talmudic references – would have been unfamiliar in the Qur'ān's late antique context.

Who was the 'servant'?

We certainly cannot definitively answer the question of the 'servant's' identity from the text of the Qur'ān itself, because the Qur'ān clearly anonymizes this figure, calling him *'abdan min 'ibādinā'*, "a servant from [among] our servants" (18:65). However, there are a few later sources of evidence, with respect to the servant figure, which we can consult.

This 'servant' earliest was identified in Arabic exegetical literature in the *tafsīr* of Mujāhid b. Jabr (d. ca. 722 CE).[130] Mujāhid's *tafsīr* is considered one of the earliest exegetical collections, traces of which, through the recension of al-Qāsim b. Nāfi' b. Abū Bazza, remain today only in references in the later *tafsīr* works of figures such as al-Ṭabarī (d. 922 CE), and Ibn Abī Hatim al-Razī (d. 925 CE).[131] In Mujāhid's *tafsīr*, the unnamed 'servant' in 18:65 was identified as "al-Khaḍir," according to the *ḥadīth* attributed to Ubayy ibn Ka'b, detailed above, and transmitted by Ibn 'Abbas or Wahb b. Munabbih.[132] "This account describes how God chides Moses for his claim to be the most knowledgeable of people, and how God tells him that it is al-Khiḍr who has greater and more esoteric knowledge than anyone else."[133]

"Al-Khaḍir" meaning, as we have seen, "the Green [One]," that Ubayy ibn Ka'b reference next was elaborated upon in the *tafsīr* of Muqātil (d. 767 CE), who did not cite Mujāhid as his source.[134] Muqātil, for his part, further identified "al-Khaḍir" with *Ilyasa'*, i.e. the biblical prophet 'Elisha', whose 'wide' (*wasī'/wāsi'*) knowledge encompassed (*yasa'u*) "the knowledge of six heavens and six earths."[135]

What we learn from these Arabic commentaries is that approximately 100 years after the appearance of 18:60–82 in the Qur'ān (presuming the Qur'ān dates to a time around the early seventh century CE), the 'servant' in 18:60–82 was identified by Mujāhid through the opaque reference to 'al-Khaḍir', 'the Green', which may have been either a name, an epithet, a pseudonym, or perhaps a shorthand reference to a particular characteristic of an already-existing figure. In the *tafsīr* of Muqātil, approximately 50 years after that of Mujāhid, 'al-Khaḍir' further was identified with the biblical prophet named Elisha. Known for the characteristic of exegetical completeness (if not source attribution), "regardless of how obvious the reference of a given pronoun might be, Muqātil is relentless in resolving it by means of some equation, paraphrase, or inserted vocative,"[136] Muqātil elaborated upon Mujāhid's earlier identification of 'al-Khaḍir' as the 'servant' in order further to identify that figure with that of the knowledgeable prophet '*Ilyasa'*', i.e., 'Elisha'.

Later exegetes, however, apparently adjusted Muqātil's reference to be instead '*Ilyās*', 'Elijah'. In Arabic, '*Ilyās*', 'Elijah', is homophonic with '*Ilyasa'*', 'Elisha'. Additionally, from a biblical perspective, the figures of Elijah and Elisha often are homologically crossed. That is, they participated in the same mission, and thus conceptually they often are paired together.[137] Muqātil's identification of 'al-Khaḍir' with '*Ilyasa'*', 'Elisha', partly was employed – it should be remembered – by Muqātil in order to rhyme with or to pun on and to identify the 'servant' whose knowledge was so 'wide' (*wasī'/wāsi'*) that it "encompassed" (*yasa'u*) the knowledge of six heavens and six earths. '*Ilyasa'*', 'Elisha', later by exegetes was equated also with '*Ilyās*', 'Elijah' – again, recall the homophonic and homological exchanges (and interchanges) that exist between these names and figures. Ultimately, however,

'*Ilyās*', i.e., 'Elijah', became the figure most often associated by Qur'ānic exegetes and in other later Arabic literature with the figure of al-Khiḍr.

Branon Wheeler cogently argued that the character of al-Khiḍr was developed by Muslim exegetes in order to *appropriate* the characteristics associated with Elijah in biblical and rabbinic stories.[138] "Elijah's association with fertility and rain production is widespread in biblical and rabbininc literature. Elijah is able to make food increase in 1 Kings 17:14–16, raise the dead in 1 Kings 17:17–24, and cause it to rain in 1 Kings 18:41–45, all of which indicate his association with fertility."[139]

In *ḥadīth* reports, "al-Khiḍr's" etymological association with the color green was attributed to his ability to make the earth fertile: in a saying attributed to Muḥammad and located in the classical *ḥadīth* and *tafsīr* collections of both Muslim and al-Ṭabarī, al-Khiḍr's name was explained "due to the fact that he [al-Khiḍr] sat on a white skin *jild* and it became green."[140] "Both al-Nawawī and al-Diyārbakrī [authors of later *ḥadīth* collections] comment that the 'skin' is symbolic of the earth, emphasizing al-Khiḍr's ability to make the earth fertile."[141]

Wheeler argues that, "like Elijah, with whom [*later*] he is associated in other contexts, al-Khiḍr personifies immortality, and in the exegesis of Q 18:60–65 is closely identified with the water of life."[142] He concludes that,

> the close similarities between the two names and the attributes of the two characters is an indication not that the Islamic sources are confused, *but that there was an effort to make the al-Khiḍr who emerged from the explanation of Q 18:60–82 a close parallel to Elijah.*[143]

This book certainly agrees with Wheeler's astute assessment that "the al-Khiḍr who emerged from the explanation of Q 18:60–82 [was] a close parallel to Elijah," but it reaches that conclusion following different reasoning. That is, Wheeler (and others) referenced several exegetical sources in order to demonstrate the "close similarities between the two names [al-Khiḍr and Elijah] and the attributes [greenness, fertility, great knowledge] of the characters."[144] However, this book argues that similarities about the names and the attributes shared between the figures – particularly in the case of the critical characteristics of 'greenness' and 'fertility', *only could have been identified by exegetes once al-Khiḍr, "the 'Green'," already (/first) had been named in earliest exegesis.* That is, similarities in greenness and fertility, between Elijah and 'al-Khiḍr' 'the Green', exist only *as a result of* the first exegetical naming of the 'servant' as 'al-Khaḍir', and *not before it.* Without that first appellative reference to 'greenness', there is no other obvious tie, either in the passage in the Qur'ān, or in the earliest *ḥadīth* and *tafsīr* narratives related to it, to the biblical figure of Elijah, and especially not to Elijah's characteristic of 'greenness'. There being no 'natural' or apparent reference to Elijah, either in the content of the Qur'ānic text or in the earliest exegetical commentary concerning it, there thus is no explanation for why exegetes would have chosen, *in the first place*, to "develop" the character of al-Khiḍr in order thereby "to appropriate the characteristics associated with *Elijah* in biblical and rabbinic stories."[145] Given such logical constraints, this book suggests, instead, that in identifying "al-Khaḍir" as the 'servant', the earliest exegete(s) were not *creating* a figure in order thereby to appropriate characteristics of Elijah, but, rather, *identifying* Elijah, himself, by using a recognizable contemporaneous epithet – "al-Khaḍir," "the 'Green [One]'" – an epithet that simultaneously referred to well-known characteristics of Elijah, and that mirrored the Qur'ān's intentional reference to an *indistinct* 'servant'.

Thus, we suggest here that one possible explanation for the exegetical identification of 'al-Khaḍir' as the 'servant' figure in the narrative at 18:60–82, *and especially for the subsequent identification of al-Khiḍr with Elisha-Elijah in the tafsīr of Muqātil*, would have been the existence of a Moses-Elijah wisdom literature story, similar to the narrative referenced in the Qur'ān, and circulating during the late antique period, during which time the figure of Elijah already widely was known for his 'greenness' and fertility aspects. Moreover, a pre-existing Elijah-Moses wisdom literature story – or, at least, a pre-existing story involving Moses and some *other* well-known figure – is the only explanation that would resolve one of the most puzzling historical aspects of this tale. Specifically, I refer here to the otherwise-inexplicable phenomenon of why no exegete, including or after Mujāhid, ever balked at the oddity of identifying or referring to the vital figure of the 'servant' – who was, it should be recalled – even wiser than the esteemed prophet Moses – by a *novel* reference to the otherwise-unattested name or figure of 'al-Khaḍir', 'the Green'. Such a pivotal identification, whether made by Mujāhid or Ubayy ibn Ka'b or anyone else – and especially the fact that such identification never was challenged by any other exegete – makes sense only if the name 'al-Khaḍir' was considered both accurate *and* corroborable, from the perspective of the person(s) making the reference. 'al-Khaḍir', as an explanatory gloss for the 'servant' figure in 18:60–82, would had to have been both pre-established in culture, and associable with this tale.

Whatever the original explanation, however, over time, al-Khiḍr and *Ilyās*/Elijah no longer were identified as the *same*, as had been the case in the early commentaries. Rather, al-Khiḍr and Elijah increasingly became identified as *distinct* (though related) figures.[146]

Links between Alexander and al-Khiḍr in later Arabic literature

Recognizing references to the Alexander tales in the 'Moses and the Servant' narrative and in the Dhū al-Qarnayn narrative immediately following, the later Arabic exegetical authors also created explanations that linked the figure al-Khiḍr – by that time an independent figure – with both the figure of Alexander and with the Alexander narratives. In the influential commentary of al-Ṭabarī (d. 922 CE), al-Khiḍr drank the 'water of life' but Alexander did not, explaining both al-Khiḍr's immortality and Alexander's early death.[147] These exegetical linkages spawned subsequent and highly popular literature and works of art involving the figure al-Khiḍr featured within the Alexander tales.[148] Thus, we see that al-Khiḍr and Elijah (again, by that time distinct figures) became linked in the medieval Arabic commentaries on three points: their great knowledge, their associations with fertility, and their immortality.

Elijah in late antique literature

From the perspective of the late antique religious milieux of the sixth to seventh century and the presence therein of rich literary traditions involving Elijah as a wise teacher and guide, the exegetical identification of 'al-Khaḍir' – as a name for Elijah – with the 'servant' from whom Moses sought knowledge, is at least not inconceivable. Elijah during the late antique period was a figure of considerable popularity among many religious communities; Jews and Christians most prominent among them. Elijah not only was associated with the biblical account in 1 and 2 Kings, but regionally was known as a herald of last days (cf. Mal 4:5),[149] as a legal authority, as a teacher of the wise, helper to those in crisis, and as a bringer of rain.[150] Elijah during the Talmudic period became a figure quite different from the Elijah of the Bible: "He is partly angelic and partly human, therefore he can connect humankind to God, serving as a supernatural mediator."[151] Onlookers at the crucifixion wondered whether Elijah would come to rescue Jesus (Mk 15:35–36, Mt 27:46–49), indicating that Elijah already was understood by the time of those Gospel narratives to be a helper who appeared to Jews in need.

Elijah in the Talmudic era was known most prominently as a teacher. Intensely popular as a subject of Talmudic narratives, Elijah frequently was depicted in a category of stories in which "a rabbi meets Elijah and asks a question … Elijah may teach or share secret knowledge on a wide variety of subjects."[152] Similarly,

> Elijah is an ideal teacher for the rabbis. Not only is he addressed as 'master and teacher', but he often acts as an ideal teacher, displaying patience and dispensing encouragement in ways that speak to the tensions between the disciples of the teachers and their earthly teachers.[153]

Finally, well-known and common associations in contemporaneous Christian scripture and lore involved the presence together of Moses and Elijah. As we saw above in Chapter Four, both Elijah and Moses became associated in the New Testament with the coming of the Messiah.[154] In the Gospel accounts, Moses and Elijah were depicted as appearing together with Jesus during his ministry at an event later referred to as the 'transfiguration' (Mk 9:4–8, Mt 17:3–8, Lk 9:30–33). Accordingly, in the tradition of Christian literature in the Near East, there was a notable precedent for the appearance together of Moses and Elijah, despite any apparent 'temporal' discrepancy between the lives of these figures (Figure 6.2).[155]

Sūrah 18 and the theological message of the Qur'ān

As we have seen in the examples of the Men of the Cave and the Dhū al-Qarnayn narratives, it seems reasonable to presume that, just as in the case of those other two narratives, any prospective late antique literary source for the 'Moses and the Servant' narrative at 18:60–82 would not have appeared verbatim in the Qur'ān. Rather, like other narratives in the Qur'ān, and certainly those in Sūrah al-Kahf, the account or tale most likely would have been shaped to align with the Qur'ān's own internal theological messages.

The argument of this section has been that a late antique literary precedent for the narrative (one that included the figure of Elijah in the role of the 'servant') is at least plausible. We have made that argument on the basis of the narrative's unusual portrayal of Moses; on the grounds that other late antique texts underlie the other primary narratives in this *sūrah*; on the basis that wisdom literature and tales with a disciple-master didactic orientation were common in late antique

Figure 6.2 Moses and Elijah together at the Transfiguration © ART Collection / Alamy Stock Photo

literature; on the evidence of the early Arabic exegetical tradition's identification of the figure of the 'servant' as "al-Khaḍir," 'the Green', and on the evidence of the subsequent exegetical identification of 'al-Khiḍr' with the figures of *Ilyasa'*/Elisha and *Ilyās*/Elijah; on the inference that 'al-Khaḍir', as an explanatory gloss for the 'servant' figure in 18:60–82, must have been a figure both pre-established in culture and associable with this tale; on the basis that tales of Elijah as a wise teacher and guide were plentiful in late antique literature; and on the basis that if indeed there had existed a contemporaneous text or tale involving Moses and Elijah with which the Qur'ān was in conversation, that too would align with late antique literary topoi in which Moses and Elijah regularly were combined (see Figure 6.2).

Moreover, the overall contention of this section is that the meaning of the narrative at 18:60–82 becomes clearer by examining the narrative as a text within its own historical context, and by placing the narrative within the larger theological arguments made in *sūrah* 18 and the Qur'ān, more generally. When we examine *sūrah* 18 as a whole, we see that, beginning with the parallel introductory and closing remarks (1–8 and 103–110), which largely are anti-trinitarian, and which promote both the Qur'ān and the mission of the prophet Muḥammad, through the parables highlighting God's coming judgment and apocalypse (27–59), and to the end of the chapter, *sūrah* 18 addressed contemporaneous late antique religious issues and narratives, and it did so in a way that would have been particularly salient for Christian and Jewish audiences of the day.

Furthermore, in contending with narratives known mainly from Syriac literature, such as the 'Men of the Cave' narrative (9–26), and the references to contemporary Alexander tales in 60–65 and the Dhū al-Qarnayn narratives (83–102), the Qur'ān engaged with compelling contemporaneous narratives in a manner that removed overt Christian and Jewish theological messages, and re-appropriated those narratives to align with its own internal theological messages.

In 18:60–82, we can identify the message that God's wisdom and justice are greater than those of man – even than those of Moses. Such a theological message about the wisdom and justice of God was made possible mainly because of the very *anonymity* of the 'servant'. This book thus agrees with Wheeler's arguments about the intention of Muslim exegesis about 18:60–82 as having been designed to demonstrate that God was wiser than Moses – and, perhaps, by extension, wiser than that of Moses' *religious community*,[156] as well – but this book argues that such a project was not limited solely to the exegesis. The Qur'ānic passage at 18:60–82 itself already promoted the message that only God is the source of all wisdom. In presenting as anonymous the identity of the 'servant', the Qur'ān also ensured that the figure – 'a servant from [among] our servants whom we have given mercy and whom we have taught from our own knowledge' – could not be linked to any specific religious community. Instead, the anonymous 'servant' only could serve the Qur'ānic theological message of God's transcendence.

Throughout *sūrah* 18, we can identify that same message of transcendent monotheism, and one that is in keeping with a greater message of the Qur'ān *vis-à-vis* its contemporaneous religious setting. The narratives in the Qur'ān promote a vision of transcendent monotheism that is anti-trinitarian, anti-rabbinic, apocalyptic, and supported by prophetic mission as exemplified by the prophet Muḥammad.

A medieval Jewish tale of Rabbi Joshua ben Levi and the strange actions of Elijah

Ultimately, the figures of al-Khiḍr and Elijah *did* become associated in both Islamic and Jewish textual sources, just as they were by Muslims and Jews in popular religious practice, as well. One interesting textual example can be seen in the Jewish legend of the Rabbi Joshua ben Levi and the strange actions of Elijah. Composed ca. 1000 CE, the tale of Rabbi Joshua and Elijah was first recorded in Arabic among the Jewish community at Kairaoun, Tunisia, as a part of the work *al-faraj ba'd al-shiddah* ('relief following distress') composed by Rabbi Nissîm b. Ya'aqobh b. Shâhîn, best known under his Arabic title, Ibn Shāhīn.[157]

In this legend, which closely parallels the 'Moses and the Servant' narrative in Q 18:65–82, Rabbi Joshua (a popular Talmudic figure who had lived in and contributed to the Talmudic academies in Palestine during the third century CE), fasted and prayed and asked to see Elijah. A common motif in rabbinic stories was the request of the sages to wish to meet Elijah,[158] and, over centuries of Talmudic lore, "Rabbi Joshua ben Levi was well known to be someone whom Elijah visited."[159]

In the tale, Rabbi Joshua met Elijah on the road (another common Jewish rabbinic motif), and R. Joshua asked to accompany Elijah on his journeys, in order to observe Elijah's wonders. Elijah agreed but warned R. Joshua that R. Joshua would not be able to endure Elijah's actions, and he, Elijah, likewise would not wish to explain his actions. R. Joshua promised not to burden Elijah with questions and Elijah agreed on the condition that once R. Joshua asked for an explanation, he, Elijah, would have to leave. After performing three seemingly unjust and otherwise inexplicable actions, the killing of a poor man's cow; the rebuilding of an unhospitable wealthy man's collapsed wall; and the wish "may God make all of you chiefs" to an inhospitable synagogue community, while making to a poor but generous community the wish "may God grant you only one chief," R. Joshua announced that he no longer could be patient, and asked Elijah to explain himself, after which time he, R. Joshua, would leave Elijah.

Before departing, Elijah explained that the poor man's wife was due to die that same day and Elijah had entreated God that the cow die in her stead; rebuilding the wall had caused a treasure underneath *not* to be discovered by the unworthy wealthy man; and a place with many chiefs is bound to be ruined, while a place with only one chief is bound to prosper. Finally, Elijah charged R. Joshua with specific advice:

> If you see a wicked man advancing and prospering, do not wonder at it, for it is to his ultimate disadvantage. Likewise, if you see a righteous man distressed or sorely tired, he is being delivered thereby from something worse. Refrain therefore from entertaining doubts in your heart about such things.[160]

Several studies have claimed this Jewish legend to be the precursor to the Qur'ānic account at 18:65–82, despite the fact that no witness to the legend has been shown to exist before Ibn Shāhīn's version ca. 1000 CE.[161] Other studies have claimed alternatively that it is Ibn Shāhīn's Jewish legend that depends upon Q 18:65–82, substituting the well-known rabbinic figure of Joshua b. Levi for that of Moses.[162] This study generally agrees with the latter proposition; i.e., that Ibn Shāhīn's narrative appears in places to have been influenced by 18:65–82. However, this study sees no reason why, if some rabbinic or other late antique text were uncovered and demonstrated to antedate the Qur'ānic account – suggesting such an account as a potential source for *both* 18:65–82 and the Ibn Shāhīn text – it could not still be the case that the Ibn Shāhīn narrative, composed in ca. 1000 CE, might have been influenced by the Qur'ānic narrative at 18:65–82, as well. By Ibn Shāhīn's time in Tunisia, 18:65–82 had become a popular Islamic and Arabic narrative, as well.[163]

Part Three: al-Khiḍr images and al-Khiḍr in the Eastern Mediterranean Al-Khiḍr in Islamic tradition

Al-Khiḍr primarily is known around the world through his identity in the Qur'ānic commentaries and later Islamic literature, including the *hadīth* traditions. His role is drawn both from the Qur'ānic account and from other sources with which he became related, such as the Persian Alexander tale the *Iskandarnāma*. In Muslim cultures around the world, al-Khiḍr is regarded as a popular folk and literary hero, renowned as a figure like Elijah in popular Jewish lore and revered highly in Sufi and mystical traditions. Al-Khiḍr in Muslim tradition is counted among the other long-living Muslim figures Enoch (cf. Gen 5:24; Enoch is associated with and known as *Idrīs* in Islamic tradition; cf. Q 19:56 and 21:85), Elijah, and Jesus, and furthermore is associated with greenness, fertility, rain, knowledge and wisdom, and immortality (in part, through association with the Alexander tales and the water of life). On account of his immortality, al-Khiḍr is said, like Elijah, to be able to appear anywhere at any time.[164]

In most places throughout the Muslim world, al-Khiḍr is known and revered for the qualities above. Again, in most places throughout the Muslim world, al-Khiḍr is associated with his role and identity in Sufi and mystical traditions. Because of his Qur'ānic narrative, al-Khiḍr is known as both deeply wise and an ideal teacher; in Sufi traditions, these qualities are highlighted, for which al-Khiḍr is considered an exemplar. Likewise, in the saint/*walī*/*pīr* tradition as it is associated with Sufism, al-Khiḍr is considered both a 'saint' and a prophet, and shrines to Khiḍr abound.

As we saw above, in the late Medieval Islamic (and especially Persianate) world, al-Khiḍr commonly was depicted as a prophet (visage ringed by fire or not depicted); commonly in his role as associated with the adventures of Alexander the Great[165] and in making the *ḥajj* annual pilgrimage, or in praying with Elijah (Figure 6.3).

Since the early modern period and in association with his majority role around the world, al-Khiḍr is most commonly depicted as a wise, bearded old man; possessing great knowledge and often on a journey. Images of al-Khiḍr as this sort often portray him as riding upon and/or holding a fish, while on or nearby the water of life. This type of imagery, popular in south Asian contexts, also may be related to depictions of a river god and Vishnu.[166] In both the medieval and modern iconographical depictions, al-Khiḍr usually is depicted wearing green clothing or robes.

Figure 6.3 Al-Khiḍr and Elijah praying together © The History Collection / Alamy Stock Photo

Al-Khiḍr in the Eastern Mediterranean

Around the Mediterranean and in Turkey – especially in the countries of the Eastern Mediterranean – popular understandings about and depictions of al-Khiḍr differ from those of south and southeast Asian contexts. In the Eastern Mediterranean, al-Khiḍr still is known as the wise servant from 18:60–82, but, also, he long has been identified there with both Elijah and with St. George.[167] In order to understand why this has been so, we need to understand al-Khiḍr in the Eastern Mediterranean in the context of regional political and religious history.

Eastern Mediterranean political and religious history

Early "Muslim"/Arabian armies spread out of the Arabian Peninsula and defeated the Byzantine armies at the Yarmouk River in 636 CE. Monastic correspondence confirms that early Arabian armies, referred to both in Greek and Syriac writings as '*muhājirūn*' (Syriac, '*Mhaggrayê*')[168] i.e., associated with a/'the' *hijra* ('migration'), took political and military control of Jerusalem in 637 CE, and were in control of Damascus by 640 CE.[169] As these early Arabian armies conquered territories in a gradually expanding pattern, their custom was not to destroy towns (there were, of course, exceptions), but to obtain the acquiescence of local leaders and to construct garrison/*miṣr* towns nearby from which to oversee particular regions.[170]

As we have seen in preceding chapters, the Eastern Mediterranean long had been home to large Christian and Jewish communities. The 'violent conquest' and 'forced conversion' models of Arab and Islamic advancement largely have been shown to be spurious, there being scant written or archaeological evidence to support such claims.[171] Indeed, archaeological and textual evidence demonstrates instead that Christian and Jewish communities in the former Byzantine areas continued on much as before.[172] Certainly, no church or synagogue records suggest that conversion to 'Islam' was demanded of Christians or Jews by these armies; *muhājirūn* armies being at that nascent stage associated more directly with transcendant monotheism and with a general affinity to the scriptures and traditions of Jews and Christians than understanding themselves as possessed of a religious identity different enough from that of Christians and Jews to necessitate those other communities' "conversion."[173]

What our extant evidence suggests is that "most communities [in Syria, Palestine, Iraq, and Egypt] which already consisted of monotheists, were not destroyed or even seriously disrupted but merely underwent a change of masters [and tax collectors]."[174] Indeed, we have early Muslim accounts of prayer taking place in churches, which must therefore have been considered suitable prayer spaces, and records of churches still being built in former Byzantine areas in the century after conquest. 'Islam', as a distinct religious tradition, thus emerged gradually in the Eastern Mediterranean (as it did everywhere),[175] and conversions to this new religious orientation from among the Christian and Jewish populations came slowly, particularly initially.[176]

Popular associations between al-Khiḍr, St. George, and Elijah

We lack records indicating exactly how popular associations between Muslim al-Khiḍr and Elijah and St. George in the Eastern Mediterranean took place. This is perhaps unsurprising, as records for such popular associations rarely exist. When we do begin to encounter records of people discussing matters such as meeting al-Khiḍr or St. George or Elijah in a dream and associating the figures together or with a common place of worship, any formalized association between them has already taken place and is presented by the writer as given.[177]

We might, however, surmise in a general way about how such associations could have taken place. As we have seen above, "Muslim" al-Khiḍr was associated early on in Arabic textual tradition with the biblical figure of Elijah, a well-known and highly popular figure throughout the Near East. Indeed, this book suggests that 'al-Khiḍr' originally may have been simply an epithet for 'Elijah'. Thus, associations between 'al-Khiḍr' and 'Elijah' naturally took place. In the Eastern Mediterranean, Elijah and St. George were themselves already related: as we have seen in Chapters Four and Five, both Elijah and St. George were known as figures who defended true religion (or true gods), and who were known as well for their similar associations with greenness, fertility, and rain. Given that al-Khiḍr ('the Green [one]') came to be understood in Islamic tradition as possessed of associations with greenness and fertility, as well as other traits similar to those of Elijah, including immortality and the ability to appear at will and to help those in need, it is perhaps unsurprising that al-Khiḍr, Elijah, and St. George – each linked in both scripture/text, and possessing shared popular traits and iconographical representations, as we have seen in preceding chapters and will see detailed in Chapter Seven – came to be associated among communities of Muslims, Christians, and Jews in the Eastern Mediterranean, as those communities developed and evolved together from the seventh–eighth century on.

Al-Khiḍr as linking figure

Indeed, during the first several Islamic centuries, al-Khiḍr may have functioned as a kind of transition or mediator figure among the changing communities of the Muslim-Byzantine political frontier.[178] Ethel Sara Wolper has argued that the very indistinctness of al-Khiḍr, as well as his clear similarities with popular religious figures, allowed him to function as a bridge or transition figure for communities, particularly in the Byzantine-Islamic frontier zone. Churches once dedicated to St. George (and other Christian figures) became associated as well with al-Khiḍr.

Wolper's research focuses primarily on the frontier zones around and within Anatolia, and this is a particularly interesting area concerning the figures in this study. Unlike most of the Eastern Mediterranean, most of the Anatolian Peninsula remained under Byzantine political control – and largely Christian in religious orientation – up through most of the 11th century CE. After the Battle of Manzikert in 1071 CE, Turkish Muslim influence began to grow throughout Anatolia. Naturally, as had been the case throughout the rest of the Christian Mediterranean, any sort of Islamization of Anatolia took place only slowly, over the course of several centuries, and not without a concomitant "Byzantinization" of Islam and of Turkish society in Anatolia.[179] Describing processes of conversion and transferal between Muslims and Christians in Anatolia, Vryonis wrote,

> the best-known equation of a Muslim with a Christian saint revolves about the figure of Khiḍr... the Turks worshipped St. George in the figure of Khidir Elias, and at Elvan Chelebi, east of Chorum, he was associated with St. Theodore. In both cases he has been identified with equestrian, military, dragon slayers.[180]

As we saw in Chapter Five, Ss. George and Theodore both were associated in the Eastern Mediterranean with the motif of mounted warrior saints who vanquished dragons. Al-Khiḍr (interestingly, primarily known in Anatolia as a composite of both al-Khiḍr and Elijah, named Khiḍr-Ilyās or Khiḍrilyas or Khizirilyas), who already had been associated with the dragon-slaying figure of St. George in the Eastern Mediterranean, naturally continued these associations with St. George in Anatolia.

Unlike al-Khiḍr in most other contexts, around the Mediterranean – and in other places with large Christian and Muslim populations together, such as in some parts of Eastern Europe – al-Khiḍr's image and identity align most closely with the popular figure of St. George. Accordingly, in the Eastern Mediterranean, images of al-Khiḍr often are identical to those of St. George (see Figure 5.1); indeed, St. George and al-Khiḍr often are understood in fact to *be* the same figure, or perhaps to refer to different aspects of the same figure. Moreover, since at least the time of extant records from the 1200s CE, Elijah-Khiḍr and George-Khiḍr have been understood to be the *same* figure, which thus has linked all three figures together in practice among Muslims, Jews, and Christians in the Eastern Mediterranean.[181] These associations, invaluable witnesses to the history of religious communities in the region, continued between communities of regional Jews, Christians, and Muslims – and other local religious communities – through the 20th century CE. Today these associations continue most prominently to exist among communities of Christians and Muslims.[182]

Al-Khiḍr sites in the Eastern Mediterranean

Numerous sites are dedicated to al-Khiḍr throughout the Eastern Mediterranean. Monuments of central importance such as the Dome of the Rock, the Masjid al-Aqṣā, and the Damascus Mosque all include smaller structures and/or spaces within them dedicated to al-Khiḍr. In addition to these conspicuous sites, several mosques throughout the region are dedicated to *Sayyidnā al-Khiḍr*, ('*sayyid*' being a Muslim honorific title) and profuse smaller shrines are dedicated to *Sayyidnā al-Khiḍr*, as well, primarily in mountain and rural areas.

Additionally, of course, Christian churches and shrines dedicated to St. George also can be considered shrines to al-Khiḍr among Muslims,[183] especially in smaller regional churches; i.e., this practice is not common in cathedrals dedicated to St. George, for instance. Sometimes, churches or other sites once dedicated to St. George or to Elijah became mosques dedicated to al-Khiḍr.[184] In other instances, a mosque to al-Khiḍr often can be built next to a church dedicated to St. George.

Recalling Ottoman partiality for the Christian figure of St. George – a fondness that existed because of the associations throughout the Levant and Anatolia between al-Khiḍr and St. George – today one finds more churches in the Levant dedicated to St. George than to any other figure (save to Mary, which of course also is due to Muslim and Ottoman fondness for the figure of Mary, who is known in Muslim tradition as *Sittnā Maryam*).[185]

Part Four: Conclusion: al-Khiḍr and the Levantine common pool

What al-Khiḍr texts, images, and sites reflect about Islamic tradition

What we see reflected in the figure of al-Khiḍr depends upon when and where we are looking. When we examine the Qur'ān and the narrative at 18:60–82, we see a religious text situated within the religious communities, political currents, and apocalyptic orientation of the wider late antique world. This text reflects a pious and monotheistically oriented community. The theological orientation of this transcendant monotheism strongly is aligned to the biblical One God, albeit from within an Arabian linguistic orientation. This community's understanding of the One God categorically rejected the contemporaneous Christian Trinitarian conception of God, aligning instead with a solemn and direct vision of transcendent, undivided monotheism.[186]

Specifically, regarding the figure of the Qur'ānic 'servant', we see reflected in him a community engaged in contemporaneous discussions and debates involving the age-old questions of theodicy, as well as the mysterious ways of God's justice. The Khiḍr narrative at 18:60–82 imparts the all-knowing, all-powerful nature of God as both unquestionable and absolute, as well as the human necessity for faith and patience in this God.

When we examine the Arabic commentaries and the medieval literary tradition, we see reflected in the figure of al-Khiḍr an expanding religious tradition incorporating into the wider Near Eastern world and defining the boundaries and components of Islamic religious identity and practice. When we examine al-Khiḍr images and sites around the world, we see reflected the influence of geography and culture. Al-Khiḍr images and sites among Sufi traditions and especially in south and central Asia reflect an Islamic religious tradition embedded within and responding to an Asian and Indian cultural context. Al-Khiḍr images and sites in the Eastern Mediterranean reflect an Islamic religious tradition embedded within and responding to a largely Christian and Jewish religious and cultural context.

Al-Khiḍr and the Levantine common pool

Compelling figures, narratives, and motifs from *the Levantine common pool*

In the Qur'ānic narrative of 18:60–82, we encounter the genre of wisdom literature, popular since the Middle Bronze Age throughout the Near Eastern world.

We see the towering biblical figure of Moses as well, fundamental to the biblical text and likewise to that of the Qur'ān, albeit in an unusual portrayal. We see as well in the narrative at 18:60–82 the presence of several late antique and agrarian religious motifs and narratives, including widespread beliefs about the nature of paradise and the geological structures of the earth, popular tales about the journeys of Alexander, and regional motifs such as the fish and the water or fountain of life.

In the later Islamic figure of al-Khiḍr, developed primarily from the Qur'ānic commentaries and later Arabic literature (and based, of course, upon the Qur'ānic narrative of 18:60–82), we see direct associations with the popular figure of Elijah, and with the motifs of greenness, immortality, and divine knowledge. Moreover, this chapter suggests Elijah as the original source for the exegetical epithet 'al-Khiḍr'; that is, 'the Green'. In later commentaries, we see al-Khiḍr – by that time no longer an epithet for Elijah but a standalone character – as connected as well with the popular figure of Alexander and his journeys. In the Eastern Mediterranean, where al-Khiḍr became intimately identified with the Christian figure St. George, we see al-Khiḍr as associated with the iconography and narrative of defeating a dragon. Naturally, St. George's geographical motifs involving rain, greenness, and fertility, likewise resonated, among local communities, with those same motifs shared by al-Khiḍr.

What the figure of al-Khiḍr contributes to *the Levantine common pool*

Al-Khiḍr became known as a popular folk and literary hero, the Green Prophet and enigmatic teacher who inspired Sufi and mystical traditions. Khiḍr was associated with the fabulous adventures of Alexander and with the water of life, as well as with the qualities of immortality and esoteric knowledge, which likewise were shared by Elijah and St. George. Al-Khiḍr was renowned as a helper to those in need who could travel great distances quickly, much like the marvelous Elijah and the miraculous St. George. And, also, like Elijah and George, al-Khiḍr became known as a powerful agricultural figure, associated with the vital geographical motifs of greenness, fertility, and crop growth.

Through this analysis of the figure al-Khiḍr, it is clear why Elijah, St. George, and al-Khiḍr became related in popular religious practice in the Eastern Mediterranean. The final chapter examines what geographically contextualizing the figures Baal-Hadad, Elijah, St. George, and al-Khiḍr explains about the linkages between these figures, and about regional religious history and its agrarian orientation.

Notes

1 The temporal designation 'late antique' and the development of this field is attributed to the pioneering work of Peter Brown. See Peter Brown, *The World of Late Antiquity: AD 150–750*, History of European Civilization Library Series (New York: Harcourt Publishers, 1971). This era is temporally construed in various ways for different purposes; in this project, the late antique period will be considered ca. 200–750 CE.

2 There is discrepancy within and among scholars and traditionalists about this date, as there are no extant records to corroborate Muḥammad's birth. In a majority of

traditional accounts – which disagree as to the year of his birth by as many as 85 years – Muḥammad's birth usually was associated with the memorable year known as the 'Year of the Elephant' *al-'ām al-fīl*. According to an account in which the Ethiopian Christian General Abraha used an army including elephant(s) for an expedition into the Ḥijāz, the date of 570 CE for the Year of the Elephant was derived by beginning with the date traditionally associated with the start of Qur'ānic revelations, ca. 610 CE, and subtracting 40 years, because of the traditional accounts that Muḥammad was age 40 when he began receiving revelation (note as well that the culturally mature age of '40' may be kerygmatic rather than historically accurate). Some scholars, such as Lawrence Conrad, using Byzantine textual evidence outside of Islamic tradition, argue for a date of *al-'ām al-fīl* closer to 552 CE. Evidence such as this, and the dating of Qur'ān fragments recently uncovered, may result in a revision of the traditional date of approximately 570 CE for the birth of Muḥammad, but because 570 CE currently remains in the scholarly mainstream, it will be employed here, as well. See Lawrence I. Conrad, "Abraha and Muḥammad: Some Observations Apropos of Chronology and Literary 'topoi' in the Early Arabic Historical Tradition," *Bulletin of the School of Oriental and African Studies, University of London* (Vol. 50, No. 2, 1987), 225–240.

3 See H. Talat Halman, *Where the Two Seas Meet: al-Khiḍr and Moses – The Qur'anic Study of al-Khiḍr and Moses in Sufi Commentaries as a Model for Spiritual Guidance* (Louisville, KY: Fons Vitae, 2013). See also Patrick Franke, *Begegnung mit Khiḍr : Quellenstudien zum Imaginären im Traditionellen Islam* (Beirut: In Kommission bei Franz Steiner Verlag Stuttgart, 2000).

4 Halman, *Where the Two Seas Meet.*

5 Robert Hoyland, *Arabia and the Arabs: From the Bronze Age to the Coming of Islam* (New York: Routledge, 2001), 8. See also Jeremiah 3:2 and Isaiah 13:19–20 and Assyrian king Sargon (r. 721-705 BCE), who wrote of "the Arabs who live far away in the desert and who know neither overseers nor officials," see D.D. Luckenbill, *Ancient records of Assyria and Babylonia*, 2 vols (Chicago: University of Chicago, 1927).

6 See Gordon Darnell Newby, *A History of the Jews of Arabia: From Ancient Times to Their Eclipse under Islam* (Columbia, SC: University of South Carolina Press), 1988, 7–8.

7 Several cities with what likely were originally Arab populations developed in this region from the period 300 BCE to 100 CE, such as at Petra, Palmyra, Hatra, and Harran. Hoyland, *Arabia and the Arabs*. In general, what is meant in this project by the term 'Arabia' equates to those portions of the Near East that are located to the east and to the south of the Levant and of the 'Fertile Crescent,' and west of Iran.

8 Hoyland, *Arabia and the Arabs*, 3–4.

9 Hoyland, *Arabia and the Arabs*, 13–16.

10 Newby, *Jews of Arabia*, 9.

11 Hoyland, *Arabia and the Arabs*, 8.

12 Hoyland, 1.

13 Newby, *Jews of Arabia*, 9, quoting Aziz Suryal Atiya, *History of Eastern Christianity* (Notre Dame, IN: University of Notre Dame Press, 1968), and Irfan Shahid, "Pre-Islamic Arabia," in *Cambridge History of Islam*, vol. 1, *The Central Islamic Lands* (Cambridge, UK: Cambridge University Press, 1970), 3–29.

14 Hoyland, *Arabia and the Arabs*, 8.

15 Hoyland, 139.

16 Aziz al-Azmeh, *The Emergence of Islam in Late Antiquity: Allāh and His People* (Cambridge, UK: Cambridge University Press, 2014), 173.

17 Al-Azmeh, 173. See also Ibn al-Kalbī, *al-Aṣnām*, as well as Ibn Ḥabīb, *al-Muḥabbar*, 315 ff., and the list of Ibn Ḥazam, *Juhara*, 491 ff.

18 al-Azmeh, *Emergence of Islam*. This point is indeed among al-Azmeh's more prominently demonstrated claims.
19 Hoyland, *Arabia and the Arabs*, 139.
20 Indeed, the name 'Mecca', known in Greek- and Roman-era maps mentioned by Ptolemy as 'Macoraba', may originate in the Semitic roots *qrb* (related to the term '*qurbān*', sacrifice, and reflecting the fact that animal sacrifice also was a part of Meccan ritual practice), and the *krb* root, via the Ethiopic place-noun *mekrâb*, meaning a 'temple' or 'synagogue'. See Gordon Newby, *Jews of Arabia*, 13 and n. 18 (attributed also to Newby's colleague J. Vanderkam). Animal sacrifice remains a component of Islamic religious practice as associated with the *Ḥajj* rituals near the Ka'ba during the *'īd al-aḍḥā* festival.
21 Hoyland, *Arabia and the Arabs*, 146–147.
22 Emran El-Badawi, *The Qur'ān and the Aramaic Gospel Traditions*, Routledge Studies in the Qur'ān, vol. 13 (New York: Routledge, 2013).
23 Nicholas de Lange, "Jews in the Age of Justinian," *in The Cambridge Companion to the Age of Justinian*, ed. Michael Maas (New York: Cambridge University Press, 2005), 411.
24 Hoyland, *Jews in Arabia*, 146.
25 Hoyland, 146–147.
26 Since the late 1970s in academic Islamic and Qur'ānic studies circles, this paradigm has begun to change. For more recent influential examples, see the work of Gabriel Said Reynolds, *The Qur'ān and Its Biblical Subtext*, Routledge Studies in the Qur'ān, vol. 10, edited by Andrew Rippin (New York: Routledge, 2010).
27 Al-Azmeh, *The Emergence of Islam in the Near East: Allāh and His People*. Al-Azmeh convincingly argues among other things that the polytheist religious composition of the community from which Muslims and Islam formed was not unlike the polytheism of wider Near Eastern communities of the time.
28 Fred Donner, "The Background to Islam," in *The Cambridge Companion to the Age of Justinian*, ed. Michael Maas (New York: Cambridge University Press, 2005), 513.
29 Patrick T. R, Gray, "The legacy of Chalcedon: Christological Problems and Their Significance," in *The Cambridge Companion to the Age of Justinian* ed. Michael Maas (New York: Cambridge University Press, 2005), 216–217.
30 Gray, 222.
31 Gray, 222.
32 Greek, CPA, and Syriac were the liturgical languages of Byzantine Orthodox churches from the fourth century. In the eighth and ninth centuries, following the establishment of Muslim political control in the Eastern Mediterranean, Arabic also became a liturgical language of some Byzantine Orthodox churches. Arabic-language Orthodox churches became identified as such by titles such as 'Rūm Orthodox [Rūm meaning 'Roman', i.e., Byzantine].
33 For other 'high places' in Persian contexts, see also the 'Ayezana' noted in Chapter Three, 73, 96n.
34 Emran El-Badawi, *The Qur'ān and the Aramaic Gospel Traditions*, 55.
35 Donner, *Muḥammad and the Believers*, 14. See also Peter Brown, "Holy Men," in *The Cambridge Ancient History*, Vol. XIV, Late Antiquity: Empire and Successors A.D. 425–600, edited by Averil Cameron, Bryan Ward-Perkins, and Michael Whitby (Cambridge, UK: Cambridge University Press, 2000), 781–810.
36 Donner, 14–15.
37 El-Badawi, *The Qur'ān and the Aramaic Gospel Traditions*, 50–51. This phenomenon has continued into the early modern and modern periods.
38 Robert G. Hoyland, *Seeing Islam as Others Saw It: A Survey and Evaluation of the Christian, Jewish and Zoroastrian Writings on Early Islam*, Studies in Late Antiquity and Early Islam, vol. 13 (Princeton, NJ: The Darwin Press, Inc., 1997), 15.
39 Donner, "The Background to Islam," 521.

40 Nicholas de Lange, "Jews in the Age of Justinian," 402–405.
41 Donner, "The Background to Islam," 521.
42 The traditional dates for the Qur'ān and for the codification of the Qur'ān are disputed within and among scholars and traditionalists. In particular, early Qur'ānic fragments, known as the *Ṣan'ā'* palimpsest and the Birmingham leaves, have been carbon-dated to substantially earlier than the traditional dates of compilation and codification. The Ṣan'ā' palimpsest has been dated to 543–643 and 433–599 (Lyon); 568–664 (Oxford); 539–669 (Zurich), 426–633 (Kiel); and the Birmingham leaves have been dated to 568–645. See also Behnam Sadeghi and Uwe Bergmann, "The Codex of a Companion of the Prophet and the Qur'ān of the Prophet" (*Arabica* 57, 4, 2010), 343–436; and Behnam Sadeghi and Mohsen Goudarzi, "Ṣan'ā' 1 and the Origins of the Qur'ān," (*Der Islam* 87, 1–2, 2012), 1–129. See also above, 2n.
43 Regarding the mainstream scholarly character of these dates, see Fred Donner, *Narratives of Islamic Origin: The Beginnings of Islamic Historical Writing*, Studies in Late Antiquity and Early Islam, vol. 14 (Princeton, NJ: Darwin Press, 1998). See also Sidney H. Griffith, *The Bible in Arabic: The Scriptures of the 'People of the Book' in the Language of Islam* (Princeton, NJ: Princeton University Press, 2013), 209.
44 Donner, *Muḥammad and the Believers*, 59.
45 Fred Donner argues in *Muḥammad and the Believers* for a notion of a gradual 'Muslim' identity formation from the general monotheist 'believer' that did not begin to formalize until the late seventh or early eighth century CE. For the reference involving frequency of occurrence of specific religious designations, see 57.
46 Griffith, *The Bible in Arabic*, 24.
47 Griffith, 57.
48 Griffith, 16.
49 For more on the usage of this term, see Sidney Griffith, "*Al- Naṣārā* in the Qur'ān: A Hermeneutical Reflection," in *New Perspectives on the Qur'ān: The Qur'ān in its Historical Context 2*, edited by Gabriel Said Reynolds, Routledge Studies in the Qur'ān, vol. 12, Andrew Rippin, series editor (New York: Routledge, 2012), 301–322.
50 Griffith, *The Bible in Arabic*, 29.
51 Adapted from El-Badawi, *The Qur'ān and the Aramaic Gospel Traditions*, 58. See Muḥammad b. 'Abd Allāh al-Azraqī, *Akhbār Mecca was mā jā'fīhā min al-āthār*, ed. 'Abd al-Malik b. Duhaysh (Mecca: maktabat al-'Asadī, 2003).
52 El-Badawi, *The Qur'ān and the Aramaic Gospel Traditions*, 5.
53 See, for instance, Q. 18:83–98, a narrative about a figure named in the Qur'ān 'Dhū al-Qarnayn', and who regularly is identified as the extra-biblical Alexander the Great.
54 See Arthur Jeffery, *Foreign Vocabulary in the Qur'ān*. Sidney Griffith furthermore points out that by the time of the Qur'ān, these words had simply *become* Arabic, see Griffith, *The Bible in Arabic*, 18.
55 Griffith, *The Bible in Arabic*, 18.
56 El-Badawi, The Qur'ān and the Aramaic Gospel Traditions, 35. El-Badawi furthermore notes that monasteries in the Sinai Peninsula also fell within the ambit of Greek influence.
57 Griffith, *The Bible in Arabic*, 20–21
58 El-Badawi, *The Qur'ān and the Aramaic Gospel Traditions*, 16, quoting William Graham, "The Earliest Meaning of Qur'ān" (*Die Welt des Islams*, 23–4, 1984), 1–28.
59 See Gabriel Said Reynolds, ed., *The Qur'ān in its Historical Context*, Routledge Studies in the Qur'ān, vol. 8, Series Editor Andrew Rippin (New York: Routledge, 2008) and See Gabriel Said Reynolds, ed., *New Perspectives on the Qur'ān: The Qur'ān in its Historical Context 2*, Routledge Studies in the Qur'ān, vol. 8, Series Editor Andrew Rippin (New York: Routledge, 2011).

60 Griffith, *The Bible in Arabic*, 26. Griffith furthermore argues that the metrically composed *mêmrê* genre of Syriac ecclesiastical practice (long metrical homiletic meditations on the significance of particular scriptural readings) may be a fruitful (and as yet largely untapped) source of study regarding Qur'ānic language and narratives. The *mêmrê* homilies often were enriched by non-biblical details from oral tradition or from apocryphal or even pseudepigraphal sources, sometimes kept in written form in texts in Syriac churches and monasteries, and sometimes widely circulated among Syriac churches. Griffith, 42–43.

61 Griffith, The Bible in Arabic, 26. The Hebrew Bible stories may be mediated ultimately by the Syriac-language Peshitta (ca. 435 CE), the Old Testament and New Testament books in Syriac. The Peshitta subsequently was revised to bring the New Testament books in line with the Greek canon as observed by Athanasius, and reached its final form, known as the Harklean version or Syriac Bible, in ca. 616 CE. See El-Badawi, *The Qur'ān and the Aramaic Gospel Traditions*, 30–33.

62 See Gabriel Said Reynolds, *The Qur'ān and its Biblical Subtext*, Routledge Studies in the Qur'ān, vol. 10, Series Editor Andrew Rippin (New York: Routledge, 2010). See also Griffith, *The Bible in Arabic*, 208.

63 Griffith, *The Bible in Arabic*, 56–57.

64 There are a few early Arabic-language rock inscriptions which pre-date the Qur'ān and the religious tradition of Islam, but these do not together constitute evidence for a developed literary tradition. There also are examples of written Islamic poetry which, in oral form, are likely to pre-date the Qur'ān and the religious tradition of Islam, but we have no surviving copies of written texts of this genre from earlier periods and thus cannot conclude that, prior to the Qur'ān, there existed a developed literary tradition of written Arabic. Indeed, it is the conclusion of Sydney Griffith's study and that of other scholars, that the Qur'ān is the first Arabic book. See Griffith, *The Bible in Arabic*, 53.

65 Griffith, *The Bible in Arabic*, 43.

66 Griffith, 43.

67 Griffith, 16.

68 Griffith, 27. Thus, the biblical communities within the purview of the Qur'ān are not likely to have been members of other sects of Jewish, Christian, or so-called Jewish-Christian communities of the day, as is sometimes argued. Griffith, 208.

69 This point is made repeatedly in small-scale research, and is made in a more broad manner by both this quotation from Sidney Griffith, *The Bible in Arabic*, 71, as well as by Emran El-Badawi, "The Qur'ān, via the lingua franca of the Near East – Aramaic – selectively challenged or re-appropriated, and therefore took up the 'dogmatic articulation' of language and imagery coming from the Aramaic Gospel Traditions, in order to fit the idiom and religious temperament of a heterogeneous, sectarian Arabian audience," *The Qur'ān and the Aramaic Gospel Traditions*, 5.

70 Griffith, *The Bible in Arabic*, 34.

71 Griffith, 33–35.

72 Griffith, 54.

73 Griffith, 3.

74 El-Badawi notes that the '*seal of the prophets*' terminology also was in use among Syriac Christian groups.

75 Griffith, *The Bible in Arabic*, 70–71.

76 Regarding the 'scrolls of Abraham', it is unclear what text is referenced here.

77 Griffith, *The Bible in Arabic*, 73. See also Roberto Tottoli, *Biblical Prophets in the Qur'ān and Muslim Literature* (New York: Routledge, 2002), 23–27.

78 See *Midrash Rabbah: Genesis*, 2 vols, translated by Harry Friedman and Maurice Simon (London: Soncino Press Ltd, 1992), and Jacob Neusner, *Confronting Creation: How Judaism Reads Genesis: An Anthology of Genesis Rabbah* (Columba, SC: University of South Carolina Press, 1991).

79 The tale of Muhammad destroying the idols in the Ka'ba is not mentioned in the Qur'ān but comes from the *sīrah*. All accounts of Muhammad's life lead back to the *sīrah* literature; in particular, to the *Sīrat Rasūl Allāh*, written about a century after Muhammad's death by Medinan scholar Ibn Isḥāq (d. 767 CE). See Alfred Guillaume, *The Life of Muhammad: A Translation of Ibn Isḥāq's Sīrat Rasūl Allāh* (Oxford: Oxford University Press, 2002 (repr. 1955)).

80 Tottoli, *Biblical Prophets in the Qur'ān*, 26.

81 Tottoli, 32–35.

82 Griffith, *The Bible in Arabic*, 77.

83 'Allāh' is likely a contraction of "*al-īlāh*," Cf. Al-Azmeh, *The Emergence of Islam*, who argues that 'Allāh' is not a contraction of '*al-īlāh*', a morphology he considers implausible because "the addition of the definite article *al-* to *Lāh* or *Īlāh* would yield different but allophonic values [i.e., phonetic variants of the phoneme] for the medial vowel /a/," (ibid., 298). Rather, Al-Azmeh argues that 'Allāh' entered the Arabic language in the absolute form of 'Allāh' and, "as it entered the Arabic language, irrespective of its origin or etymology, is an independent proper noun of the *murtajal* class," which is the class of proper nouns that exist only as integral proper names. Al-Azmeh further notes that 'Allāh' could have been "afloat" in pre-Islamic Arabia "in jurative formulae [i.e., relating to an oath] and theophoric names, and possibly among some Christians to the north," although Al-Azmeh intentionally does not suggest how, noting that we lack any map of the geographical distribution of this name and its users. See ibid., 300–301. Al-Azmeh further suggests the attractiveness of the "distinctive vagueness" of 'Allāh' which may have inspired adoption by Muḥammad, see ibid., 301–306. On the Arabic (rather than Syriac) etymology of 'Allāh', see David Kiltz, "The Relationship between Arabic *Allāh* and Syriac *Allāhā*," *Der Islam* 88 (2012): 33–50.

84 Griffith, *The Bible in Arabic*, 77–78 and 45n and 46n, referencing Daniel Madigan, "Criterion," in *Encyclopaedia of the Qur'ān*, edited by McAuliffe, vol. 1, p. 246; and Fred M. Donner, "Qur'ānic *Furqān*," *Journal of Semitic Studies* 52 (2007), 279–300. See also Uri Rubin, "On the Arabian Origins of the Qur'ān: The Case of *al-Furqān*," *Journal of Semitic Studies* 54 (2009), 421–433.

85 El-Badawi, in *The Qur'ān and the Aramaic Gospel Traditions*, argues that the "fundamental literary strategy on the part of the Qur'ān to promote a vision of strict monotheism to a sectarian Arabian audience" was a literary strategy he terms "'dogmatic re-articulation,'" ibid., 207, and that "strict monotheism," from a Qur'ānic perspective, was defined as "a type of monotheism whose nature is anti-trinitarian, post-rabbinic, and apocalyptic"; it "fundamentally rejects orthodox forms of Christian belief in God as well as the monopoly of Jewish clerics on matters of orthopraxy, and it demands urgent and austere obedience to the One true God before the coming end of the world," El-Badawi, 5.

86 For more on the Qur'ānic readings (*qirā'āt*) see Christopher Melchert, "Ibn Mujāhid and the Establishment of Seven Qur'ānic Readings," *Studia Islamica* 91 (2000): 5–22.

87 Arthur J. Droge, *The Qur'ān: A New Annotated Translation* (Bristol, CT: Equinox Publishing Ltd., 2013).

88 See also A. J. Wensinck, "al-Khaḍir," Encyclopedia of Islam, 902–903.

89 The other narratives of Chapter 18, the Sleepers and of Dhū al-Qarnayn, traditionally have garnered more interest than 'Moses and the Servant'. But on that narrative see A.J. Wensinck, "al-Khadir," Haim Schwarzbaum, "The Jewish and Moslem Versions of Some Theodicy Legends (Aa-Th. 759)" (*Fabula* Vol. 3, No. 1, 1959, 119–169); Brannon M. Wheeler, "The Jewish Origins of Qur'ān 18:65–82? Reexamining Arent Jan Wensinck's Theory," (*Journal of the American Oriental Society*, Vol. 118, No. 2, 1998, 153–171). See also Brannon M. Wheeler, *Moses in the Quran and Islamic Exegesis*, Routledge Studies in the Quran 4, edited by Andrew Rippin (New York:

Routledge, 2002). For more on the varied sources and influences on 18:60–82, see Wensinck, "al-Khadir," 902–903.

90 For information about the "storyteller" aspects of Mujāhid's early exegesis, see Claude Gilliot, "Mujāhid's Exegesis: Origins, Paths of Transmission and Development of a Meccan Exegetical Tradition in its Human, Spiritual and Theological Environment," in *Tafsīr and Islamic Intellectual History: Exploring the Boundaries of a Genre*, edited by Andreas Görke and Johanna Pink, The Institute of Ismaili Studies Qur'ānic Studies Series, 12 (Oxford: Oxford University Press, in association with the Institute of Ismaili Studies, London, 2014) 85–89.

91 Kevin Van Bladel, "Alexander Legend in the Qur'ān," 195.

92 For a view of the poetic and formal elements of sūrahs, see Angelika Neuwirth, "Form," in *Encyclopaedia of the Qur'ān*. See also Michael Zwettler, "A Mantic Manifesto: the Sūra of 'The Poets' and the Qur'ānic Foundations of Prophetic Authority," in *Poetry and Prophecy: The Beginnings of a Literary Tradition*, edited by James L. Kugel (New York: Cornell University Press, 1990). For a treatment of Sūrah 18 from a holistic linguistic and literary perspective, emphasizing the 'ring' composition of its verses and the integrated structure of its narratives, Carl W. Ernst, *How to Read the Qur'ān: A New Guide, with Select Translations* (Chapel Hill, NC: The University of North Carolina Press, 2011), 120–138.

93 *Iblīs* is "related to the Greek word *diabolos* ('accuser', cf. Eng. 'devil'), through Syriac (*dīblūs* or *diyābūlūs*). In the Septuagint *diabolos* is sometimes used to translate 'Satan' (Heb. *sāṭān*, 'accuser'), and in the New Testament the word is used to designate the chief of forces of evil (e.g. Matthew 4:1)." *Iblīs* in the Qur'ān is sometimes described as originally an angel (Q 2:36) and sometimes described as one of the *jinn* (Q 18:50). Droge, *The Qur'ān*, 5 and 44n. Additionally, 'Satan' *al-shayṭān* is referenced directly at 18:63. See also Gabriel Reynolds, "*Iblīs*," in *Encyclopaedia of the Qur'ān*.

94 *Jinn* in the Qur'ān are an ambiguous category of otherworldly beings created by God from fire (Q 15:27 and 55:15), and who both serve God (Q 51:56) and lead people astray (Q 41:29). See Droge, *The Qur'ān*, 472-473.

95 Ernst, *How to Read the Qur'ān*, 105–154.

96 See also Droge, *The Qur'ān*, 185 and associated notes.

97 See also Chapter Five, 142–144.

98 Gabriel Said Reynolds, *The Emergence of Islam: Classical Traditions in Contemporary Perspective* (Fortress Press, 2012), 131.

99 Droge, *The Qur'ān*, 185 and associated notes.

100 Reynolds, *Emergence of Islam*," 131–133.

101 See Sidney Griffith's translation in "Christian Lore and the Arabic Qur'ān: The 'Companions of the Cave' in Surat al-Kahf and in Syriac Christian Tradition," in *The Qur'ān in Its Historical Context*, edited by Gabriel Said Reynolds, Routledge Studies in the Qur'ān, series editor Andrew Rippin, vol. 8 (New York: Routledge, 2008), 128.

102 Reynolds, *Emergence of Islam*, 133. Note that Griffith argues *against* the notion that the watchdog in the Qur'ānic account is a "conceptual 'Syriacism'," but does hold that "the watch dog with its paws spread on the cave's threshold" in the Qur'ān is in keeping with the pastoral metaphors evoked by Serugh. Griffith, "Christian Lore and the Arabic Qur'ān," 128.

103 Reynolds, *Emergence of Islam*, 133, quoting Theodosius, *The Pilgrimage of Theodosius*, translated by J.H. Bernard (London: Palestine Pilgrims Text Society, 1893), 16.

104 Griffith, "Christian Lore and the Arabic Qur'ān," 130.

105 Dhū al-Qarnayn translates as "the two-horned [one]," and refers to depictions on contemporaneous regional coinage in which Alexander was depicted in profile, in the role of the Egyptian god Zeus-Ammon, wearing horns.

106 See Kevin van Bladel, "The Alexander Legend in the Qur'ān 18:83–102," in *The Qur'ān in Its Historical Context*, edited by Gabriel Said Reynolds, Routledge Studies in the Qur'ān, series editor Andrew Rippin, vol. 8 (New York: Routledge, 2008), 175–203.
107 Van Bladel, 184–185.
108 Van Bladel, 195; for accounts of oral or direct transmission, see 190.
109 Van Bladel, 188. After its appearance in 630, the Legend was used by at least three more apocalypses, the *Song of Alexander*, attributed falsely to the Syriac Christian poet-theologian Jacob of Serugh and composed between 630–636; the Syriac apocalypse *De fine mundi*, attributed falsely to the Syriac Christian poet-theologian Ephrem and composed between 640–683; and the Christian *Apocalypse of Pseudo-Methodious*, composed around 692 and possibly in reaction to the building of the Muslim Dome of the Rock monument.
110 Van Bladel, "Alexander Legend in the Qur'ān," 183.
111 For a recent examination of the narrative genre of 'parables', see Amy-Jill Levine, *Short Stories by Jesus: the Enigmatic Parables of a Controversial Rabbi*, (HarperOne, 2014).
112 Droge, *The Qur'ān*, 188 and 57n.
113 See, for instance, Suzanne Haneef, *A History of the Prophets of Islam*: *Derived from the Quran, Ahadīth and Commentaries, Vol. 2: Moses, Aaron, Joshua, Samuel, David, Solomon, Elijah, Elisha, Dhul-Kifl, Jonah, Zechariah, John, Jesus, Muḥammad*, Library of Islam (New York: University of New York Press, 1984), 157–189.
114 See Muqātil, *Tafsīr*, II, 592-597, and Ṭabarī, *Tafsīr*, XV, 271–291. See also G.H.A. Juynboll, *Encyclopedia of Canonical Ḥadīth* (Boston: Brill, 2007), 568–572.
115 Wheeler, *Moses in the Qur'an and Islamic Exegesis*, 125–127.
116 Tommaso Tesei, "Cosmological Notions from Late Antiquity in Q 18:60–65" (*Journal of the American Oriental Society* Vol. 135, no. 1, 2015) 19–32.
117 Tesei, 23.
118 Tesei, "Cosmological Notions from Late Antiquity," 20.
119 We saw notions like these in Chapter Two, 40–42.
120 Tesei, 25.
121 Griffith, *The Bible in Arabic*, 61. Griffith argues that the term *'idh'* functions as a marker for a "mode of narrative recall, utilizing a key term that recurs throughout the Qur'ān … the simple word 'when' (*idh*) impli[es] a preceding admonition 'to remember [when]'."
122 Griffith, 54–96.
123 See also Wheeler, *Moses in the Qur'an and Islamic Exegesis*, 34.
124 Halman, *Where the Two Seas Meet*, 31.
125 Schwarzbaum, *Jewish and Moslem Theodicy Legends*, 119. Note that Schwarzbaum places the narrative of 18:60–82 into the Aarne Thompson folk-literature motif category of *759, known as the angel and the hermit.
126 Schwarzbaum, *Jewish and Moslem Theodicy Legends*, 120. Cf. the same sentiment about the mysterious powers and ways of the divine, as echoed by Baal in the *Baal Cycle*, Chapter Three, 62, 43n.
127 BT *Berakoth* 7a.
128 Nicholas de Lange, "Jews in the Age of Justinian," 401–426.
129 See Michal Bar-Asher Siegal, *Early Christian Monastic Literature and the Babylonian Talmud* (Cambridge: Cambridge University Press, 2013). See also a similar argument made by Kristen H. Lindbeck, *Elijah and the Rabbis*, xvi.
130 See G.H.A. Juynboll, *Encyclopedia of Canonical Ḥadīth*, who notes that "in the Qur'ān al-Khaḍir is nowhere mentioned by name. The subject of the verb is simply left unspecified, but in all the earliest exegetical works, beginning with that of Mujāhid, al-Khadir is mentioned here by name," Juynboll, 571.
131 For a detailed explanation of the transmission of Mujāhid, see Gilliot, "Mujāhid's Exegesis," 64–112.
132 See Muqātil, *Tafsīr*, II, 592-597, and Ṭabarī, *Tafsīr*, XV, 271-291. See also G.H.A. Juynboll, *Encyclopedia of Canonical Ḥadīth* (Boston: Brill, 2007), 568–572. For the

Wahb b. Munabbih transmission of Ubayy b. Ka'b, see Wheeler, *Moses in the Quran and Islamic Exegesis*, 10.

133 Wheeler, *Moses in the Quran and Islamic Exegesis*, 10.

134 Muqātil generally did not refer to earlier exegetical sources, though he may have been aware of them.

135 G.H.A. Juynboll, *Encyclopedia of Canonical Ḥadīth*, 569; see also Muqātil, *Tafsīr*, vol. II, 594.

136 See Nicolai Sinai, "The Qur'ānic Commentary of Muqātil b. Sulaymān and the Evolution of Early *Tafsīr* Literature, in *Tafsīr and Islamic Intellectual History: Exploring the Boundaries of a Genre*, edited by Andreas Görke and Johanna Pink, The Institute of Ismaili Studies Qur'ānic Studies Series, 12 (Oxford: Oxford University Press, in association with the Institute of Ismaili Studies, London, 2014) 113–146.

137 See Chapter Four, 116–117.

138 Wheeler, *Moses in the Quran and Islamic Exegesis*, 24–25, emphasis mine.

139 Wheeler, *Moses in the Quran and Islamic Exegesis*, 24. See also Chapter Four.

140 Muslim, *Ṣaḥīḥ*, (Beirut: Dār al-Ma'rifah, 1994), vol. 5, 135; see also al-Ṭabarī, *Jāmi' al-bayān fi tafsīr al-Qur'ān*, vol 15, 168.

141 See Abū Zakarīyā' Yaḥyā al-Nawawī, *Tahdhīb al-asmā'*, ed. Wüstenfeld (Göttingen: London Society for the Publication of Oriental Texts, 1842–1847), vol. 1, 228; see also al-Diyārbakri, *Ta'rikh al-khamīs* (Cairo, 1283), vol. 1, 106. These references come from Wensinck, "al-Khaḍir," 905, and from Wheeler, "The Jewish Origins of Qur'ān 18:65–82?" 165. This ḥadīth can be found in the *Saḥīḥ* collection of Muslim, ca. 850 CE.

142 Wheeler, *Moses in the Quran and Islamic Exegesis*, 33, bracketed emphatic insertion mine.

143 Wheeler, *Moses in the Quran and Islamic Exegesis*, 25, emphasis added.

144 Wheeler, *Moses in the Quran and Islamic Exegesis*, 25.

145 Wheeler, *Moses in the Quran and Islamic Exegesis*, 24–25. The exact quote is "It is also unlikely that the association of al-Khiḍr and Elijah is the result of a confusion of the two characters, but rather than the character of al-Khiḍr was developed to appropriate the characteristics associated with Elijah in biblical and rabbinic stories."

146 See al-Ṭabarī, *Ta'rikh al-rasūl wa-l mulūk*, 415, who recorded that "Al-Khiḍr was the progeny of Persia while Elijah was an Israelite. The two meet every year during the annual festival (*mawsim*)." The theme of Elijah and al-Khiḍr meeting annually became popular in Arabic commentary, and, as Brannon Wheeler noted, this report may be the source for such traditions. See Brannon Wheeler, "Jewish Origins of Q 18:65–82?" 165 69n.

147 al-Ṭabarī, Abū Ja'far Muḥammad b. Jarīr, *Ta'rīkh al-rusul wa al-mulūk*, translated by William M. Brinner (Albany, NY: State University of New York, 1991), Vol. 3 of *The History of al-Ṭabarī*, 39 vols., edited by Ehsan Yar-Shatar.

148 See Firdawsī, *Iskandarnāma*, a Persian Alexander tale from ca. 1000 CE that specifically writes al-Khiḍr into Alexander's journey. Among many other textual and artistic references, see also the miniature paintings which depict Alexander and al-Khiḍr together at the water of life. The 16th-century miniature painting collection associated with the Alexander tales in Niẓamī Ganjavī's *Khamsa* is a good example.

149 See Chapter Four, 121.

150 See Chapter Four, 121–123; 129–130.

151 Lindbeck, *Elijah and the Rabbis*, ix.

152 Lindbeck, xix.

153 Lindbeck, 207.

154 See Chapter Four, 122–123.

155 For more on the late antique associations between Elijah and Moses, see also Chapter Four, 122–123.

156 See Brannon Wheeler, *Moses in the Quran and Islamic Exegesis*, 125–127. Emphasis in the quote mine.

157 The Arabic original was published by Julian Obermann, *Studies in Islam and Judaism: The Arabic Original of Ibn Shâhîn's Book of Comfort, known as the Ḥibbûr yaphê of r. Nissîm b. Ya'aqobh* (New Haven, CT: Yale University Press, 1933). An English translation can be found in William M. Brinner, *An Elegant Composition Concerning Relief after Adversity: by Nissim ben Jacob Ibn Shāhīn*, Yale Judaica Series, Vol. XX, edited by Leon Nemoy (New Haven, CT: Yale University Press, 1977).
158 Lindbeck, *Elijah and the Rabbis*.
159 Lindbeck, 98. For more on Rabbi Joshua ben Levi, see Ronald L. Eisenberg, *Essential Figures in the Talmud* (Lanham, MD: Jason Aronson, a subsidiary of The Rowman & Littlefield Publishing Group, Inc., 2013), "Joshua ben Levi," 137–141.
160 Brinner translation, *Composition Concerning Relief after Adversity*, 13–17.
161 See A.J. Wensinck, "El-Khiḍr," 902–903, following Julian Obermann, "Two Elijah Stories in Judaeo-Arabic Transmission," 399–400, and "Ein Werk agadisch-islamischen Synkretismus" (*Zeitschrift für Semitistik*, Vol. 5, 1927, 43–68), and Adolph Jellinek, *Bet ha-Midrasch*, (Vienna, 1873), Vol. 5, 133–35.
162 Schwarzbaum, "The Jewish and Moslem Versions of Some Theodicy Legends," for reasons of language usage and parallel structure, saw the Jewish legend as dependent upon 18:65–82, and Brannon Wheeler, "The Jewish Origins of Qur'ān 18:65–82?" argued instead that while 18:65–82 was not dependent upon the Jewish legend, the Jewish legend might be dependent upon 18:65–82, not from the Qur'ān directly, but through the medium of the Qur'ānic exegetical commentaries.
163 Compelling narratives and texts often found expression among multiple religious communities in the Near East. See above, 129n.
164 See Halman, *Where the Two Seas Meet*, 2. This work focuses on al-Khiḍr in the Sufi traditions and is thus a good source for understanding al-Khiḍr as he developed in later Arabic commentary and literature.
165 See above, 147n. and 148n.
166 Halman, *Where the Two Seas Meet*, 44 59n.
167 Written records of these correspondences go back at least to the 11th century CE.
168 Abdul-Massih Saadi, "Nascent Islam in the Seventh-Century Syriac Sources," in *The Qur'ān in its Historical Context*, edited by Gabriel Said Reynolds, Routledge Studies in the Qur'ān, vol. 8, Series Editor Andrew Rippin (New York: Routledge, 2008), 217–222.
169 Donner, *Muḥammad and the Believers*. Referencing correspondence of the Bishop Sophronius of Jerusalem from 638 CE.
170 Donner, 136–140.
171 See Richard W. Bulliet, *Conversion to Islam in the Medieval Period: An Essay in Quantitative History* (Boston, MA: Harvard University Press, 1979). See also Donner, *Muḥammad and the Believers*.
172 Donner, *Muḥammad and the Believers*, 115. Donner furthermore notes that Christian churches were still being built in the century after conquest and that early Muslim records indicate early Muslims worshipped at churches, sometimes in separate sections of the church.
173 Saadi, "Nascent Islam in Syriac Sources," 220. See also Donner, *Muḥammad and the Believers*, 114.
174 Donner, *Muḥammad and the Believers*, 115.
175 This is Donner's argument in *Muḥammad and the Believers*. Donner and others suggest that an 'Islamic' formal orientation and identity did not begin to crystalize until the 790s at the earliest. Most often this religious-identity emergence is associated with the building of monumental architectural spaces (like the Dome of the Rock in 792 CE), and the issuance of coin types which can be seen to include within them indications of a separate religious identity emerging.

176 See Richard W. Bulliet, *Conversion to Islam in the Medieval Period: An Essay in Quantitative History* (Boston, MA: Harvard University Press, 1979).

177 See Josef W. Meri, "Re-Appropriating Sacred Space: Medieval Jews and Muslims Seeking Elijah and al-Khaḍir" (*Medieval Encounters* 5, 3, 1999, 237–264); and *The Cult of Saints Among Muslims and Jews in Medieval Syria* (Oxford Oriental Monographs. Oxford: Oxford University Press, 2002). See also Chapter Four. See also Chapter Two, 45.

178 Ethel Sara Wolper, "Khiḍr and the Changing Frontiers of the Medieval World.," (*Medieval Encounters*: Jewish, Christian and Muslim Culture in Confluence and Dialogue 17, 2011, 120–146).

179 See Speros Vryonis, Jr., *The Decline of Medieval Hellenism in Asia Minor and the Process of Islamization from the Eleventh through the Fifteenth Century*, Center for Medieval and Renaissance Studies, UCLA series (Berkeley, CA: University of California Press, 1971) 444.

180 Vryonis, 485.

181 See also Taufik Canaan, *Mohammadan Saints and Sanctuaries in Palestine*. London: Luzac & Co., 1927, as well as Josef W. Meri, *The Cult of Saints Among Muslims and Jews in Medieval Syria*, Oxford Oriental Monographs (Oxford: University Press, 2002).

182 Various 20th-century factors, including the new regional political borders drawn after World War I and the establishment of the state of Israel, have led to the uprooting of traditional long-term Jewish communities in the region and to the cessation of religious practices involving communities of Jews, Muslims, and Christians together. See also Chapter Seven. On these associations between modern communities of Muslims and Christians, see for instance the name of recent Christian Bishop of the Greek Orthodox Church for the region of Mount Lebanon, Bishop George Khodor (whom I interviewed during fieldwork in 2013).

183 It should of course be noted that the names 'George' and 'Khiḍr' can be used interchangeably among and between Muslims and Christians, so one is careful not to put too fine a point on name usage between Christian and Muslim communities.

184 See, for instance, the al-Khiḍr mosque in Beirut, Lebanon. Constructed over and expanding a smaller, domed church or shrine dedicated originally to St. George, the al-Khiḍr mosque was constructed during the 19th century.

185 ARPOA website; Victor Sauma, *Sur les Pas des Saints au Liban*, 480. See also Chapter One, 2, 4n.

186 This vision of monotheism could be characterized as similar to the perspective advocated by biblical figures like Moses and Elijah.

7 Eastern Mediterranean shared religious history

On August 19, 2015, the Israeli daily newspaper *Haaretz* featured a story about the Cave of Elijah the Prophet, which is located on Mt. Carmel.[1] This is the same cave that we encountered in Chapter Two, "Levantine geography, history, and agrarian religion," and again in Chapter Four, "The Hebrew Bible and Elijah."[2] Ancient inscriptions in the cave, the article warned, are in danger of being destroyed by unwitting modern visitors. Today, the Cave of Elijah the Prophet receives visitors holding bar mitzvahs, as well as visits from local Jews, Muslims, and Druze who wish to pray in the cave of the illustrious Prophet Elijah. The cave itself has been extended and built out from the mountain wall in rectangular brick structures that are covered inside with modern Jewish religious adornments, and divided in the approximate center to create Orthodox men's and women's sides.

Following appeals from local academics, the Israeli Holy Sites Authority has initiated a two-year plan to restore the cave. The use of the cave as a religious site dates to the late Bronze Age–early Iron Age, and inscriptions inside the cave date to the Hellenistic period, reflecting an interesting example of interconnected history that has been outlined as well throughout this book. Analysis of the cave's inscriptions suggests that 'Elijah's' Cave, as it has been known since the Byzantine era and from approximately the fourth to seventh centuries CE, functioned before that as a Greek- and Roman-era shrine to the god Zeus on Mt. Carmel. Before that, researchers believe that the cave functioned as a shrine to Baal [of] Carmel.[3]

According to analysis of the cave's inscriptions, undertaken since 1966 by Asher Ovadiah, there are 180 Greek inscriptions, dating from the fourth century BCE to the third century CE, one Latin inscription, two Arabic inscriptions, and 44 Hebrew inscriptions, with some Hebrew inscriptions dating to the region's Byzantine period, and most of them dating to the 18th and 19th centuries CE, ostensibly left by Jews living nearby in Acre.

Though written at different times and directed toward different figures (different, although closely related figures, as we have seen), the inscriptions are remarkably similar in nature – dedications to family and friends, pleas for divine healing, and wishes for success in particular endeavors. One Greek inscription was left by a man called Elios, apparently an official living in Acre during the second or first centuries BCE, who wrote, "This place should be favorable to my son Kyrillos, who will not be affected by fever anymore."[4]

As we saw above in Chapter Four, Mt. Carmel, along with other prominent mountains and high places throughout the Levant, such as Mt. Sapan, long was associated with the storm-god Baal-Hadad. The account of Elijah in the Hebrew Bible at 1 Kings 18 set the iconic contest between Elijah, the prophet of Yahweh, and the 450 'prophets of Baal' on Mt. Carmel, making Elijah's spectacular victory there all the more prominent: it took place on Baal's own mountain.[5] Baal worship on the mountain gradually was subsumed during the Hellenistic era by worship of Zeus. One wall of the Cave of Elijah bears the carving of a man – today covered by the picture of a rabbi – that researchers think may have been related to Zeus, or perhaps to Baal, as Ovadiah contends. Additionally, the foot of a third-century CE statue dedicated to Zeus Heliopolitanus, as we saw above in Chapter Four, was found nearby in 1952 at the Carmelite monastery dedicated to Elijah,[6] providing further evidence of the site as associated, during the Greek and Roman eras, with the god Zeus.

Beginning in the fifth century CE, as Christian and Jewish communities in the Eastern Mediterranean began to surpass the populations of regional polytheistic communities, Christian and Jewish visitors to the cave transformed it into a site dedicated to Elijah. Among local Jewish communities of the Mt. Carmel/Acre region, of course, the cave site may have been associated with Elijah from as early as the middle of the first millennium, BCE, but the earliest extant inscriptions inside the cave that are from Jewish visitors date only to the fourth to sixth centuries CE. One carving in the northeast corner of the cave displays an equilateral Christian cross inscribed by a circle, and another displays two seven-stemmed menorahs; all three carvings date from the Byzantine period. From that time on, the site has been associated with Elijah rather than with Zeus or with Baal, as legend surrounding the cave suggests that this is the cave where Elijah stayed the night before his legendary battle with Baal (1 Kings 18: 1–46). Successive regional communities of Christians, Muslims, and Druze likewise visited over the following centuries to see and experience Elijah's cave, and often, as we saw in Chapter Four, while there to seek inspiration in dreams.[7]

Nearby, in the West Bank village of Arṭās in the region of Bethlehem, local communities of Palestinian Christians and Muslims gather annually in April for an agricultural 'lettuce' festival. At the gathering, the Muslim and Christian children of the community stage a re-enactment of the 'dragon' terrorizing local villagers (this dragon destroys their homes and pushes the villagers off their land); the dragon ultimately is vanquished in combat by the valiant 'St. George-al-Khiḍr', who restores people to their homes and land, and who is praised as well for his powers involving rain and crop growth. The reenactment thus interweaves modern themes of displacement and occupation reflective of 20th-century political history with long-term regional agrarian religious narratives. Involving the legendary defeat of a dragon and associated with the ability to control rain and make crops flourish, these geographical motifs long have been associated with this native hero, who is for the community at one and the same time both St. George and al-Khiḍr.[8]

On April 23 and May 6, the dates of the St. George festivals in the Western and Eastern churches, respectively,[9] small communities of Christians and Muslims of many sects in the Levant gather to celebrate and pay respects to the universally beloved figure St. George-al-Khiḍr. These celebrations take place in small communities all around the Eastern Mediterranean, from sites in Turkey, to villages along the Nile Delta in Egypt,[10] to mountain villages scattered throughout Lebanon, Syria, Palestine, Israel, and around Jordan. These celebrations especially are highlighted in sites such as at the St. George church in al-Khodr village in Bethlehem, where St. George's mother was said to have been born.[11] That is likewise the case at the St. George church in Lod, Israel (a town previously known as Lydda, and before that as Diospolis), where St. George's relics are said to reside, and which, as we saw in Chapter Five, has been a shrine to St. George since at least the sixth century CE.[12] From at least the late 19th century CE, that same St. George church in Lod has been appended – literally, divided by a single wall – to the al-Khiḍr mosque there.[13]

These examples of modern festivals and agrarian religious practices involving the figures of Elijah, St. George, and al-Khiḍr in the Eastern Mediterranean return our discussion to the original phenomenon that inspired this study. In the introductory chapter, we suggested that the way these figures traditionally had been studied – i.e., from a 'World Religions' perspective, in which each figure is studied as a product of their particular religious traditions – is an inadequate methodology.

Instead, we proposed to investigate each of the figures (including Baal-Hadad, suggested in earlier scholarship to be the original source of the figures Elijah, St. George, and al-Khiḍr) from the perspective of Geography of Religion theory, which suggests that religions and by extension their texts and textual personae always are a product of both the time and the place in which they originate or are manifested. In this model, religious traditions do not exist in a vacuum, but naturally are geographically contextualized: that is, influenced by contemporaneous religious, political, and geographical forces.

Geography of religion: Using a geographical lens

Regional geography

Accordingly, an understanding of regional geography is absolutely essential for a proper understanding not only of these figures, but of the geographical and meteorological motifs that have developed there and remained relevant and compelling in Levantine culture for the past few thousand years. Three main features in particular have affected geography in the Eastern Mediterranean. First, its geological structures: the Mediterranean basin, which is composed of a bedrock of limestone, weathers quickly, leaving behind an abundance of rocks, thin, rocky soils, and thousands of caves and grottoes. This kind of landscape, as we have seen, distinctly has shaped Levantine religious notions and practices. Being located exactly at the convergence of three continental plates – the African, Arabian, and Eurasian – has created the topography of the region, and resulted in three topographical zones: coastal plains in the west, a central band of mountain ranges, and plains and plateaus in the east. This continental-plate convergence also accounts for the frequency of earthquakes in the region.

The second and third major features that have affected the geography of the Levant are related to water. The climatological weather patterns of the wider Mediterranean Sea region govern seasonal wind flows, as well as precipitation. The location of the Levant, situated at the Eastern littoral of the Mediterranean Sea basin, has affected regional climate and rainfall patterns. With its mountain ranges jutting upward next to the sea and just inland of a narrow band of coastal plains, the mountainous topography of the region governs which areas of the Levant attract rainfall – the windward sides of the mountains – and which areas perennially are dry – the leeward sides of the mountains, which descend into dry plains and plateaus to the east. All of that, together with the region's water resources, of course, has affected the regional possibilities for the practice of agriculture.

Unlike in Mesopotamia, with the Euphrates and Tigris Rivers, or in Egypt, with the Nile River, the Levant lacks similarly large and annually flooding rivers that can be used as water resources and for largescale irrigation. Instead, the three main rivers in the Levant – the Orontes, the Litani, and the Jordan – as well as smaller regional rivers and hundreds of far smaller, seasonal tributaries, together with a few surface lakes and the regional aquifers, have provided the water resources necessary for life in the Levant.

These kinds of weather patterns and water resources distinctly have shaped Levantine religious notions and practices, as well. The historical names of these Levantine rivers, especially those in the north, located near Mt. Sapan, which was believed to have been the home of the storm-god, also were associated with the narratives of the storm-god Baal-Hadad. The Orontes River was known by the Greeks as Τυφῶν 'Typhon', which etymologically is related to the Greek word for 'storm', and named after the fearsome, serpent-headed storm monster who was defeated by Zeus.[14] In Latin, the Orontes River became known as the Draco, or 'dragon' river. The name of the Litani River etymologically is derived from the same Semitic root *ltn* that corresponds to the mythical sea creature Lotan ('Leviathan', from the Hebrew Bible, and whom Yahweh also defeated).[15] Recall that in the Baal Cycle, one of Baal's most memorable narratives was that of him defeating the 'twisty serpent', 'Lotan' (*ltn*), also named Yamm-Nahar, meaning both 'sea' and 'river'. Thus can one see in the historical names for the Orontes/Typhon/Draco and the Litani/'*ltn*' Rivers the attendant millennia of regional narratives that earlier were related to the regional storm-gods.[16]

In general, as we saw above in Chapter Two, the Eastern Mediterranean is arid, with rainfall totals decreasing from north to south and west to east, and with drought being a regular climatological condition. Despite that, much of the Levant falls within the 400 mm (12 inches) isohyet, and most of the region generally receives therefore sufficient annual rainfall to enable the cultivation of rain-fed agriculture. Moreover, because of the location of the Levant as the western arc of the 'Fertile Crescent' in which regional agricultural practices were spread, agriculture long has been practiced in the Eastern Mediterranean, as well. Indeed, the region primarily can be characterized by an agricultural economic base *through the mid-twentieth century* CE.[17] Thus, when we study the Levant, we are confronted with a limestone bedrock landscape, as well as an agriculturally oriented location that simultaneously is arid, and in which water from rainfall always has constituted the main source of water for crop growth and for the success or failure of its human populations. Accordingly, geographical motifs in the Levant largely have been related to and necessitated by regional agricultural needs – particularly those for rainfall from the sky.

Influence of geography

Geography does not drive religious belief, but it has a distinct shaping influence, because geography so thoroughly affects the everyday lives of people. In particular, this book reveals the considerable and long-term influence in the Levant of geography upon regional human religious orientation. The ancient Near Eastern Syro-Canaanite deity Baal-Hadad was a storm-god, whose very name meant 'lord of the storm', characterized by regional geographical and climatological patterns that included thunder and rain in the winter, Baal's disappearance in the summer, and his cyclical return to his home on Mt. Sapan in the fall. Baal-Hadad, as the dispenser of rain and the purveyor of agricultural bounty, was the dominant religious entity in the region from at least the early Bronze Age. As the manifestation of regional weather patterns, Baal-Hadad was understood as a powerful but capricious deity who thundered across the sky and showered beneficence – or cruelty – upon his human subjects, but who, properly supplicated, also might be called upon to help those in need. Baal remained dominant in regional culture through the early centuries of the Common Era, although his cult gradually began to be subsumed/supplanted by Zeus (and then sometimes Jupiter), both of whom represented similar climatological characteristics, from the fourth century BCE.[18]

Elijah, the Hebrew Bible righteous prophet of Yahweh, whose very name, אֵלִיָּהוּ, means 'my god is YHWH', bore the message that Yahweh – not Baal – was the true god in the region. Despite evidence throughout the text of the Hebrew Bible that indicates Baal-Hadad indeed had remained the god of choice among most people in the region, Elijah's prophetic mission was to promote the message that it was *Yahweh* who controlled everything, including the rain, and not the 'false' god Baal. In service of Elijah's mission on behalf of Yahweh, Elijah performed several memorable miracles, including stopping and starting the rain (and initiating an oppressive three-year drought), calling 'fire' (that is, lightning) from the sky, extending a widow's oil and flour supplies (thus demonstrating Yahweh's control over food supply in a manner similar to that of the god Baal), and disappearing miraculously in a divine chariot flown into the sky. All of Elijah's abilities in these matters ultimately were made possible only through the power of Yahweh, as the Hebrew Bible text made clear; nevertheless, Elijah became associated afterward in culture with several of the motifs of Baal which were important in regional culture: associations with powers involving the rain, storms, lightning, thunder (via celestial chariot-riding), crop growth, disappearance and return, and the ability to help those in need.

St. George, 'γεωργός', 'Georgos', the 'farmer' saint, was associated as well with several of these essential regional motifs, such as with rain, storms, fertility, crop growth, disappearance and return, and the ability to help those in need. Through pointed narratival associations in the *Acts of St. George* with the regionally popular account of Elijah from the Hebrew Bible, who had defended the 'true' god Yahweh in the face of the 'false' god Baal, George likewise came to be known as a righteous defender of 'true' faith. The cult of St. George developed an early agricultural basis that seems to have been independent of agricultural qualities associated with Elijah (although, those agricultural qualities of St. George perhaps were 'confirmed' among his cult through narratival associations with Elijah). The origin of the agricultural qualities of St. George, as articulated through his cult, and as associated regionally with the geographical motifs of greenness, fertility, rain, storms, crop growth, and with an agricultural festival date of April 23, could have stemmed from or overlapped with local cults to Zeus-Baal, and perhaps even to Zeus-Georgos, whence St. George's name could be derived.[19] Like his fellow warrior saints Theodore and Demetrius, George became associated as well in at least the sixth to eighth century CE (perhaps earlier) with the pictorial motif of vanquishing a dragon or serpent, which also may have either invited – or confirmed – conceptual associations with the agricultural qualities of a storm-god.

Al-Khiḍr, الخضر 'the Green [One]', through his name, through his associations in text with the regionally popular and agriculturally oriented figure of Elijah, and, following the seventh to eighth century, through his popular associations among Christian communities with St. George (also a revered figure with known agricultural associations), al-Khiḍr was associated as well in the Eastern Mediterranean with the compelling geographical motifs of rain, storms, greenness, fertility, crop growth, disappearance and return, and being a helper to those in need who was able to travel great distances and to appear at any time. Likewise, Khiḍr's associations in the Eastern Mediterranean with St. George, with the celebration date of April 23, and with the pictorial motif of vanquishing a dragon likely reinforced and/or confirmed his agricultural qualities, which were so important in an agrarian religious culture.

The sites in this study likewise were influenced by regional geography. As we saw above, when moisture-laden winds move up the coastal mountains of the Levant, they condense and precipitate before crossing the mountains, effectively creating a verdant area to the west and in the center of the coastal mountain ranges, and a rain shadow to the east and south. Additionally, the higher the altitude of a given mountain along the coast, the greater its attraction of both cloud formations and precipitation. To peoples in the ancient Levant, this geographical and climatological situation indicated that a storm-god was linked with high-mountain spaces. As we saw in Chapter Three, Mt. Sapan (/Kasios/Casius/*Jebl āqra'*), the highest mountain along the Levantine coast, was believed to be the home of the storm-god Baal-Hadad, and Mt. Carmel, to the south – likewise a high-mountain along the southern coast of the Levant – also was associated with many shrines to Baal. The Hebrew Bible is replete with damning references to those who venerated the 'high places', as this was a common religious practice among many mountains and high places in the Levant. Despite that, even exclusivist biblical figures such as Elijah eventually became associated with high places and mountains, as were shrines to St. George and to al-Khiḍr, as well.

The relationships between these figures as suggested by this book

These associations with rain, storms, thunder, lightning, greenness, fertility, fecundity, the ability to appear and disappear, associations with mountains and other high places, local feast or celebration days of April 23, and the motif of vanquishing a dragon or serpent, do not indicate that Elijah, George, and Khiḍr are undifferentiated or haphazard continuations of the storm-god Baal-Hadad.[20] Rather, these motifs carefully are linked both to the relationships between the figures, and to the regional geographical needs that these motifs continued to meet.

Accordingly, contrary to the perspectives of most regional religious history texts, as well as to the position advocated in the Hebrew Bible, the regional figure of the storm-god – and, by extension, 'Canaanite' religious practices – can be said to have continued through the Bronze Age, into the Iron Age and the first millennium BCE in the Levant, and lasted even for a few centuries into the Common Era.[21] Moreover, the figures of Zeus and of Jupiter *in the Levant* primarily should not be considered 'Greek' and 'Roman' religious figures, in the sense of being foreign to or separate from local Levantine religious practice and belief. Rather, this book suggests that Levantine Zeus and Jupiter *first* should be understood as embedded within their local context, and as inextricably related to and influenced by the Levantine cults to Baal-Hadad.[22] Additionally, one of the longer-lived important motifs in the region is that of the storm-god defeating a or serpent or a dragon,[23] which this book suggested in Chapter Three may originate as well in the meteorological phenomenon of waterspouts, and which also may be related to (or confirmed by) the occurrence of seasonally flooding regional rivers, as well as regional earthquakes.[24]

Given both the centrality and the dominance of the long-lived storm-god figure among religious and everyday life in the Levant, it makes sense that one of the primary theological messages of the Hebrew Bible – in particular, of that of the Deuteronomistic History – was that the worship of gods other than Yahweh leads to destruction.[25] The zealous mission of Elijah the Prophet in 1 and 2 Kings thus was the eradication of Baal worship – both in the region in general, and specifically among the Israelites. Within the Hebrew Bible, it was of course Yahweh whom the writers presented as an actual divine alternative to Baal-Hadad; however, through his mission in opposition to Baal worship, Elijah in the Hebrew Bible associatively became linked both in the text and among regional cultures with important geographical and meteorological motifs of Baal-Hadad, such as the ability to control the weather in the forms of rain and drought, associations with high places, and disappearance into the stormy sky via a celestial chariot.[26] In that way, Elijah came to function as an *antithetical alternative* to Baal-Hadad: Elijah was *not* Baal-Hadad – his mission was against Baal, in fact – but, as a figure engaged in Baal-worship-eradication, and who thereby also became associatively linked with some of Baal's most compelling geographical motifs, the figure of Elijah effectively came to function as an antithetical alternative to Baal-Hadad.

The figure of St. George is multilayered and composite, of which we have seen ample evidence throughout this book. However, given his name 'Georgos',[27] his function, as a saint for 'farmer' and agricultural communities,[28] and the motifs with which he earliest was associated, even in text – rain, greenness, fertility, fecundity, lightning, feast day of April 23, and especially the defeat of a serpent of dragon[29] – the very early cult of St. George was likely to have originated in – or at least overlapped with, or perhaps offered an alternative to – local cults to Zeus-Baal or 'Zeus-Georgos'. Such an occurrence certainly would have been in keeping with similar phenomena involving other late-third- to early-fourth-century 'warrior saints' cults, such as those of Ss. 'Demetrius' and 'Mercurius', which likely came into being when contemporaneous cults to the gods Demeter and Mercury (/Greek: Hermes) began to wane, and cults to the Christian martyrs began to rise.[30]

'Al-Khiḍr', as we suggested in extended argument in Chapter Six, likely could have been an appellative reference to Elijah during the late antique period. We argued that there was evidence in exegetical sources indicating that the identification of the anonymous 'servant' in Q 18:60–82 with the figure named 'al-Khiḍr' likely was a contemporaneous reference to and identification of Elijah."[31]

The preceding points have offered a very brief overview of major arguments made throughout this book, and the following chart tentatively details the relationships between these figures, as suggested by this study: (Figure 7.1).

This chart suggests chronological relationships between these figures, as well as conceptual relationships between them. It implies the origin of the meteorological motifs shared by Elijah, St. George, and al-Khiḍr, and it proposes why, for the past several hundred years, local agrarian religious communities in the Levant naturally would have associated and shared the 'disparate' figures of Elijah, St. George, and al-Khiḍr: these figures are not disparate; rather, they are inseparably linked.

Moreover, although this study has encompassed four distinct figures, in actuality, this chart suggests that the major points of origin for all four figures reduce only to two: those of the storm-god, Baal-Hadad, whose cult and motifs are likely to have

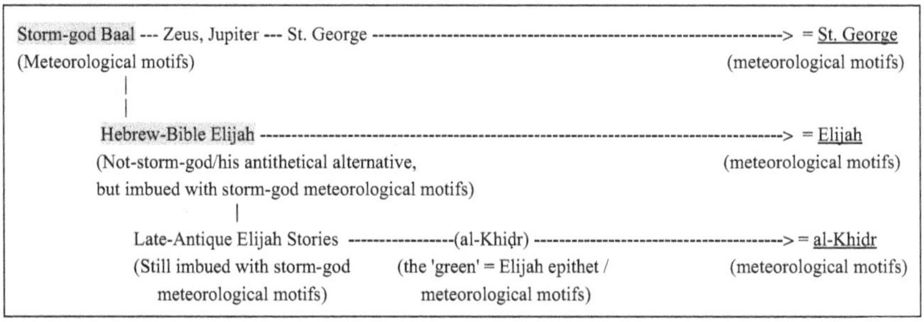

Figure 7.1 Relationships between these figures as suggested by this book

influenced the very early cult origins of St. George, and Elijah, the Hebrew Bible 'antithetical alternative' to Baal-Hadad, and who is likely, in late antique form, to be the origin of the name for the figure known as 'al-Khiḍr'. What is more, it would seem that both the storm-god Baal-Hadad, and Elijah, his antithetical alternative, revolve around the figure of the storm-god. More precisely, however, what this chart makes evident is that the figures themselves – and the meteorological motifs by which they are linked – originate not in a figure, but in *regional geographical needs*.

Thus, the associations with rain, storms, thunder, lightning, greenness, fertility, fecundity, the ability to appear and disappear, associations with mountains and other high places, local feast or celebration days of April 23, and the motif of vanquishing a dragon or serpent are examples of indispensable agricultural and meteorological *motifs* in a geographical region that long has been dominated by agricultural activity while being simultaneously dependent upon water from rainfall, characterized by aridity, and regularly blighted by drought. These motifs are related to regional needs for rainfall from the sky, for agricultural success, and for the seasonal cycle. Geographical considerations have driven these motifs, not the figure of the storm-god. Identifying regional geography as the compelling influence behind these agricultural motifs, rather than attributing these shared motifs solely to genealogical or inherited associations between figures, is a major insight of this book. Ultimately, this book argues that these geographical motifs are shared by each of the figures in this study – Baal-Hadad, Elijah, St. George, and al-Khiḍr – over a very long period of time in the region, because the figures inseparably are linked to one another, and *because they share the region*.

As the agrarian orientation of society in the Levant gradually has diminished, since the mid-20th century CE, these motifs nonetheless have persisted among regional religious figures and cultures. That is because of the long-standing religious significances of these figures between and among their respective religious communities, and because of the self-reinforcing legacy of successful cultural persistence.

Geographical contextualization: Agrarian religion and the slow development of canonical religion in the Levant

A guiding principle of this work has been the notion that texts, images, and sites function like artifacts that can tell us a great deal about the societies in which they were produced. From this perspective, every text, image, or site can be understood as a small window into history. In order to understand each of the figures in this study as a product of their own time and place, this book has investigated the figures' important texts, images, and sites for evidence within them of contemporaneous religious, political, and geographical influences. In doing this kind of geographical contextualization analysis, we see in each text, image, or site, wider evidence of the influence of geography upon the development regional religious notions and beliefs; of agrarian religion and a common pool of compelling figures, narratives, and geographical motifs in the Levant; of the interconnections between Levantine religions; and of the slow development of orthodoxies.

Where we see agrarian religion

Geography, Religion, Gods, and Saints in the Eastern Mediterranean gives us a glimpse into agrarian religion, which, as we have seen above in Chapter Two, and, far more distinctly than the perspectives of 'canonical' or 'orthodox' religion, is the orientation that dominated most people's religious understandings and practices in the Levant up through the mid-twentieth century CE. We have seen in the texts, images, and sites associated with the figures in this book several of the concepts that characterized agrarian religion.[32]

Dominated by the "essentially agrarian conditions of everyday existence,"[33] agrarian religion in the Levant directly was related to the geography of the region, and to the human needs generated therefrom. We saw this geography in the 'Sacred Landscapes' of the Levant, such as in the rocky character of the environment, its many caves and grottoes, and sacred stones.[34] We also saw the notion of caves and subterranean passageways in the Levant as being interconnected.[35] Furthermore, we see the geography of the region reflected in the persistence of agrarian water cults, generated in the Levant out of the acute need for water, and especially for rainfall from the sky.[36]

In the case of Elijah, St. George, and al-Khiḍr, in *Geography, Religion, Gods, and Saints in the Eastern Mediterranean* we encountered as well the central holy figure of agrarian religion: the 'saint', 'holy man', or 'legendary figure'.[37] Moreover, we saw abundant evidence throughout the book regarding the central religious buildings of agrarian religion: tombs and shrines.[38] Saints and holy figures in particular in agrarian religion are imbued with the power to combat demons, which we saw on repeated display throughout the book, in Levantine figures like Solomon and, in particular, St. George.

Moreover, we saw evidence of the ubiquitous presence of demons in an agrarian religious context.[39] 'Demons' in agrarian religion functioned, at least in part, as an explanation for the indiscriminate occurrence of misfortune – especially of death, and of illness. We saw the long-lived female demon, 'Abyzouth', 'Lilith', or 'al-Qarīna', who was believed to harm newborn children and their mothers,[40] as well as the agrarian religious notion that physical – and especially mental – illness was caused by demons. St. George became well known and well regarded throughout the Levant for his powers to rid people of demons – in part, because of his original spectacular defeat of a 'demon', in the form of a serpent or snake.[41]

We also saw the frequent use of talismans, amulets, and icons that were common to an agrarian religious context. In such a capricious environment, one resorted to any means possible for combatting the callous forces of nature and of the demons who lurked about, especially in the night.[42] Moreover, nighttime in an agrarian religious environment carried with it its own window into alternate realities: visions and dreams.[43] In this context, one believed that one could encounter saints and other holy figures in dreams and visions, and seeking out dream encounters with holy figures was believed to be a distinct possibility. Accordingly, we saw in this book that people of many different religious traditions, across very long periods of time, sought out the advice and assistance of Elijah – and of al-Khiḍr – at his cave on Mt. Carmel.[44]

In the main, of what we have seen frequent evidence throughout this book are the central features of agrarian religion: long-lived patterns of religious motifs and narratives, diminished sectarianism, and a common religious culture. In the shared religious practices of Levantine agrarian communities of Jews, Christians, Muslims, Druze, Alawites, and others, around the figures of Elijah, St. George, and al-Khiḍr, and in the frequent and successive use of the same holy sites among different religious groups, we see evidence of diminished sectarianism.[45] In an agrarian religious context, holidays often are built around the seasonal and celestial cycles.[46] Through shared regional holidays, such as the springtime festival date of April 23, we see the common religious culture of agrarian religion on display.

In the story of 'Astarte and the Sea', important in the region for millennia; in the form of the 'Perseus and Andromeda' story; in the form of the narrative of St. George rescuing a princess from a dragon; and, finally, in the form of the 1927 CE ritual being performed by a woman who was preparing a sheep for sacrifice 'to the sea', in return for her own fertility, we see evidence of long-lived patterns of religious motifs and narratives.[47] The stability of agrarian religion was what enabled the maintenance of stories, narratives, figures, and motifs across a very long stretch of time. That is because the needs of people, relating to rainfall, crop growth, fertility, and protection from illness and harm, have remained relatively stable in the region up through the middle of the 20th century CE. It is the stability of agrarian religion, more than anything else, that has contributed to the existence of a Levantine common pool of figures, narratives, and motifs. It is also why we see above, at the beginning of this chapter, in the Cave of Elijah story on Mt. Carmel, that although the figures venerated there may have changed over the millennia, the supplications and requests of the people visiting there largely have remained the same.[48]

Where we see the interconnections between Levantine religions, and the slow development of orthodoxies

By that same token of analysis, our geographical contextualization of each of the figures in this study also has served to demonstrate the uniqueness and specificity of each of the figures at the temporal moment in which they were presented in text. As we saw in Chapter Three, our textual analysis of the Baal Cycle demonstrated that the figure of Baal-Hadad was influenced by contemporaneous religious, political, and geographical forces. The Baal Cycle narratives were influenced by contemporaneous narratives of a storm-god overcoming a sea monster and defeating the forces of chaos.[49] What the Baal Cycle and the figure of Baal-Hadad therein reflected about contemporary Western Semitic 'Canaanite' religion was a religious environment in which water from rainfall was essential to both agricultural and human life, where gods and goddesses ruled the natural environment and helped to explain its phenomena, and where the events of human life and political power were intertwined with the favor or disfavor of the storm-god, who unmistakably was the most powerful deity in the region.

Chapter Four demonstrated that the narrative of Elijah in the Hebrew Bible reflected a religious environment that was dominated by multiple gods and goddesses, mostly Canaanite; Baal-Hadad the most prominent among them. Baal's dominance among the Canaanites and among the Israelites and Judahites as described in the Hebrew Bible was due to his preeminence over religious life in an environment where water from rainfall was essential to human agricultural life.

Elijah, a prophet of Yahweh, exemplified a main theme prevalent throughout the Hebrew Bible: Yahweh is the supreme God (not Baal), and before whom there are no other gods. Therefore, the worship of gods other than Yahweh led to destruction. Because Yahweh was the supreme god, Yahweh also did not act like other gods; he was jealous and required that his followers must worship him exclusively and do so by behaving in specific ways in specific places. Zealous dedication to Yahweh, as conveyed in the text, led to Yahweh's favor. Human worshippers of Yahweh, as portrayed by the narrative of Elijah in the text, should in fact behave like Elijah: single-minded and uncompromising in dedication to Yahweh.

The religious tradition of the Hebrew Bible revealed by the figure therein of Elijah was a tradition that thus was markedly exclusivist about its desire to distinguish itself from among other groups. This reflects, among other things, the perspective of a small kingdom(s) and minority religious tradition attempting to exist and to thrive among the larger and more powerful contemporaneous political powers in the region. The religious tradition revealed by the narrative of the prophet Elijah in the Hebrew Bible reflects a determined desire to differentiate from other groups – groups which were 'destined' to be destroyed. The Hebrew Bible narratives are in particular unique because they evince the desire to distinguish followers of Yahweh from followers of all other gods in an environment of mixture and of heterogeneous peoples.

The *Acts of St. George* allowed us to see reflected in the figure of St. George a mixed religious environment that mainly was competitive, as we saw in Chapter Five. The text included a contemporaneous environment of Jews, Christians, pagans, Jewish-Christians, and various categorizations between these. The religious environment of the first several centuries (and certainly longer, and earlier) of the Common Era in the Levant was dominated by a general belief in demons, saints, magic, and icons, alongside growing corps of 'orthodoxies' in religious organization, all of which we saw reflected in St. George texts and iconography.

St. George, a figure of multiple influences – Baal-Zeus or Zeus-Georgos perhaps prominent among these, with respect to his early cult – reflected about early Christianity a religious movement identified with biblical tradition and simultaneously differentiating from Jewish identity and practices. Moreover, early Christianity as reflected in the text was a religious tradition that, like that of Judaism, and by virtue of its association with the monotheistic biblical tradition and Hebrew Scriptures, was differentiated as well from the polytheistic traditions of the Hellenized and Roman world. The *Acts* also reveals an emerging Christian conception of God as the same as the biblical God, but with an expanded or clarified description: Trinitarian in nature, and in accordance with a contemporaneous imperial Christian position regarding Jesus following the Council of Nicaea: incorporating Jesus as the second person of the Trinity, who was considered at once both human and divine, in separate measure.

In Chapter Six, we saw that the narrative in the Qur'ān identified with the figure of al-Khiḍr reflected a religious text situated within the religious communities, political currents, and apocalyptic religious orientations of the wider late antique world. These religious communities most prominently were Melkite, Jacobite, and Nestorian Christians, rabbinic Jews, and Arab polytheists of the sixth and seventh centuries. The Khiḍr narrative in the Qur'ān reflected a pious religious community which strictly was monotheistic in its theological orientation (if not yet, perhaps, 'Muslim'). This theological perception of God strongly aligned to the biblical One God, vehemently rejecting contemporary Christian Trinitarian conceptions of God, and aligned directly with a unitary notion of monotheism.

Monotheism in the Levant: Contradistinction in Judaism, Christianity, and Islam

In addition to the influence of geography upon Levantine religious thought as demonstrated in this book, and in addition to the agrarian religious culture and the distinctive features of these figures' respective religious traditions, as reflected in their texts, this book also illuminates an interesting perspective on monotheism within these religious traditions. Specifically, this book suggests monotheism as a specific strand of religious thought that contradistinctively characterized Judaism, Christianity, and Islam in the Near East.

As we saw in Chapter Three, the storm-god, Baal-Hadad, as the manifestation of meteorological phenomena and the source, therefore, of human survival or destruction, was the preeminent deity in the Levant since at least the middle Bronze Age. A primary theological argument of the Hebrew Bible concerned the contention that it was Yahweh/YHWH who was the true God, and no other gods besides. The long-developing religious tradition reflected in the Hebrew Bible can be characterized by a determined effort to differentiate from other groups of heterogeneous peoples and multiple gods; Baal-Hadad most prominent among them. The religious tradition of the Hebrew Bible and thus of later Judaism was developed in intentional contradistinction to contemporaneous peoples, differentiating exclusivist followers of Yahweh from the followers of all other gods, and the Hebrew Bible can in part be understood therefore as a heresiological text, in that it elucidated categories of 'true' and 'false' gods.

By the first century of the Common Era, YHWH had become among communities of Jews synonymous simply with 'God' (the only). As early Christian communities began to differentiate from contemporaneous Jewish communities, a 'Christian' theological conception of God began to emerge, as we have seen above in Chapters Five and Six, one that was aligned with a notion of the God of the Bible but that also was expanded to elucidate God as Trinitarian in nature. The second 'person' of the Godhead gradually came to be understood as Jesus the 'son' of God, consubstantial with God the 'father'. In the *Acts*, 'true' and 'false' gods also were delimited, indicating the heresiological nature of this text regarding developing notions of Christian identity, as well as the development of a Christian conception of God that was formulated in contradistinction to multiple contemporaneous religious communities.

Notions of exactly how the human and divine natures of Jesus were conjoined motivated deep divisions among early Christian communities. These divided communities of Christians and their labyrinthine theological conceptions of God were unequivocally rejected in the Qur'ānic conception of God, which aligned instead with a vision of undivided monotheism more akin to that reflected in the Hebrew Bible. Because the Qur'ān created standards for 'true' and 'false' beliefs about God, it, too, could be characterized as a heresiological text.

This brief overview of monotheism as reflected in these figures' texts (outlined in more detail in each of the preceding chapters) is highlighted in the aggregate here in order to indicate an interesting implication about monotheism as reflected in this book: monotheism, as a specific strand of religious thought, in part and in different ways distinguished communities of Jews, Christians, and Muslims in contradistinction both to one another, and in contradistinction to the largely polytheistic traditions which long characterized the religious orientation of the Near East.

Furthermore, recalling the apparently Sinaitic/northern Arabian origins of the Israelite god Yahweh[50] enables one to examine the development of monotheism in its wider Near Eastern context (i.e., not exclusively Levantine). While it is not at all the claim of this project that YHWH was a monotheistic god in 'essence', this study suggests that we broaden our analysis of monotheism into the wider Near East, beyond the traditional setting of Levantine biblical history, in order to account for the influences upon YHWH of a Sinaitic and northern Arabian cultural context. Eventually combined with other regional gods, such as the Canaanite El, and perceived in a monotheistic manner as reflected in the Hebrew Bible, the Sinaitic and Arabian origins of YHWH invite a wider cultural setting for the development of monotheism.

Continuity and gradualism: Religious traditions are not born 'fully formed'

In addition to considerations of the influence of geography upon regional religious thought, and of the distinctions in respective religious traditions reflected by these figures, this study of the ways in which these figures have been constructed in texts and images argues above all for an understanding of *continuity and gradualism* in the formation of these religious traditions, over and against traditionalist portrayals of sudden and dramatic change.[51]

Founding-origins perspectives in these religious communities claim uniqueness, distinctiveness, and 'completeness' of their respective religious traditions, and often present these religious traditions in such a manner as to suggest that they were "born nearly fully formed."[52] In contrast, however, this study has demonstrated the marked *indistinctiveness* and gradual formation of each of these religious traditions. Moreover, through the study of Baal in the Baal Cycle, Elijah in the Hebrew Bible, St. George in the *Acts of St. George*, and al-Khiḍr in the Qur'ān, this study has shown that each of these traditions emerged *only gradually* from its contemporaneous religious environment, and largely in continuity with contemporaneous prevailing religious notions.

This suggests two prominent observations. First, we in religious studies would seem to misunderstand or to mischaracterize religious traditions when we consider them as 'beginning' with founding figures and early texts. In reality, it took centuries and usually some form of political control to create the orthodox(ies) by which these traditions later were characterized. Moreover, the founding figures and early texts of a tradition are, in actuality, a product far more of their contemporaneous religious contexts than they are of the religious tradition that develops after them. In that way, we should consider the texts in this study as sources of information as much about the figures themselves as they are texts in evidence of previous religious traditions.[53]

Therefore, the Baal Cycle could be considered a document in evidence of the religious context of late Bronze Age Syria-Palestine and the wider Near East as much as it is a document in evidence of Baalic history; the Hebrew Bible might be considered a document in evidence of the religious environment of Iron-Age Canaan and the greater Near East as much as it is a document in evidence of Israelite or Jewish history; the *Acts of St. George* could be considered a document in evidence of the mixed polytheistic-Christian-Jewish regional religious environment of the fourth to sixth centuries as much as it is a document in evidence of Georgic history; and the Qur'ān might be considered a document in evidence of contemporaneous late antique Arabian pagan, Jewish, and Christian communities as much it is a document in evidence of Muslim history.[54]

A second observation enabled by the evidence of continuity and gradualism in the formation of these traditions, as reflected in the figures' texts, would suggest that members of modern 'fundamentalist' religious orientations (fundamentalist in the sense of attempting to recreate communities that 'go back' to a purported religious orientation reflected in founding figures and early texts), among communities of Jews and Christians, or members of 'salafist', religious orientations, in the case of some modern Sunni Muslims, anachronistically mischaracterize their early religious traditions as *more distinctive than the historical record bears*. Indeed, were members of these types of religious orientations able to 'go back' to their traditions' earliest periods, they likely would encounter a religious environment very different from the one they had imagined.

Eastern Mediterranean shared religious culture

Linkages and similarities between the figures in this study long have been identified by the communities who venerate them. Similarities between the figures largely have revolved around shared geographical and meteorological motifs of rain, storms, thunder, lightning, greenness, fertility, fecundity, the ability to appear and disappear, associations with mountains and other high places, local feast or celebration days of April 23, and the motif of vanquishing a dragon. These motifs, as we saw above, are in the main shaped by regional geographical needs and considerations.

Linkages between these figures in text and image likewise have associated them. Elijah and St. George are known and beloved in the Eastern Mediterranean for the trait of being defenders of 'true' religion over and against 'false' gods. Al-Khiḍr and Elijah are associated especially in Islamic religious texts, and al-Khiḍr and St. George share iconographical representation in the Levant. These similarities and linkages have joined al-Khiḍr, Elijah, and St. George in popular practice among local communities of Jews, Christians, and Muslims for at least the past 800 years in the Levant.[55]

The figures have been conjoined in popular practice among communities of Jews, Christians, Muslims, Druze, Alawites, and others in the Eastern Mediterranean because these communities – and their respective religious traditions and figures – evolved there together, within an agrarian religious context. As we saw at the outset of this study, the characteristics shared by Elijah, St. George, and al-Khiḍr in the Eastern Mediterranean long have been considered 'peculiar' when these figures are studied solely as products of their respective religious traditions. When we study Elijah, St. George, and al-Khiḍr as *regional* religious figures, however, and study their texts in the context of contemporaneous religious, political, and geographical influences, their linkages and associations in text, image, and popular practice become much clearer, and their shared agricultural motifs do not appear at all peculiar.

This common geographical and cultural environment explains as well why the figures are not shared in the same way outside of the Levant. Shorn of long-term associations in community practice and in iconography, Elijah, St. George, and al-Khiḍr are known among their respective religious communities around the world mainly by the content of their canonical texts. These texts usually are interpreted in tradition-specific ways which reinforce internal theological principals and religious identities, leaving no 'natural' reason, on the basis of the texts, to understand Baal-Hadad, Elijah, St. George, and al-Khiḍr as anything other than discrete, unrelated figures from their respective religious communities.

Finally, this study underscores the importance of cultural context in religious studies. Indeed, the phenomenon of local communities of Jews, Christians, and Muslims venerating Elijah, St. George, and al-Khiḍr in the Eastern Mediterranean for at least the past 800 years is inextricable from the cultural context of the Eastern Mediterranean. Accordingly, analyses of the figures and their relationships are unworkable absent an understanding of this phenomenon as situated within the context of Eastern Mediterranean culture and religious history. All of this together suggests that we in religious studies need better to recognize regional specificity even for global religions, and that we need to recognize the existence of regionally specific relationships between religious traditions. Within the field of religious studies, these types of arguments are not made or even imagined most of the time. *Geography, Religion, Gods, and Saints in the Eastern Mediterranean* represents a critical case study for helping us better to understand this broader phenomenon.

From some point after the seventh to eighth centuries CE, linkages between all three of these figures among regional Jewish, Christian, and Muslim communities became normalized and authentic (see again Figure 7.1), as these figures were understood by their communities to be *regional* figure(s), shared by all inhabitants. Mixed religious practices of course cannot be characterized by an entirely unchanging model: "they are symbolically and practically complex activities, and their variations can be traced to political, demographic, and social conditions prevailing at the time of observation."[56] Moreover, although people can have multiple social affiliations,

> particular circumstances prompt particular identities to become more prominent at particular times. Hence, shared processions and festivals in the eleventh-century Mediterranean might blur religious boundaries during times of health crisis yet sharpen in times of political upheaval.[57]

Accordingly, this study likewise suggests that regional religious practices involving Elijah, St. George, and al-Khiḍr as among Jewish, Christian, Muslim, and other religious communities were normalized under most political conditions, but unsettled during times of upheaval, and primarily as a result of upheaval that was generated by outsiders. Potential areas for interesting research lie in an examination of the period of the 11th- to 12th-century CE Crusades, during which time Frankish Crusaders appropriated as their own the warlike and popular figure of St. George, whom they encountered in the Levant. Oblivious to the importance of St. George among multiple local religious communities, Levantine Muslims became targets of outsider Crusaders and 'their' favored saint.[58]

An additional area for potential research could involve a number of events during the turbulent 20th century, during which time new political borders were drawn, nation-states with specific religious populations were established (and in many cases, transplanted), and the political state of modern Israel was founded, largely uprooting and displacing traditional Jewish communities and their shared religious practices from locations around the Eastern Mediterranean. This event also served to displace local Christian and Muslim communities, and had the effect of creating exclusive access for specific persons to formerly open-access sites, thus disrupting traditional shared religious practices there between and among communities of Jews, Christians, Muslims, and Druze. [59]

Modern implications

At the outset of this book, we suggested that the phenomenon of communities of Jews, Christians, and Muslims venerating common figures was paradoxical and noteworthy, given that 'common wisdom', and even epistemological notions promulgated within the academic study of religion, suggest that Jews and Christians and Muslims inhabit distinct and separate religious categories, and especially so in the contentious Eastern Mediterranean.

Characterizing the Eastern Mediterranean as 'contentious' reflects turbulent 19th- and 20th-century political history in the region, which has been marked by colonialist interventions, by the establishment of nation-state borders where previously none had existed, by a legacy of authoritarian rulers, and by a reordering of traditional society and communities following World War I, which served in part to disrupt traditional religious practices involving communities of Muslims, Christians, and Jews. It should be borne in mind, however, that the considerable political changes of the 20th century have overlaid a regional culture that long has reflected a shared and stable agrarian religious history among communities of Jews, Christians, Muslims, and other religious communities in the Levant.

Tensions between modern political considerations and long-term cultural influences lie at the heart of many internal conflicts throughout the contemporary Eastern Mediterranean.[60] As the exigencies of 20th- and 21st-century political history in the region unfold, the Eastern Mediterranean often is characterized by divisions and distinctions between its *discrete* religious communities, which is both accurate and misleading. It should not be forgotten that despite these tensions, significant and long-lived areas of cultural overlap and commonality remain.

Furthermore, while today one rightly may look to the Eastern Mediterranean and identify distinct religious communities – comprised mainly of Muslims, Christians, and Jews – as we have seen in this book, the religious traditions of Judaism, Christianity, and Islam are not, textually or historically speaking, separate. Thus, this study argues for an understanding of Jews, Christians, and Muslims as distinct but not separate in their local Eastern Mediterranean context.

Although an historical record of distinct-but-not-separate religious traditions in the Eastern Mediterranean is echoed in its regional cultural traditions, and in the legacy of agrarian religion, members of religious communities today can be affected as well by unsettled political conditions and buffeted by the austerity of essentialist political and religious movements which emphasize distinction, uniqueness, and divergence.[61] None of these religious communities, however, is benefited by an incomplete or partial understanding of their shared regional histories.

Geography, Religion, Gods, and Saints in the Eastern Mediterranean demonstrates the enduring legacy of geography among peoples living in the region, and suggests that humans living in the Eastern Mediterranean have been connected by more – and for longer – on the basis of their shared geography than they have been separated by religious boundaries or changing political powers. Above all, however, this book contends that the phenomenon of al-Khiḍr, St. George, and Elijah belongs squarely within the historical heritage of the Eastern Mediterranean. Moreover, it suggests that this phenomenon reveals a great deal about the social and symbolic organization of traditional religious communities in the region.

Shared practices involving the figures of al-Khiḍr, St. George, and Elijah are an important part of a common religious and cultural heritage (Figure 7.2).[62] Today, for various political reasons, these practices usually are participated in by limited communities of Christians and Muslims, and involve mainly the figures of St. George and al-Khiḍr, and sometimes St. Elias.[63] For so many reasons relating to 20th-century history, this phenomenon is not as prevalent as it once was, and it is becoming ever rarer. As a salient part of the region's cultural heritage, however, it is important to remember that individuals still today who engage in shared practices around these figures are not engaging in practices that are in any

Figure 7.2 Muslim woman and child light candles at the church of St. George in Lod, in front of a St. George icon. (Photo by Stephanie Saldaña, 2017.)

way aberrant or abnormal, as these kinds of shared religious practices recently have been characterized.[64]

On the contrary, it is exclusivist religious practices promoted by members of modern essentialist religious orientations that today could be considered historically aberrant. Instead, shared practices involving the figures of St. George, al-Khiḍr, and Elijah – widely believed to be "everyone's inheritance"[65] as indeed these regional figures are – are authentic both to the history of these religious traditions, and to Levantine historical religious practices, as well. Shared religious practices are a natural feature of this geographical region, and of the close development therein of its religious communities.

Notes

1 Ran Shapira, "Ancient Inscriptions in Elijah the Prophet's Cave are in Danger," *Haaretz*, Aug. 19, 2015. For more on the cave itself, see Asher Ovadiah and Rosario Pierri, *Elijah's Cave on Mount Carmel and Its Inscriptions* (Oxford, UK: Archaeopress Archaeology, 2015).
2 See Chapter Two, 45, and Chapter Four, 126–128.
3 See also Chapter Four, "Elijah". The title 'Baal [of] Carmel' refers to the god Baal-Hadad. On the latter point see also Chapter Three.
4 Shapira, "Ancient Inscriptions in Elijah the Prophet's Cave are in Danger."
5 See Chapter Four, 126–128.
6 See Chapter Four, 128; see also M. Avi-Yonah, "Mount Carmel and the God of Baalbek."

7 See Chapter Two, 45.
8 For a video of this reenactment, see the YouTube link at https://youtube/Vp89_ZiFezI. See the narrative from the 3:50 minute-mark for references to St. George-al-Khiḍr's associations with rain and crop growth and his ability to cause the thunder by galloping across the sky. Please also see https://palestine-family.net/2007-artas-lettuce-festival-play-st-george-and-the-dragon-arab-educational-institute-drama-troupe/, as well as https://www.artasfolklorecenter.net/. For associations of Elijah, St. George, and al-Khiḍr with causing thunder and lightning, see Hassan S. Haddad, "'Georgic' Cults and Saints of the Levant," *Numen*, 16, Fasc. 1 (April 1969), 30.
9 The general feast or celebration day for both St. George and al-Khiḍr in the Eastern Mediterranean is April 23, except in the Orthodox churches, where the feast day of St. George is moved to May 6 if the calendar date of Easter falls on or after April 23.
10 See Helen Gibson, "St. George the Ubiquitous," *Aramco World*, 22, no. 6 (1971): 4–7 for reference to the Egyptian village of Mit Damsis. Note that these practices are not limited to the Delta region, but take place throughout Egypt and the wider Levant.
11 For a video featuring Christian and Muslim interaction around the figure of St. George-al-Khiḍr (not in a holiday setting), see the video entitled "St. George's Church," by Journeyman Pictures (https://www.youtube.com/watch?v=BwVo910B3bk)
12 Chapter Five, 147.
13 Grehan, *Twilight of the Saints*, 184–186.
14 Chapter Two, 29, and Chapter Three, 71–75; 81–83.
15 Chapter Two, 29, and Chapter Three, 62, 44n.; 81–83.
16 See also Daniel Ogden. *The Legend of Seleucus: Kingship, Narrative and Mythmaking in the Ancient World*, 117–118. See also Chapter Three, 67–75; 81–83.
17 See Chapter Two, 24–35; esp. 34.
18 See above, Chapter Three, 71–75, and Chapter Five, 140.
19 Chapter Five, 144–147.
20 Hasan Haddad should be credited for having been the first to highlight the associations between and among Elijah, St. George, al-Khiḍr, and the Storm-god Baal-Hadad in the Levant. See "'Georgic' Cults and Saints of the Levant," *Numen*, 16, Fasc. 1 (April 1969), 21–39.
21 Chapter Three, 75. See also Sergio Ribichini, "Beliefs and Religious Life," in *The Phoenicians*, Sabatino Moscati, ed. (New York: Rizzoli, 1999), 120–152. Ribichini argues that Iron Age Phoenician religion is of course not a direct and unchanged continuation of Bronze Age Syrian/Canaanite cults. However, one of the most significant differences Ribichini could identify in "Iron Age Phoenician polytheism" was that of the political tendency toward city-level religious differentiation and autonomy, rather than a change in the nature or function of the earlier gods. "A consequence, or at any rate a religious parallel, of the political subdivision of Phoenicia in the 1st millennium B.C. is therefore the new constitution or reorganization of the local city pantheon. Each city organized its own feasts and celebrations, its own traditions, its own deities, in forms which might be common to other towns, but which would not be given the same importance," 124–125.
22 Chapter Three, 71–75.
23 Chapter Three, 71–75.
24 Chapter Two, 29, 13n. See also Chapter Three, 67–70.
25 Chapter Four.
26 Chapter Four.
27 Chapter Five.
28 Chapters One and Seven, as well as Chapter Five.
29 Chapter Five, 161–169.
30 Chapter Five, 145–146.
31 Chapter Six, 216–221. See also Wheeler, *Moses in the Quran and Islamic Exegesis*, who argues in a different way that "there was an effort to make the al-Khiḍr who emerged from the explanation of Q. 18:60–82 a close parallel to Elijah," 25.

32 See Chapter Two, "Agrarian Religion". See also James Grehan, *Twilight of the Saints.*
33 Grehan, 140.
34 Chapter Two, 40–42.
35 Chapter Two; Chapter Six, 213–214.
36 Chapter Two, 24–35; 40–42. Chapter Three, 55–59; 75–77; 80–83.
37 Chapter Two, 39–40. See also Grehan, 86.
38 Chapter Two, 40.
39 Chapter Two, 43–45; Chapter Five, 147; 163–164.
40 Chapter Two, 42–43; Chapter Five, 169–170.
41 Chapter Two, 43–44; Chapter Five, 161–162; 164, 81n.
42 Chapter Two, 44–45; Chapter Five, 172, 169–176.
43 Chapter Two, 45; Chapter Five, 172, 114n.
44 Chapter Two, 45; Chapter Four, 128; Chapter Seven, 240–241.
45 Chapter Two, 45–48; Chapter Six, 227–228.
46 Chapter Two, 45–47; Chapter Five, 161–162.
47 Chapter Two, 42; Chapter Five, 174–175.
48 Chapter Two, 48–50; Chapter Seven, 240–242.
49 Chapter Three, 65–67; 75–76. See also Robert D. Miller II, *The Dragon, the Mountain, and the Nations: An Old Testament Myth, Its Origins, and Its Afterlives* (Explorations in ANE Civilizations 6. Eisenbrauns, 2018).
50 Greene, *Storm-God*, 165–166. See also Deut. 33:2, and Chapter Three.
51 I am indebted for this language to Paul R. Powers, "Review of Muḥammad and the Believers: At the Origins of Islam," *History of Religions*, 52, no. 3 (2013): 306–308.
52 Powers, 306.
53 I am indebted to Sidney H. Griffith for this language, which I have adapted. See *The Bible in Arabic*, 55.
54 Griffith argues "In other words, the chapter approaches the Qur'ān as a document in evidence of the history of Jews and Christians in Arabia, along with their scriptures and traditions, rather than as a document in Islamic history," 55.
55 Josef W. Meri, *The Cult of Saints Among Muslims and Jews in Medieval Syria* (Oxford: Oxford University Press, 2002), 4.
56 See Maria Couroucli, "Sharing Sacred Spaces – A Mediterranean Tradition," in *Sharing Sacred Spaces in the Mediterranean: Christians, Muslims, and Jews at Shrines and Sanctuaries*, Albera, Dionigi and Maria Couroucli, eds. New Anthropologies of Europe, edited by Matti Bunzl and Michael Herzfeld (Bloomington, IN: Indiana University Press, 2012), 5.
57 See Peter Gottschalk, "Introduction," in *Muslims and Others in Sacred Space Beyond Hindu and Muslim: Multiple Identity in Narratives from a Village in India* (Oxford: University Press, 2000).
58 See the Chronicle of the First Crusade *History of Antioch*, which recounts the apparition of warrior saints George, Theodore, and Demetrius (George is in the account the most beloved of them) to Crusaders at the sieges of Antioch and of Jerusalem. These saints' appearances apparently motivated the Crusaders to victory. See also Jacobus de Voragine, *The Golden Legend: Readings on the Saints*, 2 vols., William Granger Ryan, transl. (Princeton, NJ: Princeton University Press, 1993), which recounts the legend that once the Crusaders had laid siege to Jerusalem, "they did not dare mount the scaling ladders in the face of the Saracens' resistance; but Saint George appeared to them wearing white armor marked with the red cross, and made them understand that they could follow him up the walls in safety and the city would be theirs. Thus reassured, the army took the city and slaughtered the Saracens," 242.
59 See Glenn Bowman's work on Khiḍr-St. George in the Occupied Territories for an example of this kind of research. For turbulent 20th-century history, see Maria Couroucli, "Sharing Sacred Spaces – A Mediterranean Tradition," 1–9.

60 See the conundra outlined by Rami G. Khouri, “Why Aren’t Arab States More Like Individuals?,” in *The Daily Star Lebanon* (September 10, 2014).
61 See also Sami Zubaida, *Islam, the People and the State: Political ideas and Movements in the Middle East* (New York: I.B. Taurus, 2009). See in particular Chapter Five, “Components of Popular Culture in the Middle East”. See also Chapter Two of this book.
62 See similar practices as outlined by Couroucli, *Sharing Sacred Spaces*, 5.
63 For practices involving local communities of Christians and Muslims around the figure of St. Elias, see Bowman, “Identification and Identity Formations around Shared Shrines in West Bank Palestine and Western Macedonia,” in *Sharing Sacred Spaces in the Mediterranean*, 10–28. Note also that sometimes members of other religious communities, such as the Druze, participate in similar practices.
64 In addition to stories and anecdotes in contemporary news, see also Zubaida, *Islam, the People and the State*, 117–118. See also Chapter Two.
65 This was a phrase I often heard repeated by members of many religious communities during fieldwork in the Eastern Mediterranean.

Bibliography

Albera, Dionigi, and Maria Couroucli, eds. *Sharing Sacred Spaces in the Mediterranean: Christians, Muslims, and Jews at Shrines and Sanctuaries*. *New Anthropologies of Europe*, edited by Matti Bunzl and Michael Herzfeld. Bloomington, IN: Indiana University Press, 2012.

Alexander, Paul J. *The Byzantine Apocalyptic Tradition*. Edited and with an introduction by Dorothy deF. Abrahamse. Berkeley, CA: University of California Press, 1985.

Allen, Spencer. *The Splintered Divine: A Study of Ištar, Baal, and Yahweh Divine Names and Divine Multiplicity in the Ancient Near East*. Studies in Ancient Near Eastern Records 5. Munich: De Gruyter, 2015.

Alouf, Michel M. *Baalbek*, 19th edition, 8th English edition. Beirut, Lebanon: American Press, 1949.

al-Azmeh, Aziz. *The Emergence of Islam in Late Antiquity: Allāh and His People*. Cambridge, UK: Cambridge University Press, 2014.

Amiran, D. H. K. "Land Use in Israel," in *Land Use in Semi-Arid Mediterranean Climates*. Paris: UNESCO International Geographic Union, 1964.

Ando, Clifford, ed. *Roman Religion*. Edinburgh: Edinburgh University Press, 2003.

Antoniadou, Sophia, and Anthony Pace, eds. *Mediterranean Crossroads*. Athens: Pierides Foundation, 2007.

Asad, Talal. "The Construction of Religion as an Anthropological Category." In *Genealogies of Religion: Discipline and Reasons of Power in Christianity and Islam*, 27–54. Baltimore, MD: Johns Hopkins University Press, 1993.

Attwater, Donald. *The Christian Churches of the East, vol. 1: Churches in Communion with Rome*. Religion and Culture Series, edited by Joseph Husslein. Milwaukee, WI: The Bruce Publishing Company, 1946.

Attwater, Donald. *The Christian Churches of the East, vol. 2: Churches Not in Communion with Rome*. Religion and Culture Series, edited by Joseph Husslein. Milwaukee, WI: The Bruce Publishing Company, 1947.

Augustinovič, A. *'El-Khadr' and the Prophet Elijah*. Translated by Eugene Hoade. Jerusalem: Franciscan Printing Press, 1972.

Avi-Yonah, M. "Historical Outline: History and Description of Antiquities and Historical Sites." In *Steimatzky's Guides: Syria and the Lebanon*. Jerusalem and Beirut: Steimatzky's Publishing Co., 1942.

Avi-Yonah, M. "Mount Carmel and the God of Baalbek." *Israel Exploration Journal* 2(2): 118–124, 1952.

'Awadi, al- Mahmoud. *Kitāb al-ziyārāt bi-dimashq*. Edited by Salāh al-din al-Manjad. Damascus, 1956.

Badr, Habib, Slim, Suad, and Abou Nohra, Joseph, eds. *Christianity: A History in the Middle East*. Beirut, Lebanon: Middle East Council of Churches, 2005.

Balogh, Amy L. *Moses Among the Idols: Mediators of the Divine in the Ancient Near East*. Lexington/Fortress Press, 2018.

Bannister, Andrew G. *An Oral-Formulaic Study of the Qur'an*. Lanham, MD: Lexington Books, 2014.

Bauer, Walter. *Orthodoxy and Heresy in Earliest Christianity*, second German edition, with added appendices by Georg Stucker. Translated by a team from the Philadelphia Seminar on Christian Origins, edited by Robert A. Kraft and Gerhard Krodel. Philadelphia, PA: Fortress Press, 1971.

Bell, Gertrude L. *Syria: The Desert and the Sown*. New York: Tauris Parke Paperbacks, 2016 (First published London: William Heinemann, 1907).

Bernstein, Marc S. *Stories of Joseph: Narrative Migrations between Judaism and Islam*. Detroit, MI: Wayne State University Press, 2006.

Bladel, Kevin van. "The Alexander Legend in the Qur'ān 18:83-102." In *The Qur'ān in Its Historical Context*, edited by Gabriel Said Reynolds, Routledge Studies in the Qur'ān 8, series editor Andrew Rippin, 175–203. New York: Routledge, 2008.

Blömer, Michael. "Religious Continuity? The Evidence from Doliche." In *Religious Identities in the Levant from Alexander to Muhammed: Continuity and Change*, edited by Michael Blömer, Achim Lichtenberger, and Rubina Raja. Contextualizing the Sacred 4, series editors Elizabeth Frood and Rubina Raja. Turnhout, Belgium: Brepols, 2015.

Blömer, Michael, Achim Lichtenberger, and Rubina Raja. *Religious Identities in the Levant from Alexander to Muhammed: Continuity and Change*. Contextualizing the Sacred 4, series editors Elizabeth Frood and Rubina Raja. Turnhout, Belgium: Brepols, 2015.

Bowerstock, G. W., Peter Brown, and Oleg Grabar, eds. *Late Antiquity: A Guide to the Postclassical World*. Cambridge, MA: The Belknap Press of Harvard University Press, 1999.

Bowman, Glenn. "Nationalising and Denationalising the Sacred: Shrines and Shifting Identities in the Israeli-Occupied Territories (in Arabic)." *Chronos: Revue d'Histoire de l'Université de Balamand* 16: 151–210, 2007.

Bowman, Glenn. "Processus Identitaires Autour de Quelques Sanctuaires Partagés en Palestine et en Macédoine" in *Religions Traversées ; Lieux Saints Partagés Entre Chrétiens, Musulmans et Juifs en Mediterranée*. Etudes Méditerranéennes, edited by Dionigi Albera and Maria Couroucli. Arles: Actes Sud, 2009.

Boyarin, Daniel. *Border Lines: The Partition of Judaeo-Christianity*. Philadelphia, PA: University of Pennsylvania Press, 2004.

Boyarin, Daniel. *Dying for God: Martyrdom and the Making of Christianity and Judaism*. Palo Alto, CA: Stanford University Press, 1999.

Brakke, David. "Canon Formation and Social Conflict in Fourth-Century Egypt: Athanasius of Alexandria's Thirty-Ninth Festal Letter." *Harvard Theological Review* 87 (1994): 395–419.

Braudel, Fernand. *The Mediterranean: And the Mediterranean World in the Age of Philip II*. 2 vols. Translated by Siân Reynolds. Berkeley, CA: University of California Press, 1995 (1949).

Brock, Sebastian. *The Bible in the Syriac Tradition*, 2nd revised edition. Gorgias Handbooks 7. Piscataway, NJ: Gorgias Press, 2006.

Bronner, Leah. *The Stories of Elijah and Elisha: As Polemics Against Baal Worship*. Pretoria Oriental Series 6, edited by A. Van Selms. Leiden: E. J. Brill, 1968.

Brooks, E. W. *The Acts of Saint George*. Analecta Georgiana 8. Piscataway, NJ: Gorgias Press, 2006 [orig. ed. Published in Le Muséon, 1925, vol. 38].

Brotton, Jerry. "St. George Between East and West." In *Re-orienting the Renaissance: Cultural Exchanges with the East*, edited by Gerald MacLean, 50–65. New York: Palgrave Macmillan, 2005.

Brown, Peter. *The Cult of the Saints*. Chicago, IL: University of Chicago Press, 1981.

Brown, Peter. "Holy Man." In *The Cambridge Ancient History, vol. XIV Late Antiquity: Empire and Successors A.D. 425–600*, edited by Averil Cameron, Bryan Ward-Perkins, and Michael Whitby, 781–810. Cambridge, UK: Cambridge University Press, 2000.

Brubaker, Leslie, and John Haldon. *Byzantium in the Iconoclast Era (ca. 680-850): The Sources*. Birmingham Byzantine and Ottoman Monographs 7, edited by Anthony Bryer and John Haldon. Burlington, VT: Ashgate Publishing Company, 2001.

Budge, E. A. Wallis. *George of Lydda, the Patron Saint of England; A Study of the Cultus of St. George in Ethiopia*. London: Luzac & Co., 1930.

Budge, E. A. Wallis. *The History of Alexander the Great: Being the Syriac Version of the Pseudo Callisthenes, Edited from Five Manuscripts, with an English Translation and Notes*. Piscataway, NJ: Gorgias Press, 2003 [original edition published by Cambridge University Press, 1889].

Bulliet, Richard W. *Conversion to Islam in the Medieval Period: An Essay in Quantitative History*. Boston, MA: Harvard University Press, 1979.

Burckhardt, John L. *Travels in Syria and the Holy Land*. Charleston, SC: BiblioBazaar, 2008.

Burrus, Virginia, and Rebecca Lyman. "Shifting the Focus of History." In *APeople's History of Christianity, vol. 2, Late Ancient Christianity*, edited by Virginia Burrus, 1–26. Minneapolis, MN: Fortress Press, 2005.

Canaan, Taufik. *Mohammadan Saints and Sanctuaries in Palestine*. London: Luzac & Co., 1927.

Canivet, Pierre. "Christianity in the 1st Century: In the Context of Mediterranean Civilizations: Judaic, Greek, Roman and Asian." In *Christianity: A History in the Middle East*, edited by Habib Badr, Suad Slim, and Joseph Abou Nohra, 47–66. Beirut, Lebanon: Middle East Council of Churches, 2005.

Caquot, André, and Maurice Sznycer. *Ugaritic Religion*. Iconography of Religions, Section XV: Mesopotamia and the Near East, Fascicle Eight, edited by Th. P. van Baaren, L. P. van den Bosch, L. Leertouwer, F. Leemhuis, and H. Buning. Leiden: E. J. Brill, 1980.

Castelli, Elizabeth. *Martyrdom and Memory: Early Christian Culture Making*. New York: Columbia University Press, 2007.

Chaillot, Christine. *Rôle des Images et Vénération des Icônes dans Les Églises Orthodoxes Orientales*. Genève: Dialogue Entre Orthodoxes, 1993.

Chaillot, Christine. *The Syrian Orthodox Church of Antioch and All the East: A Brief Introduction to its Life and Spirituality*. Geneva: Inter-Orthodox Dialogue, 1998.

Cheyette, Frederic. "The Mediterranean Climate." In *A Companion to Mediterranean History*, edited by Peregrine Horden and Sharon Kinoshita. Wiley Blackwell Companions to World History 2, 11–25. Sussex, UK: Wiley Blackwell, 2014.

Chuvin, Pierre. *A Chronicle of the Last Pagans*. Revealing Antiquity Series, edited by G. W. Bowerstock. Translated by B. A. Archer. Cambridge, MA: Harvard University Press, 1990.

Cleave, Richard. *The Holy Land Satellite Atlas: Student Map Manual Illustrated Supplement Volume 1*. Bangkok, Thailand: Rohr Productions, Ltd., 1994.

Cline, Eric. "Tinker, Tailor, Soldier, Sailor: Minoans and Mycenaeans Abroad." *Politeia: Society and State in the Aegean Bronze Age* 12: 265–287, 1995.

Cline, Eric. *1177 B.C.: The Year Civilization Collapsed.* Princeton, NJ: Princeton University Press, 2014.

Cogan, Mordechai. *1 Kings: A New Translation with Introduction and Commentary.* The Anchor Bible, vol. 10. New York: Doubleday, 2000.

Cogan, Mordechai, and Tadmor, Hayim. *II* Kings: A New Translation with Introduction and Commentary, vol. 11. New York: Doubleday & Company, Inc., 1988.

Cohen, Howard A., and Steven Plaut. "Quenching the Levant's Thirst." *The Middle East Quarterly* 2(1): 37–44, 1995.

Cohen, Shaye J. D. *From the Maccabees to the Mishnah*, 2nd edition. Library of Early Christianity. Louisville, KY: Westminster John Knox Press, 2006.

Collins, Adela Y. *The Combat Myth in the Book of Revelation.* Missoula, MT: Scholars Press, 1976.

Conrad, Lawrence I. "The Arabs." In *The Cambridge Ancient History, vol. XIV Late Antiquity: Empire and Successors A.D. 425–600*, edited by Averil Cameron, Bryan Ward-Perkins, and Michael Whitby, 678–700. Cambridge, UK: Cambridge University Press, 2000.

Coogan, Michael D., ed. and trans. *Stories from Ancient Canaan.* Louisville, KY: The Westminster Press, 1978.

Coogan, Michael D., ed. *The New Oxford Annotated Bible, with the Apocryphal/Deuterocanonical Books, New Revised Standard Version*, 3rd edition. Oxford: Oxford University Press, 2001.

Cook, Arthur B. *Zeus: A Study in Ancient Religion, Volume i: Zeus God of the Bright Sky.* Cambridge, UK: Cambridge University Press, 1914.

Cook, Arthur B. *Zeus: A Study in Ancient Religion, Vol. ii, Zeus God of the Dark Sky (Thunder and Lightning).* Cambridge, UK: University of Cambridge Press, 1925.

Corbon, Jean. "The Churches of the Middle East: Their Origins and Identity, from their Roots in the Past to their Openness to the Present." In *Christian Communities in the Arab Middle East*, edited by Andrea Pacini, 92–110. New York: Oxford University Press, 1998.

Cormack, Margaret, ed. *Muslims and Others in Sacred Space.* AAR Religion, Culture, and History 16, edited by Jacob N. Kinnard. Oxford: Oxford University Press, 2013.

Couroucli, Maria. "Sharing Sacred Places – A Mediterranean Tradition." In *Sharing Sacred Spaces in the Mediterranean: Christians, Muslims, and Jews at Shrines and Sanctuaries*, edited by D. Albera and M. Couroucli. New Anthropologies of Europe, edited by Matti Bunzl and Michael Herzfeld, 1–9. Bloomington, IN: Indiana University Press, 2012.

Cowan, J. M. Arabic-*English Dictionary: The Hans Wehr Dictionary of Modern Written Arabic.* 4th edition. Ithaca, NY: Spoken Language Services, Inc., 1994.

Cragg, Kenneth. *The Arab Christian: A History in the Middle East.* Louisville, KY: Westminster/John Knox Press, 1991.

Cross, Frank M. *Canaanite Myth and Hebrew Epic: Essays in the History of the Religion of Israel.* Cambridge, MA: Harvard University Press, 1997.

Dalrymple, William. *From the Holy Mountain: A Journey Among the Christians of the Middle East.* New York: Henry Holt and Company, 1997.

Dar, Shimon. *Rural Settlements on Mount Carmel in Antiquity.* Oxford: Archaeopress Archaeology, 2014.

Day, John. *Yahweh and the Gods and Goddesses of Canaan*. Journal for the Study of the Old Testament Supplement Series, vol. 265, edited by David J. A. Clines and Philip R. Davies. Sheffield, UK: Sheffield Academic Press, 2000.

De Gaury, Lieut.-Colonel Gerald, M. C. "St. George of England and the Middle East." *Journal of the Royal Central Asian Society* 32: 206–208, 1945.

De Giorgi, Andrea U. *Ancient Antioch: From the Seleucid Era to the Islamic Conquest*. Cambridge, UK: Cambridge University Press, 2016.

De Lange, Nicholas. "Jews in the Age of Justinian." In *The Cambridge Companion to the Age of Justinian*, edited by Michael Maas, 401–426. New York: Cambridge University Press, 2005.

De Moor, Johannes C. *An Anthology of Religious Texts from Ugarit*. Religious Texts in Translation Series NISABA 16, edited by M. S. H. G. Heerma Van Voss, J. Knappert, R. P. Kramers, B. A. Van Proosdij, J. D. H. Waardenburg, and R. A. M. Van Zantwijk. Leiden: E. J. Brill, 1987.

Delehaye, Hippolyte. *The Legends of the Saints*. London: G. Chapman, 1962.

Dixon-Kennedy, Mike, ed. "Perun," *Encyclopedia of Russian and Slavic Myth and Legend*. Santa Barbara, CA: ABC-CLIO, 1998.

Doniger, Wendy. *The Implied Spider: Politics and Theology in Myth*. New York: Columbia University Press, 1998.

Donner, Fred M. "The Background to Islam." In *The Cambridge Companion to the Age of Justinian*, edited by Michael Maas, 510–534. New York: Cambridge University Press, 2005.

Donner, Fred M. *Muhammad and the Believers: At the Origins of Islam*. Cambridge, MA: The Belknap Press of Harvard University Press, 2010.

Donner, Herbert. *The Mosaic Map of Madaba*. Palaestina Antiqua 7. Kampen, Netherlands: Kok Pharos Publishing House, 1992.

Draper, Jonathan A., and Claytton N. Jefford. *The Didache: A Missing Piece of the Puzzle in Early Christianity*. Early Christianity and Its Literature, 14. Atlanta, GA: SBL Press, 2015.

Droge, A. J. *The Qur'ān: A New Annotated Translation*. Comparative Islamic Studies, edited by Brannon Wheeler. Sheffield, UK: Equinox Publishing Ltd., 2013.

Ducellier, Alain. "Autocracy and Religion in Byzantium, in the 4th and 5th Centuries." In *Christianity: A History in the Middle East*, edited by Habib Badr, Suad Slim, and Joseph Abou Nohra, 93–120. Beirut, Lebanon: Middle East Council of Churches, 2005.

Eberhard, Otto. "El-Chadr = der Heilige Elias = Ritter St. George. Ein Schulbeispiel palastinensischer Religionsmenagerei." *Das Altertum* 2: 82–89, 1956.

Ehrman, Bart D. *After the New Testament: A Reader in Early Christianity*. New York: Oxford University Press, 1999.

Ehrman, Bart D. *How Jesus Became God: The Exaltation of a Jewish Preacher from Galilee*. New York: HarperOne, 2014.

Eisenberg, Ronald L. *Essential Figures in the Talmud*. Plymouth, UK: Jason Aronson, 2013.

El-Badawi, Emran I. *The Qur'ān and the Aramaic Gospel Traditions*. Routledge Studies in the Qur'ān 13. New York: Routledge, 2013.

Engels, David, and Peter van Nuffelen. *Religion and Competition in Antiquity*. Brussels: Latomus, 2014.

Ernst, Carl W. *How to Read the Qur'ān: A New Guide, with Select Translations*. Chapel Hill, NC: University of North Carolina Press, 2011.

Ess, Margarete van. *Heliopolis Baalbek: 1898–1998 Rediscovering the Ruins*, 2nd edition. Berlin: Das Arabische Buch, 2001.
Faraone, Christopher A. *Vanishing Acts on Ancient Greek Amulets: From Oral Performance to Visual Design*. Bulletin of the Institute of Classical Studies Supplements, London: University of London Institute of Classical Studies, 2012.
Ferg Muhaisen, Erica. "Continuity and Contradistinction: A Geography of Religion Study of the Ancient Near Eastern Storm-God Baal-Hadad, Jewish Elijah, Christian St. George, and Muslim al-Khiḍr in the Eastern Mediterranean." PhD dissertation, University of Denver, Denver, 2016.
Finkelstein, Israel. *The Forgotten Kingdom: The Archaeology and History of Northern Israel*. Society of Biblical Literature Ancient Near East Monographs, vol. 5, edited by Ehud Ben Zvi and Roxana Flammini. Atlanta, GA: Society of Biblical Literature, 2013.
Finkelstein, Israel, and Neil Asher Silberman. *The Bible Unearthed: Archaeology's New Vision of Ancient Israel and the Origin of Its Sacred Texts*. New York: Touchstone, 2002.
Firestone, Reuven. *Journeys in Holy Lands: The Evolution of the Abraham-Ishmael Legends in Islamic Exegesis*. New York: State University of New York Press, 1990.
Fox, Robin L. *Pagans and Christians*. New York: Alfred A. Knopf, Inc., 1986.
Fox, Robin L. *Traveling Heroes: In the Epic Age of Homer*. New York: Vintage Books, 2008.
Franke, Patrick. *Begegnung mit Khiḍr : Quellenstudien zum Imaginären im Traditionellen Islam*. Beirut: In Kommission bei Franz Steiner Verlag Stuttgart, 2000.
Frend, W. H. C. *Martyrdom and Persecution in the Early Church*. Reprint. Grand Rapids, MI: Baker Book House, 1963/1980.
Frick, Frank S. "Palestine, Climate of" in *The Anchor Bible Dictionary*, vol. 5. New York: Doubleday, 1992, 126.
Fulghum, Mary M. "Coins Used as Amulets in Late Antiquity." In *Between Magic and Religion: Interdisciplinary Studies in Ancient Mediterranean Religion and Society*. Greek Studies: Interdisciplinary Approaches, edited by Sulochana Asirvatham, Corinne Pache, and John Watrous, 139–149. Lanham, MD: Rowman & Littlefield, 2001.
Georgoudi, Stella. "Sacrificing to the Gods: Ancient Evidence and Modern Interpretations." In *The Gods of Ancient Greece: Identities and Transformations*. Edinburgh Levantis Studies 5, edited by Jan N. Bremmer and Andrew Erskine, 92–105. Edinburgh, Scotland: Edinburgh University Press, 2010.
Ghanamī, al-Sayyid S. *Sayyidunā al-Khiḍr*. Cairo: Dār al-Aḥmadī, 2000.
Gibson, John C. L. *Canaanite Myths and Legends*. New York: T&T Clark Ltd., 2004.
Gilchrist, Cherry. *Russian Magic: Living Folk Traditions of an Enchanted Landscape*. Wheaton, IL: Quest Books, 2009.
Gilliot, Claude. "Mujāhid's Exegesis: Origins, Paths of Transmission and Development of a Meccan Exegetical Tradition in its Human, Spiritual and Theological Environment." In *Tafsīr and Islamic Intellectual History: Exploring the Bounds of a Genre*, edited by Andreas Görke and Johanna Pink. The Institute of Ismaili Studies Qur'anic Studies Series 12, edited by Omar Alí-de-Unzaga, 63–112. Oxford: Oxford University Press, 2014.
Ginzberg, Louis. *The Legends of the Jews*, vol. 4. Bible Times and Characters from Joshua to Esther. Philadelphia, PA: The Jewish Publication Society of America, 1968.
Glassner, Jean-Jacques. *The Invention of Cuneiform: Writing in Sumer*. Translated by Zainab Bahrani and Marc Van de Mieroop. Baltimore, MD: Johns Hopkins University Press, 2003.

Görke, Andreas, and Johanna Pink, eds. *Tafsīr and Islamic Intellectual History: Exploring the Bounds of a Genre*. The Institute of Ismaili Studies Qur'anic Studies Series 12, edited by Omar Alí-de-Unzaga. Oxford: Oxford University Press, 2014.

Goldziher, Ignaz. "Veneration of Saints in Islam." In Muslim *Studies* (Muhammedanische Studien), vol II. Translated by C. R. Barber and S. M. Stern. London: Allan & Unwin, 1971.

Goldziher, Ignaz. "On the Veneration of the Dead in Paganism and Islam." In Muslim *Studies* (Muhammedanische Studien), vol. I. Translated by C. R. Barber and S. M. Stern. New Brunswick, NJ: Aldine Transaction, 2006.

Goode, Jonathan. *The Cult of St. George in Medieval England*. Suffolk, UK: The Boydell Press, 2009.

Gottschalk, Peter. *Beyond Hindu and Muslim: Multiple Identity in Narratives from a Village in India*. Oxford: Oxford University Press, 2000.

Grant, Robert M. *Gods and the One God*. Library of Early Christianity, edited by Wayne T. Meeks. Philadelphia, PA: The Westminster Press, 1986.

Gray, Patrick T. R. "The Legacy of Chalcedon." In *The Cambridge Companion to the Age of Justinian*, edited by Michael Maas, 215–283. New York: Cambridge University Press, 2005.

Greatrex, Geoffrey. "Byzantium and the East in the Sixth Century." In *The Cambridge Companion to the Age of Justinian*, edited by Michael Maas, 477–509. New York: Cambridge University Press, 2005.

Greene, Alberto R. W. *The Storm-God in the Ancient Near East*. Biblical and Judaic Studies from the University of California, San Diego 8, edited by William Henry Propp. Winona Lake, IN: Eisenbrauns, 2003.

Gregg, Robert C. *Shared Stories, Rival Tellings: Early Encounters of Jews, Christians, and Muslims*. Oxford, UK: Oxford University Press, 2015.

Grehan, James. *Twilight of the Saints: Everyday Religion in Ottoman Syria and Palestine*. Oxford: Oxford University Press, 2014.

Griffith, Sydney H. "Christian Lore and the Arabic Qur'ān: The 'Companions of the Cave' in *Sūrat al-Kahf* and in Syriac Christian Tradition." In *The Qur'ān in Its Historical Context*, edited by Gabriel Said Reynolds. Routledge Studies in the Qur'ān 8, edited by Andrew Rippin, 109–138. New York: Routledge, 2008.

Griffith, Sydney H. "al-Nasārā in the Qur'ān: a Hermeneutical Reflection." In *New Perspectives on the Qur'ān: The Qur'ān in its Historical Context 2*, edited by Gabriel Said Reynolds. Routledge Studies in the Qur'ān 12, edited by Andrew Rippin, 301–322. New York: Routledge, 2011.

Griffith, Sydney H. *The Bible in Arabic: The Scriptures of the "People of the Book" in the Language of Islam*. Jews, Christians, and Muslims from the Ancient to the Modern World 20, edited by Michael Cook, William Chester Jordan, and Peter Schäfer. Princeton, NJ: Princeton University Press, 2013.

Guillaume, Alfred. *The Life of Muhammad: A Translation of Ibn Isḥāq's Sīrat Rasūl Allāh*. Oxford: Oxford University Press, 2002 (reprint 1955).

Gulick, John. *Social Structure and Culture Change in a Lebanese Village*. New York: Wenner-Gren Foundation for Anthropological Research, 1955.

Habel, Norman C. *Yahweh Versus Baal: A Conflict of Religious Cultures*. New York: Bookman Associates, 1964.

Haddad, Hassan S. "Baal-Hadad: A Study of the Syrian Storm-God." PhD dissertation, University of Chicago, 1960.

Haddad, Hassan S. "'Georgic' Cults and Saints of the Levant." *Numen* 16(1): 21–39, 1969.

Halman, H. Talat. *Where the Two Seas Meet: Al-Khiḍr and Moses – The Qur'anic Study of al-Khiḍr and Moses in Sufi Commentaries as a Model for Spiritual Guidance*. Louisville, KY: Fons Vitae, 2013.

Haneef, Suzanne. *A History of the Prophets of Islam: Derived from the Quran, Ahadīth and Commentaries*, vol. 2. Chicago, IL: Library of Islam, 2002.

Harris, William. *The Levant: A Fractured Mosaic*. Princeton Series on the Middle East, edited by Bernard Lewis and András Hámori. Princeton, NJ: Markus Weiner Publishers, 2003.

Harris, W. V., ed. *Rethinking the Mediterranean*. New York: Oxford University Press, 2005.

Harvey, Susan A. "To Whom Did Jacob Preach?" In *Jacob of Sarugh and His Times: Studies in Sixth-Century Syriac Christianity*, edited by George Anton Kiraz, 115–. Gorgias Eastern Christian Studies 8. Piscataway, NJ: Gorgias Press, 2010.

Hasluck, Frederick W. *Christianity and Islam Under the Sultans*, 2 vols. Oxford: Clarendon Press, 1929.

Hawting, G. R. *The Idea of Idolatry and the Emergence of Islam: From Polemic to History*. Cambridge, UK: Cambridge University Press, 1999.

Hinnels, John. Introduction to the *Routledge Companion to the Study of Religion*, 2nd edition. New York: Routledge, 2010.

Horden, Peregrine, and Nicholas Purcell. *The Corrupting Sea: A Study of Mediterranean History*. Oxford: Blackwell Publishers, Ltd., 2000.

Horden, Peregrine, and Sharon Kinoshita, eds. *A Companion to Mediterranean History*. Wiley Blackwell Companions to World History 20. Sussex, UK: Wiley Blackwell, 2014.

Horsley, Richard, and John Hanson. *Bandits, Prophets and Messiahs*. Trinity Press International, 1985.

Horsley, Richard, and John Hanson. "The Zealots: their Origin, Relationships and Importance in the Jewish Revolt." *NovT* 28: 159–182, 1986.

Hoyland, Robert G. *Seeing Islam as Others Saw It: A Survey and Evaluation of Christian, Jewish, and Zoroastrian Writings on Early Islam*. Studies in Late Antiquity and Early Islam 13. Princeton, NJ: The Darwin Press, Inc., 1997.

Hoyland, Robert G. *Arabia and the Arabs: From the Bronze Age to the Coming of Islam*. New York: Routledge, 2001.

Hoyland, Robert G. "Jews of the Hijaz in the Qur'ān." In *New Perspectives on the Qur'ān: The Qur'ān in its Historical Context 2*. Routledge Studies in the Qur'ān 12, edited by Andrew Rippin, 91–116. New York: Routledge, 2011.

Hughes, Donald J. *The Mediterranean: An Environmental History*. Nature and Human Societies Series, edited by Mark R. Stoll. Santa Barbara, CA: ABC-CLIO, 2005.

Humphreys, Stephen D. "Crosses as Water Purification Devices in Byzantine Palestine," in *Trends and Turning Points: Constructing the Late Antique and Byzantine World*, edited by Matthew Kinloch and Alex MacFarlane, 229–246. Leiden: Brill, in 2019.

Hunt, Joel H. *A Primer on Ugaritic: Language, Culture, and Literature*. New York: Cambridge University Press, 2007.

Huntington, Samuel P. "The Clash of Civilizations?" *Foreign Affairs* 72(3): 22–49, 1993.

Ibn al-Qalansi. *The Damascus Chronicle of the Crusades: Extracted and Translated from the Chronicle of Ibn al-Qalansi*. Edited and translated by H. A. R. Gibb. London: Luzac & Co., 1932.

Ibn Kathir, Isma'il bin 'Umar. *Qiṣaṣ al-Anbiā': laqad kana fi qiṣaṣihim iIbrah li-uli al-albab*. Abu al-Khayr, 'Ali 'And al-Hamid, edited by Beirut: Dar al-Khayr, 1997.

Idinopulos, Thomas A., and Brian C. Wilson, and James C. Hanges, eds. *Comparing Religions: Possibilities and Perils?* Boston, MA: Brill, 2006.

Jabr, al-Imām Mujāhīd ibn. *Tafsīr al-Imām Mujāhīd ibn Jabr: al-mutawaffá sanat 102 H.* Muhammad abd al-Salām Abu al-Nīl. Cairo: Dār al-Fikr al-Islāmī al-Ḥadīthah, 1989.

Jacobus, de Voragine. *The Golden Legend*, 2 vols. Translated by William Granger Ryan. Princeton, NJ: Princeton University Press, 1995.

Jannoray, Jean. "Nouvelles Inscriptions de Lébadée." *Bulletin de Correspondance Hellénique* 64–65: 36–59, 1940.

Jeffreys, Elizabeth, and Roger Scott. *The Chronicle of John Malalas*. Byzantina Australiensia 4. Melbourne, Australia: Australian Association for Byzantine Studies, 1986.

Juynboll, G. H. A. *Encyclopedia of Canonical Ḥadīth*. Leiden: Brill, 2007.

Kapelrud, Arvid S. *Baal in the Ras Shamra Texts*. Copenhagen, Denmark: G. E. C. Gad, 1952.

Kennedy, Hugh. "Syria, Palestine and Mesopotamia." In *The Cambridge Ancient History, vol. XIV Late Antiquity: Empire and Successors A.D. 425–600*, edited by Averil Cameron, Bryan Ward-Perkins, and Michael Whitby, 588–637. Cambridge, UK: Cambridge University Press, 2000.

Khoshnaw, Namak, Ant Adeane, and Lara El Gibaly. "Explore the IS Tunnels: How the Islamic State Group Destroyed a Mosque But Revealed a 3,000-Year-Old Palace." *BBC News*: Nov. 22, 2018. Retrieved from https://www.bbc.co.uk/news/resources/idt-sh/isis_tunnels

Kiltz, David. "The Relationship between Arabic *Allāh* and Syriac *Allāhā*." *Der Islam* 88: 33–50, 2012.

Kiraz, George A. *The Acts of Saint George and the Story of His Father*. Piscataway, NJ: Gorgias Press, 2009.

Kiraz, George A., ed. *Jacob of Sarugh and His Times: Studies in Sixth-Century Syriac Christianity*. Gorgias Eastern Christian Studies 8. Piscataway, NJ: Gorgias Press, 2010.

Kitzinger, Ernst. *Byzantine Art in the Making: Main Lines of Stylistic Development in Mediterranean Art 3rd – 7th Century*. Cambridge, MA: Harvard University Press, 1977.

Koester, Helmut. *Introduction to the New Testament, vol. 1: History, Culture and Religion of the Hellenistic Age*, 2nd edition. de Gruyter, 1995.

Korpel, Marjo C. A., and Johannes C. de Moor. *Adam, Eve, and the Devil: A New Beginning*. Hebrew Bible Monographs 65, edited by David J. A. Clines and J. Cheryl Exum. Sheffield, UK: Sheffield Phoenix Press, 2014.

Laird, Lance D. "Martyrs, Heroes and Saints: Shared Symbols of Muslims and Christians in Contemporary Palestinian Society." PhD dissertation, Harvard Divinity School, 1998. In ProQuest Dissertations and Theses, retrieved from http://proquest.umi.com (accessed June 2, 2011).

Laird, Lance D. "Boundaries and *Baraka*: Christians, Muslims, and a Palestinian Saint." In *Muslims and Others in Sacred Space*, edited by Margaret Cormack. American Academy of Religion Religion, Culture, and History Series 16, edited by Jacob N. Kinnard, 40–73. Oxford: Oxford University Press, 2013.

Le Strange, Guy. *Palestine Under the Moslems: A Description of Syria and the Holy Land from A.D. 650 to 1500*. Beirut: Khayats, 1965.

Lee, A. D. *Pagans and Christians in Late Antiquity: A Sourcebook*. New York: Routledge, 2000.

Lemaire, André, and Baruch Halpern, eds. *The Books of Kings: Sources, Composition, Historiography and Reception*. Supplements to Vestus Testamentum, vol. 129, edited by Craig A. Evans and Peter W. Flint. Leiden: Brill, 2010.

Levine, Amy-Jill. *Short Stories by Jesus: The Enigmatic Parables of a Controversial Rabbi*. New York: HarperOne, 2014.

Levine, Lee I. *Caesarea under Roman Rule*. Studies in Judaism in Late Antiquity, 7. Leiden: Brill, 1975.

Lieu, Judith, John North, and Tessa Rajak, eds. *The Jews Among Pagans and Christian in the Roman Empire*. London: Routledge, 1992.

Lindbeck, Kristen. *Elijah and the Rabbis: Story and Theology*. New York: Columbia University Press, 2010.

Lindsay, James E. *Daily Life in the Medieval Islamic World*. Greenwood Press 'Daily Life Through History' Series. Indianapolis, IN: Hackett Publishing Company, Inc., 2005.

Loosely, Emma. "Peter, Paul, and James of Jerusalem: The Doctrinal and Political Evolution of the Eastern and Oriental Churches." In *Eastern Christianity in the Modern Middle East*, edited by Anthony O'Mahoney and Emma Loosely, 1–12. Culture and Civilization in the Middle East 20, edited by Ian Richard Netton. New York: Routledge, 2010.

Luckenbill, D. D. *Ancient records of Assyria and Babylonia*, 2 vols. Chicago, IL: University of Chicago Press, 1927.

Maas, Michael, ed. *The Cambridge Companion to the Age of Justinian*. New York: Cambridge University Press, 2005.

MacMullen, Ramsay. *Paganism in the Roman Empire*. New Haven, CT: Yale University Press, 1981.

MacMullen, Ramsay. *Christianity and Paganism in the Fourth to Eighth Centuries*. New Haven, CT: Yale University Press, 1997.

MacMullen, Ramsay, and Eugene N. Lane, eds. *Paganism and Christianity 100–425 C.E.: A Sourcebook*. Minneapolis, MN: Fortress Press, 1992.

Maraval, Pierre. "Christianity in the Middle East, in the 2nd and 3rd Centuries." In *Christianity: A History in the Middle East*, edited by Habib Badr, Suad Slim, and Joseph Abou Nohra, 73–92. Beirut, Lebanon: Middle East Council of Churches, 2005.

Markus, Robert A. *The End of Ancient Christianity*. Cambridge, UK: Cambridge University Press, 1990.

Matar, Nabil, ed. and trans. *In the Lands of the Christians: Arabic Travel Writing in the Seventeenth Century*. New York: Routledge, 2003.

Mathews, Thomas F. *Byzantium: From Antiquity to the Renaissance*. New York: Harry N. Abrams, Inc., 1998.

Mazzilli, Francesca. *Rural Cult Centres in the Hauran: Part of the Broader Network of the Near East (100 BC – AD 300)*. Archaeopress Roman Archaeology 51. Summertown, Oxford, UK: Archaeopress, 2018.

McAuliffe, Jane D. *Qur'ānic Christians: An Analysis of Classical and Modern Exegesis*. New York: Cambridge University Press, 1991.

McCullough, Stewart W. *A Short History of Syriac Christianity to the Rise of Islam*. Scholars Press General Series 4. Chico, CA: Scholars Press, 1982.

McDonald, Lee M. *The Formation of the Christian Biblical Canon: Revised and Expanded Edition*. Peabody, MA: Hendrickson Publishers, 1995.

McDonald, Lee M. *The Biblical Canon: Its Origin, Transmission, and Authority*. Peabody, MA: Hendrickson Publishers, 2007.

McDonald, Lee Martin, and James A. Sanders, eds. *The Canon Debate*. Peabody, MA: Hendrickson Publishers, 2002.

McGuire, Meredith B. *Lived Religion: Faith and Practice in Everyday Life*. New York: Oxford University Press, 2008.

McKenzie, Judith S. *The Nabataean Temple at Khirbet et-Tannur, Jordan: Volume 1 – Architecture and Religion Final Report on Nelson Glueck's 1937 Excavation*. Boston, MA: American Schools of Oriental Research in collaboration with Manar al-Athar, University of Oxford, 2013.

McNeill, J. R. *The Mountains of the Mediterranean World: An Environmental History*. Studies in Environment and History, edited by Donald Worster and Alfred W. Crosby. Cambridge, UK: Cambridge University Press, 1992.

Meeks, Wayne A. *The First Urban Christians: The Social World of the Apostle Paul*, 2nd edition. New Haven, CT: Yale University Press, 2003.

Meeks, Wayne A., and Robert L. Wilken. *Jews and Christians in Antioch in the First Four Centuries of the Common Era*. Society of Biblical Literature Sources for Biblical Study, 13. Missoula, MT: Scholars, 1978.

Melchert, Christopher. "Ibn Mujāhid and the Establishment of Seven Qur'ānic Readings." *Studia Islamica* 91: 5–22, 2000.

Meredith, Anthony. *The Cappadocians*. Cresswood, NY: St. Vladimir's Seminary Press, 1995.

Meri, Josef W. "Re-Appropriating Sacred Space: Medieval Jews and Muslims Seeking Elijah and al-Khaḍir." *Medieval Encounters* 5(3): 237–264, 1999.

Meri, Josef W. *The Cult of Saints Among Muslims and Jews in Medieval Syria*. Oxford Oriental Monographs. Oxford: Oxford University Press, 2002.

Meri, Josef W., trans. A Lonely Wayfarer's Guide to Pilgrimage: 'Alī ibn Bakr al-Harawī's Kitāb al-ishārāt ilā ma'rifat al-ziyārāt. Princeton, NJ: The Darwin Press, Inc., 2004.

Mettinger, Tryggve N. D. *No Graven Image: Israelite Aniconism in its Ancient Near Eastern Context*. University Park, PA: Eisenbrauns, 2013 [1995].

Metzger, Bruce M., and Michael D. Coogan, eds. *The Oxford Guide to People & Places of the Bible*. Oxford: Oxford University Press, 2001.

Mieroop, Marc van de. *Cuneiform Texts and the Writing of History*. Approaching the Ancient World, edited by Richard Stoneman. London and New York: Routledge, 1999.

Mieroop, Marc van de. *A History of the Ancient Near East, ca.* 3000–323 *BC*. Malden, MA: Blackwell Publishing, 2004.

Millar, Fergus. *The Roman Near East 31 BC – AD 337*. Cambridge, MA: Harvard University Press, 1993.

Miller, Robert D. II. *The Dragon, the Mountain, and the Nations: An Old Testament Myth, Its Origins, and Its Afterlives*. Explorations in ANE Civilizations 6. Eisenbrauns, 2018.

Milwright, Marcus. *An Introduction to Islamic Archaeology*. The New Edinburgh Islamic Surveys, edited by Carole Hillenbrand. Edinburgh: Edinburgh University Press Ltd., 2010.

Montgomery, David R. *Dirt: The Erosion of Civilizations*. Berkeley, CA: University of California Press, 2007.

Moss, Candida. *The Other Christs: Imitating Jesus in Ancient Christian Ideologies of Martyrdom*. Oxford: Oxford University Press, 2010.

Moss, Candida. *Ancient Christian Martyrdom: Diverse Practices, Theologies, and Traditions*. New Haven, CT: Yale University Press, 2012.

Moss, Candida. *The Myth of Persecution: How Early Christians Invented a Story of Martyrdom*. New York: HarperOne, 2013.

Moss, Christopher, and Katherine Kiefer, eds. *Byzantine East, Latin West: Art-Historical Studies in Honor of Kurt Weitzmann*. Princeton, NJ: Department of Art and Archaeology, Princeton University, 1995.

Mulroy, Kevin, Editor-in-Chief. *National Geographic Atlas of the Middle East.* Washington, D.C.: National Geographic, 2003.

Narkiss, Bezalel. "'Living the Dead Became': The Prophet Elijah as a Holy Image in Early Jewish Art." In *Byzantine East, Latin West: Art-Historical Studies in Honor of Kurt Weitzmann*, edited by Christopher Moss and Katherine Kiefer. Department of Art and Archaeology, Princeton University, NJ: Princeton University Press, 1995.

Nehme, Lina M. *Phoenician Baalbek: Visiting the Temples of Roman Epoch*, 2nd English edition. Translated by Alfred Murr Beirut. Lebanon: Beirut, Aleph et Taw, 2011.

Neuwirth, Angelika. "Form." In *Encyclopaedia of the Qur'ān*, vol. 2, edited by Jane Dammen MacAuliffe, 81–84. Leiden: Brill, 2003.

Newby, Gordon D. *A History of the Jews of Arabia: From Ancient Times to Their Eclipse Under Islam*. Studies in Comparative Religion 8, edited by Frederick M. Denny. Columbia, SC: University of South Carolina Press, 1988.

Nicholson, Helen J. *Chronicle of the Third Crusade: A Translation of the Itinerarium Peregrinorum et Gesta Regis Ricardi*. Burlington, VT: Ashgate, 2001.

Nissim ben Jacob Ibn Shāhīn. *An Elegant Composition concerning Relief after Adversity*. Translated and with introduction and notes by William M. Brinner. Yale Judaica Series 20, edited by Leon Nemoy. New Haven, CT: Yale University Press, 1977.

Noegel, Scott, Joel Walker, and Brannon Wheeler, eds. *Prayer, Magic, and the Stars in the Ancient and Late Antique World.* Magic in History Series 8. University Park, PA: The Pennsylvania State University Press, 2003.

Noegel, Scott B., and Brannon M. Wheeler. *Historical Dictionary of Prophets in Islam and Judaism*. Historical Dictionaries of Religions, Philosophies, and Movements 43, edited by Jon Woronoff. Lanham, MD: The Scarecrow Press, Inc., 2002.

Obermann, Julian. *Ugaritic Mythology: A Study of its Leading Motifs*. New Haven, CT: Yale University Press, 1948.

Obermann, Julian. "Two Elijah Stories in Judeo-Arabic Transmission." In Hebrew *Union College Annual Volume XXIII* Part I, 387–404. Cincinnati, OH: Hebrew Union College, 1950.

Ocak, Ahmet Y. *İslâm-türk inançlarında hızır yahut hızır-ilyas kültü.* Ankara: Türk Kültürünü Araştırma Enstitüsü, 1985.

O'Donnell, James J. *Pagans: The End of Traditional Religion and the Rise of Christianity.* New York: Ecco/HarperCollins, 2015.

Ogden, Daniel. *The Legend of Seleucus: Kingship, Narrative and Mythmaking in the Ancient World.* Cambridge, UK: Cambridge University Press, 2017.

Omar, Irfan. "Khiḍr in the Islamic Tradition." *The Muslim World* 73, 3–4, 1993.

Onasch, Konrad, and Annemarie Schnieper. *Icons: The Fascination and the Reality.* Translated by Daniel G. Conklin. New York: Riverside Book Company, Inc., 1997.

Ortlund, Eric N. *Theophany and Chaoskampf: The Interpretation of Theophanic Imagery in the Baal Epic, Isaiah, and the Twelve*. Gorgias Ugaritic Studies 5. Piscataway, NJ: Gorgias Press, 2010.

Osborne, Robin, and Dominic Rathbone. "Farmers." In *Brill's New Pauly*, edited by Hubert Cancik and Helmuth Schneider. Brill Online, 2015.

O'Sullivan, Anthony, Marie-Estelle Rey, and Jorge Galvez Mendez. "Opportunities and Challenges in the MENA Region." *Organization for Economic Co-operation and Development (OECD)*, 1–27, 2011.

Ovadiah, Asher, and Rosario Pierri. *Elijah's Cave on Mount Carmel and its Inscriptions*. Oxford, UK: Archaeopress Archaeology, 2015.

Pacini, Andrea, ed. *Christian Communities in the Arab Middle East: The Challenge of the Future*. Oxford: Clarendon Press, 1998.

Pagels, Elaine. *Revelations: Visions, Prophecy & Politics in the book of Revelation*. New York: Viking, 2012.

Pancaroglu, Oya. "The Itinerant Dragon-Slayer: Forging paths of Image and Identity in Medieval Anatolia." *Gesta* 43(2): 151–164, 2004.

Pardee, Dennis. *Ritual and Cult at Ugarit*. Writings from the Ancient World Series, Society of Biblical Literature, vol. 10, edited by Simon B. Parker. Atlanta, GA: Society of Biblical Literature, 2002.

Parker, Simon B., ed. *Ugaritic Narrative Poetry*. Writings from the Ancient World Series, Society of Biblical Literature, vol. 9, edited by Simon B. Parker. Atlanta, GA: Scholars Press, Society of Biblical Literature, 1997.

Pastor, Jack, and Menachem Mor, eds. *The Beginnings of Christianity: A Collection of Articles*. Jerusalem: Yad Ben-Zvi Press, 2005.

Patton, Kimberly C., and Benjamin C. Ray, eds. *A Magic Still Dwells: Comparative Religion in the Postmodern Age*. Berkeley, CA: University of California Press, 2000.

Peters, F. E., ed. *The Arabs and Arabia and on the Eve of Islam*. The Foundation of the Classical Islamic World 3, edited by Lawrence I. Conrad. Brookfield, VT: Ashgate Publishing Company, 1999.

Playne, Beatrice. *St. George for Ethiopia*. London: Constable Publishers, 1954.

Pritchard, James B., ed. *The Ancient Near East: An Anthology of Texts and Pictures*. Forward by Daniel E. Fleming. Princeton, NJ: Princeton University Press, 2011.

Qleibo, Ali H. *Before the Mountains Disappear: An Ethnographic Chronicle of the Modern Palestinians*. Kornesh EL Nil: Al Ahram Press, 1992.

Radner, Karen, ed. *State Correspondence in the Ancient World, From New Kingdom Egypt to the Roman Empire*. Oxford Studies in Early Empires. New York: Oxford University Press, 2014.

Ragette, Friedrich. *Baalbek*. Park Ridge, NJ: Noyes Press, 1980.

Rebillard, Éric, and Jörg Rüpke. "Introduction: Groups, Individuals, and Religious Identity." In *Group Identity and Religious Individuality in Late Antiquity*, edited by Éric Rebillard and Jörg Rüpke. CUA Studies in Early Christianity, edited by Philip Rousseau. Washington, D.C.: The Catholic University of America Press, 2015.

Redford, Donald B. *Egypt, Canaan, and Israel in Ancient Times*. Princeton, NJ: Princeton University Press, 1992.

Reeves, John C., ed. *Bible and Qur'ān: Essays in Scriptural Intertextuality*. Society of Biblical Literature Symposium Series 24, edited by Christopher R. Matthews. Leiden: Brill, 2004.

Renard, John. "Khaḍir/Khiḍr." In *Encyclopaedia of the Qur'ān*, vol. 2, edited by Jane Dammen MacAuliffe, 81–84. Leiden: Brill, 2003.

Reynolds, Gabriel S. "*Iblīs*." in *Encyclopaedia of the Qur'ān*, vol. 3, edited by Jane Dammen MacAuliffe, 81–84. Leiden: Brill, 2003.

Reynolds, Gabriel S. *The Emergence of Islam: Classical Traditions in Contemporary Perspective*. Minneapolis, MN: Fortress Press, 2012.

Reynolds, Gabriel S., ed. *The Qur'ān in its Historical Context*. Routledge Studies in the Qur'ān 8, edited by Andrew Rippin. New York: Routledge, 2008.

Reynolds, Gabriel S. *The Qur'ān and Its Biblical Subtext*. Routledge Studies in the Qur'ān 10, edited by Andrew Rippin. New York: Routledge, 2010.

Reynolds, Gabriel S., ed. *New Perspectives on the Qur'ān: The Qur'ān in its Historical Context 2*. Routledge Studies in the Qur'ān 12, edited by Andrew Rippin. New York: Routledge, 2011.

Ribichini, Sergio. "Beliefs and Religious Life." In *The Phoenicians*, edited by Sabatino Moscati, 120–152. New York: Rizzoli, 1999.

Riches, Samantha. *St. George: Hero, Martyr and Myth*. Gloucestershire, UK: Sutton Publishing, 2000.
Robbins, Gregory A. "'Eusebius' Lexicon of 'Canonicity'." *Studia Patristica* 25: 134–141, 1993.
Robson, Laura. "Recent Perspectives on Arabic Communities in the Modern Arab World." *History Compass* 9(4): 312–325, 2011.
Rofé, Alexander. "Classification of the Prophetical Stories." *Journal of Biblical Literature* 89(4): 427–440, 1970.
Saadi, Abdul-Massih. "Nascent Islam in the Seventh Century Syriac Sources." In *The Qur'ān in its Historical Context*, edited by Gabriel Said Reynolds. Routledge Studies in the Qur'ān 8, edited by Andrew Rippin, 217–222. New York: Routledge, 2008.
Sarug, Jacob. *Jacob of Sarug's Homilies on Elijah*. Translated and introduced by Stephen A. Kaufman. Texts from Christian Late Antiquity, vol. 18, edited by George A. Kiraz. The Metrical Homilies of Mar Jacob of Sarugh, Fasc. 9–13, edited by Sebastian P. Brock and George A. Kiraz. Piscataway, NJ: Gorgias Press, 2009.
Sauma, Victor. *Sur les Pas des Saints au Liban*, 2 vols. Beirut: FMA, 1994.
The Sayings of the Desert Fathers: The Alphabetical Collection. Translated and with a forward by Benedicta Ward, SLG. Cistercian Studies Series 59. Trappist, KY: Cistercian Publications, 1975.
Schaeffer, Claude F. A. "Les fouilles de Minet-el-Beida et de Ras-Shamra: Quatrième campagne (printemps 1932). Rapport sommaire." *Syria* 14(2), 93–127, 1933.
Schaeffer, Claude F. A. "La stele du "Ba'al au foudre" de Ras-Shamra (Musée du Louvre)." *Monuments et Mémoires* 34(1–2): 1–18, 1934.
Schlumberger, Gustave. "Amulettes Byzantins Anciens: Destinés à Combattre les Maléfices et Maladies." *Revue des Etudes Grecques* 5: 73–93, 1892.
Schöck, Cornelia. "Moses." In *Encyclopaedia of the Qur'ān*, vol. 3, edited by Jane Dammen MacAuliffe, 419–426. Leiden: Brill, 2003.
Schram, Peninnah. *Tales of Elijah the Prophet*. Northvale, NJ: Jason Aronson, Inc., 1997.
Schwemer, Daniel. *Die Wettergottgestalten Mesopotamiens und Nordsyriens im Zeitalter der Keilschriftkulturen: Materialien und Studien nach derb schriftlichen Quellen*. Wiesbaden, 2001.
Schwemer, Daniel. "The Storm-Gods of the Ancient Near East: Summary, Synthesis, Recent Studies Part One." *Journal of Ancient Near Eastern Religions* 7(2): 121–168, 2007.
Schwemer, Daniel. "The Storm-Gods of the Ancient Near East: Summary, Synthesis, Recent Studies Part Two." *Journal of Ancient Near Eastern Religions* 8(1): 1–44, 2008.
Segal, Samuel M. *Elijah: A Study in Jewish Folklore*. New York: Behrman's Jewish Book House, 1935.
Sendler, Egon. *The Icon: Image of the Invisible*. Redondo Beach, CA: Oakwood Publications, 1988.
Sharkey, Heather J. *A History of Muslims, Christians, and Jews in the Middle East*. The Contemporary Middle East, edited by Beth Baron. Cambridge, UK: Cambridge University Press, 2017.
Siegal, Michael Bar-Asher. *Early Christian Monastic Literature and the Babylonian Talmud*. Cambridge, UK: Cambridge University Press, 2013.
Sinai, Nicolai. "The Qur'anic Commentary of Muqātil b. Sulaymān and the Evolution of Early Tafsīr Literature." In *Tafsīr and Islamic Intellectual History: Exploring the Bounds of a Genre*, edited by Andreas Görke and Johanna Pink. The Institute of Ismaili

Studies Qur'anic Studies Series 12, edited by Omar Alí-de-Unzaga, 113–146. Oxford: Oxford University Press, 2014.

[Sinleqqiunninni]. *The Epic of Gilgamesh.* Translated and introduced by Maureen Gallery Kovacs. Stanford, CA: Stanford University Press, 1985.

Sioutas, Michalis, Tanja Renko, Wade Szilagyi, and Alexander G. Keul. "Waterspout Climatology over the Central-Eastern Mediterranean." In *Proceedings of COMECAP 2014 –e-book of Proceedings*, vol. 3: 154–158, 2014.

Smith, Eric. *Jewish Glass and Christian Stone: A Materialist Mapping of the 'Parting of the Ways'.* Routledge Studies in the Early Christian World. New York: Routledge, 2017.

Smith, Jonathan Z. *Drudgery Divine: On the Comparison of Early Christianities and the Religions of Late Antiquity.* Chicago, IL: University of Chicago Press, 1990.

Smith, Mark S. *The Ugaritic Baal Cycle: Volume I, Introduction with Text, Translation and Commentary of KTU 1.1–1.2.* Supplements to Vestus Testamentum, vol. 55. Leiden: E. J. Brill, 1994.

Smith, Mark S. *The Origins of Biblical Monotheism: Israel's Polytheistic Background and the Ugaritic Texts.* Oxford: Oxford University Press, 2001.

Smith, Mark S. *Untold Stories: The Bible and Ugaritic Studies in the Twentieth Century.* Peabody, MA: Hendrickson Publishers, 2001.

Smith, Mark S. *God in Translation: Deities in Cross-Cultural Discourse in the Biblical World.* Forschungen zum Alten Testament, no. 57, edited by Bernd Janowski, Mark S. Smith, and Hermann Spieckermann. Tübingen, Germany: Mohr Siebeck, 2008.

Smith, Mark S., and Wayne T. Pritchard. *The Ugaritic Baal Cycle: Volume II: Introduction with Text, Translation and Commentary of KTU/CAT* 1.3–1.4. Supplements to Vestus Testamentum, vol. 114. Leiden: Brill, 2009.

Smith, Wilfred C. *What is Scripture? A Comparative Approach.* Minneapolis, MN: Augsburg Books, 2000.

Snyder, Graydon F. *Ante Pacem: Archaeological Evidence of Church Life Before Constantine.* Macon, GA: Mercer University Press, 2003.

Sokolowski, Franciszek. *Lois Sacrées des Cités Grecques.* Ecole Française d' Athèns: Trauvaux et Mémoires des Anciens Membres Étrangers de l'École et de Divers Savants 11. Paris: Éditions E. De Boccard, 1962.

Solomon, Steven. *Water: The Epic Struggle for Wealth, Power, and Civilization.* New York: HarperCollins Publishers, 2010.

Sopher, David E. *Geography of Religions.* Foundations of Cultural Geography Series, edited by Philip L. Wagner. Englewood Cliffs, NJ: Prentice-Hall, Inc., 1967.

Spier, Jeffrey. "Medieval Byzantine Magical Amulets and Their Tradition." *Journal of the Warburg and Courtald Institutes* 56: 25–62, 1993.

Stallsmith, Allaire B. "The Name of Demeter Thesmophoros." *Greek, Roman, and Byzantine Studies* 48: 115–131, 2008.

Stallsmith, Allaire B., and Allaire Brumfield. "Cakes in the Liknon: Votives from the Sanctuary of Demeter and Kore on Acrocorinth." *Hesperia: The Journal of the American School of Classical Studies at Athens* 66(1): 147–172, 1997.

Stark, Rodney. *The Rise of Christianity: How the Obscure, Marginal Jesus Movement Became the Dominant Religious Force in the Western World in a Few Centuries.* New York: Harper Collins, 1996.

Stump, Roger W. *The Geography of Religion: Faith, Place, and Space.* Lanham, MD: Rowman & Littlefield Publishers, Inc., 2008.

Sulaymān, Muqātil bin. *Tafsīr Muqātil b. Sulaymān.* Cairo: al-Haya al-Misriyya al-'Amma li-al-Kitab, 1979.

Tamari, Salim. *Mountain Against the Sea: Essays on Palestinian Society and Culture.* Berkeley, CA: University of California Press, 2009.

Tesei, Tommaso. "Some Cosmological Notions from Late Antiquity in Q 18:60–65: The Qur'ān in Light of Its Cultural Context." *Journal of the American Oriental Society* 135(1): 19–32, 2015.

Thierry, Nicole. *Haut Moyen-Âge en Cappadoce: Les Églises de la Région de Çavuşin*, tome II. Institute Français d'Archéologie du Proche-Orient, Bibliothèque Archéologique et Historique 102. Paris: Librarie Orientaliste Paul Geuthner, 1994.

Thierry, Nicole. "De la Datation des Églises de Cappadoce." *Byzantinsche Zeitschrift* 88(2): 419–455, 1995.

Thierry, Nicole, and Michel Teirry. *Nouvelles Églises Rupestres de Cappadoce: Région du Hasan Daği.* Paris: Librarie Klincksieck, 1963.

Thompson, Henry O. "Mount Carmel." In *The Anchor Bible Dictionary*, vol. 2, edited by David Noel Freedman. New York: Doubleday, 1992.

Tottoli, Roberto. *Biblical Prophets in the Qur'an and Muslim Literature.* Routledge Studies in the Qur'ān 3, edited by Andrew Rippin. New York: Routledge, 2002.

Tottoli, Roberto. "Elijah." In *Encyclopaedia of the Qur'ān*, vol. 1, edited by Jane Dammen MacAuliffe, 12–13. Leiden: Brill, 2003.

Tugendhaft, Aaron. *Baal and the Politics of Poetry.* The Ancient World, edited by Seth Sanders. New York: Routledge, 2018.

Van de Mieroop, Marc. *A History of the Ancient Near East ca.* 3000–323 BC. Blackwell History of the Ancient World. Malden, MA: Blackwell Publishing, 2003.

Vivante, Bella, ed. *Events that Changed Ancient Greece.* Westport, CT: Greenwood Press, 2002.

Vorderstrasse, Tasha, and Tanya Treptow, eds. *A Cosmopolitan City: Muslims, Christians, and Jews in Old Cairo.* Oriental Institute Museum Publications 38. Chicago, IL: The Oriental Institute of the University of Chicago, 2015.

Vyronis, Speros Jr. *The Decline of Medieval Hellenism in Asia Minor and the Process of Islamization from the Eleventh through the Fifteenth Century.* Berkeley, CA: University of California Press, 1971.

Waldmeier, Theophilus. *Appeal for the First Home of the Insane on Mount Lebanon.* London: Headley Brothers, 1897.

Walter, Christopher. "Saint Theodore and the Dragon." In *Through a Glass Brightly: Studies in Byzantine and Medieval Art and Archaeology Presented to David Buckton*, edited by Chris Entwistle, 95–106. Oxford: Oxbow Books, 2003.

Walter, Christopher. *The Warrior Saints in Byzantine Art and Tradition.* Burlington, VT: Ashgate Publishing Company, 2003.

Wansbrough, John. *The Sectarian Milieu: Content and Composition of Islamic Salvation History.* School of Oriental and African Studies University of London, London Oriental Series 34. Oxford: Oxford University Press, 1978.

Watts, Edward J. *The Final Pagan Generation: Transformation of the Classical Heritage.* Oakland, CA: University of California Press, 2015.

Weitzmann, Kurt. *The Icon: Holy Images – Sixth to Fourteenth Century.* New York: George Braziller, 1978.

Weitzmann, Kurt W. *The Monastery of Saint Catherine at Mount Sinai, The Icons, Volume One: From the Sixth to the Tenth Century.* Princeton, NJ: Princeton University Press, 1976.

Weitzmann, Kurt W. *Studies in the Arts at Sinai: Essays by Kurt Weitzmann*. Princeton, NJ: Princeton University Press, 1982.

Weulersse, Jacques. *L'Oronte: Etude de Fleuve*. Paris, 1940.

Wheeler, Brannon M. "The Jewish Origins of Qur'ān 18:65-82? Reexamining the Arent Jan Wensinck's Theory." *Journal of the American Oriental Society* 118(2): 153–171, 1998.

Wheeler, Brannon M. *Moses in the Quran and Islamic Exegesis*. Routledge Studies in the Qur'ān 4, edited by Andrew Rippin. New York: Routledge, 2002.

Wilkinson, John. *Jerusalem Pilgrims Before the Crusades*. Warminster, UK: Aris & Phillips, Ltd., 1977.

Wolper, Ethel S. *Cities and Saints: Sufism and the Transformation of Urban Space in Medieval Anatolia*. University Park, PA: The Pennsylvania State University Press, 2003.

Wolper, Ethel S. "Khiḍr and the Changing Frontiers of the Medieval World." *Medieval Encounters: Jewish, Christian and Muslim Culture in Confluence and Dialogue* 17: 120–146, 2011.

Wyatt, Nick. *Religious Texts from Ugarit*. Sheffield, UK: Sheffield Academic Press, 2002.

Yon, Marguerite. *The City of Ugarit: At Tell Ras Shamra*. Winona Lake, IN: Eisenbrauns, 2006.

Zellentin, Holger M. *The Qur'ān's Legal Culture: The Didascalia Apostolorum as a Point of Departure*. Tübingen, Germany: Mohr Siebeck, 2013.

Zijl, Peter J. van. *Baal: A Study of Texts in Connexion with Baal in the Ugaritic Epics*. Verlag Butzon & Bercker Kevelar, 1972.

Zubaida, Sami. *Islam, the People, and the State: Political Ideas and Movements in the Middle East*. New York: I.B. Tauris, 2009.

Zwettler, Michael. "A Mantic Manifesto: the Sūra of 'The Poets' and the Qur'ānic Foundations of Prophetic Authority." In *Poetry and Prophecy: The Beginnings of a Literary Tradition*, edited by James L. Kugel, 75–119. New York: Cornell University Press, 1990.

Index

Page numbers in *italics* indicate photographs/maps.

Day, John 114
Dead Sea *127*
Delehaye, Hippolyte 144
demons/sickness 43–45
Dhū al-Qarnayn 206, 208–09, 219, 221
Didache 141
Dilmun 189
disciple-master narratives 215
dogs 208
Dome of the Rock 41
Domnitziolus 175
Draco River. *see* Orontes River
dragons. *see* serpent/dragon motifs
droughts 10, 12, 27, 34–35, 44, 55–56, 76, 97, 244; Elijah Cycle 107–08, 118
Druze communities 2, 18*n*4, 241; and Ras el-Metn monastery 40
dry farming 57, *see also* rain-fed agriculture
dry years: frequency of 12, *see also* climate
Dülük (Baba Tepesi) 75
Dura-Europos 140
Dura-Europos synagogue 124, *125*

Ea 66
early Christianity, and saints/holy figures 143–44
earthquakes 29, 50*n*13, 74, 109, 112, 168, 243, 246
Eastern Mediterranean 18*n*1
Edward III (King) 175
Egypt *25*, 79, *82*, *191*; and the Baal Stele 78–79; records of Mt. Carmel 126–27
El-Badawi, Emran Iqbal 204
El/*'Ilu* 61, 63–64, 77, 93*n*117, 100–101
Elijah 2, 13, 17, 19–20*n*13, 84, 106, 110–11, 151, 169, 218–19, *220*, 244, 250, *257*; academic studies of 6; additional traits 4, 13; and al-Khiḍr 188, 216–17, 226, 229, 248; association with storms/rain 115, 130; cave associated with 240; and Christianity 122–23; compared with Moses 97, 116; as defender of the *true* faith 107, 115–16, 130; feasts 4, 20*n*18; images 123–24, *125*, 126, *220*, *224*; and Islam 123; motifs of Baal-Hadad 97, 246–47; origins 16; outside the Levant 3–4, 255; prophets of Baal 96, 107–09; and Rabbi Joshua ben Levi 222; Rabbinic-era 120–22; rise to heaven 2, 111–12, 115–16; and St. George 135, 165–66, 169, 178; within the Levant 129–30, *see also* St. Elias
Elijah Cycle 97, 105, 117, 119–20; geography 117–18; oral origins 106; summary 107–12
Elisha 110–12, 115–17, 216
Elisha Cycle 105
end of agrarian 40–50, 240–242
Enthroned Virgin between Soldier Saints icon 172–73
Enuma Elish 66, 184*n*73
environmental problems 34
Ephrem 213
Ernst, Carl 207
erosion 32–33, 51*n*30
Euphrates River 30, *82*, 243
Eusebius 142, 144, 170
exclusivist theology 13, 15, 48, 138, 251, 258

feast days 4, 20*n*18, 20*nn*18–19, 92–93*n*106, 135, 146, 161–62, 178, 241–42, 244, 259*n*9; St. Elias 125
Fertile Crescent 7
flooding 69
flora 30–31
folk religion 9, 48, *see also* popular religion
Fox, Robin Lane 73–74
fundamentalist religious groups 254

Galilee Gap 28
Gapn 62–63
geographic motifs 70–71, 84, 244
geography 244; Arabian 188–89; in the Elijah Cycle 117–18; regional 242–43; and religion 38, 49
"Geography of Religion" perspective 5–6, 13
geology 24, 27, 31, 41, 242–44
George Skylitzes 175
"'Georgic' Cults and Saints of the Levant" (Haddad) 7
Greece, associations with Mt. Sapan 71–75
Greek 71–75
Greek religious concepts 37
Gregory Nazianzus 169
Gregory of Nyssa 144, 169, 175
Grehan, James 9–10, 38–39, 49
Griffith, Sidney 200, 202

Hadda 57–58
Haddad, Hassan S. 7, 21*n*27, 146

Printed in the USA
CPSIA information can be obtained
at www.ICGtesting.com
LVHW011500110224
771554LV00011B/415